INDIA, CHINA AND AFRICA
New Partnership in Energy Security

INDIA, CHINA AND AFRICA

New Partnership in Energy Security

Dr. S.N. Yadav

JNANADA PRAKASHAN (P&D)
NEW DELHI

Published by :
JNANADA PRAKASHAN (P&D)
4837/2, 24, Ansari Road, Daryaganj
New Delhi-110002
Phone : 011-23272047 Mobile : 9212137080
Email: jnanadabooksdelhi@yahoo.com
Website: jnanadabooks.com

Assisted by :
TEXT BOOK PROMOTION SOCIETY OF INDIA
4837/2, 24, Ansari Road, Daryaganj
New Delhi-110002
Phone : 011-23272047 Mobile : 9212137080
Email: jnanadabooksdelhi@yahoo.com
Website: jnanadabooks.com

First Edition: 2025

India, China and Africa: New Partnership in Energy Security

ISBN: 978-81-7139-161-5

Typesetting by :
Vardhman Computers
New Delhi-110017

Published by Mrs. S. Chowdhary for M/s. Jnanada Prakashan (P&D) Daryaganj, Ansari Road, New Delhi-110 002 and printed at Balaji Offset, Navin Shahdara, Delhi-110032.

Preface

Essentially, this book is a comprehensive and critical investigation of the evolving partnership among India, China and Africa in the field of energy security. The author has also carefully evaluated the strategic, economic and political implications of energy security both for the energy producing as well as energy importing economies of the North and the South.

It ought to be noted that India and China are the major importers of energy in order to sustain their robust economic growth in the twenty-first century. China is the second largest consumer of energy, next only to the United State of America. India, on the other hand, is the sixth largest consumer of energy in the world.

Africa is now acquiring an entirely new role from the perspective of the energy security, mainly on account of the fact that 8 per cent of world's total oil reserves are found in this continent. Major oil reserves in Africa are found in Libya, Algeria, Sudan, Egypt, Tunisia, Nigeria, Cameroon, Gabon, Chad, Senegal, Congo, Angola, Mauritania, Kenya, Ethiopia and Equatorial Guinea. In view of the large oil deposits and mineral resources, China has crafted its Africa policy in such a way that the African continent now accounts for nearly 33 per cent of China's total oil imports.

As a matter of fact, the concept of energy security occupies prominent place in the foreign policy of China and India because, both these countries are energy deficient and heavily dependent on oil and gas import. The existing notion of energy security which focuses primarily on how to handle any disruption of oil supplies from oil producing countries was developed by the industrial world in the 1970s. Remarkably, it didn't pay attention to the prices of oil and gas. But, today the increasing prices of oil has become a major concern for oil-importing developing countries like China and India and, therefore, the very concept of energy security demands critical review in view of the changed global scenario.

Access to cheap energy has become essential to the functioning of modern economies. However, the uneven distribution of energy supplies among countries and the critical need for energy has led to significant vulnerabilities. Threats to global energy security include, the political instability of several energy producing countries, the manipulation of energy supplies, the competition over energy sources, attacks on supply infrastructure, as well as accidents and natural disasters. It is also the limited supplies of the most common forms of primary energy, *i.e.* oil and gas that changes perceptions on this issue.

Major areas of research and analysis in the work include, the critical role of energy security in the foreign policy, Energy Security and Economic Prosperity: Experiences of Energy Exporting African and Asian Economies, China's Strategy for Energy Security, India's Energy Policy, Sino-Indian Energy Cooperation in Sudan, Exploring Strategies for Sustainable Energy.

Last but not the least, I am fully convinced that this work will be an indispensable and valuable source of formation for academicians, researchers, as well as diplomats and policy-makers in the sphere of energy security and its various implications.

List of Acronyms

AABF	:	Africa-Asia Business Forum
AEC	:	Alberta Energy Corporation
AGOA	:	African Growth and Opportunity Act
APDRP	:	Accelerated Power Development and Reforms Programme
APM	:	Administered Price Mechanism
ASEAN	:	Association of South-East Asian Nations
BIMSTEC	:	Bengal Initiative for Multi Sectoral Technical and Economic Cooperation
BLF	:	Baluch Liberation Front
BP	:	British Petroleum
CASS	:	Chinese Academy of Social Sciences
CDM	:	Clean Development Mechanism
CERM	:	Coordinated Emergency Response Measures
CHP	:	Combined Heat and Power
CIS	:	Commonwealth of Independent States
CNOOC	:	China National Offshore Oil Corporation
CNPC	:	China National Petroleum Company
CPA	:	Comprehensive Peace Agreement
CPSUs	:	Central Public Sector Undertakings
CRESP	:	China Renewable Energy Scale-Up Programme
DDG	:	Decentralised Distribution Generation
E&P	:	Exploration and Production
EB	:	Executive Board
EC	:	European Commission
ECOWAS	:	Economic Community of West African States
EOSS	:	Emergency Oil Sharing System
FAO	:	Food and Agriculture Organisation
FDI	:	Foreign Direct Investment
GAIL	:	Gas Authority of India Ltd.
GDP	:	Gross Domestic Product
GOSS	:	Government of South Sudan

GSPC	:	Gujarat State Petroleum Corporation
HDI	:	Human Development Index
IAEA	:	International Atomic Energy Agency
IEA	:	International Energy Agency
ILSA	:	Iran-Libya Sanctions Act
IMF	:	International Monetary Fund
IOCs	:	International Oil Companies
IPI	:	Iran-Pakistan-India
LNG	:	Liquefied Natural Gas
MDPM	:	Market Determined Price Mechanism
NDRC	:	National Development and Reform Commission
NEC	:	National Electricity Corporation
NELP	:	New Exploration Licensing Policy
NIC	:	National Intelligence Council
NIGE Co.	:	National Iranian Gas Exports Company
OML	:	Oil Mining Licence
ONGC	:	Oil and Natural Gas Corporation Ltd.
OPEC	:	Organisation of Petroleum Exporting Countries
OPL	:	Oil Prospecting Licence
OVL	:	ONGC Videsh Ltd.
PDVSA	:	Petroleos de Venezuela
PSCs	:	Production Sharing Contracts
PSI	:	Pan-Sahel Initiative
PTI	:	Press Trust of India
REC	:	Rural Electrification Corporation
REDB	:	Rural Electricity Distribution Backbone
SAARC	:	South Asian Association for Regional Cooperation
SCO	:	Shanghai Cooperation Organisation
SERCs	:	State Electricity Regulatory Commissions
SOFAZ	:	State Oil Fund of Azerbaijan
SPLA	:	Sudan People's Liberation Army
SPR	:	Strategic Petroleum Reserve
TAP	:	Turkmenistan-Afghanistan-Pakistan
UNDP	:	UN Development Programme
UNFCCC	:	United Nations Framework Convention on Climate Change
VEI	:	Village Electrification Infrastructure
WEC	:	World Energy Council
WHO	:	World Health Organisation

Contents

1

Energy Security: Key Determinant of Foreign Policy in the Twenty-first Century

Statement of the Problem

Energy security has become one of the key determinants of the foreign policy of both the developing as well as developed world. This is mainly due to the fact that the future of economic growth now would largely depend on the supply and demand of energy, particularly oil and gas. This is more true in the case of the rising economy of China and India which import respectively 40 per cent and 70 per cent of their total energy requirements. Indeed, the future of the Chinese and Indian economy is inextricably linked to the availability of energy at reasonable prices.

Essentially, as a result of the export of oil and gas, the economic growth of the oil-rich African countries like Angola, Nigeria, Sudan and Senegal etc. have been quite impressive and in fact, have drawn the attention of the leading economists and policy-makers all over the world. For instance, in the year 2005, Angola's real Gross Domestic Product (GDP) growth rate was 14.4 per cent and the forecast GDP growth rate for the year 2006 is 14.6 per cent. More importantly, Angola's oil sector accounts for over 40 per cent of the country's gross domestic protuct.[1]

Likewise, in 2005, Sudan's real gross domestic product grew 6.4 per cent and expected to grow 5.7 per cent in 2006. Currently, 70 per cent of Sudan's total export revenues come from oil exports. Remarkably, the high oil prices have been the driving force behind Nigeria's economic growth in 2005. The country's real gross domestic product grew approximately 4.5 per cent and is expected to grow 6.2 per cent in 2006. The Nigerian economy is heavily dependent on oil sector, which accounts for 95 per cent of the government revenues.

In view of Africa's richness in mineral resources like, uranium, radium, thorium, cobalt, copper, iron ore, gold, platinum, bauxite, phosphates and diamonds as well as the vast deposits of oil and gas in over 20 African countries, the foreign policy of both China and India aims at securing these mineral and energy resources in order to sustain their robust economic growth in the 21st century.

Undoubtedly, the foreign policy of China and India towards Africa is primarily driven by their unprecedented demand for energy. Hence, energy security has emerged as one of the serious challenges for their policy-makers. Keeping this in mind, both China and India have evolved cooperative energy diplomacy in order to avoid competition and confrontation. This is clearly reflected in the case of Sudan, Nigeria and Angola. Efforts are persistently being made both by China and India to evolve cooperative framework to get access to the African mineral and energy resources.

It is remarkable to note that 8 per cent of world's total oil reserves are found in Africa. Major oil reserves in Africa are found in Libya, Algeria, Sudan, Egypt, Tunisia, Nigeria, Cameroon, Gabon, Chad, Senegal, Congo, Angola, Mauritania, Kenya, Ethiopia and Equatorial Guinea. In view of the large oil deposits and mineral resources, China has crafted its Africa policy in such a way that the African continent now accounts for nearly 33 per cent of China's total oil imports.

The concept of energy security occupies prominent place in the foreign policy of China and India because, both these countries are energy deficient and heavily dependent on oil and gas import. The existing notion of energy security which focuses primarily on how to handle any disruption of oil supplies from oil producing countries was developed by the industrial world in the 1970s. Remarkably, it didn't pay attention to the prices of oil and gas. But, today the increasing prices of oil has become a major concern for oil-importing developing countries like China and India and, therefore, the very concept of energy security demands critical review in view of the changed global situation.[2]

Not surprisingly, the oil exporting countries headed by Russia at the G-8 Summit in St. Petersburg, in July 2006 have expressed serious concern over the security of "demand of oil" and sufficient access to the market and consumer in order to justify the future investment and protect their national resources. It ought to be noted that Russia is the second-largest oil exporter after Saudi Arabia and also supplies a quarter of Europe's gas. Hence, Russia's growing concern on energy security is bound to have far-reaching impact on contemporary foreign policy.

Evolving Concept of Energy Security

The definition of *energy security* by the International Energy Agency (IEA) has evolved over the years. For example, in 1985, *Energy Technology Policy* defined it as 'an adequate supply of energy at reasonable cost.[3] By 1993, the definition had grown in complexity, as the following statement of ministers indicates:

Diversity, efficiency, and flexibility within the energy sector are basic conditions for longer-term energy security: the fuels used within and across sectors and the sources of those fuels should be as diverse as practicable. Energy systems should have the ability to respond promptly and flexibly to energy emergencies. In some cases, this requires collective mechanisms and action. Improved energy efficiency can promote both environmental protection and energy security. Continued research, development, and market deployment of new and improved energy technologies contribute to the objectives. Undistorted energy prices enable markets to work efficiently. Free and open trade and a secured framework for investment contribute to efficient energy markets and energy security. Cooperation among all energy market participants helps to improve information and understanding and helps to promote investment, trade, and confidence, necessary to achieve global energy security and environmental objectives.[4]

In its 1990 document, "Security of Supply," the European Commission cited the following definition:

> Security of supply means the ability to ensure that future essential energy needs can be met, both by means of adequate domestic resources worked under economically acceptable conditions or maintained as strategic reserves, and by calling upon accessible and stable external sources supplemented where appropriate, by strategic stocks.[5]

By 2004, the definition had broadened to include concerns about pricing: "the availability of energy at all times in various forms, in sufficient quantities, and at reasonable and/or affordable prices [and] ...the availability of oil and gas in sufficient quantities, and in particular on the risk of oil and gas supply disruptions".[6]

The following definitions from academics and policy analysts show a range in focus from physical security to the inclusion of several other aspects, including reasonable pricing, the politics of the Middle East, sustainable development, and the environmental challenge:

> If security of supply is the assurance of the physical availability of oil during a supply disruption, then a country can be said to have achieved this goal if it is always able to guarantee that a given quantity of oil is available with certainty to its domestic market, independently of possible market disturbances.[7]

> ... a condition in which a nation and all, or most, of its citizens and businesses have access to sufficient energy resources at reasonable prices for the foreseeable future, free from serious risk of major disruption of service.[8]

Energy security has three major dimensions. The first involves limiting vulnerability to disruption, given rising dependence on imported oil from an unstable Middle East. The second broader dimension is, over time, the provision of adequate supply for the rising demand at reasonable prices—in effect, the reasonably smooth functioning over time of the international energy system. The third dimension of security is the energy-related environmental challenge to operate within the constraints of "sustainable development".[9]

Increasing Importance of Energy Security in the Era of Globalisation

Access to cheap energy has become essential to the functioning of modern economies. However, the uneven distribution of energy supplies among countries and the critical need for energy has led to significant vulnerabilities. Threats to global energy security include the political instability of several energy producing countries, the manipulation of energy supplies, the competition over energy sources, attacks on supply infrastructure, as well as accidents and natural disasters.[10] It is also the limited supplies of the most common forms of primary energy, *i.e.* oil and gas that changes perceptions on this issue. Although plenty of coal, up to 155 years worth, is readily available,[11] coal is not the fossil fuel of choice for many more advanced countries, because of its highly polluting nature. The potential need to change our primary energy sources in the foreseeable future is the crux of the energy security question, leading to higher prices, more limited access to sources of energy, competitions and political troubles, which in turn make the threat even larger.

Threats to Energy Security

One of the leading threats to energy security is the significant increase in energy prices, either on the world markets—as has occurred in a number of energy crises over the years—or by the imposition of price increases by an oligopoly or monopoly supplier, cartel or country. In some cases, the threat might come from a single energy superpower—those states able to significantly influence world markets by their action alone. Rather than just manipulating prices, such suppliers might go beyond this by suspending or terminating supplies. This has been done to apply pressure during economic negotiations—such as during the Russia-Belarus energy dispute—or to apply political pressure, for example by OPEC in response to Western support for Israel in the Yom Kippur War. Suspension of supplies may also come about as a result of world-wide international sanctions against a country.

Energy plays an important role in the national security of any given country as a fuel to power the economic engine.[12] Hence, threats to energy security can also result from physical damage to the energy infrastructure either of the supplier, or of the importer, as a result of natural events, misfortune, terrorism, or warfare. The political and economic instability caused by war or other factors, such as strike action can also prevent the proper functioning of the energy industry in a supplier country.

New Threats to Energy Security

In recent years, new threats to energy security have emerged in the form of the increased world competition for energy resources, due to the increased pace of industrialisation in countries such as India and China. Although still a minority concern, the possibility of price rises resulting from the peaking of world oil production is also starting to attract the attention of at least the French government.[13]

In the future, it is possible to envisage threats to energy security, emerging not as a result of energy prices, but as a result of increases in the price of carbon emissions, within carbon emissions trading schemes, or from international political pressure to reduce emissions.

Increased competition over energy resources may also lead to the formation of security compacts to enable an equitable distribution of oil and gas between major powers. However, this may happen at the expense of less developed economies. The Group of Five, precursors to the

G8, first met in 1975 to coordinate economic and energy policies in the wake of the 1973 Arab oil embargo, a rise in inflation and a global economic slowdown.[14]

Long-term Strategy for Energy Security

Long-term measures to increase energy security centre on reducing dependence on any one source of imported energy, increasing the number of suppliers, exploiting native fossil fuel or renewable energy resources, and reducing the overall demand through energy conservation measures. It can also involve entering into international agreements to underpin international energy trading relationships, such as the Energy Charter Treaty in Europe.

The impact of the 1973 oil crisis and the emergence of the OPEC cartel was a particular milestone that prompted some countries to increase their energy security. Japan, almost totally dependent on imported oil, steadily introduced the use of natural gas, nuclear power, high-speed mass transit systems, and implemented energy conservation measures.[15] It has become one of the world leaders in the use of renewable energy.[16] The United Kingdom began exploiting North Sea oil and gas reserves, and became a net exporter of energy into the 2000s.

In other countries, however, energy security has historically been a lower priority. The United States, for example, has continued to increase its dependency on imported oil although, following the oil price increases of 2004-2006, the development of biofuels has been suggested as a means of addressing this.[17]

Increasing energy security is also one of the reasons behind the plans for an oil phase-out in Sweden, together with a block on the development of natural gas imports. Greater investment in native renewable energy technologies and energy conservation is envisaged instead. India is carrying out a major hunt for domestic oil to decrease its dependency on OPEC, while Iceland is well-advanced in its plans to become energy-independent by 2050 through deploying 100 per cent renewable energy.

Short-term Strategy for Energy Security

Many countries hold Strategic Petroleum Reserves (SPR) as a buffer against the economic and political impacts of an energy crisis. All the 26 members of the International Energy Agency hold a minimum of 90 days of their oil imports, for example.[18]

The value of such reserves was demonstrated by the relative lack of disruption caused by the 2007 Russia-Belarus energy dispute, when Russia indirectly cut exports to several countries in the European Union.

Natural Gas

Compared to petroleum, reliance on imported natural gas creates significant short-term vulnerabilities, Many European countries saw an immediate drop in supply, when Russian gas supplies were halted during the Russia-Ukraine gas dispute in 2006.

Improving Energy Security Via Decentralisation

One possible way of simultaneously contributing to international energy and climate security is by investing in decentralized energy. By building electricity generating capacity close to the source of demand, one can improve combustion efficiency (by capturing waste heat) and reduce imports of natural gas and other fuels. Using on-site renewable powered energy can go even further in reducing and fuel imports and emissions responsible for climate change and air pollution.

Guidelines for Figures 1 - 3

Unit: *Thousand metric tons of coal equivalent and kilograms per capita*

Figure Notes:
For figure 1 to 3

Data on individual energy commodities are aggregated and presented in these figures.

Production

Included in the production of commercial primary energy for **Solids** are hard coal, lignite, peat and oil shale; **Liquids** comprised crude petroleum, natural gas liquids, biodiesel and alcohol; **Gas** comprised natural gas and primary steam/heat; and **Electricity** comprised primary electricity generation from hydro, nuclear, geothermal, wind, tide, wave and solar sources.

Stocks, International Trade and Bunkers

Changes in stocks, imports and exports refer to all primary and secondary forms of commercial energy (including condensate and feedstocks); **Air bunkers** refer to bunkers of aviation gasolene and jet fuel; **Sea bunkers** refer to bunkers of hard coal, gas-diesel oil and residual fuel oil.

Consumption

Included in the consumption of commercial energy for **Solids** are consumption of primary forms of solid fuels, net imports and changes in stocks of secondary fuels; **Liquids** comprised consumption of energy petroleum products including feedstocks, natural gasolene, condensate, refinery gas and input of crude petroleum to thermal power plants; **Gases** include the consumption of natural gas, input of heat to thermal power plants, net imports and changes in stocks of gasworks and coke-oven gas; and **Electricity** comprised production of primary electricity and net imports of electricity.

Unallocated

An unallocated column has been created in figures 1-3 in order to balance out the difference between the results of the above formula for consumption and the total consumption column. This inequality occurs primarily because of the exclusion of non-energy petroleum products as well as inadequate or unavailable stock data.

Changes in methodology

Beginning with the forty-eighth edition of this publication, the following products were added: steam/heat, alcohol and biodiesel.

FIGURE 1

Global Pattern of Energy Production and Consumption

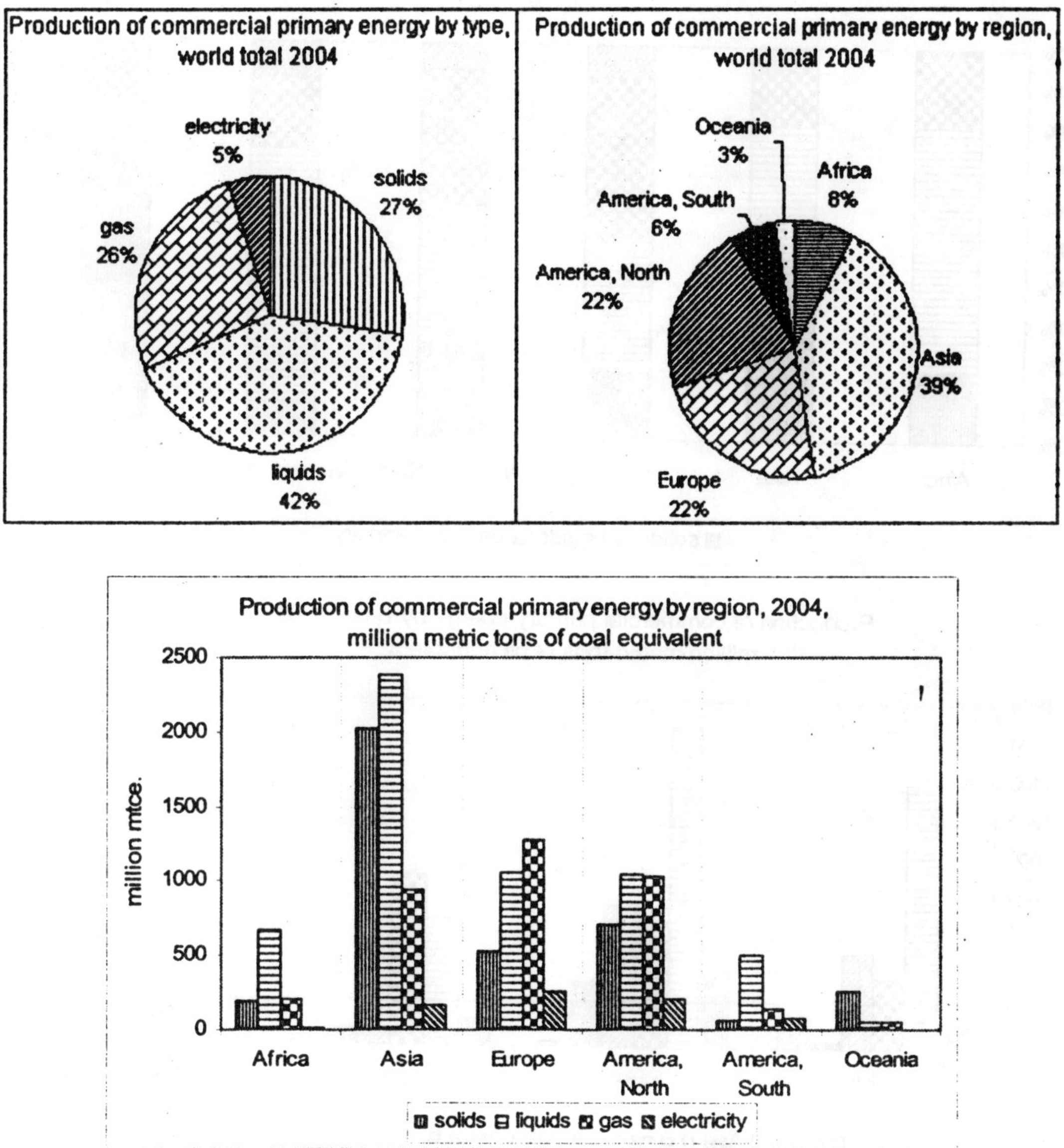

Source: 2004 Energy Statistics Yearbook United Nations, New York, 2007.

FIGURE 2

Production, trade and consumption of commercial energy

Unit: *Thousand metric tons of oil equivalent and kilograms per capita*

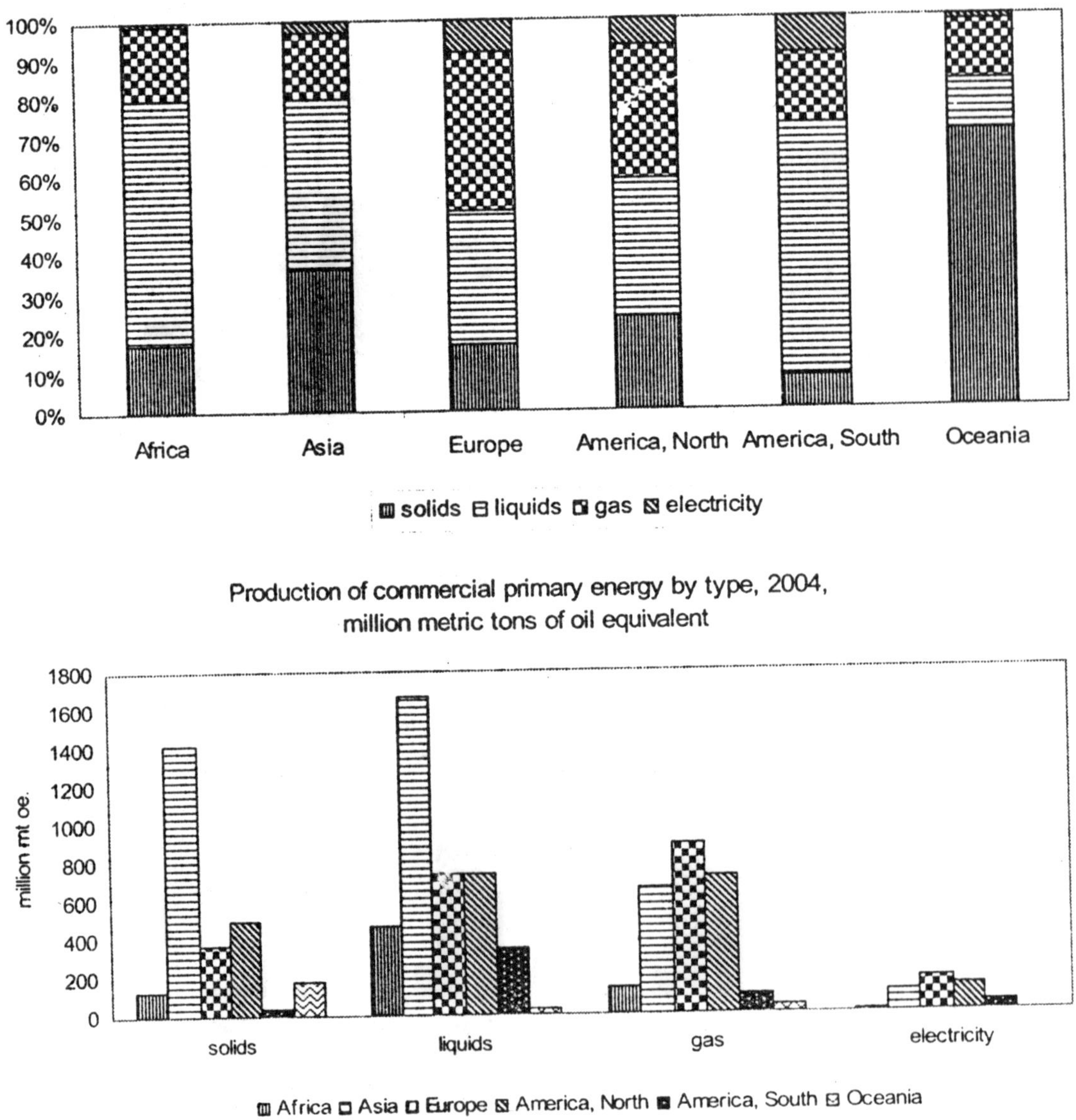

Source: 2004 Energy Statistics Yearbook United Nations, New York, 2007.

FIGURE 3

Production, trade and consumption of commercial energy

Unit: *Thousand terajoules and gigajoules per capita.*

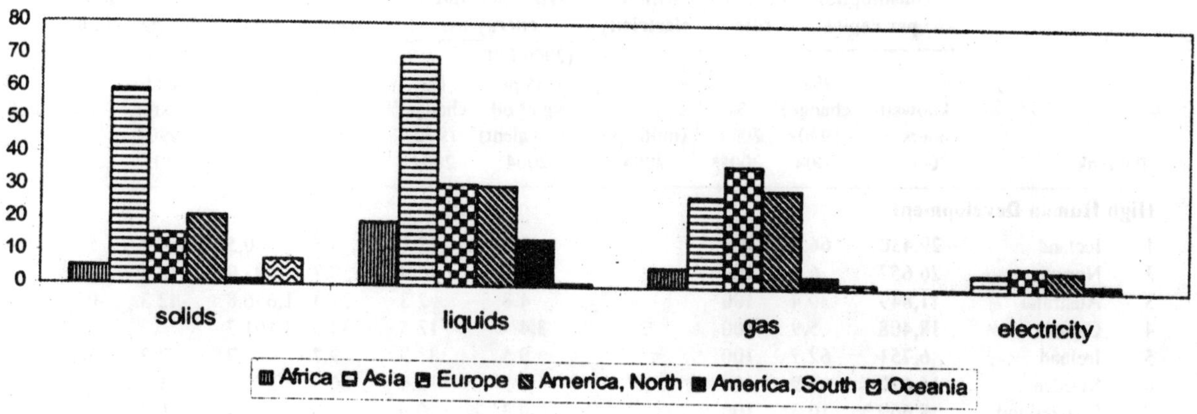

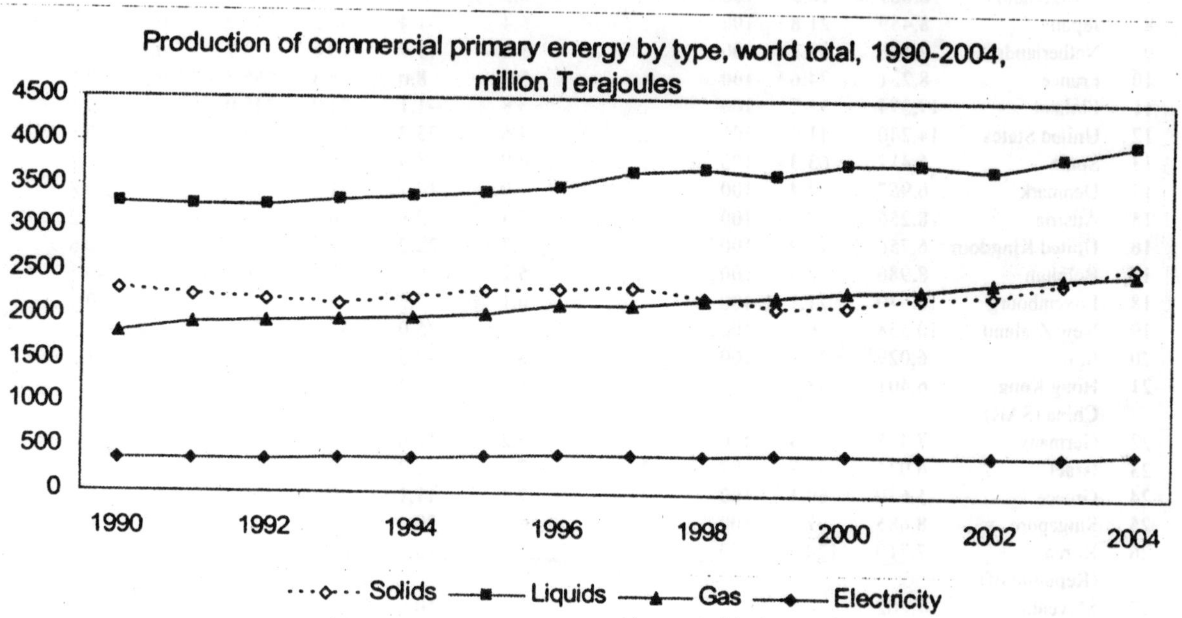

Source: 2004 Energy Statistics Yearbook United Nations, New York, 2007.

TABLE 1

Global energy consumption pattern

HDI rank		Electricity consumption per capita		Electri-fication rate	Population without electricity	GDP per unit of energy use		Forest area			
								% of total land area	Total	Total change	Average annual change
		kilowatt-hours) 2004	(% change) 1990-2004	% 2000-2005[a]	(millions) 2005	(2000 PPP US$ per kg of oil equivalent) 2004	(% change) 1990-2004	(%) 2005	(thou-sand sq km) 2005	(thou-sand sq km) 1990-2005	(%) 1990-2005
High Human Development											
1	Iceland	29,430	66.4	100	..	2.5	-12.1	0.5	0.5	0.2	5.6
2	Norway	26,657	6.5	100	..	5.9	15.9	30.7	93.9	2.6	0.2
3	Australia	11,849	30.4	100	..	4.8	2.3	21.3	1,636.8	-42.3	-0.2
4	Canada	18,408	5.9	100	..	3,4	12.5	33.6	3,101.3	..	..
5	Ireland	6,751	62.7	100	..	9.5	81.9	9.7	6.7	2.3	3.4
6	Sweden	16,670	-1.9	100	..	4.5	13.0	66.9	275.3	1.6	(.)
7	Switzerland	8,669 [b]	10.3[b]	100	..	8.3	0.9	30.9	12.2	0.7	0.4
8	Japan	8,459	21.8	100	..	6.4	-1.4	68.2	248.7	-0.8	(.)
9	Netherlands	7,196	32.7	100	..	5.8	11.7	10.8	3.7	0.2	0.4
10	France	8,231[c]	24.6 [c]	100	..	5.9	8.0	28.3	155.5	10.2	0.5
11	Finland	17,374	33.2	100	..	3.8	-1.1	73.9	225.0	3.1	0.1
12	United States	14,240	11.9	100	..	4.6	25.3	33.1	3,030.9	44.4	0.1
13	Spain	6,412	63.3	100	..	6.9	-4.9	35.9	179.2	44.4	2.2
14	Denmark	6,967	7.4	100	..	7.9	14.7	11.8	5.0	0.6	0.8
15	Austria	8,256	27.7	100	..	7.3	2.9	46.7	38.6	0.9	0.2
16	United Kingdom	6,756	15.9	100	..	7.3	22.2	11.8	28.5	2.3	0.6
17	Belgium	8,986	33.4	100	..	5.2	10.3	22.0	6.7	-0.1	-0.1
18	Luxembourg	16,630	21.1	100	..	6.1	77.5	33.5	0.9	(.)	0.1
19	New Zealand	10,238	6.7	100	..	5.1	25.0	31.0	83.1	5.9	0.5
20	Italy	6,029[d]	36.1[d]	100	..	8.2	-2.5	33.9	99.8	16.0	1.3
21	Hong Kong, China (SAR)	6,401	34.4	..	..	11.5	6.4	..	..	..	..
22	Germany	7,442	10.4	100	..	6.2	31.6	31.7	110,8	3.4	0.2
23	Israel	6,924	62.8	97	0.2	7.3	4.7	8.3	1.7	0.2	0.7
24	Greece	5,630	60.1	100	..	7.4	11.1	29.1	37.5	4.5	0.9
25	Singapore	8,685	67.7	100	0.0	4.4	30.6	3.4	(.)	0.0	0.0
26	Korea (Republic of)	7,710	178.3	100	..	4.2	-6.3	63.5	62.7	-1.1	-0.1
27	Slovenia	7,262	..	..	..	5.4	10.6	62.8	12.6	0.8	0.4
28	Cyprus	5,718	97.2	..	..	5.9	8.5	18.9	1.7	0.1	0.5
29	Portugal	4,925	69.9	100	..	7.1	-9.8	41.3	37.8	6.8	1.5
30	Brunei Darussalam	8,842	80.9	99	0.0	..	..	52.8	2.8	-0.4	-0.7
31	Barbados	3,304	85.0	..	..	..	..	4.0	(.)	..	..
32	Czech Republic	6,720		..	..	4.0	30.8	34.3	26.5	0.2	(.)

Contd....

Contd...table no.1

33	Kuwait	15,423	75,0	100	0.0	1.9	63.1	0.3	0.1	(.)	6.7
34	Malta	5,542	53.4	..	..	7.5	47.9	1.1	..	..	..
35	Qatar	19,840	101.8	71	0.2	..	(.)	..	..	..	..
36	Hungary	4,070	6.7	..	..	5.9	40.6	21.5	19.8	1.8	0.6
37	Poland	3,793	6.9	..	..	51	74.8	30.0	91.9	3.1	0.2
38	Argentina	2,714	70.6	95	1.8	7.4	15.8	12.1	330.2	-22.4	-0.4
39	United Arab Emirates	12,000	41.5	92	0.4	2.2	15.7	3.7	3.1	0.7	1.8
40	Chile	3,347	138.7	99	0.2	6.1	11.9	21.5	161.2	8.6	0.4
41	Bahrain	11,932	52.3	99	0.0	1.8	21.5	0.6	..	..	..
42	Slovakia	5,335	..		..	3.9	45.3	40.1	19.3	0.1	(.)
43	Lithuania	3,505	..		..	4.5	60.5	33.5	21.0	1.5	0.5
44	Estonia	6,168	..		..	3.5	113.2	53.9	22.8	1.2	0.4
45	Latvia	2,923	..		..	5.6	122.6	47.4	29.4	1.7	0.4
46	Uruguay	2,408	52.4	95	0.2	10.4	5.3	8.6	15.1	6.0	4.4
47	Croatia	3,818	..	..	..	5.6	12.0	38.2	21.4	0,2	0.1
48	Costa Rica	1,876	54.4	99	0.1	10.0	2.9	46.8	23.9	-1.7	-0.4
49	Bahamas	6,964[e]	87.0	..	..	..	..	51.5	5.2	..	..
50	Seychelles	2,716[e]	88.2	..	..	..	..	88.9	0.4	0.0	0.0
51	Cuba	1,380	0.6	96	0.5	..	..	24.7	27.1	6.6	2.1
52	Mexico	2,130	46.5	..	..	5.5	8.5	33.7	642.4	-47.8	-0.5
53	Bulgaria	4,582	-10.3	..	..	3.0	44.7	32.8	36.3	3.0	0,6
54	Saint Kitts and Nevis	3,333[e]	115.3	..	..	..	..	14.7	0.1	0.0	0.0
55	Tonga	327[e]	30.8	..	..	..	..	5.0	(.)	0.0	0.0
56	Libyan Arab Jamahiriya	3,147[e]	-22.2	97	0.2	..	..	0.1	2.2	0.0	0.0
57	Antigua and Barbuda	1,346[e]	-10.7	..	..	..	..	21.4	0.1	..	..
58	Oman	5,079	83.2	96	0.1	3.0	-29.9	(.)	(.)	0.0	0.0
59	Trinidad and Tobago	4,921	67.1	99	0.0	1.3	-5.3	44.1	2.3	-0.1	-0.3
60	Romania	2,548	-19.9	..	..	4.5	80.9	27.7	63.7	(.)	0.0
61	Saudi Arabia	6,902	57.9	97	0.8	2.0	-28.2	1.3	27.3	0.0	0.0
62	Panama	1,807	51.0	85	0.5	8.4	13.5	57.7	42.9	-0.8	-0.1
63	Malaysia	3,196	129.6	98	0.6	4.1	-5.1	63.6	208.9	-14.9	-0.4
64	Belarus	3,508	..	..	..	2.4	89.6	38.0	78.9	5.2	0.5
65	Mauritius	1,775	147.2	94	0.1	..	..	18.2	0.4	(.)	-0.3
66	Bosnia and Herzegovina	2,690	..	..	..	5.3	..	43.1	21.9	-0.3	-0.1
67	Russian Federation	6,425	..	..	..	2.0	28.3	47.9	8,087.9	-1.6	0.0
68	Albania	1,847	82.3	..	..	5.9	55.2	29.0	7.9	0.1	(.)
69	Macedonia (TFYR)	3,863				4.6	13.7	35.8	9.1	0.0	0.0
70	Brazil	2,340	39.5	97	6.5	6.8	-6.7	57.2	4,777.0	-423.3	-0.5
Medium Human Development											
71	Dominica	1,129	170.7	..	..	..	..	61.3	0.5	(.)	-0.5
72	Saint Lucia	1,879	136.6	..	..	..	..	27.9	0.2	0.0	0.0

Contd...

Contd...table no.1

73	Kazakhstan	4,320	..	..	..	1.9	86.7	1.2	33.4	-0.9	-0.2
74	Venezuela (Bolivarian Republic of)	3,770	23.6	99	0.4	2.6	0.5	54.1	477.1	-43.1	-0.6
75	Colombia	1,074[e]	3.1	86	6.3	10.9	29.6	58.5	607.3	-7.1	-0.1
76	Ukraine	3,727	..	..	..	2.0	11.7	16.5	95.8	3.0	0.2
77	Samoa	619[e]	103.0	..	..	..	..	60.4	1.7	0.4	2.1
78	Thailand	2,020[e]	141.1	99	0.6	4.9	-14.0	28.4	145.2	-14.5	-0.6
79	Dominican Republic	1,536	197.7	93	0.7	7.6	7.0	28.4	13.8	..	..
80	Belize	686[e]	13,8	..	..	..	..	72.5	16.5	..	..
81	China	1,684	212.4	99	8.5	4.4	108.6	21.2	1,972.9	401.5	1,7
82	Grenada	1,963	225.0					12.2	(.)	..	..
83	Armenia	1,744	..	..	..	5,6	122.8	10.0	2.8	-0.6	-1.2
84	Turkey	2,122	109.5	..	..	6.2	6.4	13.2	101.8	5.0	0.3
85	Suriname	3,437	-9.9	..	..	..	..	94.7	147.8	0.0	0.0
86	Jordan	1,738	53.4	100	0.0	3.6	4.3	0.9	0.8	0.0	0.0
87	Peru	927	44.6	72	7.7	10.9	30.0	53.7	687.4	-14.1	-0.1
88	Lebanon	2,691	374.6	100	0.0	3.5	29.9	13.3	1.4[f]	0.2	0.8
89	Ecuador	1,092	77.3	90	1.3	4.8	-17.7	39.2	108.5	-29.6	-1.4
90	Philippines	677	68.8	81	16.2	7.9	-12.7	24.0	71.6	-34.1	-2.2
91	Tunisia	1,313	93.7	99	0.1	8.2	22.2	6.8	10.6	4.1	4.3
92	Fiji	926[e]	44.9	..	..	..	..	54.7	10.0	0.2	0.1
93	Saint Vincent and the Grenadines	1.030114.1		..	..	..	..	27.4	0.1	(.)	1.5
94	Iran (Islamic Republic of)	2,460	126.7	97	1.8	3.1	-13.6	6.8	110.8	0.0	0.0
95	Paraguay	1,146	99.3	86	0.9	6.4	-2.0	46.5	184.8	-26.8	-0.8
96	Georgia	1,577		..	..	4.1	236.3	39.7	27.6	..	..
97	Guyana	1,090	155.3	..	..	..	..	76.7	151.0'	..	..
98	Azerbaijan	2,796'				2.5		11.3	9.4	..	..
99	Sri Lanka	420	127.0	66	6.7	8.3	13.8	29.9	19.3	-4.2	-1.2
100	Maldives	539	385.6					3.0	(.)	0.0	0.0
101	Jamaica	2,697	160.8	87	0.3	2.5	-18.2	31.3	3.4	-0.1	-0.1
102	Cape Verde	529	330.1	..	..	..	..	20.7	0.8	0.3	3.0
103	El Salvador	732	62.7	80	1.4	7.0	-3.1	14.4	3.0	-0.8	-1.4
104	Algeria	889	40.7	98	0.6	6.0	4.5	1.0	22.8	4.9	1.8
105	Viet Nam	560	324.2	84	13.2	4.2	26.5	39.7	129.3	35.7	2.5
106	Occupied Palestinian Territories	513	..	..	..	..	..	1.5	0.1[f]	0.0	0.0
107	Indonesia	476[e]	75.0	54	101.2	4.1	-0.1	48.8	885.0	-280.7	-1.6
108	Syrian Arab Republic	1,784	88.4	90	1.9	3.4	19.9	2.5	4.6	0.9	1.6
109	Turkmenistan	2,060	..	..	..	1.3[g]	-21.3	8.8	41.3	0.0	0.0
110	Nicaragua	525	37.1	69	1.7	5.2	-2.3	42.7	51.9	-13.5	-1.4
111	Moldova	1,554	..	..	..	2.0	40.8	10.0	3.3	0.1	0.2
112	Egypt	1,465[e]	93.0	98	1.5	4.9	-2.2	0.1	0.7	0.2	3.5
113	Uzbekistan	1,944	..	..	..	0.8	11.1	8.0	33.0	2.5	0.5
114	Mongolia	1,260	-25.2	65	1.0	..	..	6.5	102.5	-12.4	-0.7
115	Honduras	730	79.4	62	2.7	4.8	-3.9	41.5	46.5	-27.4	-2.5

Contd...

Contd...table no.1

116	Kyrgyzstan	2,320	..	..	..	3.3	92.3	4.5	8.7	0.3	0.3
117	Bolivia	493	42.1	64	3.3	4.5	-10.6	54.2	587.4	-40.6	-0.4
118	Guatemala	532	100.0	79	2.7	6.4	-3.6	36:3	39.4	-8.1	-1.1
119	Gabon	1,128	5.4	48	0.7	4.9	3.1	84.5	217.8	-1.5	(.1)
120	Vanuatu	206 [e]	18.4	..	..	..	..	36.1	4.4	0.0	0.0
121	South Africa	4,818 [h]	20.8[h]	70	14.0	3.7	-4.5	7.6	92.0	0.0	0.0
122	Tajikistan	2,638	..	..	..	2.1	139.6	2.9	4.1	(.)	(1.)
123	Sao Tome and Principe	99 [e]	-23.8	..	..	..	..	28.4	0.3	0.0	0.0
124	Botswana	..[i]	..[i]	39	1.1	8.6	40.0	21.1	119.4	-17.8	-0.9
125	Namibia	..[i]	..[i]	34	1,4	10.2	-16.5	9.3	76.6	-11.0	-0.8
126	Morocco	652	84.7	85	4.5	10.3	-13.9	9.8	43.6	0.8	0.1
127	Equatorial Guinea	52 [e]	0	..	..	..	..	58.2	16.3	-2.3	-0.8
128	India	618	77.6	56	487.2	5.5	37.1	22.8	677.0	37.6‘	0.4
129.	Solomon Islands	107 [e]	13.8	..	..	..	..	77.7	21.7	-6.0	-1.4
130	Lao People's Democratic Republic	126 [e]	80.0	..	..	..	..	69.9	161.4	-11.7	-0.5
131	Cambodia	10 [e]	-44.4	20	10.9	..	..	59.2	104.5	-25.0	-1.3
132	Myanmar	129	111.5	11	45.1	..	..	49.0	322.2	-70.0	-1.2
133	Bhutan	229 [e]	126.7	..	..	..	..	68.0	32.0	1.6	0.4
134	Comoros	31 [e]	3.3	..	..	..	..	2.9	0.1	-0.1	-3.9
135	Ghana	289	-22.3	49	11.3	5.4	18.3	24.2	55.2	-19.3	-1.7
136	Pakistan	564	61.6.	54	71.1	4.2	7.7	2.5	19.0	-6.3	-1.6
137	Mauritania	112 [e]	60.0	..	..	..	..	0.3	2,7	-1.5	-2.4
138	Lesotho	..[i]	..[i]	11	1.9			0.3	0.1	(.)	4.0
139	Congo	229	-2.1	20	3.2	3.3	45.4	65.8	224.7	-2.6	-0.1
140	Bangladesh	154	111.0	32	96.2	10.5	7.2	6.7	8.7	-0.1	-0.1
141	Swaziland	L	..[i]	..	..	..	..	31.5	5.4	0.7	1.0
142	Nepal	86	104.8	33	18.1	4.0	18.4	25.4	36.4	-11.8	-1.6
143	Madagascar	56	5.7	15	15.2	..	..	22.1	128.4	-8.5	-0.4
144	Cameroon	256	8.9	47	8.7	4.5	-4.4	45.6	212.5	-33.0	-0.9
145	Papua New Guinea	620 [e]	28.1	..	..	..	..	65.0	294.4	-20.9	-0.4
146	Haiti	61	-17.6	36	5.5	6.2	-39.9	3.8	1.1	-0.1	-0.6
147	Sudan	116	123.1	30	25.4	3.7	33.2	28.4	675.5	-88.4	-0.8
148	Kenya	169	26.1	14	29.4	2.1	-3.8	6.2	35.2	-1.9	-0.3
149	Djibouti	260 [e]	-46.8	..	..	..	..	0.2	0.1	..	..
150	Timor-Leste	294 [e]	..	..	..	..	..	53.7	8.0	-1.7	-1.2
151	Zimbabwe	924	-10.1	34	8.7	2.6	-13.4	45.3	175.4	-46.9	-1.4
152	Togo	102	1.0	17	5.1	3.1	-26.9	7.1	3.9	-3.0	-2.9
153	Yemen	208	34.2	36	13.2	2.8	-6.0	1.0	5.5	0.0	0.0
154	Uganda	63 [e]	61.5	9	24.6	..	..	18.4	36.3	-13.0	-1.8
-155	Gambia	98 [e]	30.7	..	..	..	..	41.7	4.7	0.3	0.4
Low Human Development											
156	Senegal	206	70.2	33	7.8	6.5	28.2	45.0	86.7	-6.8	-0.5
157	Eritrea	67	..	20	3.5	..	..	15.4	15.5	-0.7	-0.3

Contd...

Contd...table no.1

158	Nigeria	157	-1.9	46	71.1	1.4	22.7	12.2	110.9	-61.5	-2.4
159	Tanzania (United Republic of)	69	4.5	11	34.2	1.3	-12.5	39.9	352.6	-61.8	-1.0
160	Guinea	87[e]	3.6	..	..	..	..	27.4	67.2	-6.8	-0.6
161	Rwanda	31[e]	24.0	..	..	..	..	19.5	4.8	1.6	3.4
162	Angola	220	161.9	15	13.5	3.3	-12.4	47.4	591.0	-18.7	-0.2
163	Benin	81	72.3	22	6.5	3.3	25.8	21.3	23.5	-9.7	-1.9
164	Malawi	100[e]	14.9	7	11.8	..	..	36.2	34.0	-4.9	-0.8
165	Zambia	721	-7.8	19	9.5	1.5	1.4	57.1	424.5	-66.7	-0.9
166	Côte d'Ivoire	224	7.7	50	9.1	3.7	29.1	32.7	104.1	1.8	0.1
167	Burundi	22[e]	-4.3	..	..	..	..	5.9	1.5	-1.4	-3.2
168	Congo (Democratic Republic of)	92	-42.1	6	53.8	2.2	-55.8	58.9	1,336.1	-69.2	-0.3
169	Ethiopia	36	..	15	60.8	2.8	5.8	11.9	130.0	-21.1	-0.9
170	Chad	11[e]	-31.3	..	..	..	..	9.5	119.2	-11.9	-0.6
171	Central African Republic	28[e]	-12.5	..	..	..	..	36.5	227.6	-4.5	-0.1
172	Mozambique	545	856.1	6	18.6	2.6	105.8	24.6	192.6	-7.5	-0.2
173	Mali	41[e]	36.7	..	..	..	..	10.3	125.7	-15.0	-0.7
174	Niger	40[e]	-13.0	..	..	..	..	1.0	12.7	-6.8	-2.3
175	Guinea-Bissau	44[e]	4.8	..	..	..	..	73.7	20.7	-1.4	-0.4
176	Burkina Faso	31[e]	55.0	7	12.4	..	..	29.0	67.9	-3.6	-0.3
177	Sierra Leone	24	-54.7	..	..	..	..	38.5	27.5	-2.9	-0.6
Developing countries		1,221	..	68[j]	1,569.0	4.6	..	27.9	21,147.8	-1,381.7	-0.4
Least developed countries		119	..	..	..	..	..	27.5	5,541.6	-583.6	-0.6
Arab States		1,841	..	..	..	3.4	..	7.2	877.7	-88.0	-0.6
East Asia and the Pacific		1,599	..	..	..	..	..	28.6	4,579.3	-75.5	0.1
Latin America and the Caribbean		2,043	..	90[j]	45.0[j]	6.2	..	45.9	9,159.0	-686.3	-0.5
South Asia		628	..	..	..	5.1	..	14.2	911.8	12.5	0.1
Sub-Saharan Africa		478	..	26[j]	547.0[j]	..	..	26.8	5,516.4	-549.6	0.6
Central and Eastern Europe and the CIS		4,539	..	..	..	2.6	..	38.3	8,856.5	22.7	(.)
OECD		8,795	..	100	..	5.3	..	30.9	10,382.4	67.9	0.1
High-income OECD		10,360	..	100	..	5.3	..	31.2	9,480	105.6	0.1
High human development		7,518	..	99	..	5.0	..	36.2	24,327.1	-366.8	-0.1
Medium human development		1,146	..	72	:	4.5	..	23.3	10799.6	462.4	-0.2
Low human development		134	..	25	..	..	..	29.8	4,076.5	-379.5	-0.5
High income		10,210	..	100	..	5.2	..	29.2	9,548.4	107.1	0.1
Middle income		2,039	..	90	..	4.2	..	33.8	23,132.3	-683.1	-0.2
Low income		449	..	45	..	..	..	23.9	6,745.6	-676.2	-0.6
World		2,701[j]	..[j]	76[j]	1,577.0[j]	4.8[j]	..	30.3[j]	39,520.3[j]	1,252.7[j]	-0.2

Source: Human Development Report 2007-2008

NOTES

a. Data refer to the most recent year available during the period specified.
b. Includes Liechtenstein.
c. Includes Monaco.
d. Includes San Marino.
e. Data are estimates produced by the UN Statistics Division.
f. Estimate produced by the Food and Agriculture Organization based on information provided by the country.
g. Data refer to a year or period other than that specified.
h. Data refer to the South African Customs Union, which includes Botswana, Lesotho, Namibia and Swaziland.
i. Included in data for South Africa.
j. Data are aggregates provided by original data source.

Sources
Column 1: UN2007d.
Column 2: calculated based on data from UN 2007b,
Columns 3-4: IEA 2002 and IEA 2006.
Column 5 : World Bank 2007b, based on data from IEA.
Columns 6: calculated based on data from World Bank 2007b.
Columns 7-8: FAO 2006,
Columns 9-10: calculated based on data from **FAO 2006.**

TABLE 2

Energy Sources

				Share of TPES[a]													
				Fossil fuels						*Renewable energy*[b]				*Other*			
		Tpes (Mt of oil equivalent)		*Coal*[c] (%)		*Oil*[d] (%)		*Natural gas* (%)		*Hydro, solar, wind and geothermal* (%)		*Biomass and waste*[e] (%)		*Nuclear* (%)	
HDI rank		*1990*	*2005*	*1990*	*2005*	*1990*	*2005*	*1990*	*2005*	*1990*	*2005*	*1990*	*2005*	*1990*	*2005*		
High Human Development																	
1	Iceland	2.2	3.6	3.0	2.7	32.6	24.6	0.0	0.0	64.5	72.6	0.0	0.1	0.0	0.0		
2	Norway	21.5	32.1	4.0	2.4	39.8	44.1	9.2	16.1	48.5	36.6	4.8	4.1	0.0	0.0		
3	Australia	87.5	122.0	40.0	44.5	37.1	31.1	16.9	18.9	1.5	1.2	4.5	4.3	0.0	0.0		
4	Canada	209.4	272.0	11.6	10.3	36.9	35.8	26.1	29.6	12.2	11.5	3.9	4.6	9.3	8.8		
5	Ireland	10.4	15.3	33.3	17.6	47.0	56.0	18.1	22.7	0.6	1.0	1.0	1.6	0.0	0.0		
6	Sweden	47.6	52.2	6.2	5.0	30.8	28.5	1.2	1.6	13.1	12.7	11.6	17.2	37.4	36.2		
7	Switzerland	25.0	27.2	1.4	0.6	53.8	47.1	6.5	10.2	10.5	10.5	3.7	7.1	24.7	22.5		
8	Japan	444.5	530.5	17.4	21.1	57.4	47.4	9.9	13.3	2.3	2.0	1.1	1.2	11.9	15.0		
9	Netherlands	66.8	81.8	13.4	10.0	36.5	40.2	46.1	43.1	(.)	0.3	1.4	3.2	1.4	1.3		
10	France	227.8	276.0	8.9	5.2	38.3	33.1	11.4	14.9	2.1	1.7	5.1	4.3	35.9	42.6		
11	Finland	29.2	35.0	18.2	14.1	35.1	30.6	7.5	10.3	3.2	3.9	15.6	19.6	17.2	17.3		
12	United States	1,927.5	2,340.3	23.8	23.7	40.0	40.7	22.8	21.8	2.0	1.5	3.2	3.2	8.3	9.0		
13	Spain	91.1	145.2	21.2	14.1	51.0	49.1	5.5	20.5	2.4	2.5	4.5	3.5	15.5	10.3		
14	Denmark	17.9	19.6	34.0	18.9	45.7	41.8	10.2	22.4	0.3	3.0	6.4	13.2	0.0	0.0		
15	Austria	25.1	34.4	16.3	11.8	42.4	42.2	20.7	24.0	10.9	9.7	9.8	11.6	0.0	0.0		
16	United Kingdom	212.2	233.9	29.7	16.1	38.9	36.2	22.2	36.3	0.2	0.3	0.3	1.7	8.1	9.1		
17	Belgium	49.2	56.7	21.7	9.0	38.1	40.2	16.6	24.9	0.1	0.2	1.5	2.8	22.6	21.9		
18	Luxembourg	3.6	4.8	31.7	1.7	45.9	66.2	12.0	24.7	0.2	0.3	0.7	1.2	0.0	0.0		
19	New Zealand	13.8	16.9	8.2	11.8	28.8	40.3	28.3	18.9	30.7	23.8	4.0	5.1	0.0	0.0		
20	Italy	148.0	185.2	9.9	8.9	57.3	44.2	26.4	38.1	3.8	4.3	0.6	2.3	0.0	0.0		

Contd...

Contd...table no.2

21	Hong Kong, China (SAR)	10.7	18.1	51.5	36.8	49.4	47.7	0.0	12.1	0.0	0.0	0.5	0.3	0.0	0.0
22	Germany	356.2	344.7	36.1	23.7	35.5	35.8	15.4	23.4	0.4	1.3	1.3	3.5	11.2	12.3
23	Israel	12:1	19.5	19.8	39.2	77.3	51.2	0.2	6.6	3.0	3.7	(.)	(.)	0.0	0.0
24	Greece	22.2	31.0	36.4	28.9	57.7	57.1	0.6	7.6	1.0	2.1	4.0	3.3	0.0	0.0
25	Singapore	13.4	30.1	0.2	(.)	99.8	80.3	0.0	19.7	0.0	0.0	0.0	0.0	0.0	0.0
26	Korea (Republic of)	93.4	213.8	27.4	23.1	53.6	45.0	2.9	12.8	0.6	0.2	0.8	1.0	14.8	17.9
27	Slovenia	5,6	7.3	25.4	20.2	31.7	35.8	13.6	12.7	4.5	4.1	4.8	6.7	21.5	21.0
28	Cyprus	1.6	2.6	3.7	1.5	95.9	96.3	0.0	0.0	0.0	1.6	0.4	0.6	0.0	0.0
29	Portugal	17.7	27.2	15.5	12.3	66.0	58.5	0.0	13.8	4.5	2.4	14.0	10.8	0.0	0.0
30	Brunei Darussalam	1.8	2.6	0.0	0.0	6.8	29.7	92.2	69.6	-0.0	0.0	1.0	0.7	0.0	0.0
31	Barbados	..	..	..	..	..	..	..	..	..	..	..	..	..	..
32	Czech Republic	49.0	45.2	64.2	44.7	18.3	22.1	10.7	17.0	0.2	0.5	0.0	3.9	6.7	14.3
33	Kuwait	8.5	28.1	0.0	0.0	40.1	66.5	59.8	33.5	0.0	0.0	0.1	0.0	0.0	0.0
34	Malta	0.8	0.9	23.8	0.0	76.2	100.0	0.0	0.0	0.0	0.0	0.0	0.0	0.0	0.0
35	Qatar	6.3	15.8	0.0	0.0	12.1	15.7	87.8	84.3	0.0	0.0	0.1	(.)	0.0	0.0
36	Hungary	28.6	27.8	21.4	11.1	29.8	26.0	31.2	43.6	0.4	0.4	1.3	4,0	12.5	13.0
37	Poland	99.9	93.0	75.5	58.7	13.3	23.8	9.0	13.2	0.1	0.2	2.2	5.1	0.0	0.0
38	Argentina	46.1	63.7	2.1	1.4	45.7	36.7	40.8	50.4	3.4	4.6	3.7	3.5	4.1	2.8
39	United Arab Emirates	22.5	46.9	0.0	0.0	39.9	27.9	60.1	72.1	0.0	0.0	0.0	(.)	0.0	0.0
40	Chile	14.1	29.6	18.4	13.9	45.8	39.2	10.6	23.8	6.2	7.0	19.0	15.5	0.0	0.0
41	Bahrain	4.8	8.1	0.0	0.0	26.5	23.2	73.5	76.8	0.0	0.0	0.0	0.0	0.0	0.0
42	Slovakia	21.3	18.8	36.7	22.5	21.1	18.4	23.9	31.2	0.8	2.2	0.8	2.4	14.7	24.8
43	Lithuania	16.2	8.6	4.9	2.3	42.2	29.1	28.9	28.8	0.7	2.4	1.8	8.3	27.8	31.9
44	Estonia	9.6	5.1	59.9	59.3	31.7	15.5	12.8	15.7	0.0	0.1	2.0	12.1	0.0	0.0
45	Latvia	7.8	4.7	6.3	1.3	45.3	29.7	30.6	28.8	5.4	6.1	8.5	30.2	0.0	0.0
46	Uruguay	2.3	2.9	(.)	0.1	58.6	59.4	0.0	3.1	26.8	19.9	24.2	15.4	0.0	0.0
47	Croatia	9.1	8.9	9,0	7.5	53.4	50.7	24.2	26.7	3.6	6.1	3.4	4.0	0.0	0.0
48	Costa Rica	2.0	3.8	0.1	0.5	48.3	51.4	0.0	0.0	14.4	41.1	36.6	7.0	0.0	0.0
49	Bahamas	..	..	..	..	..	..	..	..	..	..	..	..	..	..
50	Seychelles	..	..	..	..	..	..	..	..	..	..	..	..	..	..
51	Cuba	16.8	10.2	0.8	0.2	64.1	73.4	0.2	6.0	(.)	0.1	34.3	20.3	0.0	0.0
52	Mexico	124.3	176.5	2.8	4.9	67.0	58.8	18.6	25.0	5.2	4.9	5.9	4.7	0.6	1.6
53	Bulgaria	28.8	20.1	32.1	34.6	33.7	24.6	18.7	14.0	0,6	2.0	0.6	3.7	13.3	24.3
54	Saint Kitts and Nevis	..	..	..	..	..	..	..	..	..	..	..	..	..	..
55	Tonga	..	..	..	..	..	..	..	..	..	..	..	..	..	..
56	Libyan Arab Jamahiriya	11.5	19.0	0.0	0.0	63.8	72.2	35.1	27.0	0.0	0.0	1.1	0.8	0.0	0.0
57	Antigua and Barbuda	..	..	..	..	..	..	..	..	..	..	..	..	..	..
58	Oman	4.6	14.0	0.1	0.0	466	33.3	53.4	66.7	0.0	0.0	0.0	0.0	0.0	0.0
59	Trinidad and Tobago	6.0	12.7	0.0	0.0	21.4	13.6	77.8	86.2	0.0	0.0	0.8	0.2	0.0	0.0
60	Romania	62.4	38.3	20.7	22.7	29.2	24.6	46.2	36.4	1.6	4.7	1.0	8.5	0.0	3.8
61	Saudi Arabia	61.3	140.3	0.0	0.0	64.7	63.6	35.3	36.4	0.0	0.0	(.)	(.)	0.0	0.0
62	Panama	1.5	2.6	1.3	0.0	57.1	71.7	0.0	0.0	12.8	12.3	28.3	16.1	0.0	0.0
63	Malaysia	23.3	61.3	4.4	9.6	55.8	43.3	29.2	41.8	1.5	0.8	9.1	4.5	0.0	0.0
64	Belarus	42.2	26.6	5.6	2.4	62.2	27.9	29.7	63.7	(.)	(.)	0.5	4.8	0.0	0.0

Contd...

Contd...table no.2

65	Mauritius	..	..	..	..	..	..	..	..	..	..	..	..	..	..
66	Bosnia and Herzegovina	7.0	5.0	59.4	55.3	29.0	26.6	5.5	7.4	3.7	9.5	2.3	3.7	0.0	0.0
67	Russian Federation	878.3	646.7	20.7	16.0	31.0	20.6	41.8	54.1	1.6	2.4	1.4	1.1	3.6	6.1
68	Albania	2.7	2.4	23.7	1.0	45.2	68.1	7.6	0.6	9.2	19.3	13.6	9.6	0.0	0.0
69	Macedonia (TFYR.)	2.7	2.7	57.6	48.7	40.6	33.2	0.0	2.3	1.6	5.1	0.0	5.6	0.0	0.0
70	Brazil	134.0	209.5	7.2	6.5	43.9	42.2	2.4	8.0	13.3	13,9	31.1	26.5	0.4	1.2
Medium Human Development															
71	Dominica	..	..	..	..	..	..	..	..	..	..	..	..	..	..
72	Saint Lucia	..	..	..	..	..	..	..	..	..	..	..	..	..	..
73	Kazakhstan	73.7	52.4	54.2	52.6	28.2	14.5	14.5	33.5	0.9	1.3	0.2	0.1	0.0	0.0
74	Venezuela (Bolivarian Republic of)	43.9	60.9	1.1	0.1	43.2	50.4	47.2	38.1	7.2	10.6	1.2	0.9	0.0	0.0
75	Colombia	24.7	28.6	12.4	9.4	42.0	43.3	13.6	21.4	9.6	12,0	22.3	14.4	0.0	0.0
76	Ukraine	251.7	143.2	32.0	26.0	24.1	10.3	36.5	47.1	0.4	0.7	0.1	0.2	7.9	16.1
77	Samoa	..	..	..	..	..	..	..	..	..	..	..	..	..	..
78	Thailand	43.9	100.0	8.7	11.2	45.2	45.5	11.6	25.9	1.0	0.5	33.4	16.5	0,0	0.0
79	Dominican Republic	4.1	7.4	0.3	4.0	74.8	75.1	0.0	0.1	0.7	2.2	24.2	18.6	0.0	0.0
80	Belize	..	..	..	..	..	..	..	..	..	..	..	..	..	..
81	China	863.2	1,717.2	61.2	63.3	12.8	18.5	1.5	2.3	1.3	2.0	23.2	13.0	0.0	0.8
82	Grenada	..	..	..	..	..	..	..	..	..	..	..	..	..	..
83	Armenia	7.9	2.6	3.1	0.0	48.9	16.6	45.2	52.3	1.7	6.0	(.)	(.)	0.0	27.7
84	Turkey	53.0	85.2	31.9	26,4	44.6	35.1	5.4	26.7	4.6	5.6	13.6	6.3	0.0	0.0
85	Surinam	..	..	..	..	..	..	..	..	..	..	..	..	..	..
86	Jordan	3.5	7.1	0.0	0.0	95.3	78.5	2.9	19.5	1.7	1.0	0.1	(.)	0.0	0.0
87	Peru	10.0	13.8	1.5	6.7	58,5	53.5	4.1	10.6	9.0	12.8	26.9	16.4	0.0	0.0
88	Lebanon	2.3	5.6	0.0	2.4	93.7	92.9	0.0	0.0	1.9	1.8	4.4	2.3	0.0	0.0
89	Ecuador	6.1	10.4	0.0	0.0	75.9	83,5	3.7	4.4	7.0	5.7	13.5	5.1	0.0	0.0
90	Philippines	26.2	44.7	5.0	13.6	45.9	35.4	0.0	5.9	20.0	20.7	29.2	24.4	0.0	0.0
91	Tunisia	5.5	8.5	1.4	0.0	57.5	50.0	22.3	36.6	0.1	0.2	18.7	13.3	0.0	0.0
92	Fiji	..	..	..	..	..	..	..	..	..	..	..	..	..	..
93	Saint Vincent and the Grenadines	..	..	..	..	..	..	..	..	..	..	..	..	..	..
94	Iran (Islamic Republic of)	68.8	162.5	0.9	0.7	71.9	47.5	25.4	50.5	0.8	0.9	1.0	0.5	0.0	0.0
95	Paraguay	3.1	4.0	:	..	..	..	..	..	..	..	..	..	..	..
96	Georgia	12.3	3.2	4.8	0.5	47.1	25.3	36.9	33.5	5.3	17.0	3.7	20.1	0.0	0.0
97	Guyana	..	..	..	..	..	..	..	..	..	..	..	..	..	..
.98	Azerbaijan	26.0	13.8	0.3	0.0	45.2	38.6	54.7	58.7	0.2	1.9	(.)	(.)	0.0	0.0
99	Sri Lanka	5.5	9.4	0.1	0.7	24.0	43.2	0.0	0.0	4.9	3.2	71.0	52.9	0.0	0.0
100	Maldives														
101	Jamaica	2.9	3.8	1.1	1.0	82.4	86.5	0.0	0.0	0.3	0.3	16.2	12.2	0.0	0.0
102	Cape Verde	..	..	..	..	..	..	..	..	..	..	..	..	..	..
103	El Salvador	2.5	4.6	0.0	(.)	32.0	44.4	0.O	0.0	19.8	22.6	48.1	32.4	0.0	0.0
104	Algeria	23.9	34.8	2.6	2.0	40.6	31.7	56.7	66.0	(.)	0.1	0.1	0.2	0.0	0.0
105	Vietnam	24.3	51.3	9.1	15.8	11.3	24.3	(.)	9.6	1.9	3.6	77.7	46.7	0.0	0.0

Contd...

Contd...table no.2

106	Occupied Palestinian Territories	..	..	...	..	..	..	..	..	..	..	..	..	..	..
107	Indonesia	103.2	179.5	3.8	14.2	33.2	36.6	17.9	17.1	1.5	3.7	43.6	28.5	0.0	0.0
108	Syrian Arab Republic	11.7	17.9	0.0	(.)	86.3	65.3	11.7	33.0	2.0	1.7	. (.)	(.)	0.0	0.0
109	Turkmenistan	19.6	16.3	1.5	0.0	38.0	26.5	62.4	75.0	0.1	(.)	0.0	0.0	0.0	0.0
110	Nicaragua	2.1	3.3	. 0.0	0.0	29.2	41.4	0.0	0.0	17.3	8.1	53.2	50.5	0.0	0.0
111	Moldova	10.0	3.6	20.0	2.1	49.3	19.0	32.8	69.0	0.2	0.2	0.4	2.1	0.0	0.0
112	Egypt	31.9	61.3	2.4	1.5	70.5	49.2	21.1	45.3	2.7	1.9	3.3	2.3	0.0	0.0
113	Uzbekistan	46.4	47.0	7.3	2.2	21.8	12.1	70.0	84.6	1.2	1.1	(.)	(.)	0.0	0.0
114	Mongolia	3.4	2.6	73.6	75.0	24.5	22.7	0.0	0.0	0.0	0.0	1.3	1.7	0.0	0.0
115	Honduras	2.4	3.9	(.)	2.9	31.1	51.0	0.0	0.0	8.1	4.0	62.0	42.0	0.0	0.0
116	Kyrgyzstan	7.6	2.8	33.2	19.7	40.5	22.5	19.9	22.1	11.3	43.8	0.1	0.1	0.0	0.0
117	Bolivia	2.8	5.3	0.0	0.0	46.5	56.2	22.6	25.8	3.7	4.0	27.2	14.0	0.0	0.0
118	Guatemala	4.5	8,0	0.0	3.1	28.8	40.5	0.0	0.0	3.4	3.5	67.9	53.2	0.0	0.0
119	Gabon	1.2	1.7	0.0	0.0	28.2	31.0	7.2	6.1	49	4.1	59.7	58.8	0.0	0.0
120	Vanuatu	:	:	:	..	..	..	..	..	..	..	..	..	..	..
121	South Africa	91.2	127.6	72.9	72.0	11.6	12.2	1,6	2.8	0.1	0.2	11.4	10.5	2.4	2.3
122	Tajikistan	5.6	3.5	11.2	1.3	36.8	42.6	24.8	14.0	25.4	41.5	0.0	0.0	0.0	0.0
123	Sao Tome and Principe	..	..	..	..	..	..	..	..	..	..	..	..	..	..
124	Botswana	1.3	1.9	39.4	31.5	26.9	36.5	0.0	0.0	(.)	(.)	33.1	24.1	0.0	0.0
125	Namibia	..	1.4	..	0.2	..	66.8		0.0		10.3		13.5	..	0.0
126	Morocco	6.7	13.8	16.8	32.3	76.1	60.2	0.6	2.8	1.6	1.0	4.7	3.3	0.0	0.0
127	Equatorial Guinea	..	..	..	..	..	..	..	..	..	..	..	..	..	..
128	India	319.9	537.3	33.2	38.7	19.6	23.9	3.1	5.4	1.9	1.7	41.7	29.4	0.5	0.8
129	Solomon Islands														
130	Lao People's Democratic Republic	..	..	..	..	..	..	..	..	..	..	..	..	..	..
131	Cambodia	..	4.8	..	0.0	..	26.6	..	0.0	..	0.1	..	73.2	..	0.0
132	Myanmar	10.7	14.7	0.6	0.6	6.9	13.7	7.1	14.4	1.0	1.8	84.4	69.6	0.0	0.0
133	Bhutan	..	..	..	..	..	..	..	..	..	..	..	..	..	..
134	Comoros	..	..	..	..	..	..	..	..	..	..	..	..	..	..
135	Ghana	5.3	8.9	0.0	0.0	18.9	28.7	0.0	0.0	9.2	5.1	73.1	66.0	0.0	0.0
136	Pakistan	43.4	76.3	4.8	5.3	25.2	21.9	23.2	33.0	3.4	3.5	43.2	35.5	0.2	0.8
137	Mauritania	..	..	..	..	..	..	..	..	..	..	..	..	..	..
138	Lesotho	..	..	..	..	..	..	..	..	..	..	..	..	..	..
139	Congo	1.1	1.2	0.0	0.0	26.5	38.2	0.0	0.0	4.0	2.5	69.4	56.3	0.0	0.0
140	Bangladesh	12.8	24.2	2.2	1.4	14.7	19.1	29.0	44.7	0.6	0.5	53.5	34.3	0.0	0.0
141	Swaziland														
142	Nepal	5.8	9.2	0.8	2.0	4.5	9.2	0.0	0.0	1.3	2.3	93.4	86.6	0.0	0.0
143	Madagascar														
144	Cameroon	5.0	7.0	0.0	0.0	19.5	16.6	0.0	0,0	4.5	4.8	75.9	78.6	0.0	0.0
145	Papua New Guinea	..	..	..	..	..	..	..	..	..	..	..	..	..	..
146	Haiti	1.6	2.5	0.5	0.0	20.5	23.2	0.0	0.0	2.5	0.9	76.5	75.8	0.0	0.0
147	Sudan	10.6	18.4	0.0	0,0	17.5	19,9	0.0	0.0	0.8	0.6	81.7	79.5	0.0	0.0
148	Kenya	12.5	17.2	0.7	0.4	16.8	19.1	0.0	0.0	4.0	5.9	78.4	74.6	0.0	0.0
149	Djibouti	..	..	..	..	..	..	..	..	..	..	..	..	..	..
150	Timor-Leste	..	..	..	..	..	..	..	..	..	..	..	..	..	..

Contd...

Contd...table no.2

151 Zimbabwe	9.4	9.7	36.6	23.1	8.7	7.1	0.0	0.0	4.0	5.2	50.4	61.9	0.0	0.0
152 Togo	1.4	2.0	0.0	0.0	15.6	18.2	0.0	0,0	0.6	0.3	82.6	79.4	0.0	0.0
153 Yemen	2.6	6.7	0.0	0.0	97.0	98.8	0.0	0.0	0.0	0.0	3.0	1.2	0.0	0.0
154 Uganda	..	..	..	..	..	..	..	..	..	..	..	..	..	..
155 Gambia	..	..	..	..	..	..	..	..	..	..	..	..	..	..
Low Human Development														
156 Senegal	2.2	3.0	0.0	3.1	39.2	55.3	0.2	0.4	0.0	2.0	60.6	39.2	0.0	0.0
157 Eritrea	..	0.8	..	0.0	..	35.2	..	0.0	..	(.)	..	64.8	..	0.0
158 Nigeria	70.9	103.8	0.1	(.)	15.0	13.9	4.6	7.5	0.5	0.7	79.8	78.0	0.0	0.0
159 Tanzania (United Republic of)	9.8	20.4	(.)	0.2	7.6	6.3	0.0	0.6	1.4	0.7	91.0	92.1	0.0	0.0
160 Guinea	..	..	..	..	..	..	..	..	..	..	..	..	..	..
161 Rwanda	..	..	..	..	..	..	..	..	..	..	..	..	..	..
162 Angola	6.3	9.9	0.0	0.0	23.2	28.5	7.0	6.2	1.0	1.5	68.8	63.8	0.0	0.0
163 Benin	1.7	2.6	0.0	0.0	5.8	33.3	0.0	0.0	0.0	(.)	93.2	64.7	0.0	0.0
164 Malawi	..	..	..	..	..	..	..	..	..	..	..	..	..	..
165 Zambia	5.5	7.1	4.0	1.3	12.6	9.6	0.0	0.0	12.5	10.7	73.4	78.7	0.0	0.0
166 Cote d'Ivoire	4.4	7.8	0.0	0.0	24.8	33.9	0.0	17.8	2.6	1.6	72.1	58.3	0.0	0.0
167 Burundi	..	..	..	..	..	..	..	..	..	..	..	..	..	..
168 Congo (Democratic Republic of)	11.9	17.0	1.8	1.5	10.1	3.2	0.0	0.0	4.1	3.7	84.0	92.5	0.0	0.0
169 Ethiopia	15.2	21.6	0.0	0.0	6.6	8.2	0.0	0.0	0.6	1.1	92.8	90.6	0.0	0.0
170 Chad	..	..	..	..	..	..	..	..	..	..	..	..	..	..
171 Central African Republic	..	..	..	..	..	..	..	..	..	..	..	..	..	..
172 Mozambique	7.2	10.2	0.5	0.0	4.6	5.2	0.0	0.2	0.3	11.2	94.4	85.4	0.0	0.0
173 Mali	..	..	..	..	..	..	..	..	..	..	..	..	..	..
174 Niger	..	..	..	..	..	..	..	..	..	..	..	..	..	..
175 Guinea-Bissau	..	..	..	..	..	..	..	..	..	..	..	..	..	..
176 Burkina Faso	..	..	..	..	..	..	..	..	..	..	..	..	..	..
177 Sierra Leone	..	..	..	..	..	..	..	..	..	..	..	..	..	..
Developing countries	..T	..T	30.3	32.5	30.5	31.0	9.4	14.1	2.7	2.9	26.3	18.0	0.8	1.4
Least developed countries	..T	T	..	..	..	17.4	..	..	..	..	..	..	..	..
Arab States	237.4T	477.1T	1.1	1.3	59.5	54.2	33.9	40.2	0.7	0.4	4.8	3.8	0.0	0.0
East Asia and the Pacific	..T	..T	..	..	..	25.1	..	..	..	..	..	..	..	..
Latin America and the Caribbean	..T	..T	4.5	4.8	51.9	48.7	16.8	21.7	7.9	9.0	17.7	14.3	0.7	1.1
South Asia	456.2T	818.9T	23.9	26.1	27.7	28.3	9.0	17.9	1.9	1.7	37.1	25.3	0.4	0.5
Sub-Saharan Africa	T	T	..	..	..	13.8	..	..	..	..	..	..	..	..
Central and Eastern Europe and the CIS	1751.5T	1266.3T	27.6	22.6	29.8	20.5	36.1	46.0	1.4	2.2	1.2	2.1	4.0	7.0
OECD	4525.5T	5547.6T	23.5	20.4	42.0	40.5	18.6	21.8	2.92.7	3.1	3.5	9.9	11.0	
High-income OECO	4149.4T	5101.1T	22.2	19.9	42.3	40.6	19.0	21.7	2.9	2.6	3.0	3.4	10.6	11.6

Contd...

Contd...table no.2

High human development	5950.8T	6981.2T	21.7	18.3	40.9	39.3	22.8	26.0	2.8	2.9	3.4	3.9	8.3	9.5
Medium human development	..T	3816.T	36.8	40.6	24.7	25.1	12.9	13.8	2.0	2.5	22.7	16.8	1.0	1.2
Low human development	..T	..T	..	..	..	13.1	..	..	..	..	..	..	..	..
High income	4300.4T	5423.2T	21.7	19.0	42.9	41.5	19.5	22.7	2.8	2.5	2.9	3.2	10.2	11.0
Middle income	3556.4T	4594.4T	31.6	34.3	31.0	28.3	21.7	2.3	3.1	11.4	10.1	2.1	2.4	
Low income	..T	T	..	23.3	..	20.6	..	11.6	..	2.3	..	41.8	..	0.5
World	8757.7T[f]	11433.9T	25.3	25.3[g]	36.8[g]	35.0[g]	19.1[g]	20.7[g]	2.5[g]	2.6[g]	10.3[g]	10.0	6.0[g]	6.3[g]

Source: Human Development Report 2007-2008

NOTES

a. Total primary energy supply (TPES) is made up of indigenous production + imports - exports -international marine bunkers ± stock exchanges, TPES is a measure of commerical energy consumption. In some instances, the sum of the shares by energy source may not sum up to 100% because pumped storage generation has not been deducted from hydroelectricity generation.

b. In 2005, 12.6% of the world's energy needs were supplied by renewable sources. Hydro-electric power constitutes 17% of this total, solar/wind/ other1%, geothermal 3% and biomass and waste 79%. Shares for individual waste 79%. Shares for individual

c. Coal and coal products.

d. Crude, natural gas liquids (NGLs), feedstocks and petroleum products

e. Biomass, also referred to as traditional fuel, comprised animal and plant materials (wood, vegetal ethanol, animal materials/wastes and sulphite lyes). Waste comprised municipal waste (wastes produced by the residential, comme -rcial and public service sectors that are collected by local authorities for disposal in a central location for the production of heat and/or power) and industrial waste.

f. Data is a world aggregate from IEA from IEA 2007.

g. Data calculated based on world aggregates from IEA 2007

Sources

Columns 1-2: IEA 2007

Columns 3-14 : calculated based on data on primary energy suppy from IEA 2007

Energy Security and the Foreign Policy of China and India *vis-à-vis* Africa

Since the industrial revolution, the geopolitics of energy—who supplies it, and securing reliable access to those supplies—have been a driving factor in global prosperity and security. Over the coming decades, energy politics will determine the survival of the planet.

The political nature of energy, linked to the sources of supply and demand, comes to public attention at moments of crisis, particularly when unstable oil markets drive up prices and politicians hear constituent protests. But, energy politics have become yet more complex. Transport systems, particularly in the United States, have become largely reliant on oil, so disruption of oil markets can bring a great power to a standstill. Access to energy is critical to sustaining growth in China and India not only to lift these countries out of poverty, but to keep pace with burgeoning populations. Failure to deliver on the hope of greater prosperity could unravel even authoritarian regimes, and even more so democratic ones, as populations become more educated and demanding. And it is these very factors that have turned the market power of energy suppliers into political power. Importers have come to compete for supplies, driving up prices, supplier wealth and the capacity to play roles in regional and international politics that go well-beyond the GDP of countries, such as Russia, Venezuela and Iran.

These traditional geopolitical considerations have become even more complex with global climate change. The United Nations' Intergovernmental Panel on Climate Change (IPCC) has irrefutably documented that the use of fossil fuels is the principal cause of greenhouse gases that are driving up the temperature of the planet. Climate change will create severe flooding and droughts, which will devastate many countries' food production, lead to the spread of various illnesses, and cause hundreds of thousands of deaths per year, particularly for those living in the developing world. Nearly two billion people were affected by climate related disasters in the 1990s and that rate may double in the next decade. At the very same time, that countries are competing for energy, they must radically change how they use and conserve energy. The politics of that debate, particularly how to pay for the costs and dissemination of new technologies, and how to compensate those who contribute little to climate change but, will most severely experience its tragedies, are emerging as a new focal point in the geopolitics.

Ironically, high oil and gas prices and the actions that must be taken to address climate change—namely, pricing carbon at a cost that will drive investment, new technology and conservation to control its emission—will drive another existential threat: the risk of nuclear proliferation. Higher energy and carbon prices will make nuclear power a more attractive option in national energy strategies, and the more reliant that countries become on nuclear power, the more they will want to control the fuel cycle. The risk of breakout from civilian power to weaponisation would increase dramatically, as well as the risk of materials and technology getting into the hands of terrorists.

Confronting these challenges requires an understanding of the fragility of international oil and gas markets, but also of the nexus among energy security, climate change, and nuclear energy and proliferation. This chapter seeks to address these interconnections, and the kinds of measures that will be needed to ensure sustainability, prosperity and security.

Phenomenal Rise in China's Energy Consumption

China's blistering economic growth has made access to adequate energy supplies an increasingly important priority. It is the world's second largest consumer and third largest producer of primary energy. From 2000 to 2005, China's energy consumption rose by 60 per cent, accounting for almost half of the growth in world energy consumption. The country is able to meet more than 90 per cent of its energy needs with domestic supplies—largely because of abundant coal reserves and a coal-based economy. However, it imports almost half of the oil it consumes.

Self-sufficient in oil as recently as 1993, China became the world's second largest consumer of oil behind the United States in 2003. A year later, it was the number three importer of oil after the United States and Japan. Between 2000 and 2005, China was responsible for about one quarter of the growth in world oil demand, but only accounted for less than 8 per cent of global consumption. However, imports are projected to account for 60-80 per cent of China's oil consumption by 2020.

International Implications of China's Energy Explosion

China is grappling with its new role as a major importer of oil. The country's loss of self-sufficiency, substantial increases in the volume and cost of its oil imports after the turn of the century, and its emergence as an important factor in the world oil market and accompanying international scrutiny all caught China's leaders by surprise. For the past decade, Beijing has been struggling to cope with the domestic and foreign consequences of rapid demand growth.

During the past several years, China experienced an economic explosion that has triggered a frantic scramble for natural resources to sustain its growth. Currently, the world's second largest consumer of oil, only thirteen years ago, China did not import any oil at all. In 2004, oil imports to China are said to have increased by 37 per cent, which contributed to soaring oil prices around the world.[19] In 2005, China consumed an average of 6.9 million barrels per day (mbd) of oil.[20] By 2025, that amount is projected to increase to approximately 13.2 mbd.[21] That same year, China's production level is expected to be approximately 4.0 mbd, which will require the country to have a net import of at least 9.2 mbd.[22]

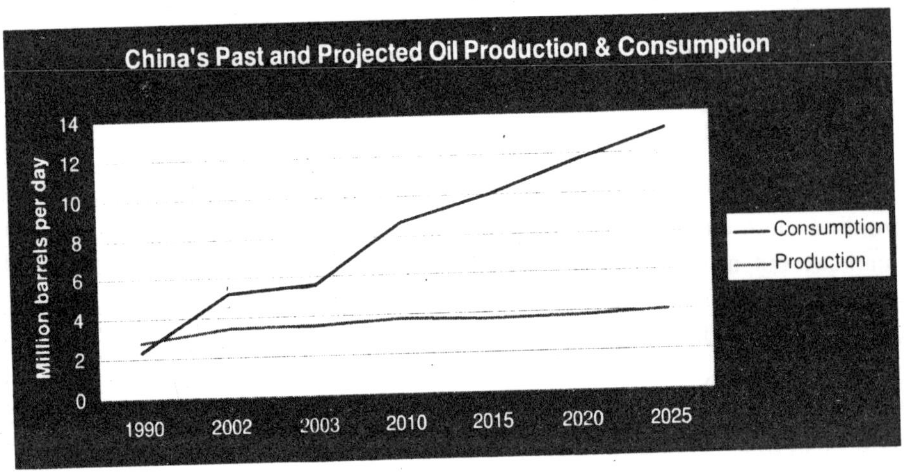

China had managed to be self-sufficient until 1993, meeting all its internal consumer oil needs for the previous five decades, due to the discovery of massive oil reserves at the Daqing oilfields in the far north of the country during the 1950s. With the increase in oil consumption, the Daqing oilfields can no longer be relied upon to fully sustain the country in the years to come. With economic growth running at a rate of about nine per cent per year, China is now engaged in a massive effort to reach beyond its borders and grab as much oil as possible to ensure its future economic growth. To this end China is directing much of its attention to Russia, Canada, South America, the Middle East and Africa.

Across the globe, China's efforts to acquire oil are far-reaching and aggressive. However, all along the way, China's efforts are being met with political, economic, strategic and environmental roadblocks. Faced with the challenge of trying to overcome many hurdles, China has been taking many steps, some more controversial than others, to achieve its goals.

Sino-Russian Linkages

Just north of China is neighbouring Russia, a major non-OPEC oil-producing country endowed with huge hydrocarbon resources. Currently, Russia holds the world's largest natural gas reserves, of which it is also the largest exporter, and the eighth largest oil reserves, of which it is the second largest oil exporter.[23] However, Russian oilfields, located mostly in the Western Siberia were established in the 1970s and desperately need capital and technology to stabilise their production. Russia needs at least a $25 billion overall investment to accomplish this and approximately $6-7 billion annually.[24]

During the 1950s, China and Russia maintained a close alliance. Between 1960 and 1985, China's relationship with Russia was defined as deeply hostile. After 1985, there was a gradual normalisation during the Gorbachev regime. Then, after 1991, which marked the end of the Cold War, Russia maintained a political distance from China because China remained communist and had publicly endorsed a 1991 coup attempt by Soviet communist hardliners. However, Boris Yeltsin changed his policy in April 1996, when China urged Russia to agree to a "strategic partnership." In July 2001, Presidents Vladimir Putin and Jiang Zemin signed a treaty of alliance, which formalised and expanded Chinese-Russian cooperation and strategic coordination.

The rapprochement created the conditions for China to turn to Russia for some of its oil needs. While Russia has the oil to provide China, China has the capital to help improve some of Russia's poor infrastructure. However, the exchange is not without difficulties. Russian internal affairs are fraught with politics that can make construction processes slow and complex, and, therefore, no immediate significant solution is being offered to China to quench its thirst for oil.

Since 2001, China has been involved in talks with Russia to try to negotiate building a major pipeline that would take oil from the Western Siberia to Daqing. Japan, which was interested in having the pipeline terminate at Nakhodka instead, began bidding for the project. Russia teetered between China and Japan, which were locked in a fierce struggle over access to the Russian oil. In late 2004, Japan appeared to have won the deal by offering to finance a substantial amount of the project. Then, in September 2005, President Putin announced that the pipeline would first go to China's Daqing and then continue to the Pacific Coast. This appeared to be an ideal solution for various reasons. First, since China had resolved its border issues for the first time in 40 years with Russia, the relationship between the two countries has improved dramatically. Second, sending oil to both locations would allow Russia to diversify its export routes.

Construction and the continued planning on the pipeline are now underway. The complete project cost was estimated at $11.5 billion. The first stage, which will originate at Taichet and continue to Skovorodino, is expected to be completed some time during the second half of 2008.[25] China's view, the cost of building pipelines is worth the price because, it lessens China's dependence on imports by sea, something that is of growing concern due to potential security implications.[26]

Central Asia and Caspian Sea

Since the breakup of the former Soviet Union, the Caspian Sea, which borders Russia, Azerbaijan, Iran, Turkmenistan and Kazakhstan, has become one of the world's hottest new oil zones. The Caspian Sea has mostly untapped oil and natural gas sources. Some experts have previously predicted that the Caspian Sea region could one day become the next Middle East. However, this is highly unlikely, as production levels, currently roughly 1.8 mbd, are expected to reach only 4 mbd by 2015, compared to 45 mbd for the Middle Eastern countries that year.[27]

China's proximity and insatiable appetite for oil makes it an ideal partner for Central Asia's energy market. Kazakhstan has the Caspian Sea region's largest percentage of recoverable crude oil reserves. Its production accounts for approximately two-thirds of the overall region. In 2005, Kazakhstan produced approximately 1.3 mbd.[28] Kazakhstan's net exports have been increasing steadily since 1992, which then totalled 129,900 barrels per day (bpd). Today, net exports have passed the 1 mbd mark.[29] Kazakhstan's current infrastructure has allowed it to export the oil to world markets via the Black Sea (via Russia); the Persian Gulf (via swaps with Iran); northward to Russia via pipeline and rail;[30] and most recently to China, via a newly constructed pipeline.

China and Kazakhstan began energy cooperation in 1997 and, prior to the Sino-Kazakhstan oil pipeline, the two countries relied on railway shipments of oil. During the first five months of 2006, 45,000 bpd were shipped via train from Kazakhstan to China.[31] Then on July 29, 2006, the Sino-Kazakhstan pipeline, jointly constructed by CNPC and construction companies from Kazakhstan, delivered its first batch of crude oil to the northwestern Xinjiang Autonomous Region. The pipeline currently runs from Atasu, in western Kazakhstan, and enters China at Alashankou port on the Chinese border before reaching its final destination at PetroChina Dushanzi Petrochemical Company.

Construction on the pipeline had been broken into three phases. The first phase was completed in 2003 and runs westward across western Kazakhstan from the oil fields of Aktobe region to the oil hub of Atyrau. The second phase of the pipeline, the Atasu-Alashankou section, was actually completed in May 2006, but suffered some minor setbacks, attributed to differences in measuring standards, before oil was finally transported through the pipeline. The final phase will entail completing the Kenkiyak-Kumkol pipeline in central Kazakhstan. The entire pipeline project is expected to be completed by 2011.

Previously, there was doubt as to whether or not China would be able to fill the pipeline enough to make the project worthwhile. But in August 2005, CNPC scored a major victory when it won a bid to purchase Petro Kazakhstan Inc, a Canadian oil producing company, for $4.8 billion. Not only will owning PetroKazakhstan give China access to probable reserves of approximately 550 million barrels of oil, it will also give Beijing more influence in Central Asia, an area of focus in part, due to the available natural resources.

In October 2005, the deal was finalised with Kazakhstan approving the purchase after CNPC agreed to sell one-third of PetroKazakhstan to Kazakhstan. A political significance of the victory for Kazakhstan is that it breaks some of its reliance on Russia, something a number of countries in Central Asia long to do. Had India won the bid, the oil would likely have to be shipped through Russia. Instead, CNPC will be able to transport the oil via pipeline directly to China.[32]

The advantages China has in its proximity to the Caspian region cannot be denied. By sharing the same borders with Central Asian countries, China has a common concern over regional security. The Shanghai Cooperation Organization (SCO), whose members comprise China, Russia, Kazakhstan, Kyrgystan, Tajikistan and Uzbekistan, came about in an effort to fight what is commonly referred to as the three forces—terrorism, separatism and extremism—to safeguard peace and stability in the region. A lack of regional stability could put current and future oil infrastructure at risk.

On the other hand, conflict can play in China's favour. For example, in 2001 the U.S. formed an alliance with Uzbekistan to fight terrorism from neighbouring Afghanistan. However, after the Andijan tragedy, which occurred in May 2005 and is believed to have claimed up to 500 lives, Western-Uzbek relations deteriorated, when the U.S. criticised the killing. What Western countries were calling a tragedy and a violation of human rights, China was justifying as an appropriate response to terror understood to be the work of religious extremists. This helped further relations between China and Uzbekistan and paved a way into further oil and gas deals. In June 2005, a joint-venture agreement was signed that called for CNPC to invest up to $600 million in the country in a partnership with state-owned Uzbekneftegaz. Then, in September, CNPC joined a consortium that included companies from Malaysia, South Korea and Russia, to carry out exploration near the Aral Sea.

Iran

Iran is becoming a major oil supplier to China. With an estimated 125.8 billion barrels, Iran is said to have the second-largest pool of untapped conventional petroleum in the world after Saudi Arabia, which has an estimated 260 billion barrels. One advantage Iran has over Saudi Arabia is a tremendous potential for future production capacity. Currently, Saudi Arabia is reported to be producing at nearly its maximum sustainable rate, which is between nine and 10 mbd. This means that it likely will not be able to raise its output significantly over the next 20 years even as global demands continue to rise. Iran, on the other hand, while currently producing approximately 4 mbd, is thought to be capable of boosting that amount to 7 mbd. Few other countries have this increase potential.[33]

Under the Executive Order 12959, signed by President Bill Clinton in 1995 and renewed by President Bush in March 2004, U.S. companies are prohibited from doing business in Iran.

Furthermore, the U.S. has threatened to punish foreign firms that do business in Iran, under the Iran-Libya Sanctions Act (ILSA) of 1996, which penalises foreign companies investing more than $20 million in Iran's oil and gas industry, but this has not deterred China. In 2000, China is said to have imported some 170,000 bpd of oil from Iran.[34] According to the U.S. Department of Energy, in 2003, Iran supplied China with roughly 13 per cent of its oil imports. Last year, China imported approximately 244,000 bpd of crude from Iran. More recently, the two countries signed a memorandum of understanding that will commit Sinopec, one of China's largest integrated energy and chemical companies, to buying 250 million tons of liquefied natural gas from Iran over 30 years. While the U.S. may frown on these actions, it has little recourse without adequate support from the United Nations.

The primary concern is that Iran's massive oil reserves give it the ability to influence countries in need of the oil into selling arms to Iran or providing good financing on arms deals. This serves as a sweetener for China in that it is able to provide both financing and weapons or weapons technology to Iran. Iran has the leverage to obtain the technology and arms because China wants what Iran has.

Additionally, China's steps to conduct business with Iran in deals that will bypass the ILSA paves the way for other countries to partake in similar kinds of deals. For example, India is on track to have a $4.16 billion pipeline that will carry gas from Iran through Pakistan to India. With countries such as China and India backing Iran, the U.S. begins to fight a losing battle. China's backing provides a strong support system to Iran. This backing could hurt U.S. objectives of curbing any potential nuclear activity.

Saudi Arabia

Much of China's strategy lies in pursuing natural resources with countries in which they can obtain a strong geopolitical foothold. The political tide in the Middle East has been turning in China's favour because relations between the U.S. and Saudi Arabia have been marred by events stemming from the September 11, 2001 attacks.

Saudi Arabia has one-fourth of the world's proven oil reserves and it will most likely remain the world's largest oil exporter in the years to come. Until 1996, Saudi Arabia was the number one exporter of crude oil to the U.S. However, over the past decade, Canada, Venezuela and Mexico, with their proximity and increasing production rates, have become major sources of imported oil. From January to May of this year, the U.S. imported 14 per cent of its oil from Saudi Arabia, 12 per cent from Venezuela, 17 per cent from Mexico and 18 per cent from Canada.[35]

Following the September 11 attacks in New York, finger pointing began, and a number of lawsuits against members of the Saudi government were born. Accusations such as that the Saudi government funded the 9/11 attacks and the Saudi regime was responsible for nourishing most of the hijackers (Osama bin Laden and 15 of the 19 hijackers were born in Saudi Arabia) were predominant. Although the September 11 Commission concluded that the Saudi government did not fund al-Qaeda, it did criticize the country as being "a problematic ally in combating Islamic extremism".[36] Saudi Arabia continues to claim its allegiance to fighting terrorism. However, should these accusations be left to fester, it could cause serious damage to the U.S.-Saudi relationship.

Meanwhile, China has been stepping up its relations with the Saudi government. According to China's Foreign Ministry, total trade between the two countries, mostly Saudi oil bought by China, grew by 59 per cent during the first 11 months of 2005.[37] After the two countries signed cooperative agreements in January 2006, Xinhua reported that Saudi Arabia had become China's largest crude oil provider, largest trade partner and second largest export market in the regions of West Asia and Africa. According to the report, in 1999 bilateral trade between the two countries was below $2 billion. By 2005, that figure had risen to $15 billion. In four to five years, the bilateral trade volume is expected to reach $40 billion.[38]

Venezuela

China is also busily strengthening bilateral relations for oil, south of the U.S., in Venezuela, which has maintained a tense relationship with the U.S. since Hugo Chavez took office in 1999. The fifth largest oil exporter in the world, Venezuela exports approximately 60 per cent of its oil to the U.S.[39]

Since coming into power, Chavez has visited China on five different occasions. Both countries have been striving to strike up cooperation deals that would not only bolster Venezuela's economy and oil infrastructure but also provide increased oil exports to China. In 2004, Chavez signed eight agreements on energy cooperation with China. In 2004, Venezuela exported 12,300 bpd to China. Currently, Venezuela is exporting some 150,000 bpd to China. Through recent agreements, China hopes to increase this amount to 200,000 bpd by the end of 2006.[40] Some reports are saying recent agreements between the two countries will increase imports to China to 500,000 bpd.[41]

In addition to various business arrangements between Venezuela's state-run oil company and China Petroleum that include purchasing Venezuelan fuel oil and power plant fuel, Chinese companies are seeking to invest in oil exploration and production in the country. In return, Chavez expects and is receiving Chinese assistance in the areas of telecommunications, food production and culture.

China and Venezuela are planning to cooperate on various oil projects, including the exploration and development of new fields as well as the development of older fields.[42] Chavez visited China in December 2004, where he declared that Venezuela was ready to help China establish its own strategic petroleum reserve. He also spoke "of a budding strategic alliance between the two countries[43] and signed an agreement that would allow Chinese companies to gain developmental rights to 15 oilfields in eastern Venezuela.[44] Chough this would appear to be an excellent opportunity for China, there are still a number of hurdles to overcome before the full export potential can be realised.

One issue facing China is that of transporting the oil. While Chavez is opening the doors and allowing China access to Venezuela's oil, transporting the oil could prove to be costly. A tanker capable of hauling 500,000 barrels would be profitable if it is for a short haul. However, that same size tanker will undoubtedly lose money hauling oil all the way to Asia. China requires supertankers capable of hauling 2 million barrels in order to be profitable. However, profitability diminishes as oil prices rise. Supertankers are not permitted to pass through the Panama Canal, which would save time and money. There is ongoing discussion on widening the Panama Canal. However, not only would this be an expensive proposition but it would also take several years to accomplish.

Another alternative is to build a pipeline from Venezuelan oilfields across Colombia to Pacific ports in Colombia or Ecuador. Unfortunately such a pipeline would currently be vulnerable to sabotage because it would run across a war zone where rebels have long made a habit of attacking the country's existing pipelines. Additionally, the necessary Pacific port facilities currently do not exist and would have to be constructed. A third alternative would be an existing, refurbished inter-oceanic pipeline located in Panama. However, large-scale oil shipments from Venezuela to China would dramatically increase the pipeline's use. Additionally, the Venezuelan and Panamanian governments have been negotiating the use of the pipeline to pump the oil for quicker access to China. The pipeline reportedly has a capacity of 800,000 bpd. However, the pumps were installed to move oil from the Pacific to the Atlantic and would require modification or reversal to send the fuel the other direction.[45]

Chavez has also signed a contract to have China construct a number of supertankers, which will eliminate its dependency on renting these tankers. It will also, according to Chavez, allow him to create one of the greatest fleets in the world.[46] Additionally, Venezuela plans to manufacture parts for the tankers, which will enable it to conduct much of its own maintenance.

China's interest in Venezuela's oil poses a potential threat to U.S. interests. This year, Venezuela is the U.S. fourth largest oil supplier after Canada, Mexico and Saudi Arabia. Tensions between the U.S. and Venezuela have been flaring since an April 2002 coup briefly removed Chavez from office. Chavez put the blame on the U.S., accusing Washington of sponsoring the attempted overthrow as well as a devastating oil lockout in 2002-2003. With a severe distrust of the Bush administration, and a marked "anti-imperialist viewpoint," Chavez has voiced concerns that President Bush had plans to have him assassinated, adding that if he were killed the U.S. could "forget Venezuelan oil.[47]

As the Venezuelan economy stands today, there is very little likelihood that Venezuela would stop exporting oil to the U.S. Venezuela depends too heavily on its oil industry. In a recent study, it was estimated that over 60 per cent of Venezuela's population lived in poverty, earning less than $2 per day. Using the revenues from Venezuela's oil industry, Chavez has been able to offer a number of programmes promoting literacy, job training, land reform, subsidised food and small loans. He has also used the revenue for health care and to import Cuban doctors.

Should Venezuela find an alternate export partner in China to replace the U.S., it could hurt the U.S., which depends on Venezuela to provide oil for 12 to 15 per cent of its consumption rate.[48] Despite statements made by Venezuelan officials, such as Ali Rodriguez, president of Venezuela's state-owned oil company, PDVSA, who called the assumption of replacing its U.S. business with China "absurd," Chavez has made a number of threats, including that of putting an embargo on oil shipments to the U.S. According to the Government Accountability Office, which is the investigative arm of Congress, should Venezuelan supplies of oil to the U.S. be disrupted, it could cause an immediate 15 per cent spike in international crude oil prices that could disrupt U.S. economic growth.[49] The U.S. currently has the infrastructure in place, such as refineries capable of processing Venezuela's crude. Refineries in China are not currently capable of processing Venezuela's heavy crude oil. Under the current situation, it would be in Venezuela's best interest to maintain the U.S. as its natural market for oil. However, as China and Venezuela continue to work together, oil might easily be turned into a geopolitical weapon.

Canadian Oil

Canada has been the largest foreign supplier of oil to the U.S. since 1998. According to figures given by the EIA, so far this year, Canada has produced an average of 3.22 mbd. Of this, an average of just over 2.2 mbd has been exported to the U.S. The vast bulk of Canada's proven crude reserves are located in Alberta's huge oil sands deposits, an estimated 178 billion barrels.

Within the past two years, in an effort to increase its own energy security, China has begun flexing its muscles to strike various deals with Canada to win access to some of the most prized oil reserves in North America. In April 2005, CNOOC, through its wholly owned subsidiary CNOOC Belgium BVBA, signed an agreement with MEG Energy Corp., a Canada-based company, to buy 16.67 per cent of MEG for $135 million. MEG has the rights to an oil sands lease in a 52-section (32,900 acres) oil sands block that is believed to contain 2 billion barrels of recoverable oil.[50] This acquisition is expected to help pave the way for further investment into Canada's huge oil sands resources. In another deal, Sinopec has acquired 40 per cent of the Northern Lights Oil Sands Project in Alberta, where production is expected to begin sometime in 2009 or 2010.[51]

China has also been concentrating on creating export routes from Canada. In another business transaction, PetroChina Co. Ltd. and Enbridge Inc., Canada's number two pipeline company, signed a memorandum of understanding to cooperate on the development of the Gateway pipeline which is expected to transport approximately 400,000 bpd of oil produced from the Alberta oil sands from Edmonton to a port on the west coast of British Columbia, where it can then be shipped via tanker to China, as well as other Asia-Pacific markets and California. China will possibly sign up for as much as half of the pipeline's capacity of (200,000 bpd), while Enbridge will broker the supply deals between PetroChina and oil sands producers.[52]

In 2003, the U.S. bought over 50 per cent of Canada's oil production, which equates to 1.5 mbd or 553,000,000 barrels for the year. That same year China imported a mere 376,000 barrels the entire year, most likely in one or two small shipments during the winter.[53] Although China's involvement may seem insignificant thus far, further encroachment into neighbouring Canada's oil supply could potentially cause uneasiness between Canada and the U.S., which have shared a smooth energy relationship since the 1970s. Historically, almost all of Canada's exported oil had been sent via a pipeline heading south.

Now, China is busy striking up deals with Canadian companies that could ultimately cause it to begin gaining market share. Like any capitalistic business, Canadian firms would not likely reject offers made by the Chinese simply to protect U.S. imports. Additionally, Canada is capitalising on China's growth in other areas as well. For example, economic growth in the U.S. has been slowing. As a result of this slowing, the U.S. is not importing as much from Canada. This would have a negative impact on the Canadian economy, if it weren't for China offsetting this with its purchases of metallic minerals, machinery and electrical equipment exports. While exports to the U.S., which account for 64 per cent of Canada's exports, drop in areas, such as the forestry sector, China is picking up the slack in other areas. In April 2005, the Canadian government released its International Policy Statement which stated, "Internationally, we will secure and enhance Canada's place in the U.S. market, anchoring our position in a globally competitive North American economy, and further develop our trade investment links with new economic powerhouses such as China, India and Brazil.[54]

With a newfound interest in expanding its economic reach to further its exports, coupled with the slowing economies of the U.S. and Japan, Canada could easily feel justified in increasing its oil supplies to China. Should China become aggressive enough, it would be plausible to cause the U.S. to lose part of its market share. This is not likely to happen any time soon, however. There are a number of hurdles China first needs to overcome. Long-term agreements to sell oil to the Chinese need to be signed. Supply deals with other potential shippers need to be signed. Canada must figure out which port will best support supertankers. Canada currently prohibits oil-tanker traffic along most of its Western Coast, which could pose a problem to China. Finally, Chinese refineries are better suited for handling Middle-Eastern crude than Canadian crude. If China hopes to diversify its oil sources, this will have to change significantly.

China's Security Challenges of Importing Oil

Currently, the majority of oil imports to China are shipped in via tankers and supertankers. As much as 80 per cent of its oil passes through the 630 mile-long Strait of Malacca in Southeast Asia, where 40 per cent of the world's piracy occurs. According to some reports, China is stepping up efforts to secure sea-lanes and transport routes vital for oil shipments.

One method by which to step up its security is through closer relations with key countries. India is one such country; it can patrol the Indian Ocean, Bay of Bengal and Arabian Sea as tankers transport oil from locations such as Africa or the Middle East. Along with offering support at sea, improved relations with India now offer a secondary method to safely transport oil, specifically, via pipelines traversing critical countries. China offers pipeline construction experience coupled with engineering and petrochemical processing experience, while India and Pakistan can offer security within their borders.

China is also reportedly trying to modernise its military, in what has been described as a multi-year military modernisation effort, that will take up to a decade to accomplish. Soldiers are being better trained to use high-technology weapons and more effective cruise and anti-ship missiles for use in the waters surrounding Taiwan. China has been trying to update its military for more than two decades to come into the age of computers, satellites and electronic weapons. Although progress has been slow, several programmes will likely come into play simultaneously in the next few years, which will offer China new firepower against Taiwan. For example, China is rapidly developing cruise and other anti-ship missiles.[55] This modernisation and weapons build-up in the Taiwan Strait is a means by which China can project a threat of force should Taiwan's rulers take steps toward formal independence. It can also be seen as a means, by which to ensure that oil is safely transported through the South China Sea and the Taiwan Strait in the event of a conflict with Taiwan. Not only is China's improved military capability aimed at Taiwan but, it is also aimed at the U.S., should the U.S. intervene.

According to a report purportedly written for the Department of Defence, entitled "Energy Futures in Asia," China believes the U.S. Navy controls sea-lanes in the South China Sea and that America would disrupt Chinese energy imports in any conflict over Taiwan. China sees the U.S. as an unpredictable country that violates the sovereignty of others. Not only would China like to build a blue-water navy but they are reportedly looking at developing undersea mines and missile capabilities to deter any potential disruption of its energy supplies from potential threats, especially those that could arise from a conflict with Taiwan. According to the report, China had already developed electronic eavesdropping posts, from the Pakistani port of Gwadar to Myanmar, to monitor shipping traffic through Strait of Hormuz and the Arabian Sea. It had provided Myanmar, which is the closest point to the Strait of Malacca, with billions of dollars in military assistance, according to American Foreign Policy Council (AFPC).[56]

China has been exploring options to bypass the Strait of Malacca by constructing a pipeline to Myanmar as well as Bangladesh, Pakistan or Thailand. In early 2004, China was pursuing a land bridge project in southern Thailand which would give Asian oil importers an alternative to shipping oil through the Strait of Malacca. This project would include the construction of a $3 billion oil refinery and $881 million worth of oil depots with a 143-mile pipeline running from Phangnga to Nakhon Si Thammarat.[57] However, after a dramatic increase in steel prices, which accounts for 60-70 per cent of the project's construction cost, Chinese investors began getting cold feet and in April 2005 the project was put on hold. Myanmar is another option China has been considering. Since at least 2004, China has been looking at the possibility of building a 775-mile oil pipeline from Sittwe on the Bay of Bengal to Kunming in Yunnan province. This project is still in its planning stages.

Geographically and logistically, Pakistan would be an ideal choice. However, a pipeline through that country could be subject to terrorist attacks. Despite this, China and Pakistan have been progressing in their discussions on energy cooperation. Pakistani President Pervez Musharraf was discussing the possibility of giving China direct access to Gwadar port, which is located near the Strait of Hormuz through which 40 per cent of the world's oil passes.[58] China had contributed $198 million while Islamabad contributed $50 million to the port's construction, the first phase of which was completed in April 2005. China reportedly will finance phase two as well. In order to give China direct access to Gwadar port, Pakistan is researching the prospect of transporting crude oil through its mountainous terrain to China's border. This could be accomplished via railway or pipeline. Musharraf is also trying to convert Pakistan into an energy corridor for China through Gwadar seaport by developing new rail and road networks. Musharraf said that by linking the two countries by rail and gas pipeline it would ensure rapid trade and energy development, which would be mutually beneficial.[59]

Should a crisis occur that disrupts the flow of oil into China, it could prove to have a powerful negative impact. With China's exploding economy, fuelled by an increase in oil demand and decreasing domestic supplies of oil, China could be faced with an economic and socio-economic crisis, if it is not able to obtain the resources necessary to support it. Oil is at the forefront of its requirements list, being integral to myriad industrial and consumer needs. China's oil stockpiles are currently very low. Should China somehow lose part of its oil supply, it would probably impose strict fuel rationing. Fuel would be allocated to food transportation and other essential means of transport while private citizens would be denied. China is extremely vulnerable to that.

In February 2005, Chinese oil officials said they were planning to set up a Strategic Petroleum Reserve (SPR) as a buffer against price rises and supply shortages. According to Chinese state-owned media, the reserve, located in four locations in Zhejieng, Shandong and Liaoning provinces, would cost the national government $1.6 billion, plus the cost of the oil. This stockpile would last 20 to 30 days.[60] China currently holds less than 10 days of imports.

Competition with India

China faces competition with other countries to be the first to tie the knot on oil exploration projects throughout the world. India has been going to toe with China in its global pursuit of oil. Given their current situations, China and India are the two countries developing the greatest new thirst for oil. While China imports approximately 40 per cent of its oil, India imports more than 70 per cent of its oil.[61] Neither country has the domestic oil fields capable of supplying their domestic needs, making them equally dependent on oil from abroad. Therefore, the race for equity oil is on, and given the highly aggressive nature of the Chinese bidders, India has learned the hard way, that it needs to act quickly to seal its oil contracts.

The concept of equity oil, or securing acreages abroad, is not a new one. Several decades ago, U.S. and European countries began using this idea. Exxon, Mobil and Chevron are past examples of companies that came to dominate the oil business using the concept of equity oil. And each time they pursued concessions in new oilfields abroad, they were actively aided by the respective governments.

China is feeling the crunch, as India is competing more and more for oil and natural gas fields around the world. Following China's example, India is also pursuing oil in remote areas.

With 37 per cent of the world's population, India and China are both in a desperate race to catch up with the U.S., Europe and Japan industrially. To meet its growing oil demand, India, like China, is tapping into countries that have been isolated by the West, giving China more competition in those areas.[62]

Early in 2004, the Indian state-owned Oil and Natural Gas Corporation Limited (ONGC) had almost closed a deal with Sudan to pick up an 11 per cent stake in the Block 3 oilfield in Sudan. The oilfield was already producing 400,000 bpd. As India waited for the Union Cabinet's nod, CNPC swooped down and offered 17 per cent more than ONGC's bid, and a deal was signed immediately.[63] By learning from its mistakes, ONGC is getting better at the game and has since been able to win a number of bids.

China has figured out early on that the best way to tap into equity oil is to focus on oilfields of the relatively crisis-ridden countries shunned by Western oil majors. This explains its pursuit of oil in areas, such as Sudan, Venezuela and Iran. However, companies, such as ONGC are right on China's heels, engaged in bidding wars to win equity as well in these countries. By picking up equity in oilfields around the world, China is able to ensure cheap and reliable oil supplies. By acquiring equity in foreign oilfields and sharing the cost of development and production, China can cut its oil purchase cost.

China's Strategy for Energy Abroad

Inevitably, China's dependence on oil and gas resources abroad will increase with time. With more and more consumers purchasing automobiles and tens of thousands of factories across the country now running on stand-alone diesel-oil generators (a reliable source but one that eats up fuel), China has entered a race for its life. To win this race, China has developed a multi-faceted, geo-economic and geo-strategic approach to its global pursuit of oil. The two primary factors that drive China's geo-strategic approach are its increasing oil needs coupled with security needs. These approaches can be further broken down into three major strategic elements that comprise China's search for oil:

(*i*) China is increasingly looking at state-to-state oil deals to secure its oil supplies rather than buying on the open market. With a slowdown of global oil production and fewer discoveries of major fields, this puts key importing countries (the U.S., India, China and Japan) in greater competition for oil on the world market, with prices higher as a result.

(*ii*) Chinese oil companies are taking more risks in order to acquire oil assets overseas. These risks are already having major geo-political consequences. For example, in deals made with Sudan, China has become the country's chief arms supplier and diplomatic ally, as Sudan wages a genocidal war against its African tribes. In another example, China's deals with Iran, going against the Iran-Libya Sanctions Act (ILSA) of 1996, have paved the way for other countries to do the same, opening up more opportunities for trade in arms and weapons of mass destruction. The selling of arms and weapons technology is a growing trend used by countries, such as China and Russia, to meet their own economic needs.

(*iii*) Finally, a strong political undercurrent can be seen in China's pursuit of oil. China and Russia have been striving for a strong alliance. But, the dominant purpose behind the China-Russia relationship can be seen as a way to control the power of the U.S. As both countries feel they are threatened by the U.S., they aim to use a strategic alliance as a means to overcome their strategic isolation through cooperation. Russia sells advanced weaponry and oil to China, while China returns hard currency.

Part of China's geo-economic strategy goes beyond its alliance with just Russia. China has joined forces with Brazil, Russia and India in a new coalition of emerging superpowers proposed by President Putin, called the BRIC alliance. There has also been talk of other countries, such as Iran, South Africa and Venezuela joining the pack as well. The current coalition encompasses over 40 per cent of the total world population. The idea of BRIC came about due to growing concerns of U.S. and European domination over the world economy and political scene. There is a sense of uneasiness and a fear that the U.S. has too much control over, among other things, the world's oil. One of the shared goals of the BRIC alliance could very well be to lessen Western influence over many of the world's sources of oil by joining together in a coalition of countries growing in economic strength and capability, one that will one day outgrow the economic strength of the Western powers.

Another factor, driving China's relentless pursuit of oil, is the general consensus that the supply will one day be diminished. Currently, supplies are able to meet demands. However, some markets are beginning to dry up. The EIA predicts that developing nations like China will push worldwide demand up 47 per cent to 121 mbd by 2030. This will have a tremendous impact on oil companies around the world trying to keep up with demand. Oil companies will have to spend an estimated $3 trillion to develop new supplies to keep up the pace of world demand.[64]

Worldwide, oil production had peaked for more than 50 oil-producing countries. The discovery of new oil sources, which has declined over 40 years, had almost ceased. In 2002, the world consumed four times more than the amount of newly discovered oil. Global demand is projected to reach 119 mbd in 2025. Analysts do not agree on the world outlook for oil production. Some believe that world oil production has already peaked. Others calculate a decline in production by 2010. Some more optimistic analysts predict that output will level off by 2036. Improvements in drilling technology and exploitation of unconventional oil sources, such as Canada's oil sands, could delay an inevitable declined.[65] Either way, buying up oil and oil deals is the equivalent to buying time. This time will be necessary to develop new technologies, providing alternatives to oil and gas.

Global Implications of China's Increasing Energy Demand

- China has a growing role in Central Asia, Russia, ASEAN countries, the Middle East and Africa. Additionally, its role could grow closer to the U.S. border as it reaches agreements with countries in South America and even Canada.
- China is emerging as a competitor against Japan and the U.S. for imported oil.

- China's increasing demand for oil is strongly influencing world commodity prices and markets, driving prices up to dramatic levels.
- The growing pollution caused by China's industrialisation is becoming a regional and international concern.
- China's influence in certain countries could eventually backfire against the U.S., as certain major U.S. oil supplying nations find an oil export substitute in China. The Venezuelan government and its political disagreements and strong words with the Bush administration provides a perfect example of a country that could potentially cut off the U.S. in favour of doing business with China. Should China be able to carry the Venezuelan oil business with adequate purchases, oil could be used as a weapon of diplomacy against the U.S.

Finally, China, knowing that it could face a bleak future if its appetite is not curbed, is also searching for technology that will stretch its resources.

Measures Undertaken by China to Stretch its Oil Reserves

- Seeking smarter technology to squeeze out more oil from oil wells.
- Seeking new refining technologies. Although China does not import oil from South Africa, it could benefit from South Africa's technology in the energy sector and Sasol's, a South African-based global company, strong refining and coal to liquids infrastructure, which would be essential to China's future development. Sasol signed a letter of intent with China in August 2004 to investigate the feasibility of establishing two coal liquefaction plants within the Asian country.
- Exploring alternatives to oil in the transportation sector by developing a market for alcohol fuels like ethanol, methanol and biodiesel as well as battery technology that facilitates electrification of transportation.

Measures the U.S. should Undertake

In an effort to maintain a strong foothold on energy, there are three steps the U.S. should take. First, it should continue to carefully monitor China's involvement in global energy. Second, the U.S. should take the necessary steps to maintain a strong political hold on its current global resources. Finally, the U.S. should continue to seek ways to diversify its energy sources. Part of this diversification strategy should entail increased research into energy alternatives, such as renewable energy. This research can be expanded through cooperation. Cooperation with China in renewable energy could prove to be fruitful in many ways. Increased renewable sources of energy would decrease dependency on oil. It would also help to increase China's own sense of energy security. By cooperating with China to improve its energy security, the U.S. could help reduce the overall wariness of both countries and form a stronger bond.

China's Growing Trade with Africa Indicative of Sino-Western Energy Conflicts

Trade between China and Africa jumped 39 per cent to $32.17 billion in the first 10 months of 2005, fuelled by increased oil imports and the export of Chinese goods, largely textiles. This follows rises of 59 per cent in 2004 and 50 per cent in 2003.

The rate of increase in Sino-African trade could see China threatening the United States' predominant position in the next period. US-Africa trade was $44.5 billion in 2004.

Energy is China's main concern and over the last few years it has struck or expanded on existing oil deals with Angola, Algeria, Chad, Equatorial Guinea, Gabon, Nigeria and Sudan. Africa now supplies around one quarter of China's energy imports.

China is expected to overtake both the UK and France this year to become the world's fourth largest economy, and is growing at around 9.3 per cent per year. China's trade surplus was $90.8 billion for the first 11 months of 2005, three times the level of 2004. This was boosted by textile exports following the end of the quota system. China's excess capacity and reliance on exports is antagonising both the US and European Union.

In 2003, China overtook Japan to become the world's second largest consumer of oil after the US. Demand is increasing rapidly and its oil consumption is growing by 7.5 per cent per year, seven times more than the US. China's energy needs accounted for 40 per cent of the total growth in global oil demand over the past four years. It currently imports about one-third of its consumption, but is projected to import two-thirds by 2025.

By 2010, China is expected to have 90 times more cars than it had in 1990, and is projected to surpass the total number of cars in the US by 2030. China is also attempting to increase and diversify supplies, particularly away from the Middle East, where it currently sources about 58 per cent of its oil. Areas of interest include Russia, the Caspian Basin, the Americas, the East China Sea and particularly Africa.

Africa contains about 8 per cent of the world's proven oil reserves, 70 per cent of which is off the west coast in the Gulf of Guinea, which stretches from the Ivory Coast to Angola. The low sulphur content of West Africa's oil makes it of further strategic importance.

Last year, China displaced Japan as the second largest importer of African oil after the US, which currently imports about 15 per cent of its oil from Africa. China first established a presence in Sudan's Muglad oilfields 10 years ago, and filled the vacuum when the US broke diplomatic ties with Sudan in 1997. Currently between half and 60 per cent of Sudan's oil exports go to China, amounting to around 7 per cent of China's imported oil.

China has invested more than $8 billion in joint exploration contracts in Sudan, including the construction of a pipeline from the southern oilfields to the Red Sea and a tanker terminal at Port Sudan. About 10,000 Chinese people work in the country.

China has greatly increased its investments throughout the continent in booming sectors such as mining, fishing, precious woods and telecoms, but also in less profitable sectors neglected or abandoned by the West, e.g., Zambia's Chambezi copper mines and the supposedly exhausted oil reserves in Gabon.

There are currently around 700 Chinese firms operating in 49 African countries. According to the IMF, Africa should experience growth of 5.8 per cent this year, the highest for 30 years, fuelled in large part by China's trade with the continent.

"China is competing for anything and everything at this stage," explains Dianna Games, a South African economic and political analyst. "They know Africa is wide open to them."

China also exports manpower and technical expertise, sends doctors and nurses to the continent establishes scholarships for African students at Chinese universities, trains African businessmen and trade officials, and encourages Chinese businessmen to invest in Africa.

China has invested heavily in privatisations and infrastructure projects intended to aid trade and the movement of goods, including: trains, roads, buildings, electricity and phone lines, mining prospects and oil refineries. It has also invested in tourism and has launched Nigeria's first satellite.

Since the China-Africa Forum in 2000, China has scrapped tariffs on 190 kinds of imported goods from 28 of the least developed African countries, and cancelled $1.2 billion in debt.

China's export bank has recently given a soft loan to Angola, which has given it a stake in oil exploration in shallow waters off the coast. The loan is to be used for infrastructure projects, many of which facilitate the development of the petroleum industry and wider trade.

Projects under way include, railways, roads, a fibre-optic network, schools, hospitals, offices and housing developments of up to 5,000 units. A new airport with direct flights from Luanda to Beijing is also planned.

The deal guarantees Angola just 30 per cent of the construction contracts, with Chinese companies expected to win the remainder. This has caused some concern in Angola's unions, but not in the government. "Why would you stop these guys coming?" asks Isaac Maria dos Anjos, a ruling party MP. "It absolutely will help the ruling party. We have to build hospitals. We have to build bridges. And we will do a lot of it in just one year," *i.e.*, before the next election.

Angolan Finance Minister, Jose Pedro de Morais explained that Angola's infrastructure is being rebuilt quickly, which has helped it to normalise relations with other banks who are now ready to expand their lines of credit.

China's loan, and its policy of non-interference, has made Angola less interested in accepting an IMF conditional loan, which calls for economic transparency and the opening up of its books to corporate governance concerning its oil contracts.

The multinationals who have traditionally and historically exploited the continent's resources are alarmed at China's rapid incursions into African trade, as are US policymakers and the Western press.

Western analysts have criticised China by claiming that Chinese money is enriching corrupt leaders, buying influence, gaining access to resources, and is being used as a means to garner support regarding Taiwan and United Nations Security Council issues.

Gal Luft of the neo-conservative think tank Institute for the Analysis of Global Security, complains along these lines, saying that "it will be much easier for [some African] countries to work with Chinese companies, rather than American and European companies, which are becoming more restricted by the publish-what-you-pay initiative and others calling for greater transparency."

The US Council on Foreign Relations has also issued a bipartisan report accusing the Bush administration of lacking a comprehensive, long-term strategy for dealing with Africa and urging policymakers to give it greater attention. It calls for an upgrade in diplomatic and intelligence capabilities by appointing an ambassador to the African Union and opening more missions in key African cities, particularly in energy-producing countries.

The report criticises the shortcomings of a humanitarian approach, and calls for a comprehensive elaboration of US interests. "The United States must recognise and act on its rising national interests on the continent through a far higher mobilisation of leadership and focused resources that target Africa's new realities."

It lists a hierarchy of US interests: oil and gas; growing competition with China; war on terrorism; HIV/AIDS pandemic; conflict resolution and peacekeeping; democracy and human rights; and long-term economic development.

The report hypocritically bleats that China "does not share US concern for issues of governance, human rights or economic policy." Duncan Innes-Ker, of the Economist Intelligence Unit, concurs. He believes "Chinese firms are a little less ethically constrained" than their Western counterparts.

China has become more forthright in its arms sales in line with its growing economic influence. It sold an estimated $1 billion worth of arms to Ethiopia and Eritrea during their border conflict between 1998 and 2000, comparable to the US selling arms to both sides during the Iran-Iraq war. It has also sold arms to both Zimbabwe and Sudan whilst they have been under Western arms embargoes, and has sold helicopters to Mali and Angola, arms to Namibia and Sierra Leone, and army uniforms to Mozambique.

In 2004, China contributed more than 1,500 troops to UN peacekeeping across the continent, primarily in the Democratic Republic of Congo and Liberia. Chinese peacekeepers were sent to Liberia two months after Liberia switched its diplomatic recognition from Taiwan to China. "The centre of gravity of oil is shifting," believes Daniel Yergin, chair of the Cambridge Energy Research Associates. "Last year, Asia consumed more oil than North America". This shift is having an impact on Africa, where it will stimulate more intense rivalries for access to that continent's resources.

Indo–African Energy Cooperation

Growth demands energy. It is no wonder that India—with an economy expected to grow at over 5 per cent a year for the next twenty-five years—has developed a ravenous appetite for energy. India is the world's fifth largest consumer of energy, and by 2030 it is expected to become the third largest, overtaking Japan and Russia.

The country's demand for oil alone is expected to increase at an average rate of 2.9 per cent annually over the next quarter century. Yet, India has only 0.4 per cent of the world's proven oil reserves, and domestic production is expected to remain constant, if not decline. Absence of the discovery of major reserves—which most analysts view as unrealistic—it is clear that India will remain a net importer of oil. If consumption follows the current trajectory, India is also projected to run out of coal, its primary source of energy, in forty years. Its domestic natural gas reserves are limited as well.

India's import dependence has intensified concerns that without reliable and affordable energy, it will be unable to sustain high economic growth. India imports (to varying degrees) its three major sources of energy, and its dependence on imported oil is expected to increase even further. The situation is complicated by a number of factors: (1) major oil suppliers are in unstable regions in the Middle East and Africa; (2) oil prices are high, spurring higher gas prices; (3) geo-political uncertainty stokes fears of a possible supply disruption and volatility in oil prices; (4) slow market reform has limited investment; and (5) few or no viable energy alternatives currently exist: India's civilian nuclear programme has regularly fallen behind schedule and large-scale development of hydroelectricity generation facilities has been stymied. Development of non-conventional energy sources has progressed; but their use is currently limited.

India Joins the Scramble for Oil

India has recently joined the global scramble for oil and natural gas alongside other Asian states, including China, South Korea and Japan. Through diplomatic manoeuvres aimed at securing transnational pipeline routes and overseas crude oil and natural gas production deals, India is seeking to lay claim to a larger share of the world's energy resources. It is also carrying out a major restructuring of the national energy industry.

Though India's thirst for oil is rooted in economic imperatives, the emergence of India as a major player in foreign energy ventures will have a profound impact on world geo-politics. It takes place under conditions, in which oil is already the object of the most intense competition between the US, the European Union, China, Japan and Russia.

The country's international oil policy is becoming a growing point of friction with the United States. In particular, the US is determined to scuttle Indian negotiations with Iran over a pipeline to India via Pakistan. The development of closer ties between India, China and Russia, as well as India's courting of oil-rich Venezuela, are also potential threats to American interests.

Energy needs and control over energy supplies are central to the strategic calculations of all the major powers. They are no less important for the Indian bourgeoisie, which, having abandoned its post-independence national development strategy in 1991, is seeking to transform India into a platform for global manufacturing, office processing and research production, and use its increasing weight in the world capitalist economy and its nuclear, space and military capacities to lay claim to great power status.

In terms of global oil consumption, India is still a relatively small player. Although India is home to more than 15 per cent of the world's population, it accounts for only 3 per cent of world oil consumption. China, by contrast, consumes 7.6 per cent of the world's oil. India's energy needs are rising sharply, however. Last year alone, India's crude oil consumption increased by 10 per cent. Moreover, India is highly dependent on oil imports. Some 70 per cent of India's oil is imported and oil imports account for one third of the total value of all India's imports. By 2020, India is expected to have to import 80 per cent of its energy needs.

India has the world's fastest-growing car market, which is driving oil consumption and imports. Economic growth, rising oil prices and recent disruptions in oil supplies due to the US military interventions in Iraq and Afghanistan are propelling the Indian government to join the hunt for cheap and secure sources of oil and natural gas.

Much of the urgency behind India's current drive to secure and diversify its sources of oil and natural gas is due to fear of falling behind other countries, especially China. The chairman of the partly privatised Oil and Natural Gas Corporation (ONGC), Subir Raha, said in a recent interview with Bloomberg.com that India was concerned that it had lost oil bids in Sudan and Indonesia to China. During "the three to four years" China had a "lead" on India in aggressively seeking foreign energy resources, the Chinese "got lots of oil and gas projects" when crude oil prices "had fallen to single digits," complained Raha. "When we came to the international market, crude reached record levels and no one was selling properties."

But the, US drive to control world oil supplies is an even bigger concern. New Delhi well-recognises that the US, by projecting its military power into the Middle East and Central Asia through the invasions of Afghanistan and Iraq, is seeking to gain a stranglehold over the world's oil supplies, and that this constitutes a potentially grave threat to the interests of the Indian bourgeoisie.

Since the end of the Cold War and the abandonment of national economic regulation, the Indian government has developed a new relationship with Washington, an Indian-US strategic partnership. The United States is currently India's largest trading partner and, due to bilateral defence agreements made in the aftermath of the September 11th attacks, the Indian and US militaries have mounted joint exercises in the Indian Ocean and South China Sea.

In spite of these ties, India's urgent need to secure energy resources is contributing to the development of major fault lines in the Indo-US relations and lending further urgency to the moves New Delhi took in the wake of the US invasions of Afghanistan and Iraq to improve relations with other Asian states, including, China, Russia and Iran, in the hopes of constraining US power.

The economic and geo-strategic conflicts between India and China run deep. However, in keeping with the steps initiated by the previous Bharatiya Janata Party-led government, the present Congress-led United Progressive Alliance government is seeking to mend fences with China. India is wary of Washington's aims to make India a frontline state in any future confrontation between the US and China. It is also increasingly eager to avoid direct confrontation with China over energy resources. The two countries have pursued joint ventures for oil extraction, including in Russia, Iran and Sudan, and China has proposed even closer cooperation.

Reflecting these recent shifts, Indian Prime Minister Manmohan Singh recently declared, "Diplomacy has changed and today it is about economics, trade and petroleum." These words were echoed by China's deputy foreign minister, Zhou Wenzhong, who said, "Business is business. We try to separate politics from business."

There has been some talk of an unofficial Indo-Chinese-Russian alliance aimed at curbing US penetration in Asia. On April 11, India and China announced the formation of a "strategic partnership," with Singh declaring, "India and China can together reshape the world order." The deal includes pledges to boost bilateral trade, improve diplomatic relations and work together to address "global challenges and threats."

Energy Security Pact between India and Russia

Last year, during Russian president Putin's visit to India, the two countries signed a memorandum of understanding for joint exploration and distribution of natural gas in the Caspian Basin, as well as for building underground gas storage facilities in India and technology transfers to India from Russia.

While visiting Moscow last October, India's Petroleum and Natural Gas Minister Manishankar Aiyar stated, "In the half-century of Indian independence, Russia has guaranteed our territorial integrity, and in the second half it may be able to guarantee our energy security. What I am talking about is the strategic alliance with Russia in energy security, which is becoming for India at least as important as national security."

India already holds a 20 per cent stake in Russia's energy-rich Sakhalin-1 block. ONGC Videsh Ltd. (OVL), the overseas arm of India's Oil and Natural Gas Corporation Ltd. (ONGC), has made an investment of $1.7 billion, which is expected to go up to $3.5 billion later this year.

Reportedly, India is to consider investing a further $1.5 billion in the Sakhalin-3 gas field and another $1.5 billion in the joint Russian-Kazakh Kurmangazy oilfield, both in the Caspian Sea. The Russian invitation to India to join the Sakhalin-3 project is especially noteworthy, since it occurred shortly after Moscow removed a major US oil company from the same project.

As one of the planned Indo-Sino joint ventures, Indian and Chinese oil firms lined up together as Asian customers for the possible purchase of the some of the assets of the Russian Yukos Oil Co., confiscated by the Putin regime in Russia.

These moves are clearly aimed at establishing some sort of counterweight to American dominance over energy production. On February 14, inaugurating the third Asian gas buyers summit in New Delhi, the Indian petroleum minister Manishankar Aiyer proclaimed that Asian natural gas players should come together to form an Asian gas grid. The aim of such a grid would be to enable the countries in the region to take full advantage of oil profits and thereby end the "wretched western dominance" that has prevented energy security and economic growth in Asia.

Energy Diplomacy with Iran and Pakistan

The suggestion by Iran to the previous BJP-led Indian government about the construction of a pipeline to supply oil and gas from Iran to India is once again on the table. Iran is scurrying to secure diplomatic ties with Asian powers via energy deals in order to counteract US threats of economic sanctions and military invasion. A $40 billion deal was drafted on the 7th of January with the National Iranian Oil Co. (NIOC). The deal would allow India to import natural gas over a period of 25 years, starting in 2009. NIOC would also develop two Iranian oilfields and a gas field.

The Indian government had reconfirmed that it will not stop its dealings with Iran because of US objections, including those voiced by US Secretary of State Condoleezza Rice during her recent trip to India. Talking to reporters on the sidelines of the Confederation of the Indian Industries, Aiyar said, "We have noted what US concerns are, and I think US is well aware of what our energy requirements are... . We need 100 million standard cubic metres per day of natural gas by 2025. Can America supply us that? I am only looking at securing energy security for the country."

Iran is the second largest crude oil producer among the Organization of Petroleum Exporting Countries (OPEC). It owns 10 per cent of the world's proven oil reserves and also has the world's second largest natural gas reserves. India perceives Iran as a viable corridor to access the natural resources and economic opportunities of Central Asia and the Middle East. During the third gas buyer's summit in February, officials of the National Iranian Gas Exports Company (NIGE Co.) began their preliminary discussions on the delivery of Iran gas via a pipeline at the India-Pakistan border, expected to be signed in Teheran by June.

The development of an Indo-Pakistani-Iranian pipeline is seen by New Delhi, as a means of both helping to meet its energy needs and fostering a closer economic relationship with Pakistan. The Indian political elite calculates that this will cut across Pakistan's ability to pursue a policy of geo-political confrontation with India and enable Indian business to dominate the Pakistani market.

However, to bypass a direct agreement with Pakistan, India has proposed two separate agreements—one between India and Iran on purchasing the gas and another between Iran and Pakistan for the pipeline. During the summit the initial construction plan was revised to include plans to extend the pipeline to Southern China.

Energy Security and India's "Look East" Policy

Dropping the earlier policy of isolationism practised by New Delhi in relation to the military junta in Burma (formerly Rangoon), the Indian government hosted a week-long visit from the

Burmese military general Than Shwe last October. The visit aimed to accelerate closer diplomatic ties with Myanmar and also neighbouring Bangladesh, in part to pave the way for a pipeline to bring Burma's natural gas to India via Bangladesh.

The Burmese pipeline agreement has been hailed in India as a major step toward regional cooperation. It is particularly seen as a landmark in India-Bangladesh relations. According to the Indian petroleum minister, it is the first time in over 30 years that Bangladesh has agreed to its territory being used for transport of any commodity to the Indian market.

India's recent initiative for a leading position in closer regional collaboration among the Association of South-East Asian Nations (ASEAN) and the Bay of Bengal Initiative for Multi Sectoral Technical and Economic Cooperation (BIMSTEC) states is part of New Delhi's attempt to penetrate regions to its east traditionally dominated by China and Japan.

To the West, India has secured energy deals in Africa. including in Libya, Sudan and in the Ivory Coast. Even further off, India is looking to establish long-standing relationships with a number of South American states. Among these countries, Venezuela has become prominent. "Venezuela is our arrowhead in Latin America," assured the Indian petroleum minister, saying that India would use Venezuela to enter other South American countries' energy markets.

Closer relations, between India and Venezuela run directly counter to US attempts to isolate the regime of Hugo Chavez. During his four-day visit to India this month, Venezuela's President Hugo Chavez and Prime Minister Manmohan Singh signed six energy and cooperation agreements. The ONGC Ltd. and GAIL Ltd. is to take a 49 per cent stake in the Venezuelan oilfield of San Cristobal and PDVSA. Venezuela's state-run oil company is to invest in India's Mangalore Refinery in the state of Karnataka.

Venezuela, the world's fifth-largest oil exporter, is currently seeking to diversify its markets as a means to reduce its dependence on the United States, which currently buys over 60 per cent of Venezuelan oil. Venezuela has recently deepened cooperation and signed a number of agreements in the petroleum sector with Russia, China, Brazil and Argentina.

Energy Cooperation between India and West Africa

This has been something significant on the economic and trade diplomacy front that has largely gone unnoticed. But for a few mandarins in the Indian commerce and foreign ministries and some officials in the CII headquarters, the story has remained under wraps. It started around three years back and it is about India and West Africa. A new paper by Chatham House titled "India and West Africa—A burgeoning relationship" brings out some startling facts.

India's involvement in West Africa is expanding beyond its traditional Commonwealth partners like Nigeria and Ghana. Although Nigeria is India's largest trading partner (worth $3 billion in trade—mostly oil), Indian investment in Côte d'Ivoire will grow to $1 billion during the period 2006 to 11 - 10 per cent of what Indian companies have invested abroad in the last decade.

Benin accounted for more than half of India's exports to francophone Africa in the 1980s; its main import—the so-called real Madras handkerchief or 'Madras George'—was, in fact, handloom material cut in strips measuring 8 yards × 1 yard, which were used to make women's dresses.

At present, India is the largest investor in Ghana, the second largest trade partner of Senegal and the third largest export destination for Nigeria, after the United States and Spain; it obtains about 20 per cent of its oil requirements from Nigeria. More than half of India's imports of cashew nuts are from Côte d'Ivoire and Guinea-Bissau, while Mali, Benin and Burkina Faso export high-quality cotton to India.

Moreover, of the twelve fastest-growing emerging markets in the world, six are in Africa and no fewer than five in West Africa. Thus, India launched an initiative in 2004 called Techno-Economic Approach for Africa-India Movement (TEAM-9), together with eight energy-and resource-rich West African countries, including, Senegal, Mali, Guinea-Bissau, Côte d'Ivoire, Ghana, and Burkina Faso. Within the framework of TEAM-9, India extended lines of credit totalling $500 million to the eight West African countries. It has become so successful that at least six other countries are interested in joining the initiative.

India faces fierce competition from the West and other Asian countries to secure West African resources. India's quest for energy in West Africa is not a core component of the government's energy security policy; rather, it is part of its bid to diversify energy sources. India is prepared to offer package deals offering infrastructural investments in addition to cash bonus payments on signature of contracts. There has also been controversy in Liberia over a $900 million deal to mine ore with Mittal, whose contract allowed the company to opt out of national human rights and environmental laws.

The contract is currently being reviewed by the Liberian Senate. The United States currently derives 15 per cent of its oil supplies from Africa as compared to 22 per cent from the Persian Gulf. Within the next ten years, the United States could be depending on Africa for a quarter of its oils supplies, according to the US National Intelligence Council. Nigeria alone is the fifth biggest source of US oil imports, with the United States accounting for half of Nigeria's oil exports. In recent years, China's political, economic and military relations have been subordinated to its quest to secure energy resources in the African continent as energy resources are being secured in exchange for aid, arms or infrastructure investment.

A major deal that India lost to China in 2004 illustrates the intense Chinese-Indian competition over energy in Africa. Angola's state-owned Sonangol reportedly blocked an Indian move to buy Anglo-Dutch energy giant Shell's 50 per cent share in Block 18 for about US$620 million. India's state-run Oil and Natural Gas Corporation (ONGC) had almost closed with Shell, but the Chinese evidently cut a deal with the Angolan government at the last minute, resulting in Sonangol exercising its pre-emption rights. This stymied Shell's move to sell its stake to ONGC, a deal which would have yielded about 5 million tonnes of crude oil daily for New Delhi from

2008 to 2009. It is widely believed that, China managed to swing the deal by offering aid to the tune of US$2 billion for a variety of projects to Angola, compared to India's offer of US$200 million for developing railways.

So far, African leaders have responded to China's interest in West Africa positively, seeing it as an alternative source of investment and countervailing force to Western interests and influence. But when the tide turns against China, India may be more welcome in the region for similar reasons *vis-à-vis* China as China is against the Western powers. India also has the relative advantage that English is one of its official languages. While the 'softness' of the Indian state and its democratic procedures as well as its incoherent approach are considered liabilities today, they may prove its biggest assets. Indeed, India should guard against blindly copying the Chinese model in West Africa and allow its own distinct policy towards the region to evolve.

In January 2005, the US National Intelligence Council (NIC) convened a group of leading US experts on Sub-Saharan Africa to discuss likely trends in the region in the medium term. The NIC report assumes that India has no Africa policy—'Over the next 15 years, there is probably a greater possibility of India developing a distinct foreign policy with political interests toward Africa'.

Today, the growth in economic ties between India and West Africa seems dramatic because it started from a very low base; indeed, it is likely to flatten in the coming years. India is in direct competition not only with the old colonial masters in the region (such as France) but also with cash-rich China for a share of the West African pie. The unstable security climate, the patterns of conflict, the fragile political state, weak democratisation, religion, terrorism and the high prevalence of HIV/AIDS all have the potential to derail the Indian success story.

Whatever role India ultimately plays in West Africa, perhaps the most important element it introduces is competition. 'For Africans, it is quite a welcome change from the approach they get from Western governments that manages to be both patronising and demeaning at the same time', Duncan Green, head of research at the British aid organisation Oxfam, commented recently.

The immediate reaction is to compare it to the IT revolution in India- substantial, silent and largely unnoticed. But there is a significant difference—the government has played a major role in kickstarting this process; and that too over two different ruling formations and under three different foreign ministers. Will it sustain and lead to something significant? The jury is still out on that.

India Provides West Africa US$250 m to Develop Biofuels

The Indian government will give US$250 million towards a fund to boost biofuel production in 15 West African countries. Ghana's vice president Alhaji Aliu Manama announced the fund on 14 November 2006, at a workshop held in Accra, Ghana, to discuss biofuel financing in West Africa.

The fund will be set up by the Bank for Investment and Development (EBID) of the Economic Community of West African States.

Biofuel is an attractive source of energy for West African states because it can protect their economies against rising crude oil prices on the world market. It is also seen as a viable source of climate-friendly energy. In theory the Clean Development Mechanism under the Kyoto Protocol could be used to fund biodiesel production, but West African countries lack the expertise needed to apply for the scheme.

"There is an acute shortage of expertise to develop such proposals," said Ghana's Minister for Lands, Forestry and Mines, Dominic Fobih.

Fobih welcomed the fund, but said that procedures for developing Clean Development Mechanism proposals should still be properly studied.

The workshop was co-sponsored by EBID and the UN Conference on Trade and Development (UNCTAD).

EBID pledged to foster private-public partnerships, with support from UNCTAD, and to finance agricultural and industrial production for biofuels.

As a first step in this direction, EBID will provide US$35 million for a jatropha biodiesel project, in Ghana, in conjunction with the country's commercial banks and financial institutions.

Benin, Mali, Nigeria and Senegal, led by Ghana, have pioneered research on biofuel and jatropha plantations. Jatropha oil's low cost and ease of cultivation make it an attractive crop for biofuel production.

But, biofuel production is still a relatively young technology, and more research is needed, notably to make sure it is geared towards the needs of small farmers for whom biofuel use on a local scale — for village power or agro-processing could be highly promising.

In addition, to be competitive on the international market. West Africa will need to find viable sources of funding to invest in plantations of between 50,000-150,000 hectares, and into processing, transport and storage facilities. It will also have to reduce its production costs and improve its farming techniques to reduce the risk of low yields, pests and disease.

India and West Africa to Strengthen Bilateral Ties

India decided on October 16 to extend a line of credit of 250 million US$ and 100 million US$ worth of agricultural and industrial supplying for the Economic Community of West African States (ECOWAS).

In a move to renew its cooperative partnership with Africa, India has also decided to increase the number of scholarships for Nigerian students to study in India from 50 to 75, according to the Press Trust of India (PTI).

The decisions came following talks between visiting Indian Prime Minister Manmohan Singh and Nigerian President Yar'Adua on October 15.

After the talks, India and Nigeria issued a joint declaration on strategic partnership that covers a wide range of areas of cooperation from security, trade and economy to education, science and technology.

The two sides also signed a memorandum of understanding on defence cooperation and three other documents on foreign affairs consultation and cooperation.

It was agreed that the two countries would sign within the next six months an extradition treaty, agreements on double taxation avoidance and bilateral investment promotion and protection.

Also in the declaration, India and Nigeria agreed to enhance mutually beneficial trade and investment exchanges with each other in sectors such as infrastructure, agriculture, food processing, small and medium enterprises, power generation, fertilisers, information and communication technology, pharmaceuticals, automobiles, auto-components and other sectors.

India Pledges $500 m to the West African Nations

India today pledged $500 million in the form of concessional credit facilities to eight West African countries—Burkina Faso, Chad, Côte d'Ivoire, Equatorial Guinea, Ghana, Guinea-Bissau, Mali and Senegal—who, together with India, form TEAM-9 or Techno-Economic Approach for Africa-India Movement.

TEAM-9 Ministers, who signed a memorandum of understanding (MoU), agreed that a Heads of State/Government meeting would be held regularly.

The MoU also set up a Council of Ministers comprising Foreign Ministers or any other Minister, as well as a Joint Business Council under the new regional cooperation mechanism.

"It was decided that the TEAM-9 cooperation mechanism will operate at Government, institutional and private sector levels, sharing various types of expertise, intellectual and physical resources as well as economic opportunities for promoting welfare, growth and prosperity of the people," a joint statement issued after the meeting said.

Stressing that transfer of technologies was envisaged under the TEAM-9 mechanism, the statement spoke of specific projects in areas such as agriculture, small-scale industries, rural development, pharmaceuticals, telecommunications and energy.

According to the MoU, the new regional cooperation mechanism was being created "recognising" the crucial role that South-South cooperation can play in this era of globalisation, liberalisation and privatisation.

In remarks to the press, the External Affairs Minister, Yashwant Sinha, said after the meeting: "We have talked about food security and freedom from hunger, which will mean cooperation in agriculture and water management."

Denying that India looked to African countries in terms of votes at the United Nations, Mr. Sinha said: "As far as political issues are concerned, we have not discussed them here today. We will let that evolve as we go along."

India's Quest for Energy Security Sees Decisive Steps Forward

The volatility in global crude market continued to pose a major threat to India's energy security and eroded the bottomlines of many oil companies in 2007, even as several new hydrocarbon discoveries were made and oil assets acquired overseas to secure the country's fuel needs.

To tide over a part of the crisis, the government also launched another round of auctions for its oil and gas assets, the seventh under the new policy, and hoped to attract $3-3.5 billion in investments, over and above $8 billion attracted in exploration in the previous six rounds.

'From a year back, India's energy sector has seen notable progress on policy and reforms front,' said Arvind Mahajan, director, national industry infrastructure and government, for global consultancy KPMG. 'While in some sectors policy initiatives have moved forward, in others, actual private participation has also made progress,' he said in a report titled 'India Energy Report - 2007'.

The consultancy said the Indian energy sector would need investments of $120-150 billion over the next five years as demand was expected to more than double over the period.

As global crude prices continued to surge during 2007 and threatened to breach the psychologically important level of $100 per barrel, policymakers were at pains to address the situation. Political compulsions, such as elections to some state assemblies, had prevented them from biting the bullet to raise prices of energy fuels, which led to what is called under-recovery of prices of transport and cooking fuels.

With the country dependent on overseas sources for about 74 per cent of its oil needs, India's oil bill import also surged despite the 12.5 per cent rise in the value of the Indian rupee *vis-à-vis* the dollar.

Some global think tanks in the energy industry ranked India fifth in the world in terms of petroleum demand and said that by 2010, the country was projected to replace South Korea and emerge as the fourth-largest consumer of energy, after the US, China and Japan. And by 2025, it is also forecast to overtake Japan.

The International Energy Agency (IEA), a global forum on energy security, even projected that India's dependence on oil imports will grow to more than 90 per cent by 2020. And as per the 11th Five Year Plan, too, India's crude oil needs would rise to 145 million tonnes in 2011-2012 from the 127 million tonnes in 2006-07, while domestic production should rise to 40 million tonnes from 34 million.

The next 10 years will be crucial for all countries, including China and India, because of the rapid expansion of energy-supply infrastructure,' Nobuo Tanaka, executive director of the agency, said recently.

'We need to act now to bring about a radical shift in investment in favour of cleaner, more efficient and more secure energy technologies,' he added, while releasing the latest edition of the World Energy Outlook.

During the year 2007, several companies, both domestic and multinationals, reported new discoveries, notably in the Krishna-Godavari, Cauveri and Mahanadi basins. Yet, India's dependence on the world energy markets only surged during the year.

Earlier the month of December 2007, the government also offered 57 exploration and production (E&P) blocks to both domestic and multinational companies in deepwater, shallow waters as well as on land.

This followed 49 discoveries made by private and joint venture companies in 15 blocks under the previous six rounds of auctions, inviting an investment to the tune of $8 billion.

'Indian sedimentary basins are still poorly explored in terms of well density, which means, higher opportunity for the E&P companies and more chances to get oil and gas in the country,' Petroleum Minister Murli Deora said.

This year, key oil and gas discoveries were made by the state-run Oil and Natural Gas Corporation (ONGC) and the Mukesh Ambani-led Reliance Industries Ltd. (RIL) in the Krishna-Godavari (K-G), Cauveri and Mahanadi basins.

The Reliance discovery was the first in the Krishna deep-water basin, which was awarded to the company under the first round of auctions under the new policy.

Reliance also struck oil and gas in a deep-water block in the east coast—again a first time in the Cauvery deep-water basin. This contract was awarded under the third round and the company holds 100-per cent participating interest in this block.

ONGC made its second discovery in the Mahanadi basin, for which the company had bid exclusively without any partners under the first round. The state-run firm also struck oil and gas overseas and led the Indian companies that acquired hydrocarbon assets abroad.

The company's overseas arm ONGC Videsh Ltd. (OVL) won two exploration blocks in Brazil through international competitive bidding in November and signed production-sharing contracts for some deep-water exploration blocks in Myanmar, with participating interests.

Before that, the newly-formed joint venture between the investment arm of the London-based steel tycoon L.N. Mittal and OVL, named ONGC Mittal Energy Ltd., acquired 30 per cent participating interest in an exploratory block in Turkmenistan, as also in Trinidad and Tobago.

'The benefits of ONGC's expertise and global hydrocarbon presence and the networking of Mittal Steel have been synergised to make big forays in our joint quest for securing oil equity for India,' said ONGC chairman R.S. Sharma.

'We are trying to set footholds in E&P business in 21 countries across the world,' Mittal said. 'We will contribute significantly to the energy security of India.'

While India's dependence on imports for crude oil continued to grow during 2007, the country emerged as net exporter of fuel products like petrol and kerosene. As per industry estimates, oil-refining companies, which had a capacity for 143 million tonnes, were expected to add 90-100 million tonnes over the next four to five years.

'This large-scale commissioning of capacities, when viewed against the expected demand of 196 million tonnes, suggests that India's petroleum product exports are slated to rise from the current 17 per cent of fuel processed in the country,' the KPMG report said.

The year also saw Indian oil companies joining hands with international oil and gas majors for technological and business collaborations, both in India and abroad.

ONGC and British Petroleum (BP) signed a pact for collaboration in oil and gas exploration and production business. The company tied up with Norway's Norsk Hydro to develop its deep-water oil and gas blocks in India.

The year also witnessed key regulatory changes in the domestic oil and gas sector, even as the government announced new gas pipeline policy that provides for setting aside 33 per cent of the pipeline capacity by the owner for providing open access to other users.

The government set up the Petroleum and Natural Gas Regulatory Board with L. Mansingh as the first chairperson to act as an independent watchdog for the downstream petroleum sector.

In the area of cross-border pipelines, although talks continued for importing gas from Iran via Pakistan, little progress was made, as several issues still remained to be resolved, especially on pricing and access charges.

'The general theme of private participation and competition has advanced in the past one year with some concrete examples on the ground to substantiate it. Going forward, we expect these themes to manifest on a wider scale', Mahajan said.

India Moves to Recover Lost Ground in the International Energy Game

In the words of Indian Prime Minister Manmohan Singh, "China is ahead of us in planning for its energy security—India can no longer be complacent." These words conveyed the sense of urgency that India holds over meeting its energy needs. India is playing catch-up with other major players in the global energy game. This realisation has not come a moment too soon given the advent of rising oil prices, India's unprecedented growth levels, lack of energy-efficient technologies and reliance on energy-heavy industries for its development. Power shortages and blackouts continue to plague India's major cities and undermine the confidence of investors and foreign companies operating in India. These power shortages have been fuelled by a combination of burgeoning growth rates, inefficiencies by the state-run power sector and power being stolen or siphoned for votes. The growing popularity of gas-guzzling sports utility vehicles and multi-purpose vehicles in India is also placing strains on its energy needs.

India, as the world's number six energy consumer, is also in a more desperate situation compared to its peers. For example, oil imports account for two-thirds of India's oil consumption while China imports one-third of its crude oil consumption. Furthermore, China's proven oil reserves stand at 18 billion barrels compared to five billion barrels in India. Indian-owned Oil and Natural Gas Corporation (ONGC) has invested $3.5 billion in overseas exploration since 2000 while Chinese-owned China National Petroleum Corporation (CNPC) has made overseas investments of an estimated $40 billion.

Indian policymakers have initiated numerous policies to address India's growing energy needs. For example, India is pushing for the creation of 15-45 days of emergency reserves in Rajkot, Mangalore and Visakhapatnam. India is also diversifying beyond oil to access other energy resources such as nuclear power, coal, natural gas and renewable energy resources as well as stepping up exploration activities within its borders.

Nevertheless, for the short to medium term India will have to rely on an increasing amount of imported oil and gas to meet its energy needs. As a result, India is stepping up energy diplomacy with states in the South Asia region as well as states further afield in Central Asia, Russia, and the Middle East and as far away as Latin America and Africa. ONGC, for example, has invested in offshore gas fields in Vietnam, as well as energy projects in Algeria, Kazakhstan, Indonesia, Venezuela, Libya and Syria, while Indian Oil Corporation is looking to invest in deep-water exploration in Sri Lanka. Reliance Industries, India's largest private sector oil firm, also has stakes in an offshore field in Yemen and a liquefied natural gas project in Iran and is in talks to acquire energy assets in Nigeria, Chad, Angola, Cameroon, Congo and Gabon in Africa as well as in South America and the Middle East.

However, this quest for energy security is being impeded by India's sometimes tense relations with energy suppliers, energy transit countries and energy competitors. For example, just as India and China have for centuries engaged in competition for leadership in Asia, the developing world and status on the world stage, so the need for energy security has now raised the possibility of further competition and confrontation in the energy sphere. India's tense relations with Pakistan also have an added dimension with the question of a gas pipeline from Turkmenistan or Iran to India, which will have to traverse Pakistani territory. Nationalism and oil are proving to be a volatile mix. Resolving territorial disputes and improving relations with traditional adversaries will become increasingly important for India if it is to meet its energy import needs by peaceful means.

India's Neighbourhood: Festering Disputes Prevent Access to Energy Resources

While China has either resolved or shelved its border disputes, India has active conflicts on almost all of its borders with neighbouring states. Apart from India's poor relations with Pakistan on its western borders, the ongoing violence in India's northeast with sporadic attacks on pipelines and India's poor relations with natural gas-rich Bangladesh and China-friendly Myanmar have prevented it from fully exploiting its proximity to a region rich in energy resources on its eastern borders. Frosty relations between Bangladesh and India are rooted in accusations by India that Bangladesh is fuelling terrorist movements in India's northeast in the presence of rising Islamic fundamentalism and anti-India sentiment in Bangladesh under the Bangladesh National Party

(BNP)-led coalition government, illegal migration between both states, and Bangladesh accusing India of re-routing the Ganges and Brahmaputra river systems that traverse both states. These disagreements have slowed the progress for discussions on a natural gas pipeline from Myanmar to India, which will have to pass through Bangladeshi territory forcing India to look into the expensive option of creating a deep-sea pipeline through the Bay of Bengal that would bypass Bangladesh.

Disagreements have recently given way to progress as a joint statement was issued at a meeting of the energy ministers from India, Bangladesh and Myanmar in Yangon, which agreed to the construction of a 900 km gas pipeline from Myanmar's offshore Shwe field to Kolkata passing through Myanmar's Arakan state, the Indian states of Mizoram and Tripura, and Bangladesh. As part of the deal, Bangladesh will also get access to the gas as well as $125 million in transit fees. In exchange for agreeing to the project, Bangladesh is also pushing for a trade and transport corridor linking Nepal and Bangladesh through Indian territory as well as access to hydroelectric power generated in Bhutan and Bangladesh using India's power grid.

Nevertheless, several potential glitches remain. Given that the pipeline will be traversing insurgency-infested areas across the three states adds an element of instability to the project. Furthermore, relations between Bangladesh and India remain strained, as seen most recently with Bangladesh's disappointment to India unilaterally withdrawing from the 13th South Asian Association for Regional Cooperation (SAARC) summit, which was due to be held in Dhaka. India cited the suspension of democracy in Nepal and the deteriorating security situation in Bangladesh as its reasons for withdrawing, which ultimately resulted in the postponement of the summit.

While India's relations with Myanmar have seen considerable improvement in recent years, Myanmar clearly remains within the Chinese sphere of influence. India has moved from voicing its opposition to the military junta's crackdown on pro-democracy activists and the arrest of Aung San Suu Kyi, the leader of the National League for Democracy to a more pragmatic, non-interventionist policy. This change in policy by India has been prompted by its desire to access the region's energy resources, gain access to the vast markets of Southeast Asia, balance the influence of China and counter Indian insurgent groups operating from Myanmar.

Notably, Myanmar has helped Indian security forces to crackdown on northeast Indian insurgent groups on at least three occasions over the past ten years. India's more conciliatory approach with Myanmar's military regime was demonstrated most recently when India became the first country to host General Than Shwe, the hardline chairman of Myanmar's ruling State Peace and Development Council, since the ousting of moderate Prime Minister Khin Nyunt at the end of October. However, India's warming relationship with Myanmar is making Myanmar a potential stage for Sino-Indian energy competition. For example, China is also in discussions with Myanmar for a 1250 km pipeline from the deep-water port of Sittwe in Myanmar on the Bay of Bengal coast to Kunming in Yunnan province.

China is also looking at the possibility of pipelines traversing Pakistani and Bangladeshi territory, as part of its "String of Pearls" strategy to bypass the narrow Straits of Malacca, which experiences 40 per cent of the world's piracy and through which 80 per cent of China's oil imports flow. Construction has recently been completed on a deep-sea port in Gwadar in the Pakistani province of Baluchistan, in which China has provided technical expertise and financing. China's involvement has been fuelled by the proximity of the port city to the Straits of Hormuz, through which 40 per cent of the world's oil passes. The port would compete with a port facility at Chabahar in Iran, which is being jointly developed by India and Iran to access the landlocked states of Central Asia and Afghanistan. China's "String of Pearls" strategy also forms part of a wider Chinese policy to encircle India.

India's plans to generate hydroelectric power through damming and re-routing several river systems have also been delayed by changes in state and central governments and disputes with upstream and downstream states such as Nepal, Bangladesh and Pakistan. Most recently, Pakistan has been pushing for international arbitration to resolve a dispute over the Baglihar dam, which India is constructing to generate power across the Chenab River running through Kashmir. Pakistan claims this project is a violation of the 1960 Indus Water Treaty. The dispute now threatens to derail the peace initiatives between India and Pakistan.

Nevertheless, India has made significant progress in tapping into energy resources within its borders including oil discoveries in Rajasthan by U.K.-based Cairn Energy and gas discoveries by India's Reliance Industries off the coast of Andhra Pradesh in the Bay of Bengal. In August 2003, ONGC also announced a deep-sea project, "Sagar Samriddhi," to look for oil and gas reserves in the Arabian Sea and the Bay of Bengal. In the last two years, India has reported 21 oil and gas discoveries amounting to 800 million tons of oil and gas, although domestic oil production has still been stagnant at about 32 million tons annually for the past few years.

Indo-Iranian Energy Cooperation: The "Peace Pipeline"

The inability to resolve the Kashmir dispute between Pakistan and India has undermined the viability of an Iran-Pakistan-India natural gas pipeline. A Memorandum of Understanding was signed between Iran and India in 1993 for a $4 billion 1700 km pipeline from Iran's South Pars field with 700 km passing through Pakistani territory. Pakistan stands to benefit with gas to meet its own energy needs and $500 million in transit fees. The international community has also shown growing interest in the Iran-Pakistan-India pipeline, with the World Bank and Japan's Sumitomo Mitsui Banking Corporation willing to finance the project. Russia also supports the project although the U.S. opposes it, instead pushing for the competing trans-Afghan pipeline project.

However, in the presence of sporadic tensions between India and Pakistan, both states have often proposed separate pipeline projects with Iran, with India sometimes pushing for the expensive option of a deep-sea pipeline that bypasses Pakistan altogether. Rising oil prices and a recent improvement in Indo-Pakistani relations following a commitment to resume a "Composite

Dialogue" in January 2004 has revived hopes for the "peace pipeline," which has now become one of the confidence-building measures being pursued by both states. Notably, Pakistan has offered security guarantees for the pipeline, vowing that gas flow will not be "switched off" even during periods of Indo-Pak tensions or hostilities. However, the future of the pipeline project is once again in doubt due to periodic violence across the Line of Control in Kashmir and rising tensions in Pakistan's Baluchistan province with attacks by the Baluch Liberation Front (BLF) on energy infrastructure.

At the beginning of 2005, India also completed a $40 billion deal with Iran to import 7.5 million tons of liquefied natural gas annually over a 25-year period as well as obtaining stakes in the development of Iran's largest onshore oilfield, Yadavaran, as well the Jufeir oilfield. The Yahavaran oilfield is a Sino-Indian-Iranian collaboration with India holding a 20 per cent stake, China a 50 per cent stake and 30 per cent with Iran. In exchange for Iranian gas, India is investing in Iran's ports and energy infrastructure. Iran and India have agreed to jointly develop the Iranian port at Chabahar as well as the road linking the port to Afghanistan and Central Asia, and grant India exclusive rights to the port.

Cooperation in the energy arena is influencing relations in other arenas, including trade and military cooperation. Bilateral exchanges of defence and intelligence officials are routine and in 2003 both states conducted joint naval exercises. These developments have not only concerned India's traditional adversaries, China and Pakistan, but also its newly found allies, Israel and the United States, who fear that military technology supplied to India could be diverted to Iran.

India and Central Asia

India is at a geographic disadvantage in Central Asia, when compared to China. While China shares borders with Kazakhstan, Kyrgyzstan, and Tajikistan, as well as Russia, India does not share a land border with any of the Central Asian states. That being said, however, India's warm relations with the Soviet Union during the Cold War have provided it with influence in Central Asia. Further, India also has its soft power to exercise, with historical links that go beyond the Indo-Soviet Treaty of Friendship to the Mughal period and Silk Road, as well as the popularity of Indian mass culture in the region such as Bollywood films and music.

However, the presence of two unfriendly regimes standing between India and Central Asia has slowed the progress of Indo-Central Asian cooperation in the economic, transportation and energy spheres. For example, progress on the $3.3 billion U.S.-backed Turkmenistan-Afghanistan-Pakistan (TAP) or Trans-Afghan pipeline that is to supply gas from the Daulatabad fields in southeast Turkmenistan has been delayed by instabilities in Afghanistan and poor Indo-Pak relations. With the ousting of the Taliban regime in Afghanistan, the instalment of a pro-U.S. regime and improving Indo-Pak relations, the TAP project is back on the table. Nevertheless, progress has been impeded by the competing Iran-Pakistan-India pipeline, sporadic violence in Afghanistan, Turkmenistan's isolationism and questions over whether Turkmenistan has sufficient gas to meet India's and Pakistan's needs given its competing energy agreements with Ukraine, Russia, Iran and its own domestic consumption needs.

India's increasing interest in Central Asia's energy resources has been accompanied by a growing involvement in the region's security. India has expanded military contacts in Central Asia, allegedly establishing a military and medical facility in Tajikistan. Other major world powers have followed similar trends. Since 9/11 the United States has forged closer relations with Central Asia and established a military presence in Afghanistan, Tajikistan, Kyrgyzstan and Uzbekistan. China has led in the creation of the Shanghai Cooperation Organization, which is fighting the "three evils" of extremism, terrorism and fundamentalism and promoting greater economic integration and development in Central Asia and China's West. Meanwhile, Russia has reasserted its presence in Central Asia under President Vladimir Putin, as seen most recently with Russia becoming a member of the Central Asian Cooperation Organization. Russia has also established a permanent military presence in Tajikistan replacing its 201st division and border guards, who had been in the region since the 1992-1997 Tajik Civil War, as well as maintaining a military presence at Kant airbase in Kyrgyzstan.

Numerous formal and informal overlapping power blocs are emerging in the region, which spillover into the energy arena. For example, Iran, Russia and India are pushing for a north-south oil and gas pipeline and transportation corridor to link Asia with Europe, which is in competition with a U.S.-led initiative to create an east-west corridor on the historic Silk Road through Baku, Tbilisi and Ceyhan. A growing military presence in the region coupled with increasing desperation to access the region's energy resources makes Central Asia a stage for potential great power conflicts.

Indo-Russian Energy Cooperation: Revival of the "Strategic Triangle"

India has recently stepped up efforts to access energy resources in Russia, the world's second largest oil producer and leading gas producer. India's ONGC Videsh Ltd (OVL) holds a 20 per cent stake in Sakhalin-1 of $1.7 billion, which is set to begin production this year eventually generating 2.3 billion barrels of oil and 17.3 trillion cubic feet of gas. India is also looking to invest in the Sakhalin-3 project, which is estimated to hold 4.6 billion barrels of oil and 770 billion cubic meters of gas as well as investing in the joint Russian-Kazakh Kurmangazy oilfield in the Caspian Sea. During Russian President Vladimir Putin's visit to India in December, the two countries also signed a Memorandum of Understanding for joint exploration and distribution of natural gas from the Caspian basin as well as building underground gas storage facilities in India.

The controversy over the sale of the Yugansk, which produces 60 per cent of Yukos' oil output and pumps 11 per cent of Russia's oil, has also highlighted India's growing interest in Russian energy assets. While the mysterious buyer, Baikal Finance Group, ended up selling its stake in Yugansk to Rosneft in December, which has been acquired by Russian state-owned Gazprom, this does not preclude the possibility of Yukos' assets being acquired by India's ONGC ONGC has been considering a $2 billion investment for a 10-15 per cent stake in Yugansk.

Indo-Russian energy cooperation is being further cemented by political and military cooperation. Just as India increasingly relies on Russian energy resources, so it also constitutes one of the biggest buyers of Russian military hardware. During Indian Petroleum Minister Mani Shankar Aiyar's visit to Moscow in October 2004, he voiced similar sentiments stating that "in the first half-century of Indian independence, Russia has guaranteed our territorial integrity, and in the second half it may be able to guarantee our energy security."

In fact, growing Indo-Russian energy cooperation resurrects former Russian Prime Minister Yevgeny Primakov's idea for a strategic triangle between Russia, India and China. These states are bound together by their shared interests in the fight against terrorism, the push for a multipolar world, and respect for the principles of state sovereignty and non-intervention with regards to their respective separatist movements in Chechnya, Kashmir and Taiwan. Now the energy sector can be added to this list of shared interests. India and China are already collaborating in the development of the Yahavaran oilfield in Iran and India's leading state-owned gas company, Gas Authority of India Limited (GAIL), has acquired a 10 per cent stake in China Gas Holdings. With India and China vying for assets in Yukos, Sino-Indian-Russian collaboration in the energy sphere could be further cemented. On December 3, 2004 during Russian President Vladimir Putin's meeting with Indian Prime Minister Manmohan Singh in New Delhi, a joint statement was released which included a proposal for greater cooperation with China, stating that "the sides express their conviction in favour of a progressive increase in trilateral cooperation, which also leads to social and economic development amongst the three countries."

As India has made limited progress in accessing energy resources on its doorsteps, due to poor relations with neighbouring states, it has shown a growing interest in accessing energy resources further a field, including in Africa and Latin America. In many cases, India is vying for energy resources in some of the most unstable parts of the world such as Sudan where India has invested $1.5 billion. In July 2004, India's OVL signed a $194 million contract with the Sudanese government for the construction of a 741-km petroleum product pipeline from Khartoum refinery to Port Sudan. Khartoum refinery is currently owned by the Sudanese government and China's CNPC.

While India has made nowhere near the progress of China on the international energy stage, it is conceivable that India could become a major player in the near future thus bringing it into competition with other major energy consuming countries. Furthermore, India's and China's attempts to engage "rogue states" such as Myanmar, Iran and Sudan in order to access their energy resources is undermining attempts by the West to isolate these regimes. The quest for energy resources on the world stage could eventually be added to the outsourcing debate as an area of contention between India and the West.

However, conflict over increasing energy needs is not inevitable. The need to access energy resources on the world stage can be as much a catalyst for cooperation as it can for conflict. For example, the Iran-Pakistan-India and Myanmar-Bangladesh-India natural gas pipelines raise the stakes for regional states to resolve their differences. Conversely, India's plans for generating hydroelectric power through rerouting several river systems adds an additional element of instability in relations between India and downstream and upstream states such as Bangladesh, Nepal and Pakistan.

Furthermore, the increasing interdependence between China and India as a result of their burgeoning trade relationship reduces the possibility of conflict over energy resources. Sino-Indian bilateral trade reached $13.6 billion in 2004 making China India's second largest trading partner. It should be noted, however, that expanding trade relations do not necessarily preclude the possibility of conflict, as seen by the fact that China is Japan's largest trading partner, with trade up 26 per cent in 2004, while relations in the political and security arena have continued to plummet over historical animosities and territorial disputes rooted in nationalism and energy resources. India faces this same volatile combination in many of its disputes with neighbouring countries. Thus, the cards are still out over whether India's quest for energy security will undermine international security.

Sino-Indian Discussion on Energy Security

Chinese Premier Wen Jiabao visit to India in April 2005, appearing on the forefront of a dialogue soon opening between the two most populous nations in the world. It is likely the two nations will engage in a growing race to gain access to energy resources they need for their soaring economic expansion.

The premier was received by Tata Consultancy Services CEO Mr. Ramadorai during his visit to Bangalore. He then visited the TCS Global Development Center for General Motors (GM). The CEO of TCS was quoted saying "Premier Wen's visit is a significant milestone that has added a further impetus to our presence in China".

Both countries seek to secure oil from multiple locales around the globe, where most Western nations cannot compete, including Sudan and Myanmar. China also is courting support from Venezuela, currently one of the largest suppliers of oil to the US. If successful, Chinese and Indian demand has the potential to create increasing difficulties for the US to fulfil its energy needs from traditional sources.

China and India, whose relations are sometimes troubled by border disputes, are warming up to each other. Analysts suggest that an agreement reached during the dialogues could preempt competition and conflict over oil in the future.

India and China are partners in Sudan's Greater Nile Project, but cooperation between the two may not come easily. Indian industry may seek to shy away from extending assistance to a nation some view as an economic rival during the ascendancy of the subcontinent's GNP.

These events come at a time when the United States recently announced its intention to help India, a past rival of China, become a "superpower." India has also been planning military expansion and modernisation.

China and India Seek Cooperation in Global Oil Quest

The race between the world's two most populous nations to secure the energy they need to fuel their growing economies likely to be on the agenda during the visit of Chinese Premier Wen Jiabao visit to India during April 2005.

With rapidly growing oil demand and increasing dependence on imports—last year over 40 per cent of China's crude and some 70 per cent of India's came from abroad—the two countries have more than just their rivalry in common. They are linked by similar business models, with cash-rich, State-controlled oil firms seen having more appetite for risk than companies beholden to earnings-conscious shareholders.

"Although there is competition, both sides share a common aim," said Zhou Fengqi, a high-level adviser in the Energy 'Research Institute of China's National Development and Reform Commission. "There is a basis for cooperation between the two sides, because they are both developing countries with oil demand ... but the specifics of any cooperation still needs to be researched."

A deal could include agreements for each country to refrain from trying to buy certain assets to prevent bidding wars, or working on joint projects in areas of interest, analysts said. "We are pitted against each other almost always to the advantage of the third country," Indian Oil Minister Mani Shankar Aiyar said.

Although Chinese and Indian companies are partners in Sudan's Greater Nile Project, widespread cooperation could be a long way off with both countries on a global prowl for assets. "The Chinese in particular, I think, would be reluctant to start excluding themselves from ... areas of certain countries just so they could avoid having Indians bidding on one or two assets," said Gavin Thompson, a Beijing-based analyst with Wood Mackenzie. "It's just a little bit too competitive for that to happen."

If China and India can cooperate over oil and gas deposits, there may still be a future for lower-level cooperation. "Both countries have large populations without access to modern forms of energy and we need to work together developing technologies appropriate for rural areas," said R.K. Pachauri, Director General of the Tata Energy and Resources Institute in New Delhi. Cleaner coal-burning techniques would offer another opportunity for cooperation, but neither side had promoted this kind of deal amid the jostling about overseas oil resources, he said.

China and India Manoeuvre to Secure Energy Supplies

"We look on China not as a strategic competitor but as a strategic partner," said the Indian Petroleum Minister Mani Shankar Aiyar during his January 10-13, 2006 visit to Beijing.

While in China, Aiyer, who was accompanied by representatives of major Indian petroleum firms, signed five memoranda on energy cooperation with the Chinese National Development and Reform Commission. And on January 12, the Indian delegation met with top officials from

China's main energy companies, including the China National Petroleum Corporation (CNPC), China Petrochemical Corporation, and China National Offshore Oil Corporation.

In his public appearances while in China, Aiyar repeatedly argued that China and India, both of which have a burgeoning need for oil and natural gas imports, have a common interest in seeking to lessen competition for energy supplies and in working together to discover and develop new energy supplies,

Aiyar observed that China and India are in a similar position in the energy sector—both have substantial coal resources but are highly dependent on imported oil and gas—and urged co-operation between them in bidding for oil resources in third countries.

India is currently pursuing energy production and exploration projects in more than 50 countries, often in competition with Beijing.

On several occasions in the past two years India has lost significant bids to China, including in Angola, Kazakhstan, Ecuador and Burma. Chinese oil firms, meanwhile, are reputed to have made several deals in which they overpaid for energy assets. Last August, CNPC paid $4.18 billion to acquire Canadian oil company PetroKazakhstan. India's Oil and Natural Gas Corporation (ONGC) had bid $3.9 billion.

"The Chinese have learned," said Aiyar, "that if we constantly compete, they [often] have to pay more than a billion dollars over [the] ideal price. As it is, the assets they acquire are often of uncertain value in risky countries."

Aiyar also warned that competition for energy resources, if not checked, could enflame relations between Asia's two rising powers. "It is clear to me," said Aiyar, "that any imitation of the 'Great Game' between India and China is a danger to peace. We cannot endanger each other's security in our quest for energy security."

Aiyar's call for cooperation between India and China in the energy field was seconded by the director of the China Energy Strategy Centre, a government think-tank. Unbridled competition between India and China for oil and natural gas "will be harmful to all concerned," said Xia Yisehn, "and so the necessity of co-operating to share risks and reduce costs in a multilateral way is gaining currency here"

State-owned Chinese and Indian energy companies have already launched several joint exploration ventures, including in Russia, Iran and Sudan, with China generally taking the larger stake.

In December, a further step toward Sino-Indian energy cooperation was taken when China's CNPC and India's ONGC, respectively their countries largest state-owned oil companies, mounted a successful $573 million joint bid to acquire Petro-Canada's 37 per cent stake in the al-Furat oil and gas fields in Syria.

The India-Chinese energy talks complement India's efforts to develop an Asian oil and gas grid. The grid, which is intended to ensure reliable delivery networks and "energy security" for

Asia, was formally inaugurated at a conference held in New Delhi in November 2004, that brought together ministerial representatives of the North and Central Asian energy producing countries, including Russia, Uzbekistan, Kazakhstan and Azerbaijan, and their counterparts from the principal Asian consumer nations—China, Japan, South Korea and India.

"The era when our [energy] production was controlled by others is now behind us, the era when the bulk of consumers lived in other continents is also over," Aiyar told the November conference.

Energy Security and Sino-Indian Relations

The current co-operation on energy matters between China and India arises out of a recent thawing of relations between the two countries. (During the latter decades of the Cold War, China was allied with the US and Pakistan, while India enjoyed close military, geopolitical and economic relations with the USSR.) Shortly after the 2003 US invasion of Iraq, India's National Democratic Alliance government, led by the strongly pro-US Hindu supremacist Bharatiya Janata Party (BJP), launched a concerted drive to repair relations with China. The first-ever Sino-Indian Strategic Dialogue was held in January 2005 to deal with common issues regarding "globalisation, energy security and the democratisation of international relations."

In April 2005, the Chinese premier Wen Jiabao visited India and the two countries announced a "strategic partnership" to make advances in economic cooperation and trade issues. This also agreed to strive for "closer political initiatives and to engage in joint exploration for oil and gas in other countries". The same month the first China-India Business Cooperation Conference was held to expand the current bilateral trade of $US14 billion per year. China is already India's second-largest trading partner.

To further the cooperation between the two countries, their governments recently designated 2006 as "India-China friendship year". Just days before Aiyar's visit to China, Indian foreign secretary Shyam Saran was in Beijing to conduct the second round of strategic dialogue after the upgrading of bilateral ties to a "strategic and cooperative level."

The Indian foreign secretary focussed his discussions on gaining Chinese backing for India's bid for a permanent seat on the United Nations Security Council and the resolution of the longstanding border dispute. India is also taking steps to join the Chinese and Russian-led Shanghai Cooperation Organisation, through which Moscow and Beijing are seeking to counter US influence in Asia, especially in Central Asia.

Behind these moves lies the common concern of the Indian and Chinese regimes over the Bush administration's military interventions in Iraq and Afghanistan and Washington's attempt to gain a strategic stranglehold over the oil-rich regions of the Middle East and Central Asia. Recent US statements threatening Iran and Syria have only further fuelled these concerns.

While pursuing closer ties with China, India's United Progressive Alliance has also sought to enter into a "strategic partnership" with the US, including accepting a US offer of assistance in helping India to become a "great power."

The Indian elite is acutely aware of the fact that Washington has identified India as a potential counter-weight to China, and is hoping to benefit from the readiness of the US to provide it with support. It calculates, however, that it can do so, without becoming dependent on or subordinate to the US.

While in Beijing, India's foreign secretary Shyam Saran made direct reference to the geopolitical manoeuvring, declaring that China and India "are too big to contain each other or be contained by any other country" and that the perception that the two countries might be seeking the containment of each other is outdated. "India would be happy to work closely with China towards the progressive realisation of an East Asian Community and, eventually, a larger Asian Economic Community."

TABLE 3

Sino-Indian Energy Cooperation *vs.* Competition

Competition

Asset	*India's bid*	*China's bid*	*Winner*	*Date*
Sonangol—50% state, offshore block 18 (Angola)	ONGC—$310 million	Sinopec—$725 million	China	Nov-04
PetroKazakhstan (Kazakhstan)	ONGC-Mittal—$3.9 billion	CNPC—$4.18 billion (Initial bid — $3.6 billion)	China	Aug-05
EnCana Corp (Ecuador)	ONGC—$1.4 billion (Bid withdrawn)	Andes Petroleum (CNPC, CNOOC)—$1.42 billion	China	Sep-05
South Atlantic Petroleum—45% stake (Nigeria)	OVL—$2 billion (Bid withdrawn)	CNOOC — $2.3 billion	China	Jan-06

Cooperation

Asset	*Sino-Indian bid*	*Date*
Greater Nile Oil Project (Sudan)	OVL—25% ($750 million), CNPC—40% ($441 million)	OVL—March 2003, CNPC—1996
Petro-Canada—37% (Syria)	$573 million (OVL-CNPC—Himalaya Energy)	Dec-05
Omimex de Colombia Ltd.—50% (Columbia)	$850 million (OVL-Sinopec)	Aug-06
Yadavaran oilfield (Iran)	OVL—29%, Sinopec—51 per cent	Sep-06

CNPC—China National Petroleum Corporation (China)
CNOOC—China National Offshore Oil Corporation (China)
ONGC—Oil and Natural Gas Corporation (India)
OVL—ONGC Videsh Limited (India)

The US is not prepared, however, to sit idly, while China and India seek to develop a *modus vivendi* for cooperation in the energy sector.

The Bush administration, which is already exerting strong pressure on India to abandon plans to jointly develop a pipeline with Pakistan to bring Iranian natural gas to South Asia, sent a demarche to New Delhi this month demanding that it "reconsiders" ONCG's Syrian investment. It justified this action on the grounds the India's purchase of the oil and gas property will undermine the United Nations'—read US and European Union—efforts to isolate the Syrian regime.

The *Hindu* quotes a senior Indian official as expressing outrage over the US move: "Today, it is Iran and Syria, tomorrow it may be Sudan or Myanmar or Venezuela or some place else. At stake is not just our energy security but also our right to take decisions by ourselves."

In a cabinet reshuffle, Mani Shankar Aiyar was replaced as Petroleum Minister and given the portfolio of Youth Affairs and Sports. The Indian press is all but unanimous in terming this a demotion and linking it to Aiyar's outspoken advocacy of the Iran-Pakistan-India gas pipeline.

India and China must Develop Viable Strategies for Energy Cooperation

India and China must widen their options for energy availability and develop viable strategies for energy security, Prime Minister Dr. Manmohan Singh said during his visit to China in January 2008.

Addressing the Chinese Academy of Social Sciences (CASS) here, Singh said: "We can do much more to jointly develop clean and energy efficient technologies through collaborative research and development. India seeks international cooperation in the filed of civilian nuclear energy, including with China."

The other areas that merited the attention of both countries were food security and protecting the environment, as it is a common heritage that could not be abandoned or squandered.

The Strategic and Cooperative Partnership for Peace and Prosperity, established in 2005, was aimed at seeking a purposeful engagement in all of these areas, Dr. Singh said.

As far as the boundary question was concerned, India and China were both determined to keep it peaceful, and their Special Representatives have been instructed to arrive at a mutually satisfactory solution.

He concluded by saying that he looked forward to India and China playing a significant role in the transformation of Asia.

REFERENCES

1. Surya Narain Yadav, "Energy Security and Foreign Policy: A Comparative Study of China and India in African Perspective", Approach Paper presented at the Institute of Chinese Studies, Delhi, April 10, 2007.

2. *Ibid.*

3. International Energy Agency, "Energy Technology Policy", *IEA*, Paris, 1985.

4. —, "Shared Goals", *IEA*, Paris, 1993.

5. European Commission, "Security of Supply", 1990.

6. Chingendael International Energy Programme, "Study on Energy Supply Security and Geopolitics", The Hague, Netherlands, 2004.

7. Lacasse, Chantale and André Plowde "On the Renewal of Concern for the Security of Supply", *Energy Journal,* 16(2), 1995.

8. Barton, Barry, Catherine Redgwell, Anita Ronne and Donald N. Zillman, "Energy Security: Managing Risk in a Dynamic Legal and Regulatory Enrolment", Oxford University Press, New York, 2004.

9. Martin, William Flynn, Ryukichi Imai, Helga Steeg, "Maintaining Energy Security in a Global Context", Trilateral Commission, New York, 1996.

10. Power Plays: Energy and Australia's Security (http://www.aspi.org.au/publications/publication_details.aspx?ContentID=142&pubtype=5)

11. World Coal Institute (http://www.worldcoal.org/pages/content/index.asp?PageID=21)

12. http://www.emeraldinsight.com/Insight/ViewContentServlet? Filename=/published/emeraldfulltextarticle/pdf/3280010106.pdf.

13. BBC News: 'Peak Oil' Enters Mainstream Debate (http://news.bbc.co.uk/1/hi/business/4077802.stm).

14. Panoptic World: "Globocops of Energy Security" (http://www.maavak.net/maavak/maavak070.html) Mathew Maavak, originally published in The Korea Herald on July 18, 2006.

15. Oil Crisis, US Senator Bob Bennett, September 27, 2000 (http://bennett.senate.gov/press/record.ctm?id=226465)

16. US Energy Information Administration; Country Analysis Brief, Japan: Environmental Issue, January 2004 (http://www.eia.doe.gov/emeu/cabs/japanenv.html)

17. CNN: Oil Majors Question Bush Biofuel Plan, February 15, 2007 (http://money.cnn.com/2007/02/15/news/companies/bush_biofuel.reut/index.htm)

18. http://www.iea.org/Textbase/work/2002/beijing/KUOLT2.PDF and Reauthorisation of the Energy Policy and Conservation Act (http://www.agiweb.org/gap/legis 106/reauthspr.html)

19 "IEA Raises 2005 China Oil Demand to 6.8 Mln bpd," *AFX News Limited,* 11 March 2005.

20. "World Petroleum (Oil) Demand, 2002-2006," *Energy Information Administration,* (9 Aug 2006).

21. "World Oil Consumption by Region, Reference Case, 1990-2030," *Energy Information Administration,* 9 August 2006.

22. International Energy Outlook 2006," *Energy Information Administration,* Appendix E, p. 160.

23. "Russia: Country Analysis Brief," *Energy Information Administration,* February 2005, (9 Mar 05).

24. Ding Ying, "Russia Gets Mileage with Oil Diplomacy," *Beijing Review,* March 2005, (9 Mar 2005).

25. "Terminal of Eastern Siberia-Pacific Pipeline is Determined," *The Russian Oil and Gas Report* [Russia], 2 August 2006.

26. Greg Priddy, telephone interview, 21 March 2005.
27. "Caspian Sea: Background," *Energy Information Administration,* September 2005, (14 Aug 2006).
28. Kazakhstan," *CIA World Factbook,* 29 June 2006, (12 July 2006).
29. "Kazakhstan," *Energy Information Administration,* Country Analysis Briefs, July 2005.
30. "Kazakhstan," *Energy Information Administration, Department of Energy,* July 2005.
31. "First Kazakh Crude Arrives in China," *Pipeline Asia,* 13 July 2006.
32. "China Beats India for Kazakhstan Oil Firm," *China National News,* 22 August 2005.
33. Michael T. Klare, "Oil, Geopolitics and War with Iran," *Asia Times,* 13 April 2005.
33. "MOFTEC Paper Profiles Zhuhai Corporation's Visit to Iran in 2000," *Beijing Guoji Shangbao,* Open Source Center, 5 January 2001.
35. "Year-to-Date Imports of Crude Oil and Petroleum Products into the United States by Country of Origin, January-May 2006," *Energy Information Administration,* 2006.
36. "Port Authority to Join Lawsuit Against Saudi Arabia over 9/11 Attack," *USA Today,* 10 September 2004.
37. King to Sign Saudi-China Oil Deals," *Aljazeera.net,* 23 Jan 2006.
38. "Saudi Arabia becomes China's Largest Oil Provider," *People's Daily Online,* 26 January 2006.
39. Chavez Se Reunira En China Con Presidente Y Primer Ministro," *Laverdad,* 21 August 2006.
40. Chavez Se Reunira En China Con Presidente Y Primer Ministro," *Laverdad.*
41. "China, Venezuela Sign Energy Deal," *China National News,* 25 August 2006.
42. Chavez Se Reunira En China Con Presidente Y Primer Ministro," *Laverdad.*
43. Charles Roth, "Venezuela Plan to Sell US Oil Ops Flawed - Ex-PdVSA Pres," *FWN Select,* 2 February 2005, Rigzone, <http://www.rigzone.com>.
44. Chris Buckley, "China Gains Access to Venezuelan Oil," *The International Herald Tribune,* 28 December 2004.
45. Eric Jackson, "China-Venezuela Oil and Telecom Deals will Affect Panama," *The Panama News,* 9 January 2005.
46. Chavez Se Reunira En China Con Presidente Y Primer Ministro," *Laverdad.*
47. Nikolas Kozloff, "Latin America: Venezuela's Chavez: 'Oil is a Geopolitical Weapon,'" *Triniscenter.com,* 6 April 2005.
48. Energy Information Administration.
49. Patricia I. Vasquez, "US Unprepared for Venezuela Oil Embargo," *Oil Daily,* 15 July 2006.
50. Canada Oil Sands Vital to Chinese Energy Security," *Platts Energy Economist,* 1 June 2006.
51. "Canada Oil Sands Vital to Chinese Energy Security," *Platts Energy Economist.*
52. Ibid.
53. Greg Stringham, Canada Association of Petroleum Producers, 10 May 2005.

54. Government of Canada Releases International Policy Statement," *Canada News Wire,* 19 April 2005.
55. Edward Cody. "China Builds a Smaller, Stronger Military," *Washington Post,* 12 April 2005.
56. Arnold Gay, "Oil Fuelling China's Naval Build-Up," *Straits Times,* 2 May 2005.
57. Chinese and Korean Firms Invited to Invest in Landbridge Project," Thailand-China Business Link, 27 July 2004.
58. Pakistan Considers Energy Route for China," *The Post Chronicle, 22* February, 2006.
59. President Musharraf Promises to Make Pakistan 'Energy Corridor for China,'" *BBC Monitoring International Reports,* 4 July 2006.
60. China Plans Oil Reserves to Manage Prices," *United Press International,* 2 February 2005.
61. Manjeet Kripalani, Dexter Roberts and Jason Bush, "India and China: Oil-Patch Partners?," *Business Week Online,* 7 February 2006.
62. Keith Bradsher, "India Joins China in Stepped-up Thirst for Oil," *International Herald Tribune,* 18 February 2005.
63. Anup Jayaram, "ONGC Videsh Faces a Chinese Challenge in its Global Search for Equity Oil," *Business World* [India], 16 August 2004.
64. Marianne Lavelle, "Hostage to Oil," *U.S. News & World Report,"* 10 January 2005.
65. Petroleum and Natural Gas, Crude." *Encyclopedia of Global Industries.* Online Edition, Thomson Gale, 2005. Reproduced in Business and Company Resource Center, Farmington Hills, Mich.: Gale Group, 2005.
66. http://www.wsws.org/articles/2006/jan2006/chin-j24_prn.shtml
67. http://www.wsws.org/articles/2005/jan2005/ind1-a12_prn.shtml
68. http://indianeconomy.org/2007/06/09/india-and-west-africa/
69. http://www.scidev.net/news/index.cfm?fuseaction=printarticle&itemid=3243&language=1
70. http://www.bilaterals.org/article-print.php3?idarticle=9995
71. http://www.hinduonnet.com/thehindu/thscrip/print.pl?file=200430202791200.htm&date...
72. http://www.mumbainews.net/story/312559
73. http://www.progress.org/2005/energy42.htm
74. http://www.en.wikinews.org/wiki/India_and_China_to_discuss_energy:_cooperation_or_comp...
75. http://www.chinaembassy.org.in/eng/ssygd/SinoIndiaRelations/t189990.htm
76. http://www.wsws.org/articles/2006/jan2006/indi-j23_prn.shtml
77. http://www.wsws.org/articles/2006/jan2006/indi-j31_prn.shtml
78. http://www.andhranews.net/Intl/2008/January/15/India-China-must-29698.asp

• • •

2

Energy Security and Economic Prosperity: Experiences of Energy Exporting African and Asian Economies

Geography of Production and Consumption of Strategic Minerals

The world mineral market is characterised by an uneven geographical concentration of resources, production and consumption. The major producers are mainly from developing and transition economies and are net exporters, while the major consumers are mainly from developed countries and rely heavily on imports. Since the 1990s, some Asian developing countries have significantly increased their consumption of minerals to help fuel their booming economies, and are now among the leading consumers and importers.

Oil and gas reserves are highly concentrated in West Asia. Its share in world total proven and probable reserves was 62 per cent for oil and 40 per cent for gas at the end of 2005. However, in terms of oil and gas production, West Asia's share was only 23 per cent in 2005. In contrast, developed countries that only accounted for 6 per cent and 8 per cent of global reserves of oil and gas respectively, had a significant 25 per cent share in global oil and gas production (Table 4). For natural gas, the Russian Federation has the largest reserves (27 per cent of the world total) and the highest production (22 per cent of the world total). The Persian Gulf region, which accounts for only 10 per cent of world gas production is set to increase this share as trade in LNG expands.[1]

Developed countries and South, East and South-East Asia are two groups of countries for which the share in world consumption is greater than in world production and reserves. The gap is larger for developed countries, but is growing rapidly for Asian countries (Table 4).[2] This explains why exploration activity is highly concentrated in developed countries where around 70 per cent of new fields are drilled. Among developing countries, exploration activities are mostly concentrated in South, East and South-East Asia (Table 4).

For metallic minerals, the picture varies by commodity. However, with few exceptions, developed countries and developing Asia consume more metals than they produce, while the converse applies to Africa, Latin America and the Caribbean, as well as to South-East Europe and the Commonwealth of Independent States (CIS). It is interesting to note, however, that the share of developed countries in the consumption of iron, copper and zinc fell significantly in 2005 from that of a decade ago.

TABLE 4

Reserves, production, consumption, and exploration of oil and natural gas, by region, 1995 and 2005 (per cent)

	Oil and gas						*Reserves at end 2005*	
	Exploration		*Production*		*Consumption*			
	1995	*2005*	*1995*	*2005*	*1995*	*2005*	*Oil*	*Gas*
Economy	*Share in total number*				*Share in total volume*			
Developed countries	67	71	31	25	56	52	6	8
Developing countries	29	23	49	54	29	36	84	59
Africa	4	6	8	10	3	3	10	8
Latin America	7	6	10	11	7	7	10	4
Developing Asia	17	11	41	33	20	26	65	47
West Asia	2	3	21	23	7	9	62	40
South, East and South-East Asia	15	6	10	10	18	17	3	7
South-East Europe and CIS	5	6	19	201	4	12	10	31
Russian Federation	3	3	16	16	8	8	6	27
Total world	100	100	100	100	100	100	100	100

Source: UNCTAD, based on data from CIS Energy and BP 2006

a Shares calculated on the basis of the number of new fields drilled.

b Shares calculated on the basis of volume

c The reserves are proven and probable **

This was compensated by a strong increase in the share of developing Asian countries for these metals. Also worth nothing is the strong increase in the participation of developed countries in iron ore production to the detriment of Latin American countries and economies in transition and of developing Asia gold zinc and bauxite production (Table 5).

For many developing countries, minerals are the most important export products. The heavy reliance on minerals is particularly pronounced among oil-producing countries in Africa and West Asia (Table 9). African and Latin American countries are endowed with diverse minerals, ranging from precious minerals to ferrous and industrial minerals. Africa dominates the world's supply of precious metals and stones, such as platinum, diamonds and gold, of which it is the leading producer, while Latin America is the leading producer of such metals as copper and silver (USGS, 2005).

Commodity Price Boom and its Impact on Investments

Mineral markets are volatile. The most recent commodity price boom has had a major impact on corporate investment behaviour as well as on government policies. It is therefore important to understand the underlying forces behind the recent.

TABLE 5

Production and consumption of selected metallic minerals, 1995 and 2005

(per cent)

Metal	*Developed countries*		*Africa*		*Latin America and the Caribbean*		*Developing Asia*		*South-East Europe and the CIS*		*All regions*	
	1995	*2005*	*1995*	*2005*	*1995*	*2005*	*1995*	*2005*	*1995*	*2005*	*1995*	*2005*
Iron ore production	17	29	6	4	31	24	27	29	19	14	100	100
Pig iron production[a]	37	29	2	1	8	5	39	52	14	13	100	100
Copper production	41	43	6	9	19	21	12	6	22	21	100	100
Copper consumption[b]	64	46	1	1	5	6	28	42	2	5	100	100
Gold production	34	28	30	21	12	18	14	23	10	10	100	100
Gold consumption	37	39	3	4	2	2	56	53	2	2	100	100
Nickel production	31	30	6	5	12	17	28	26	23	22	100	100
Nickel consumption	52	50	5	3	10	13	10	12	23	22	100	100
Zinc production	45	36.	4	4	23	21	22	32	6	7	100	100
Zinc consumption	57	42	2	2	15	8	19	39	7	9	100	100
Bauxite production	39	36	15	10	28	27	12	19	6	8	100	100
Alumina production[c]	40	48	2	1	28	20	14	19	16	12	100	100

Source: UNCTAD, based on data from the Raw Materials Group, Virtual Metals and Bloomsbury Minerals Economics Limited

a Pig iron production (iron content) is used as a proxy for iron ore consumption.

b The first column's data for each region are for 1996.

c Aluminium production is used as a proxy for bauxite consumption.

TABLE 6

Developing and transition economies with highest dependency on exports of minerals

(per cent of total exports, 5-year average (2000-2004))

Sorted by fuels [a]			*Sorted by non-fuel minerals* [a]		
Economy	*Fuels*	*Product description*	*Economy*	*Ores and metals*	*Product description*
Algeria	97.8	Oil and gas	Guinea[bc]	89.8	Bauxite, alumina, gold and diamonds
Nigeria[b]	97.8	Oil	Botswana[d]	87.2	Diamonds, copper, nickel
Libyan Arab Jamahiriya	96.9	Oil	Surinam[b]	70.0	Alumina (aluminium oxide)
Yemen	93.3	Oil and gas	Zambia[b]	61.5	Copper, cobalt
Kuwait[b]	92.9	Oil	Jamaica	60.8	Alumina, bauxite
Angola	92.2	Oil	Niger[b]	46.1	Uranium and gold

Contd...

Contd...table 6

Qatar	89.1	Oil, petro-chemicals	Chile	45.0	Copper
Saudi Arabia[b]	88.9	Oil	Mozambique[b]	42.3	Aluminium
Brunei Darussalam[b]	88.3	Oil	Papua New Guinea[b]	38.6	Gold, copper
Azerbaijan	86.6	Oil	Congo Republic[g]	34.0	Various metals
Iran, Islamic Rep of[b]	86.3	Oil and gas	Ghana[h]	33.3	Gold
Venezuela	83.4	Oil	Cuba	33.2	Nickel
Turkmenistan	81.0	Gas	Peru	32.9	Gold copper, zinc
Oman	80.6	Oil	Rwanda [bi]	32.2	Various metals
Gabon	79.5	Oil	Uzbekistan	30.3	Gold
Sudan[b]	74.2	Oil	Georgia	24.9	Various metals
Syrian Arab Republic	72.8	Oil	South Africa[c]	21.7	Platinium, gold
Bahrain	70.5	Oil	Bolivia	19.1	Zinc, gold
Trinidad and Tobago[b]	61.3	Oil and gas	Kazakhstan	18.0	Various metals
Kazakhstan	56.1	Oil and gas	Bahrain	16.8	Aluminium

Source: UNCTAD, based on COMTRADEdatabase and other sources

a Fuels include SITC 3. Ores and metals include SITC 27+28+68 and when relevant diamond ore has been added

b 2 to 4-year average

c The Economist Intelligence Unit

d Bank of Botswana Financial Statistics

e Derived from OPEC Annual Statistical Bulletin

f IMF Staff Reports

g IMF Direction of Trade Statistics

h IMF Ghana statistical annex

i IMF Direction of Trade Statistics

FIGURE 4

Production, trade and consumption of crude petroleum

Unit: *Thousand metric tons; kilograms per capita; reserves production ratio (R/P) in years*

Figure Notes:

For Bolivia and Venezuela, data on crude petroleum include condensate.

Total consumption for Brunei excludes the amounts of natural gasolene and condensate blended with crude oil.

For Canada, Germany and Greece, data include inputs other than crude petroleum and natural gas liquids.

For South Africa, crude oil production data refer to synthetic oil from coal.

For Bahrain, crude oil production and imports data have been revised including, production from Abu Saafa field.

Data on reserves were taken from the Survey of Energy Resources, World Energy Council.

Production, trade and consumption of crude petroleum

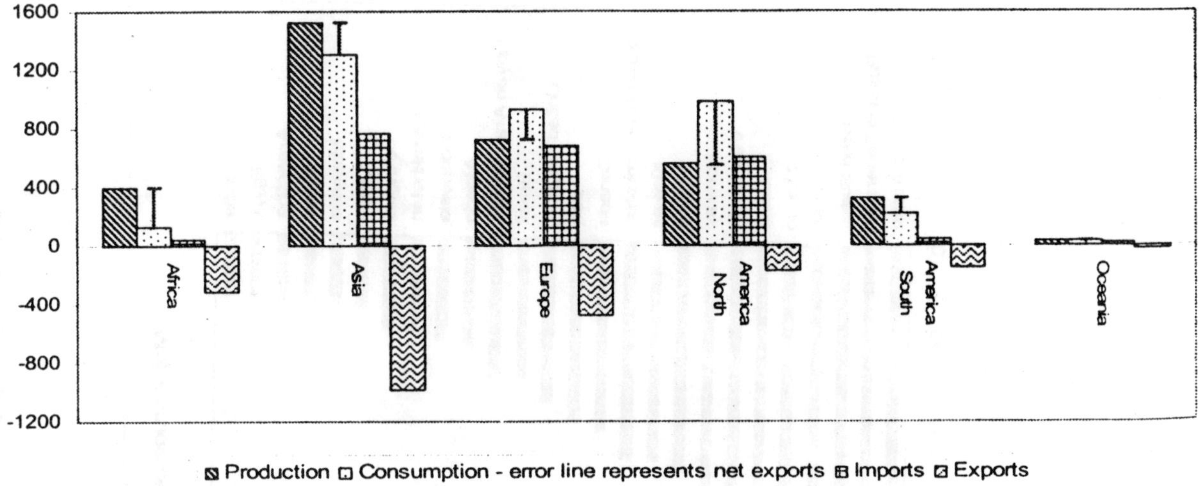

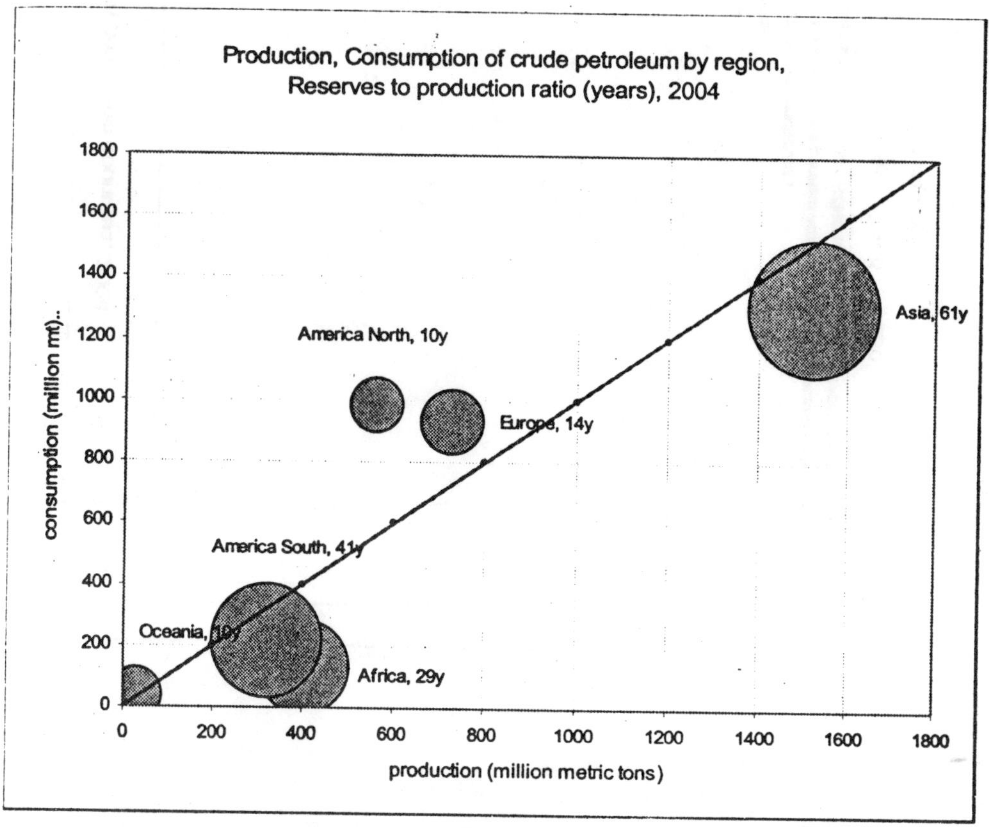

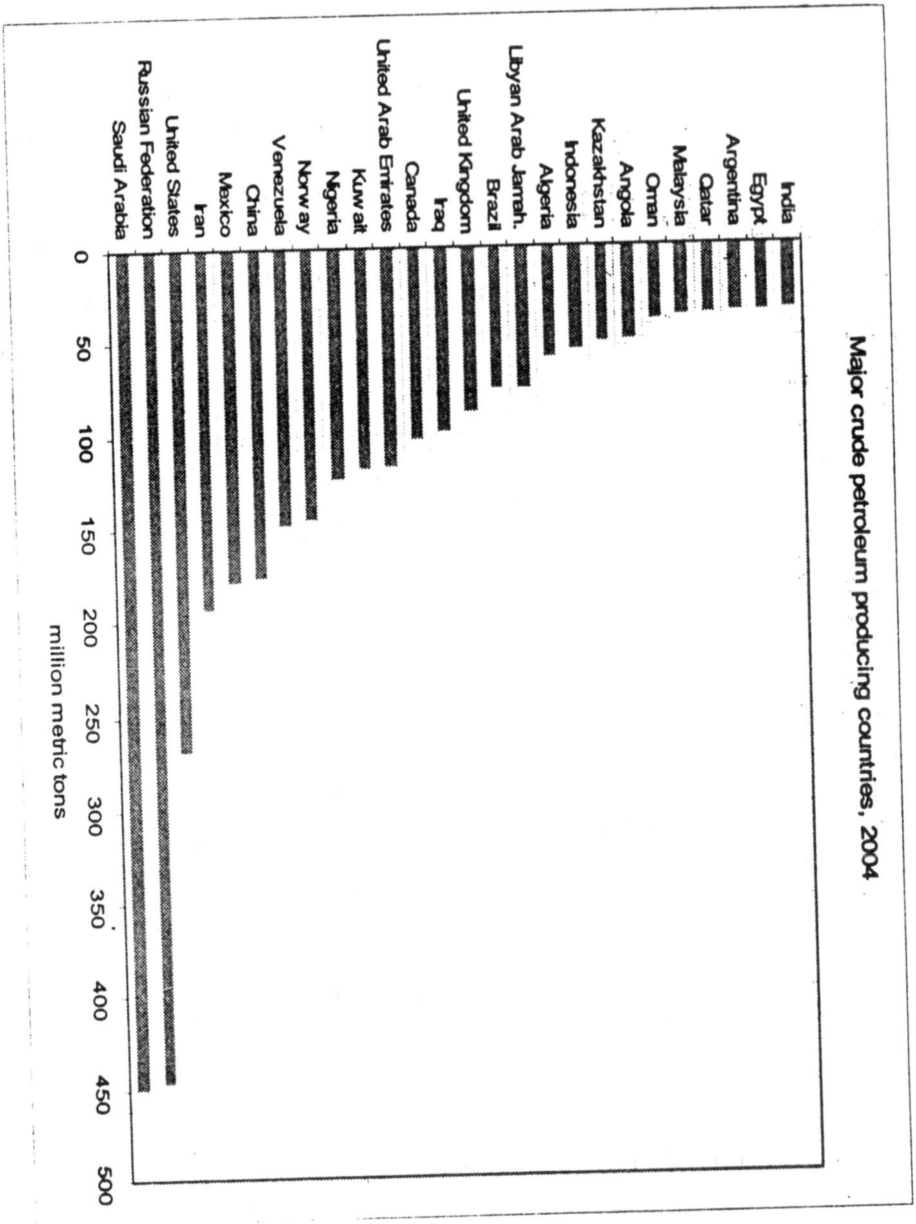
Major crude petroleum producing countries, 2004
India
Egypt
Argentina
Qatar
Malaysia
Oman
Angola
Kazakhstan
Indonesia
Algeria
Libyan Arab Jamah.
Brazil
United Kingdom
Iraq
Canada
United Arab Emirates
Kuw ait
Nigeria
Norw ay
Venezuela
China
Mexico
Iran
United States
Russian Federation
Saudi Arabia
0
50
100
150
200
250
300
350
400
450
500
million metric tons

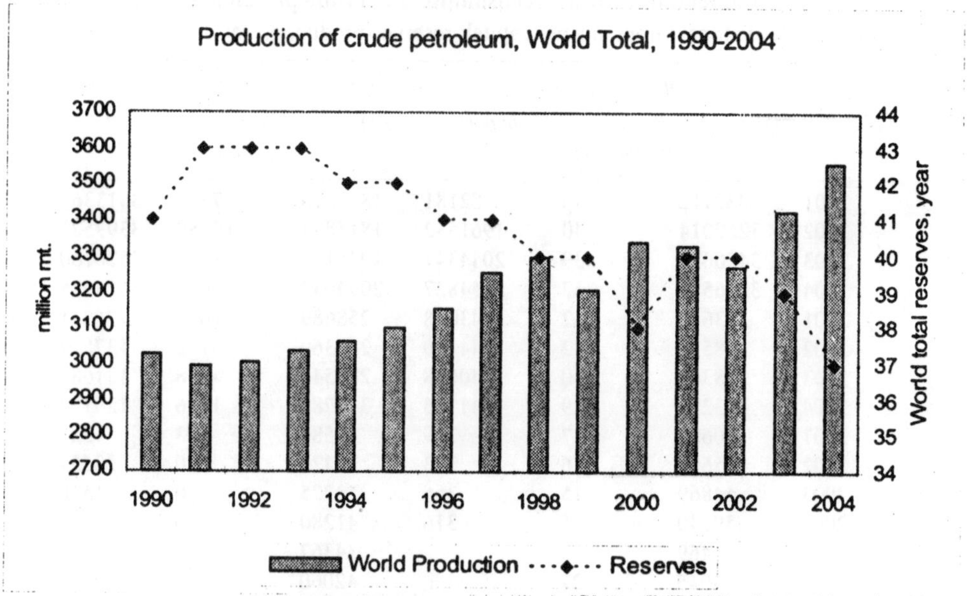

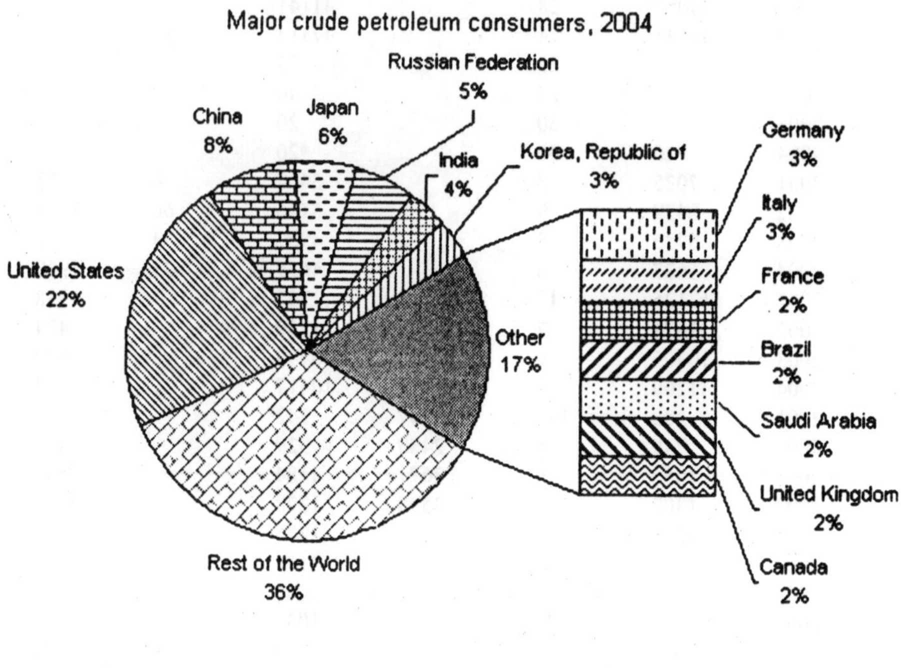

Source: 2004 Energy Statistics Yearbook United Nations, New York, 2007.

TABLE 7

Production, trade and consumption of crude petroleum

Thousand metric tons; kilograms per capital; reserves/production ratio (R/P) in years

		Production					*Consommation*	
Country or area	*Year*	*Total*	*Reserves/ Production*	*Imports*	*Exports*	*Changes in stocks*	*Total*	*Per capita*
World	2001	3332112	40	1982181	1893216	7783	3413365	545
	2002	3267014	40	1961532	1815836	15189	3397521	536
	2003	3420027	39	2044347	1936155	8058	3520160	549
	2004	3566519	37	2154827	2094047	12671	3614628	557
Africa	2001	353640	32	43018	258689	1658	136311	169
	2002	348525	32	44180	255360	-172	137517	166
	2003	378308	30	40638	287544	-278	131680	156
	2004	403276	29	41715	314780	1016	129194	148
Algeria	2001	40609	17	209	19583	-293	21528	654
	2002	45601	16	373	25420	0	20554	611
	2003	54869	15	366	33725	0	21510	625
	2004	59340	15	316	41280	0	18376	522
Angola	2001	36469	33	..	34367	124	1978	186
	2002	44045	27	..	42060	-80	2065	190
	2003	43083	28	..	41141	-166	2108	188
	2004	49443	24	..	47114	780	1549	136
Benin	2001	35	29	..	35	..	0	0
	2002	40	25	..	40	..	0	0
	2003	20	50	..	20	..	0	0
	2004	*20	50	..	*20	..	0	0
Cameroon	2001	7025	8	..	5452	0	1573	104
	2002	6439	9	..	5146	60	1233	80
	2003	6735	8	..	4957	-54	1832	116
	2004	6637	8	..	4657	31	1949	122
Congo	2001	12125	17	..	11587	..	538	166
	2002	11674	17	..	11250	..	424	127
	2003	10705	19	..	10133	..	572	168
	2004	11209	18	..	10417	..	792	226
Côte d'Ivoire	2001	302	126	2547	242	..	2607	153
	2002	749	51	2488	329	..	2908	168
	2003	1055	36	2671	1184	..	2542	144
	2004	1302	29	3598	1278	..	3622	203
Dem. Rep. of Congo	2001	1225	21	..	1225	..	0	0
	2002	1151	23	..	1151	..	0	0
	2003	1083	24	..	1083	..	0	0
	2004	1033	25	..	1033	..	0	0
Egypt	2001	34602	13	..	2409	689	31504	487
2002	34473	12	..	2229	0	32244	489	
	2003	35954	12	..	2100	0	33854	503
	2004	34909	13	..	1896	0	33013	481

Contd...

Contd... table 7

Equatorial Guinea	2001	10440	14	..	*10440	..	0	0
	2002	11597	13	..	11597	..	0	0
	2003	10299	14	..	10299	..	0	0
	2004	7453	20	..	7098	..	355	685
Ethiopia	2001	..	..	755	..	..	755	11
	2002	..	..	759	..	..	759	11
	2003	..	..	*763	..	..	*763	*11
	2004	..	..	*767	..	..	*767	*11
Gabon	2001	14995	23	..	14184	*1	810	639
	2002	13975	24	..	13157	*3	815	627
	2003	11056	31	..	10364	*1	691	519
	2004	10736	32	..	10015	..	721	529
Ghana	2001	..	..	1576	..	..	1576	78
	2002	..	..	1719	..	..	1719	84
	2003	..	..	1960	..	..	1960	93
	2004	..	..	1813	..	..	1813	84
Kenya	2001	..	..	1966	..	..	1966	63
	2002	..	..	1466	..	..	1493	47
	2003	..	..	1649	..	..	1649	50
	2004	..	..	2044	..	..	2044	61
Libyan Arab Jamah.	2001	64730	70	..	47510	..	17220	2948
	2002	60584	75	..	43620	..	16964	2817
	2003	68736	66	..	52135	..	16601	2669
	2004	75280	61	..	58522	..	16758	2610
Madagascar	2001	..	..	..	..	..	470	29
	2002	..	..	..	..	..	470	29
	2003	..	..	*472	..	..	*472	•28
	2004	..	..	*475	..	..	*475	•27
Morocco	2001	10	22	7259		257	7012	240
	2002	13	17	6309	..	-18	6340	214
	2003	10	22	4467	..	57	4420	147
	2004	11	20	6133		-67	6211	203
Nigeria	2001	112715	36	..	101022	698	10995	93
	2002	97957	42	..	87402	-191	10746	89
	2003	113914	36	..	108096	-278	6096	49
	2004	122948	33	..	117583	233	5132	40
Senegal	2001	..	..	968	..	48	920	87
	2002	..	..	925	..	0	925	85
	2003	..	..	1179	..	39	1140	102
	2004	..	..	1113	..	-58	1171	103
Sierra Leone	2001	..	..	*252	..	..	*252	*55
	2002	..	..	*260	..	..	*260	*55
	2003	..	..	*262	..	..	*262	*50
	2004	..	..	*265	..	..	*265	*46

Contd...

Contd.. talble 7

South Africa Customs Union	2001	4615	1	25452	184	..	29883	586
	2002	4706	1	27712	106	..	32312	631
	2003	4369	1	25221	0	..	29590	577
	2004	4642	1	23590	1	..	28231	549
Sudan	2001	10394	7	..	7697	119	2578	82
	2002	12035	6	..	8946	0	3089	96
	2003	13250	6	..	9849	0	3401	103
	2004	15000	5	..	11150	0	3850	115
Tunisia	2001	3349	12	1120	2752	15	1702	176
	2002	3486	11	1197	2907	54	1722	176
	2003	3170	13	1120	2458	123	1709	173
	2004	3313	12	1057	2717	97	1556	157
Zambia	2001	..	..	444	..	..	444	42
	2002	..	..	475	..	..	475	44
	2003	..	..	508	..	..	508	47
	2004	..	..	544	..	..	544	47
America, North	2001	547050	10	568900	154324	4372	957254	1946
	2002	552408	10	552596	158335	3102	942367	1890
	2003	568228	10	584779	171435	5392	976180	1938
	2004	558658	10	607876	177436	6268	983829	1930
Aruba	2001	120	..	*325	..	..	*445	*6357
	2002	120	..	*330	..	..	*450	*6988
	2003	120	..	*335	..	..	*455	*6423
	2004	120	..	*335	..	..	*455	*6389
Barbados	2001	63	16	..	63	..	0	0
	2002	80	13	..	80	..	0	0
	2003	74	14	..	74	..	0	0
	2004	84	12	..	84	..	0	0
Canada	2001	88279	6	45384	56844	632	76187	2456
	2002	91110	6	43533	57150	285	77208	2462
	2003	99256	5	44522	60993	917	81868	2586
	2004	102564	5	45842	66970	-388	81824	2561
Costa Rica	2001	..	..	282	..	-11	293	73
	2002	..	..	484	..	25	459	112
	2003	..	..	531	..	-17	548	131
	2004	..	..	527	..	0	527	124
Cuba	2001	2886	40	1715	..	..	4601	409
	2002	3628	32	1479	..	..	5107	453
	2003	3680	32	2296	..	..	5975	528
	2004	3253	36	1600	..	..	4853	428
Dominican Republic	2001	..	..	1924	..	..	1924	225
	2002	..	..	1975	..	..	1975	228
	2003	..	..	2088	..	..	2088	237
	2004	..	..	2137	..	..	2137	239

Contd...

Contd... talble 7

El Salvador	2001	..	..	1041	..	0	1041	163
	2002	..	..	984	..	46	938	144
	2003	..	..	974	..	27	947	143
	2004	..	..	994	..	28	966	143
Guatemala	2001	1149	70	861	1061	..	94	81
	2002	1344	60	599	1259	..	684	57
	2003	1347	59	0	1347	..	0	0
	2004	1007	79	248	953	..	302	24
Jamaica	2001	..	..	1059	..	0	1059	408
	2002	..	..	1159	..	8	1151	439
	2003	..	..	883	..	0	883	333
	2004	..	..	731	..	0	731	273
Martinique	2001	..	..	*825	..	..	*825	*1972
	2002	..	..	*890	..	..	*890	*2108
	2003	..	..	*595	..	..	*595	*1397
	2004	..	..	*600	..	..	*600	*1397
Mexico	2001	162559	13	..	92740	-6	69825	696
	2002	165964	13	..	96860	-267	69371	681
	2003	176612	12	..	104702	-463	72373	701
	2004	176280	12	..	105180	507	72593	693
Netherlands	2001	..	..	12968	..	..	12968	74529
Antilles	2002	..	..	11018	..	..	11018	63322
	2003	..	..	11011	..	..	11011	61514
	2004	..	..	10861	..	..	10881	49913
Nicaragua	2001	..	..	972	..	11	961	185
	2002	..	..	828	..	-31	859	161
	2003	..	..	893	..	37	856	162
	2004	..	..	844	..	-38	879	164
Panama	2001	..	..	2334	..	12	2322	773
	2002	..	..	967	..	-61	1028	336
	2003	..	..	0	..	0	0	0
	2004	..	..	0	..	0	0	0
Trinidad and	2001	5844	15	4779	2589	69	7965	6127
Tobago	2002	6767	13	4564	3828	-6	7809	5979
	2003	6943	12	4436	3688	69	7622	5853
	2004	6336	13	3220	2891	-86	6751	5167
United States	2001	286150	10	494431	1027	3665	775889	2724
	2002	283395	10	483786	458	3103	763620	2648
	2003	280196	10	516216	631	4822	790959	2720
	2004	268014	11	539917	1368	6243	800330	2723
America, South	2001	325338	40	38456	153037	262	210495	597
	2002	310637	42	34835	141436	8246	195790	547
	2003	305579	43	33920	137162	761	201577	556
	2004	320846	41	40288	146584	-19	214549	583
Argentina	2001	40089	9	1421	14767	46	26697	712
	2002	38907	9	539	13683	25	25738	678

Contd...

Contd... talble 7

	2003	38125	9	252	11802	0	26575	702
	2004	35551	10	520	9013	-133	27191	711
Bolivia	2001	1561	31		243	-192	1510	177
	2002	1549	33	..	369	-315	1495	172
	2003	1670	30	..	126	0	1544	171
	2004	1939	27	..	579	0	1360	147
Brazil	2001	65562	20	21188	5618	-2320	83452	480
	2002	73795	18	19372	11917	-889	82139	466
	2003	76059	17	17379	12262	-312	81488	455
	2004	75336	17	22866	12282	91	85849	473
Chile	2001	256	41	9683	..	218	9721	631
	2002	213	44	9583	..	129	9667	620
	2003	173	48	10009	..	115	10067	632
	2004	170	48	10410		524	10056	625
Colombia	2001	31159	8	275	15258	0	16176	376
	2002	29806	8	176	14545	0	15437	352
	2003	27908	9	59	11589	144	16234	364
	2004	26714	9	176	11025	0	15865	350
Ecuador	2001	21101	31	..	12758	63	8280	643
	2002	20458	32	..	12058	328	8072	616
	2003	21422	30	..	12937	585	7900	615
	2004	27386	24	..	18483	-306	9209	707
Paraguay	2001	..	..	101	..	-1	102	18
	2002	..	..	104	..	5	99	17
	2003	..	..	84	..	-2	86	14
	2004	..	..	50	..	-16	67	11
Peru	2001	5026	8	4000	1009	-222	8239	313
	2002	5006	8	3982	1156	193	7640	286
	2003	4929	8	4499	1560	166	7703	284
	2004	4599	8	4046	841	-298	8102	294
Surinam	2001	643	40	..	85		558	1332
	2002	615	42	..	76		539	1280
	2003	588	44	..	76		512	1210
	2004	612	42	..	88		524	1194
Uruguay	2001	..	..	1788	..	33	1755	522
	2002	..	..	1079	..	–192	1271	375
	2003	..	..	1638	..	65	1573	462
	2004	..	..	2200	..	94	2106	614
Venezuela	2001	159941	64	..	103299	2637	54005	2182
	2002	140288	72	..	87632	8963	43693	1732
	2003	134705	77	..	86810	0	47895	1863
	2004	148540	70	..	94293	26	54221	2075
Asia	2001	1429898	66	670667	898744	-1228	1203049	323
	2002	1348140	70	671378	809457	3857	1206204	320
	2003	1436397	65	707107	871703	2485	1269317	334
	2004	1527666	61	763478	967427	1824	1321893	343

Contd...

Contd... talble 7

Azerbaijan	2001	14779	64	..	8440	29	6310	779
	2002	15209	63	..	6872	-32	6369	783
	2003	15251	62	..	8997	-53	6307	777
	2004	15348	62	..	9048	40	6260	754
Bahrain	2001	9096	2	2883	..	10	11969	18273
	2002	9215	2	3174	..	-14	12403	18457
	2003	9408	2	3283	..	1	12690	18391
	2004	9393	2	3326	..	64	12655	17874
Bangladesh	2001	..	86	1403	..	78	1325	9
	2002	..	93	1276	..	50	1226	9
	2003	..	80	1335	..	-93	1428	11
	2004	..	89	1252	..	-39	1291	9
Brunei	2001	9384	18	..	9050	16	318	949
	2002	9736	17	..	9511	6	219	642
	2003	9952	17	..	9809	-32	175	504
	2004	9695	17	..	9552	53	90	246
China	2001	163959	20	60260	7550	1297	215372	169
	2002	167000	20	69406	7665	1052	227689	177
	2003	169600	19	91020	8133	616	251871	195
	2004	175873	19	122720	5492	2978	290123	223
Cyprus	2001	..	..	1154	..	-2	1156	1656
	2002	..	..	1078	..	-8	1086	1538
	2003	..	..	969	..	-2	971	1358
	2004	..	..	243	..	-35	278	381
Georgia	2001	99	51	2	70	6	25	5
	2002	74	68	4	51	-1	28	5
	2003	140	36	1	72	0	69	13
	2004	98	51	0	61	..	37	7
India	2001	31972	21	77554	..	..	109526	106
	2002	32894	20	81907	..	..	114801	109
	2003	33015	20	87027	..	..	120042	112
	2004	34082	20	95310	..	..	129392	120
Indonesia	2001	60176	8	15397	32617	..	42956	206
	2002	55586	9	15880	27990	..	43476	205
	2003	56860	8	15303	21605	..	50558	236
	2004	54605	9	16471	20592	..	50484	232
Iran (Islamic Rep. of)	2001	183493	67	..	106154	..	77339	1196
	2002	168595	72	..	92970	..	75625	1154
	2003	187814	64	..	113767	..	74047	1114
	2004	195698	61	..	121943	..	73755	1101
Iraq	2001	116107	132	..	90189	0	25918	1045
	2002	99112	154	..	71281	0	27831	1089
	2003	65270	235	..	39973	0	25297	960
	2004	98127	157	..	74766	0	23361	861
Israel	2001	4	250	9828	..	-70	9902	1521
	2002	5	200	9596	..	-212	9813	1480

Contd...

Contd... talble 7

	2003	3	333	10552	..	*55	10500	1556
	2004	2	500	10536	..	-342	10880	1584
Japan	2001	286	16	201529	..	77	201738	1587
	2002	252	15	201649	..	1322	200579	1574
	2003	294	14	204444	..	-649	205387	1611
	2004	293	14	200397	..	-496	201186	1576
Jordan	2001	2	..	3875	..	62	3815	736
	2002	2	..	3869	..	9	3862	725
	2003	2	..	3824	..	0	3826	698
	2004	1	..	4248	..	67	4182	742
Kazakhstan	2001	36060	31	2335	28525	0	9870	665
	2002	42067	26	2985	34911	0	10141	682
	2003	45376	24	2332	38638	0	9070	608
	2004	50672	21	3250	41738	..	12184	813
Korea,	2001	..	..	117400	..	-102	117502	2482
Republic of	2002	..	..	108059	..	572	107487	2256
	2003	..	..	109947	..	2986	106961	2227
	2004	..	..	112813	..	-104	112917	2348
Korean	2001	..	..	581	..	..	581	26
Democratic	2002	..	..	582	..	..	582	26
Peple's Republic	2003	..	..	566	..	..	566	25
	2004	..	..	571	..	..	571	25
Kuwait	2001	98646	126	..	62937	0	35709	15696
	2002	93520	133	..	54695	0	38825	17164
	2003	106782	116	..	63098	0	43684	19287
	2004	117957	106	..	73689	..	44268	16549
Kyrgyzstan	2001	76	66	0	..	-56	132	27
	2002	76	66	10	..	-28	114	23
	2003	69	72	2	..	-23	94	19
	2004	74	68	7	..	-10	91	18
Malaysia	2001	33997	11	9200	18647	-256	24806	1116
	2002	36054	10	7330	18732	1024	23628	1043
	2003	38318	10	8197	19401	-250	27364	1185
	2004	36758	11	7685	18596	-427	26274	1117
Myanmar	2001	653	10	530	..	2	1181	24
	2002	862	8	463	..	-124	1449	30
	2003	967	7	0	..	-56	1023	21
	2004	1002	7	0	..	-58	1060	21
Oman	2001	47593	17	..	45228	-910	3275	1322
	2002	44685	18	..	41767	-1336	4254	1676
	2003	40808	19	..	37997	-1495	4306	1847
	2004	38934	20	..	35967	-752	3719	1643
Other Far East	2001	36	28	39483	..	145	39374	1765
	2002	46	22	40686	..	-75	40807	1817
	2003	41	24	46103	..	218	45926	2032
	2004	40	25	52080	..	356	51764	2281

Contd...

Contd... talble 7

Pakistan	2001	2828	13	7036	433	0	9431	67
	2002	3112	12	7075	239	0	9948	69
	2003	3147	12	7143	240	0	10050	68
	2004	3232	11	8277	41	134	11334	75
Philippines	2001	63	95	14980	..	-304	15347	197
	2002	277	22	12877	..	*-550	13704	172
	2003	20	300	12525	..	114	12431	154
	2004	19	316	9988	..	-343	10350	127
Qatar	2001	31836	52	..	30056	-573	2353	4064
	2002	33321	50	..	27535	1860	3926	6353
	2003	33594	49	..	26651	2598	4345	6832
	2004	35902	47	..	30930	496	4476	6711
Saudi Arabia	2001	393208	85	..	313404	-74	79878	3808
	2002	353452	93	..	274130	1585	77737	3617
	2003	419192	78	..	337227	226	81739	3712
	2004	449192	74	..	*365170	*150	83872	3699
Singapore	2001	..	..	40817	0	0	40817	9840
	2002	..	..	40660	0	0	40660	9781
	2003	..	..	37502	0	0	37502	8584
	2004	..	..	44195	1	0	44194	10423
Sri Lanka	2001	..	..	1955	..	-54	2009	107
	2002	..	..	2281	..	55	2226	117
	2003	..	..	1996	..	.33	2029	106
	2004	..	..	2206	..	-20	2226	115
Syrian Arab Republic	2001	28959	15	3613	19613	..	12959	775
	2002	31150	14	491	18700	..	12941	755
	2003	28000	15	200	15700	..	12500	711
	2004	23300	18	450	11300	..	12450	692
Tajikistan	2001	18	111	..	5	..	13	2
	2002	16	125	..	4	..	12	2
	2003	18	111	..	3	..	15	2
	2004	18	111	..	3	..	15	2
Thailand	2001	3093	11	35610	1827	-737	37613	599
	2002	3787	10	36378	2435	-1722	39452	621
	2003	4785	8	38741	3028	-2159	42657	679
	2004	4297	8	43535	2827	-1680	46685	733
Timor-Leste	2001	..	..	..	..	..	..	..
	2002	*130	0	..	*130	..	0	0
	2003	*130	0	..	*130	..	0	0
	2004	*135	0	..	*135	..	0	0
Turkey	2001	2520	15	23242	..	125	25637	374
	2002	2420	16	23662	..	2	26080	375
	2003	2351	17	24095		-40	26486	377
	2004	2251	17	23918	..	184	25985	368
Turkmenistan	2001	8020	9	..	1500	..	6520	1429
	2002	9400	7	..	2810	..	6590	1423

Contd...

Contd... talble 7

	2003	9600	7	..	2970	..	6630	1411
	2004	9350	7	..	3000	..	6350	1332
United Arab Emirate	2001	111234	104	..	89097	0	22137	6347
	2002	94730	119	..	81618	0	13112	3493
	2003	114026	99	..	91390	0	22636	5608
	2004	117366	96	..	108292	0	9074	2077
Russian Federation	2001	337199	24	5118	162109	909	179299	1239
	2002	368203	22	6232	188385	1011	185039	1285
	2003	409211	20	5737	227856	-1207	188299	1315
	2004	446088	18	4209	257624	1381	191292	1330
Serbia and Montenegro	2001	899	24	1871	..	..	2770	255
	2002	812	27	2582	..	..	3394	313
	2003	773	28	2910	..	..	3683	340
	2004	652	34	3314	..	..	3966	366
Slovakia	2001	46	9	5404	17	-59	5492	1021
	2002	44	10	5553	14	-34	5617	1044
	2003	42	13	5594	17	-37	5656	1051
	2004	38	24	5858	108	75	5713	1062
Slovenia	2001	0	..	..	0	..	0	0
	2002	1	..	..	1	..	0	0
	2003	0	..	..	0	..	0	0
	2004	0	..	..	0	..	0	0
Spain	2001	338	6	56792	..	769	56361	1396
	2002	316	6	56449	..	287	56478	1383
	2003	322	6	57298	..	389	57231	1377
	2004	255	8	59167	..	-460	59882	1386
Sweden	2001	..	..	19891	..	214	19677	2215
	2002	..	..	18550	..	-377	18927	2124
	2003	..	..	20332	..	410	19922	2228
	2004	..	..	20743	..	-23	20766	2314
Switzerland Liechtenstein	2001	..	..	4732	..	5	4727	651
	2002	..	..	4805	..	-3	4808	656
	2003	..	..	4523	..	23	4500	613
	2004	..	..	5078	..	.11	5089	683
The Former Yugoslavia Republic Macedonia	2001	..	..	637	..	-5	642	315
	2002	..	..	552	..	15	537	264
	2003	..	..	812	..	-16	828	408
	2004	-	..	827	..	-4	831	409
Ukraine	2001	2617	53	13127	83	..	15661	319
	2002	2625	53	18858	418	..	21065	435
	2003	2814	50	22453	1438	..	23829	500
	2004	3003	46	21693	427	..	24269	511
United Kingdom	2001	108387	5	48992	80907	926	75546	1262
	2002	107430	5	52041	81198	-33	78306	1324
	2003	97835	5	48589	68823	-1182	78783	1328
	2004	87516	6	55858	60724	136	82514	1382

Contd...

Contd... talble 7

Oceania	2001	29372	8	25373	23097	759	30889	1004
	2002	32765	9	25668	22703	-384	36114	1155
	2003	30108	10	25075	18814	209	36160	1131
	2004	29214	10	24678	17199	-136	36829	1133
Australia	2001	25331	8	21153	19421	874	26189	1351
	2002	28849	9	21152	19128	-293	31166	1585
	2003	26628	9	20282	15556	81	31273	1570
	2004	25800	9	20257	14043	-92	32106	1588
New Zealand	2001	1509	5	4220	1204	-115	4640	1200
	2002	1364	5	4516	1083	-91	4888	1249
	2003	1053	6	4793	896	128	4822	1194
	2004	914	7	4421	721	-44	4658	1141
Papua New	2001	2332	12	..	2472	..	60	12
Guinea	2002	2552	12	..	2492	..	60	12
	2003	2427	13	..	2362	..	65	12
	2004	*2500	12	..	*2435	..	*65	*12

Source: 2004 Energy Statistics Yearbook United Nations, New York, 2007

TABLE 8

International trade of crude petroleum (Principal importers/exporters)

Thousand metric tons 2003

Importers	**Exporters**							
	World	*Iran (Islamic rep. of)*	*Russian Federation*	*Norway,*	*Kuwait*	*Unted Arab Emirates*	*Venezuela*	*Nigeria*
Australia	20282	39	..	..	145	1835	..	..
Belarus	14885	..	14885	..	..	..	..	..
Belgium	36245	4689	11624	4711	..	..	896	1265
Brazil	17816	34	..	194	..	..	27	6251
Canada	44522	..	1223	12226	..	..	1393	1572
China	91020	12394	5254	932	907	864	444	122
Finland	10931		7595	910	..	..	..	..
France incl. Monaco	85366	5821	17625	16189	2113	:	143	5323
Germany	106464	23	41591	22281	..	..	961	2883
Greece	19782	4244	7699	..	..	..	..	23
India	88623	*14000	..	..	*16000	*17000	..	*3500
Indonesia	16817	246	..	..	..	..	..	..
Italy and San Marino	84337	9913	20904	4692	..	..	214	1717
Japan	204444	32461	1444	160	19329	50592	..	3012
Korea, Republic of	109947	8516	1516	262	8704	18580	..	381
Netherlands	48526	2311	10862	6753	4002	..	..	1293

Contd...

Contd...table 8

]Netherlands Antilles	11011	..	..	..	..	11011	..	..
Philippines	12525	2850	177	..	..	1909	:	..
Poland	17448	..	17202	..	..	..	..	..
Portugal	12733	258	1481	640	..	..	..	2988
Singapore	37502	1319	62	64	5433	4189	..	..
Spain	57298	4264	10230	2553	..	..	816	6456
Sweden	20332	3151	4049	7650	..	..	817	..
Thailand	38741	46	..	..	130	8492	..	125
Turkey	24095	7029	4619	..	..	..	..	..
United Kingdom	48589	..	4420	32578	..	..	1124	130
United States	516216	..	7959	11595	10545	453	76516	41984

2003

United Kingdom	*Mexico*	*Libyan Arab Jamah.*	*Canada*	*Indonesia*	*Qatar*	*Algeria*	*Angola*	*Saudi Arabia*
..	..	..		4276	153	..	..	1703
..	..	..	..	..	..	..	..	..
4142	..	..	..	312	45	249	..	6144
383	..	..	..	..	..	3343	..	3559
9401	1399	..	..	..	..	6422	..	3143
202	..	129	55	3333	676	128	10103	15080
158	..	..	...	..	..	..	..	..
8883	155	3623	..	..	..	5864	3028	11245
11594	..	8968	..	..	:.	3727	381	3880
..	..	989	..	..	..	..	..	6184
	*1478	..	..	*100	..	..	..	*29000
..	..	236	..	..	..	700	383	5152
74	..	21948	..	..	..	3466	814	10564
..	529	..	:.	7181	18687	..	127	50581
..	..	..	131	4561	6331	..	992	33515
9787	..	..	..	..	..	..	42	10592
..	..	..	..	..	..	..	..	..
..	..	..	..	155	508	..	..	5698
..	..	..	..	..	..	..	..	..
1056	668	1741	..	..	..	..	..	1694
..	:.	..	..	..	6173	..	..	10537
922	7265	7621	..	..	..	1502	..	6994
958	..	..	..	..	..	..	..	..
..	..	..	..	767	1782	257	..	5950
..	..	4580	..	..	..	240	..	3868
..	583	..	..	..	..	1072	..	2669
19041	80035	..	78678	1282	..	5184	18727	86944

2004

Importers	Exporters							
	World	*Iran (Islamic rep. of)*	*Russian Federation*	*Norway,*	*Kuwait*	*Unted Arab Emirates*	*Venezuela*	*Nigeria*
Australia	20257	39	..	..	145	1835	..	..
Belarus	17814	..	17814	..	..	..	..	..
Belgium	34407	4620	13953	2949	331	..	915	433
Brazil	22866	..	..	..	..	..	26	11430
Canada	45842	..	..	12304	..	..	2563	1315
China	122720	18070	13350	2614	1419	1877	328	1868
Finland	11035	..	7595	910	..	..	..	..
France incl. Monaco	85103	6374	19193	15599	1687	..	..	2645
Germany	110126	405	46227	21804	60	..	783	914
Greece	20297	4244	7699	..	..	..	..	23
India	95310	15000	..	..	17000	18000	..	5000
Indonesia	18930	*250	..	..	..	..	..	*3600
Italy and San Marino	86867	9556	23297	3337	..	..	38	1443
Japan	200397	28736	1353	140	17705	51158	..	3498
Korea, Republic of	112813	8773	1156	275	8773	19973	..	1577
Netherlands	52074	2432	15788	7772	4527	..	..	94
Netherlands Antilles	10881	..	..	..	..	10881	..	..
Philippines	9988	3290	81	..	..	73	..	..
Poland	17316	..	17203	..	..	..	..	..
Portugal	12769	258	1481	643	..	..	..	2988
Singapore	44195	..	..	..	6407	4515	..	..
Spain	59167	3469	9631	3494	..	..	454	6238
Sweden	20743	3151	4049	7650	..	..	817	..
Thailand	43535	..	69	..	226	12293	..	..
Turkey	23918	5821	6551	..	..	..	..	..
United Kingdom	55858	..	7909	39771	..	..	1249	248
United States	539917	..	8043	10451	12281	..	84526	54582

FIGURE 5

Production, trade and consumption of natural gas

Unit: *Terajoules and megajoules per capita*

Figure Notes

Production

Refers to net production: gross production minus re-injected, minus flared and vented, minus extraction loss shrinkage.

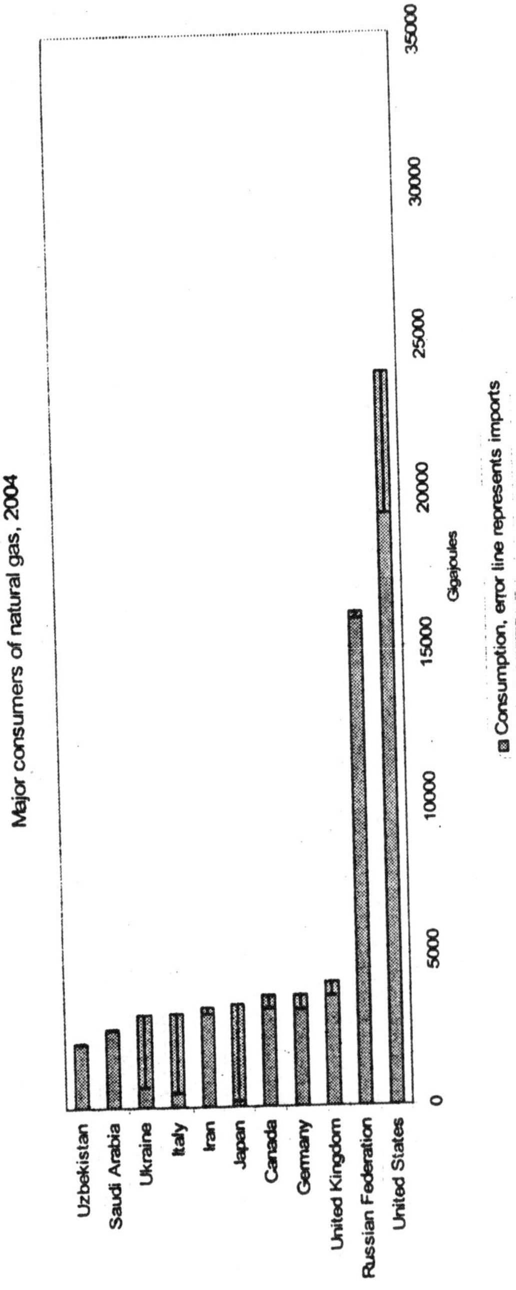
Major consumers of natural gas, 2004
Uzbekistan
Saudi Arabia
Ukraine
Italy
Iran
Japan
Canada
Germany
United Kingdom
Russian Federation
United States
0
5000
10000
15000
20000
25000
30000
35000
Gigajoules
Consumption, error line represents imports

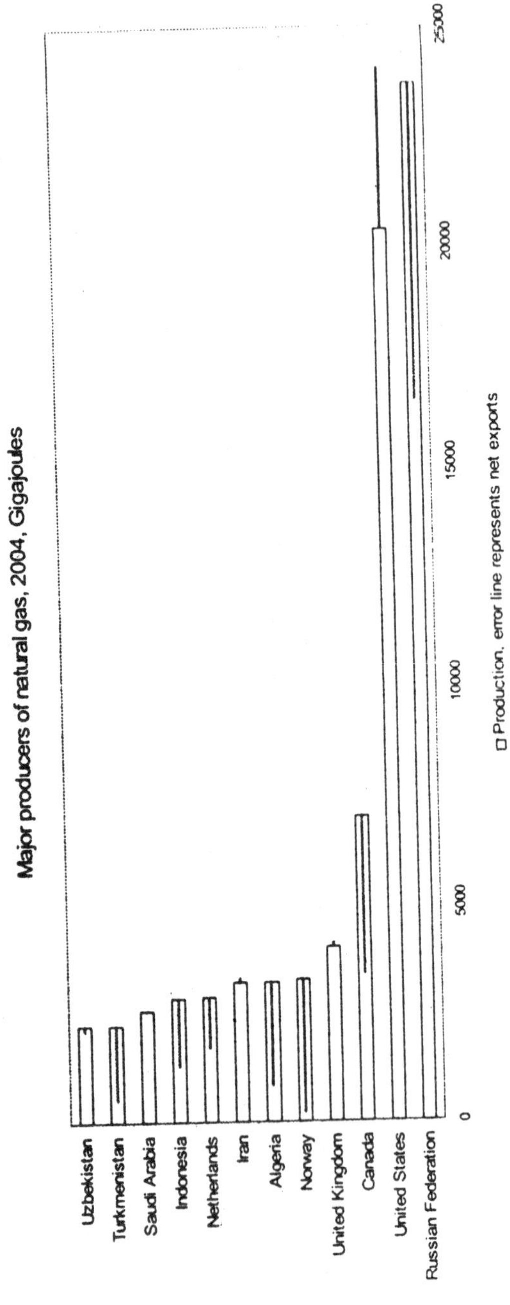
Major producers of natural gas, 2004, Gigajoules
Uzbekistan
Turkmenistan
Saudi Arabia
Indonesia
Netherlands
Iran
Algeria
Norway
United Kingdom
Canada
United States
Russian Federation
0
5000
10000
15000
20000
25000
Production, error line represents net exports

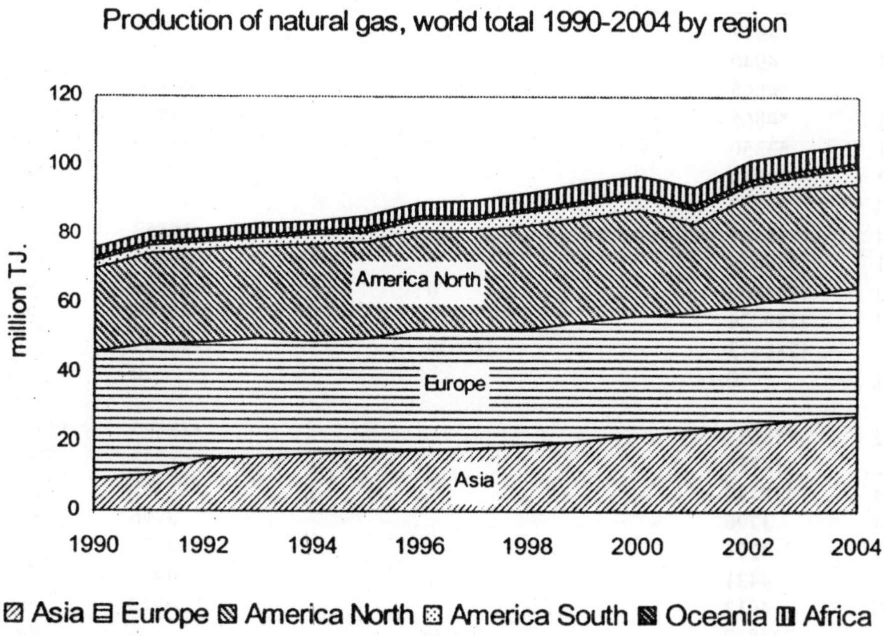

TABLE 9

Production, trade and consumption of natural gas

(Terajoules and megajoules per capita)

Country or area	*Year*	*Production*	*Imports*	*Exports*	*Changes stocks*	*Consumption Total*	*Consumption Per capita*
World	2001	98580711	25645554	25713647	928044	97504574	15576
	2002	101714081	27449222	27044962	92419	102025921	16092
	2003	104295926	29220335	28491741	512420	104512101	16313
	2004	106821594	30935723	30773664	447601	106536052	16411
Africa	2001	4994533	59668	2631359	..	2422842	2997
	2002	5396878	. 59525	2656027	..	2800376	3388
	2003	5660937	64393	2894626	..	2830704	3343
	2004	5966704	82543	3135799	..	2913448	3340
Algeria	2001	3068448	..	2234390	..	834058	25344
	2002	3213741	..	2306043	..	907698	26961
	2003	3248416	..	2353418	..	884998	26017
	2004	3216262	..	2378557	..	837705	23819
Angola	2001	*20140	..	..	..	*20140	*1896
	2002	23560	..	..	..	23560	2168
	2003	*27360	..	..	..	*27360	*2446
	2004	28500	..	..	.	28500	2502

Contd...

Contd...table 9

Congo	2001	4877	..	..	..	4877	1506
	2002	4940	..	..	..	4940	1484
	2003	*4865	..	..	..	*4865	*1425
	2004	*4865	..	..	..	*4865	*1389
Côted'Ivoire	2001	53350	..	..	.	53350	3129
	2002	54353	..	..	..	54353	3135
	2003	47770	..	..	..	47770	2714
	2004	35157	..	..	..	35157	1967
Egypt	2001	856436	..	0	..	856436	13247
	2002	1051806	..	0	..	1051806	15939
	2003	1189024	..	30666	..	1158358	17209
	2004	1288413	..	140030	.	1148383	16699
Equatorial Guinea	2001	0	..	..	..	0	0
	2002	*18537	.	..	..	*18537	*37373
	2002	18773	..	..	..	18773	37028
	2004	*18730	..	..	..	*18730	*36163
Gabon	2001	3796	..	..	..	3796	2994
	2002	4271	..	..	..	4271	3288
	2003	4421	..	..	..	4421	3322
	2004	4912	..	..	..	4912	3606
Libyan	2001	234839	..	30020	..	204819	35060
Arab	2002	235980	..	23940	..	212040	35217
Jamah.	2003	243200	..	28500	..	214700	34512
	2004	266001	..	41800	..	224201	34922
Morocco	2001	1749	..	..	..	1749	60
	2002	1633	..	..	..	1693	57
	2003	1633	..	..	..	1693	54
	2004	1977	..	..	..	1977	65
Mozambique	2001	47	..	..	..	47	3
	2002	92	.	..	..	92	5
	2003	96	..	..	..	96	5
	2004	52312	..	52189	..	123	6
Nigeria	2001	581413	..	342596	..	238817	2030
	2002	623048	..	305760	..	317288	2623
	2003	742296	..	459810	.	282486	2271
	2004	873602	..	496350	..	377252	2931
Rwanda	2001	*13	..	..	..	*13	*2
	2002	*13	..	..	..	*13	*1
	2003	*13	..	..	..	*13	*1
	2004	*7	..	..	..	*7	*1
Senegal	2001	25	..	..	..	25	2
	2002	114	..	..	..	114	10
	2003	423	..	..	..	423	38
	2004	506	..	..	..	506	44
South Africa	2001	84478	..	..	..	84478	1655
Customs Un.	2002	83764	..	..	..	83764	979

Contd...

Contd...table 9

	2003	50218	..	..	..	50218	1636
	2004	77172	..	..	..	77172	1501
Tunisia	2001	84922	59668	24353	..	120237	12429
	2002	80966	59525	20284	..	120207	12290
	2003	82428	64393	22232	..	124590	12617
	2004	95312	82543	26873		150982	15205
United Rep.	2001	0	..	..	..	0	0
Tanzania	2002	0	..	..	..	0	0
	2003	0	..	..	..	0	0
	2004	4975	..	..	..	4975	132
America,	2001	30497324	4614370	4656275	1052456	29402963	59766
North	2002	30811452	4883582	4853376	-703525	31545183	€3263
	2003	30391212	5094259	5120025	24689	30340757	60241
	2004	30069994	5486557	5461162	-22873	30118262	59078
Barbados	2001	1257	..	1257	4690	..	..
	2002	1139	..	..	..	1139	4234
	2003	1020	..	..	..	1020	3778
	2004	973	..	..	..	973	3589
Canada	2001	7084850	148953	4120413	-230424	3343814	107792
	2002	7133466	251548	4103366	-130528	3412176	108800
	2003	7032164	369794	3876239	-183243	3708962	117150
	2004	7011348	414979	4015014	-220123	3631436	113674
Cuba	2001	23217	..	..	..	23217	2066
	2002	22827	..	..	..	22827	2025
	2003	25675	..	..	..	25675	2271
	2004	27470	..	..	..	27470	2423
Dominican	2001	..	0	..	..	0	0
Republic	2002	..	0	..	..	0	0
	2003	..	181	..	..	181	21
	2004	..	207	..	..	207	23
Mexico	2001	1469563	146213	9534	1090	1605152	15992
	2002	1506981	278231	1777	0	1783435	17511
	2003	1579524	375146	0	1811	1952859	18905
	2004	1651290	434882	0	52638	2033534	19416
Puerto Rico	2001	..	24568	..	..	24568	6398
	2002	..	24568	..	..	24568	6366
	2003	..	28860	..	..	28860	7440
	2004	..	26534	..	..	26534	6812
Trinidad and	2001	548129	..	128447	..	419682	322832
Tobago	2002	638636	..	199091	..	439545	336558
	2003	971764	..	507206	..	464558	356749
	2004	1024185	..	536381	..	487804	373338
United States	2001	21370308	4294636	397881	1281790	23985273	84219
	2002	21508403	4329235	549142	-572997	25861493	89682
	2003	20781065	4320278	736580	206121	24158642	83073
	2004	20354728	4609955	909767	144612	23910304	81341

Contd...

Contd...table 9

America, South	2001	3652513	384195	390417	19203	3627088	10286
	2002	3586321	417596	416664	15526	3571727	9975
	2003	3715622	440165	426256	11224	3718307	10250
	2004	4115018	561479	604373	0	4072125	11064
Argentina	2001	1558100	0	240639	..	1317461	35144
	2002	1496647	3923	227635	..	1272935	33548
	2003	1664109	3539	258475	..	1409173	37211
	2004	1820534	2920	313272	..	1510182	39507
Bolivia	2001	179577	..	149778	..	29799	3499
	2002	218691	..	189029	..	29662	3407
	2003	255726	..	167781	..	87945	9745
	2004	355620	..	291101	..	64519	6992
Brazil	2001	286688	178459	..	..	465147	2676
	2002	367896	207931	..	..	575827	3264
	2003	397527	195770	..	..	593297	3315
	2004	420030	313155	..	..	733185	4038
Chile	2001	81777	204423	..	19203	266997	17335
	2002	83772	204853	..	15526	273099	17519
	2003	73681	238369	..	11224	300826	18885
	2004	*73280	241084	..	0	314364	19528
Colombia	2001	269559	..	.	..	269559	6259
	2002	269287	..	..	..	269287	6146
	2003	257762	..	..	..	257762	5784
	2004	*271346	..	..	..	*271346	*5990
Ecuador	2001	9760	..	..	..	9760	758
	2002	9869	..	..	..	9869	753
	2003	16234	..	..	..	16234	1264
	2004	17056	..	..	..	17056	1309
Peru	2001	29696	..	..	..	29696	1127
	2002	31377	..	..	..	31377	1173
	2003	33696	..	..	..	33696	1241
	2004	*48761	..	..	..	*48761	*1770
Uruguay	2001	..	1313	..	..	1313	391
	2002	..	889	..	..	889	263
	2003	..	2487	..	..	2487	730
	2004	..	4320	..	..	4320	1259
Venezela	2001	1237356	..	..	..	1237356	49994
	2002	1108782	..	..	..	1108782	43947
	2003	1016887	..	..	..	1016887	39552
	2004	1108392	..	..	..	1108392	42426
Asia	2001	23242524	5739013	6165708	38493	22777337	6115
	2002	24869774	6210000	6335814	40869	24703091	6553
	2003	26403777	6760701	6840220	74889	26249369	6895
	2004	27706190	7245619	7549869	52014	27349927	7107
Afghanistan	2001	*4250	..	..	..	*4250	*192
	2002	285	..	..	..	285	14

Contd...

Contd...table 9

	2003	242	..	..	..	242	11
	2004	119	..	..	..	119	5
Armenia	2001		53082	0	..	53082	15926
	2002		39887	0	..	39887	12003
	2003		45278	0	..	45278	11918
	2004		50782	490	..	50292	16620
Azerbaijan	2001	208670	125804	..	-2451	336925	41616
	2002	193928	148350	..	4411	337867	41522
	2003	193326	153778	..	452	346652	42707
	2004	194905	187218	..	3551	378572	45578
Bahrain	2001	242921	..	..	..	242921	370872
	2002	255748	..	..	..	255748	380577
	2003	263779	..	..	..	263779	382288
	2004	274330	..	..	..	274330	387472
Bangladesh	2001	384256	..	..	..	384256	2728
	2002	404256	..	..	..	404256	2811
	2003	434849	..	..	..	434849	3205
	2004	467723	..	..	..	467723	3360
Brunei Darussalam	2001	445654		386604	..	59050	176269
	2002	447477	..	389562	..	57915	169839
	2003	482490	..	423510	..	58980	169971
	2004	477318	..	411413	..	65905	180068
China	2001	1459431	..	94210	..	1365221	1069
	2002	1571720	..	89502	..	1482218	1154
	2003	1685000	..	57553	..	1627447	1260
	2004	1544800	..	90914	..	1453886	1119
China, Hong Kong SAR	2001	..	94271	..	..	94271	14018
	2002	..	89560	..	..	89560	13245
	2003	..	57590	..	..	57590	8457
	2004	..	83197	..	..	83197	12137
Georgia	2001	1537	36535	..	284	37788	7234
	2002	650	30957	..	0	31607	6105
	2003	712	35169	..	0	35881	7000
	2004	461	41575	..	0	42036	8081
India	2001	885699	..	..	..	885699	857
	2002	958122	..	..	..	958122	912
	2003	1016146	..	..	..	1016146	951
	2004	1007951	..	..	..	1007951	934
Indonesia	2001	2845020	..	1666663	..	1178357	5653
	2002	3065116	..	1470469	..	1594647	7528
	2003	3192073	..	1537388	..	1654685	7708
	2004	2837254	..	1543980	..	1293274	5&44
Iran (Islamic Rep. of)	2001	2400165	177692	14089	..	2563768	39731
	2002	2721192	207721	50140	..	2878773	43924
	2003	3051153	225549	134322	..	3142380	47279
	2004	3198059	238385	135848	..	3300596	49258

Contd...

Contd...table 9

Iraq	2001	104880	..	..	..	104880	4227
	2002	87400	..	..	..	87400	3419
	2003	59280	..	..	..	59280	2251
	2004	101455	..	..	..	101455	3738
Israel	2001	365	..	..	..	365	56
	2002	335	..	..	..	335	51
	2003	321	..	..	..	321	48
	2004	43585	..	..	..	43585	6345
Japan	2001	229287	2965929	..	-17059	3212275	25268
	2002	236027	2999513	..	23462	3212078	25212
	2003	220188	3190273	..	-2847	3413308	26766
	2004	214508	3155823	..	7846	3362485	26334
Jordan	2001	9586	..	..	..	9586	1850
	2002	9000	..	..	..	9000	1689
	2003	10200	..	..	..	10200	1861
	2004	10400	..	..	..	10400	1846
Kazakhstan	2001	471773	166954	216054	..	422673	28499
	2002	550604	319003	407179	..	462428	31121
	2003	647698	339292	429494	..	557496	37393
	2004	862531	454587	674340	..	642778	42869
Korea,	2001	..	879644	..	43774	835870	17656
Republic of	2002	..	950690	..	16878	933812	19601
	2003	..	1057600	..	78301	979299	20394
	2004	..	1205570	..	50116	1155454	24031
Kuwait	2001	347806	..	..	..	347806	152882
	2002	311914	..	..	..	311914	137893
	2003	363426	..	..	..	363426	160453
	2004	378504	..	..	..	378504	141497
Kyrgyzstan	2001	1288	25987	..	27275	5505	..
	2002	1171	33401	..	..	34572	6924
	2003	1054	27470	..	..	28524	5661
	2004	1132	30017	..	..	31149	6116
Malaysia	2001	*1732929	..	745338	..	*987591	*44428
	2002	*1787405	..	790818	..	*996587	*43976
	2003	*1870708	..	852155	..	*1018553	*44107
	2004	2180862	..	1008475	..	1172388	49842
Myanmar	2001	244015	..	198790	..	45225	938
	2002	252967	..	206193	..	46774	957
	2003	306893	..	244747	..	62146	1256
	2004	317937	..	253555	..	64382	1288
Oman	2001	572951	..	326308	..	246643	99533
	2002	630632	..	318942	..	311690	122809
	2003	691553	..	354757	..	336796	144486
	2004	706149	..	*393225		312924	138217
Other Far	2001	31642	257374	..	9174	279842	12547
East	2002	33045	290174	..	21	323198	14394

Contd...

Contd...table 9

	2003	30961	302611	..	-2090	335662	14850
	2004	32374	372921	..	-8242	413537	18226
Pakistan	2001	800401	..	..	0	800401	5659
	2002	836631	..	..	0	836631	5774
	2003	897330	..	..	0	897330	6045
	2004	1119118	..	..	-308	1119426	7362
Philippines	2001	5283	..	..	..	5283	68
	2002	66367	..	..	..	66367	835
	2003	101146	..	..	..	101146	1253
	2004	96743	..	..	..	96743	1185
Qatar	2001	1099633	..	599374	..	500259	864005
	2002	1207536	..	699495	..	508041	822073
	2003	1262086	..	740121	..	521965	820700
	2004	1605919	..	947540	..	658379	987075
Saudi Arabia	2001	2095045		..	..	2095045	99878
	2002	2236692	..	..	..	2236692	104076
	2003	2343609	..	..	..	2343609	106436
	2004	2562899	..	..	..	2562899	113033
Singapore	2001	..	83090	..	83090	20031	..
	2002	..	134872	..	134872	32445	..
	2003	..	208631	..	208631	47753	..
	2004	245965	..	245965	58011	..	
Syrian Arab Republic	2001	*210743	..	..	..	*210743	*12604
	2002	•256360	..	..	..	..	..
	2003	*256360	*14947	•258245	..	..	..
	2004	267670	14887	..	..	..	..
Tajikistan	2001	1506	21470	..	..	22976	3745
	2002	1130	28083	..	..	29213	4622
	2003	1246	20140	..	..	21386	3424
	2004	1250	20737	..	..	21987	3419
Thailand	2001	686719	236303	..	..	923022	14705
	2002	716194	270677	..	..	986871	15546
	2003	707276	293327	..	..	1000603	15922
	2004	701157	315779	..	..	1016936	15957
Turkey	2001	11950	614878	..	4771	622057	9077
	2002	14477	667112	..	-3903	685492	9845
	2003	21448	803993	..	1073	824368	11748
	2004	26350	843063	..	-949	870362	12312
Turkmenistan	2001	1943706	..	1409471	..	534235	117054
	2002	2023273	..	1460538	..	562735	121541
	2003	2241513	..	1644383	..	597130	127103
	2004	2235451	..	1701216	..	534235	112093
United Arab Emirates	2001	1535886	..	291097	..	1244790	356878
	2002	1693142	..	277556	..	1415586	377087
	2003	1748141	..	280444	..	1467697	363651
	2004	1787162	..	274983	..	1512179	346195

Contd...

Contd...table 9

Uzbekistan	2001	2175359	..	217710	..	1957649	78419
	2002	2191336	..	175420	..	2015916	79467
	2003	2173692	..	141346	..	2032346	77889
	2004	2235451	..	113890	..	2121561	80948
Viet Nam	2001	52168	..	..	..	52168	659
	2002	107642	..	..	..	107642	1350
	2003	125993	..	.-	..	125993	1548
	2004	214663	..	..	..	214663	2613
Europe	2001	34588450	14848308	11460251	-182104	38158611	44539
	2002	35399638	15878519	12369660	739550	38168947	44584
	2003	36464965	16860817	12784875	401612	40159295	46914
	2004	37311026	17559525	13591940	418443	40860168	47467
Albania	2001	327	..	..	.	.	327
	2002		544	..	..	..544	155
	2003	544	..	..	..	544	154
	2004	636	..	..	.	636	204
Austria	2001	68413	248152	16184	-21004	321385	40068
	2002	74295	258276	21053	-13515	325033	40432
	2003	82603	317283	40567	7889	351430	43564
	2004	77550	331352	51847	2568	354487	43548
Belarus	2001	9849	666847	..	4326	672370	67419
	2002	9501	678898	..	3862	684537	68971
	2003	9810	699560	..	-3128	712498	72159
	2004	9942	758652	..	-4673	773267	78712
Belgium	2001	..	610993	..	-2130	613123	59741
	2002	..	635134	..	12792	622342	60363
	2003	..	662591	..	-7390	669981	64695
	2004	..	677290	..	-506	677796	65195
Bosnia and Herzegovina	2001	..	11286	..	..	11286	2980
	2002	..	11726	..	..	11726	3064
	2003	..	12232	..	..	12232	3192
	2004	..	14289	..	..	14289	3655
Bulgaria	2001	853	127044	..	482	127415	16102
	2002	752	116222	..	5132	111842	14213
	2003	597	109593	..	-6136	116326	14868
	2004	12432	111129	..	7602	115959	14864
Croatia	2001	76395	41162	9329	528	107700	24273
	2002	80572	41207	13764	-2253	110268	24818
	2003	83205	43274	12996	3876	109607	24675
	2004	83528	40037	13209	-3997	114353	25745
Czech Republic	2001	5671	359894	0	-8091	373656	36397
	2002	5338	368354	38	12564	361090	35377
	2003	6098	360045	1928	-604	364819	35753
	2004	7555	333350	3329	-24717	362293	35479
Denmark	2001	353062	..	142090	-4461	215433	40275
	2002	353693	..	138837	-408	215264	40101

Contd...

Contd...table 9

	2003	335062	..	120692	-2445	216815	41032
	2004	395033	..	171722	7748	215563	39937
Estonia	2001	..	33050	..	..	33050	24177
	2002	..	27714	..	..	27714	20363
	2003	..	31635	..	..	31635	23330
	2004	..	36032	..	..	36032	26669
Finland	2001	..	172446	..	..	172446	33195
	2002	..	171371	..	..	171371	32918
	2003	..	171371	..	..	171371	36399
	2004	..	183779	..	..	183779	35209
France incl.	2001	70222	1663132	37181	-50563	1746736	29263
Monaco	2002	67438	1744261	35068	32860	1743771	29084
	2003	59621	1788025	38937	-23331	1832040	30426
	2004	51530	1857438	57079	-17279	1869168	30156
Germany	2001	741143	2951423	244115	-68040	3516491	42748
	2002	743728	3063709	269209	22680	3515548	42644
	2003	740615	3187328	282769	-39600	3684774	44644
	2004	685342	3389857	324436	88200	3662563	44378
Greece	2001	1870	77680	..	1255	78295	7163
	2002	1973	81622	..	-192	83787	7625
	2003	1442	93138	..	319	94261	8555
	2004	1337	101125	..	-1220	103682	9391
Hungary	2001	115224	362207	134	-20962	498259	48849
	2002	109582	404952	0	11627	502907	49426
	2003	106329	462396	0	15786	552939	54520
	2004	110100	431618	0	-3135	544853	53857
Ireland	2001	30639	136078	..	0	166717	43575
	2002	31519	139612	..	0	171131	43880
	2003	25293	145769	..	1145	169917	42865
	2004	32025	137683	..	143	169565	42099
Italy and San	2001	580723	2086927	2365	-37490	2702775	46703
Marino	2002	557137	2259025	1981	129692	2684489	46320
	2003	529017	2392454	14516	-52692	2959647	51006
	2004	493813	2587295	15050	-5145	3071203	53054
Latvia	2001	..	50582	..	-8506	59088	24995
	2002	..	53210	..	-6870	60080	25610
	2003	..	65403	..	2728	62675	26876
	2004	..	80880	..	18897	61983	26726
Lithuania	2001	..	101015	..	..	101015	28969
	2002	..	102123	..	..	102123	29379
	2003	..	110900	..	..	110900	32024
	2004	..	110335	..	..	110335	32020
Luxembourg	2001	..	32315	..	..	32315	73610
	2002	..	48986	..	..	48986	110329
	2003	..	49499	..	.-	49499	110489
	2004	..	55794	..	..	55794	123547

Contd...

Contd...table 9

Netherlands	2001	2591786	712810	1651219	-276	1653653	103437
	2002	2524867	892010	1750281	-774	1667370	103531
	2003	2428905	849263	1603074	447	1674647	103418
	2004	2864924	628124	1784604	-925	1709369	105140
Norway,	2001	2273483	..	2022071	.	251412	55832
Svlbd.	2002	2751407	..	2561226	..	190181	42038
J.Myn. 1	2003	3081659	..	2835323	..	246336	54116
	2004	3274692	..	3068945	..	205747	44947
Poland	2001	162449	335498	1573	13655	482719	12491
	2002	166037	312390	1605	6356	470466	12178
	2003	167997	350607	1767	-7010	523847	13706
	2004	182618	379467	1753	7728	552604	14470
Portugal	2001	..	104769	..	-137	104906	10222
	2002	..	126847	..	-122	126969	12292
	2003	..	122968	..	328	122640	11783
	2004	..	153733	..	57	153676	14671
Republic of	2001	..	108297	..	40	108257	29815
Moldova	2002	..	95929	..	-79	96008	26500
	2003	..	101685	..	-100	101785	28172
	2004	..	106513	..	-40	106553	25261
Romania	2001	501496	107387	..	-4242	613125	27703
	2002	493064	145601	..	4656	634009	29090
	2003	485135	197100	..	-2974	685209	31527
	2004	482759	191269	..	25664	648364	29863
Russian	2001	21807667	155556	6796667	32222	15134334	104617
Federation	2002	22308334	271333	6972000	458111	15149556	105232
	2003	23252111	329000	7116778	526556	15937777	111262
	2004	23693333	258889	7530000	295556	16126666	112108
Serbia and	2001	21153	59362	..	..	80515	7415
Montenegro	2002	16946	64030	..	.	80976	7476
	2003	13723	70955	..	..	84678	7824
	2004	11951	79420	..	..	91371	8442
Slovakia	2001	7009	263569	0	-16374	286952	53347
	2002	6754	273122	0	6927	272949	50743
	2003	7745	256076	151	-38	263708	49025
	2004	6603	264166	39	14944	255786	47543
Slovenia	2001	244	39301	..	..	39545	19872
	2002	222	37914	..	..	38136	19125
	2003	199	41982	..	..	42181	21143
	2004	201	41608	..	..	41809	20942

Contd...

Contd...table 9

Spain	2001	21904	736262	..	-4758	762924	18895
	2002	21718	880596	..	30009	872305	21353
	2003	9149	984756	..	565	993340	23907
	2004	14398	1145112	..	-11478	1170988	27108
Sweden	2001	..	40720	..	..	40720	4584
	2002	..	41439	..	..	41439	4651
	2003	..	41322	..	..	41322	4622
	2004	..	41142	..	..	41142	4584
Switzerland,	2001	..	117824	..	..	117824	16216
Liechtenstein	2002	..	115643	..	..	115643	15787
	2003	..	122238	..	..	122238	16651
	2004	..	126105	..	..	126105	16925
T.F. Yug. Rep.	2001	..	3346	..	-5	3351	1647
Mecedonia	2002	..	3477	..	13	3464	1706
	2003	..	3082	..	-8	3090	1524
	2004	..	2725	..	5	2720	1340
Ukraine	2001	715529	2221701	39683	..	2897547	59089
	2002	728882	2194017	61964	..	2860935	59108
	2003	748794	2357979	78040	..	3028733	63585
	2004	799130	2424391	159124	..	3064397	64580
Unitd	2001	4431339	109673	497640	12427	4030945	67336
Kingdom	2002	4345335	217769	542634	26482	3993988	67534
	2003	4309312	310675	637337	-12571	3995221	67340
	2004	4019594	478926	410803	22446	4065271	68095
Oceania	2001	1605367	..	409637	-4	1195734	38864
	2002	1650018	..	413421	-1	1236598	39579
	2003	1639414	..	425739	6	1213669	37964
	2004	1652662	..	430522	17	1222123	37597
Australia	2001	1354543	.	409637	..	944906	48739
	2002	1411424	..	413421	..	998003	50755
	2003	1456588	..	425739	..	1030849	51736
	2004	1488699	..	430522	..	1058177	52351
New Zealand	2001	*247524	..	..	-4	*247528	*64027
	2002	*235294	..	..	-1	*235295	*60147
	2003	*179476	..	..	6	*179470	*44434
	2004	*160633	..	..	17	*160616	*39328
Papua New	2001	*3300	..	..	..	*3300	*671
Guinea	2002	*3300	..	..	..	*3300	*656
	2003	*3350	..	..	..	*3350	*633
	2004	*3330	..	..	..	*3330	*614

Source: 2004 Energy Statistics Yearbook United Nations, New York, 2007

TABLE 10

International trade of natural gas (Principal importers/exporters)

Thousand metric tons

2003

Importers					**Exporters**			
	World	*Russian Federation*	*Canada*	*Algeria,*	*Netherlands*	*Indonesia*	*Norway*	*Turkmenistan*
Belarus	699560	*699560	..	..	..	..	..	..
Belgium	662591	..	..	126371	240797	..	215374	..
Canada	369794	..	..	..	..	..	..	..
Czech Republic	360045	265394	..	..	..	..	94651	..
Finland	190004	190004	..	..	..	..	..	..
France incl. Monaco	1788025	422132	..	389188	287395	..	542125	..
Germany	3187328	1398271	..	..	644370	..	987800	..
Hungary	462396	419493	..	..	..	..	..	..
Italy and San Marino	2392454	740131	..	896150	283578	..	284759	
Japan	3190273	..	..	..	..	953205	..	..
Korea, Republic of	1057600	..	..	9215	..	279595	..	..
Mexico	375146	..	..	...	...	..	..	..
Netherlands	849263	..	..	..	..	..	282365	..
Poland	350607	275629	..	..	..	..	19555	..
Portugal	122968	..	..	100816	..	..	..	..
Russian Federation	329000	..	..	..	..	..	..	*329000
Slovakia	256076	256076	..	..	...	..	..	.
Spain	984756	..	..	565396	..	..	97848	..
Turkey	803993	475732	..	148386	..	..	..	..
Ukraine	2156791	*2156791	..	..	..	..	..	..
United Kingdom	310675	..	..	..	..	..	258317	4320278
United States	4320278	..	3752184	61440	..	..	..	

Exporters

Malaysia	*Qatar*	*Brunei Darussalam*	*Australia*	*United Arab Emirates*	*United States*	*Nigeira*	*Trinidad and Tobago*
..	..	..	..	..	..	..	..
..	..	..	..	..	..	..	..
..	..	..	..	..	369794	..	..
..	..	..	..	..	..	..	..
..	..	..	..	..	..	..	..
..	..	..	..	..	..	..	..
..	..	..	..	..	..	..	..
..	..	..	..	..	..	..	..
..	..	..	..	..	..	163068	..

662370	360128	346970	416614	286436	67697	..	..
152842	317758	29841	6710	..	..	..	..
..	..	..	..	..	375146	..	..
..	..	..	..	..	..	..	..
..	..	..	..	..	..	..	..
..	..	..	..	..	..	22152	..
..	..	..	..	..	..	..	..
..	..	..	..	..	..	..	..
..	80414	..	..	15820	..	166592	1365
..	...	...	..	..	..	4330	..
..	..	..	..	..	..	..	..
..	..	..	..	..	..	..	..
3130	16170	..	..	..	..	58637	419245

2004

Importers				**Exporters**				
	World	*Russian Federation*	*Canada*	*Algeria,*	*Netherlands*	*Indonesia*	*Norway*	*Turkmenistan*
Belarus	758652	*758652	..	..	..	..	..	
Belgium	677290	15322	..	113551	282935	..	251582	..
Canada	414979	..	..	..	..	..	..	..
Czech Republic	333350	245182	..	..	..	..	88168	..
Finland	183779	*183779	..	..	..	..	..	..
France incl. Monaco	1857438	384911	..	226428	355680	..	484274	..
Germany	3389857	1466679	..	..	748779	..	1038277	..
Hungary	431618	347748	..	..	..	..	..	13968
Italy and San Marino	2587295	900074	..	..	307619	..	197739	..
Japan	3155823	..	..	..	..	847203	..	..
Korea, Republic of	1205570	..	..	12196	..	294483	..	..
Mexico	434882	..	..	..	..	..	..	..
Netherlands	628124	..	..	..	..	..	230012	..
Poland	379467	236370	..	..	..	..	19376	..
Portugal	153733	..	..	97138	..	..	..	..
Russian Federation	258889	..	..	..	..	..	..	*258889
Slovakia	264166	*264166	..	..	..	..	..	..
Spain	1145112	..	..	587007	..	..	93200	..
Turkey	843063	531645	..	130956	..	..	..	..
Ukraine	2424391	*2424391	..	..	..	..	..	..
United Kingdom	478926	..		..	..	...	..	343323
United States	4609955	..	3877564	138402	..	..	..	...

Malaysia	*Qatar*	*Brunei Darussalam*	*Australia*	*United Arab Emirates*	*United States*	*Nigeira*	*Trinidad and Tobago*
..	..	..	..	..	..	..	..
..	..	..	..	..	..	..	..
..	..	..	..	..	..	..	..
..	..	..	..	..	414979	..	..
..	..	..	..	..	..	..	..
..	..	..	..	..	..	..	..
..	..	..	..	..	..	150952	..
..	..	..	..	..	..	..	..
..	..	..	..	..	..	..	..
..	..	..	..	..	..	..	..
716870	368498	346425	469362	278300	65945	..	3036
250071	320891	48934	25665	3316	..	6398	..
..	..	..	..	.	434882	..	..
..	..	..	..	..	.	..	..
..	..	..	..	..	..	..	..
..	..	..	..	..	..	..	..
..	..	..	..	..	..	56595	..
..	..	..	..	..	..	..	..
..	..	..	..	..	..	..	..
..	160170	..	..	13223	..	202713	..
..	...	..	..	..	..	42855	..
..	..	..	..	..	..	..	..
..	..	..	..	..	..	..	..
23148	14071	..	18552	..	..	13841	512427

Source: 2004 Energy Statistics Yearbook United Nations, New York, 2007

TABLE 11

Cross-border M&A sales, by sector and by group of economies, 2005-2006

(Millions of dollars)

	2005				*2006*			
Group of economies	*All industries*	*Primary*	*Manufacturing*	*Services*	*All industries*	*Primary*	*Manufacturing*	*Services*
World	716 302	115420	203730	397152	880457	86133	274406	519918
Developed economies	604882	110474	171020	323388	727955	65119	247233	415602
Developing economies	94101	2858	25963	65280	127372	16639	22603	88130
Transition economies	17318	2088	6747	8483	25130	4374	4570	16185

Source: UNCTAD, cross-border M&A database

This section examines the trends and patterns of FDI in 2006 by major regions. The discussion in the following sections focuses on recent trends in FDI flows to and from each region, as well as their subregions and countries, and provides a picture of the changing geographical, sectoral and industrial patterns of FDI flows by region. Policy developments underlining these patterns, and prospects for each region are also analysed.

Developing Countries

Africa

FDI to Africa amounted to $ 36 billion in 2006—a new record level. The surge was in large part related to investments in extractive industries, but FDI also rose in various service industries. As a result, inflows as a percentage of the region's gross fixed capital formation increased to 20% in 2006, from 18% in 2005. As in other years, there were wide variations among the different African countries. FDI inflows rose in 33 countries and fell in 21. Some Asian developing countries have become major sources of cross-border M&As and other forms of FDI in Africa. Outward FDI from Africa also reached a record level in 2006 largely driven by TNCs from South Africa. Policy developments indicate a further opening up to foreign investment, although some countries have also made changes in their regulatory frameworks with a view to securing greater benefits from inward FDI.

Geographical trends

(i) Inward FDI natural resources drove the surge

In 2006, FDI inflows to Africa rose by 20 per cent to $36 billion twice their 2004 level. Following substantial increases in commodity prices, many TNCs, particularly those from developed countries already operating in the region, significantly expanded their activities in oil. Gas and mining industries. TNCs from Asia expanded even more rapidly, through both greenfield investments and cross-border M&As (Table 12). At the same time, the services sector continued to attract considerable FDI, in particular in transport, storage and communications. An estimated 442 greenfield investments were undertaken in Africa in 2006, 258 by developed-country TNCs, particularly Europe (161), 175 by developing economies (134 from Asia and the remaining from within Africa), a few from South-East Europe and the CIS[3]. The value of cross-border acquisitions of African enterprises reached a record level ($18 billion) in 2006, almost half of this in the form of M&As by Asian TNCs, which represents a huge expansion of activity since the start of the decade (Table 12), particularly in oil, gas and mining activities. Despite the increased FDI inflows, however, Africa's share in global inflows fell from 3.1 per cent in 2005 to 2.7 per cent in 2006.

FDI inflows contributed to a strengthening of the balance of payments in several African countries. In 2006, foreign reserves in the region as a whole grew by some 30 per cent, and by even move in some major oil-exporting countries such as Nigeria and the Libyan Arab Jamahiriya.[4] Income on inward FDI grew by 14 per cent, which was more than in Asia and Oceania (9 per cent) but much less than in Latin America and the Caribbean (36 per cent).[5]

The extractive industries accounted for most of the increase in inflows to Africa in 2006. While such investments can help boost exports and government revenues, concerns have arisen in several mineral-rich countries about the impact on exchange rates and the prospects for other export-oriented activities (EIU, 2007a). In Zambia, for instance, a ten-fold increase in copper exports since 2000 to $2.7 billion in 2006 led to an appreciation of the real exchange rate.[6] As a consequence, Zambia's attractiveness for FDI suffered in export-oriented clothing and horticulture, as well as in those products that are entitled to preferences under the African Growth and Opportunity Act (AGOA)[7] and the Euro-Mediterranean Partnership. Similar concerns have been raised for Algeria, the Libyan Arab Jamahiriya, Mauritania, Nigeria, South Africa, Swaziland and Uganda. Moreover, the appreciation of the real exchange rate exacerbated the situation even further in countries with already high costs of production, capacity shortage or low competitiveness. This may have led to the closure of some foreign-owned production facilities in garments and other manufactures, for example in Kenya, Lesotho, Mauritius and Swaziland.[8] These disinvestments were partly offset in some cases by higher inflows into new natural resource exploration activities, particularly in some Least Developed Countries (LDCs) (Box 1).

TABLE 12

Distribution of cross-border M&A purchases in Africa by home region, 1999-2006
(Millions of dollars)

Acquiring regions	*1999*	*2000*	*2001*	*2002*	*2003*	*2004*	*2005*	*2006*
World	3117	3199	15524	4684	6427	4595	10509	17569
Developed economies	2534	2380	14964	3668	3156	2571	9564	7173
Developing economies	583	819	559	1016	3270	2024	470	9791
Africa	52	769	520	809	569	1849	360	746
Latin America and Caribbean	373	..	..	67	166		-	125
Asia	158	50	39	141	2536	175	116	8850

Source: UNCTAD, cross-border M&A database

The top 10 FDI recipients in Africa accounted for $32 billion (or nearly 90 per cent) of the region's inflows in 2006, up from $20 billion in 2005. Eight of them attracted FDI in excess of $1 billion in 2006, the same as the previous year; and in four of them such flows were higher than $3 billion: Egypt, Nigeria, Sudan and Tunisia (Table 16). Both cross-border M&As and greenfield investments contributed to increased inflows to several of the top host countries particularly Egypt, Nigeria, Sudan, Tunisia and Morocco.[9] While most of the FDI to the region as a whole went to extractive industries, in Egypt—the top FDI recipient in 2006—20 per cent of the more than $10 billion of its inflows were in non-oil activities such as agriculture, manufacturing, banking and tourism.

BOX 1

FDI flows to African LDCs[a] rise, led by investment in extractive industries

FDI flows to African LDCs increased from $6 billion in 2005 to $8 billion in 2006 (box figure 1) following two consecutive years of decline. The increase was driven by investors seeking new mining locations in response to rising global demand and high commodities prices. As a result, the share of LDCs in FDI to Africa rose from 21 per cent in 2005 to 23 per cent in 2006, and, as with many other African host economies, such investment was mainly from developed countries and Asian developing countries. TNCs in telecommunications activities have also started to invest in African LDCs, especially those LDCs that were previously considered risky due largely to conflicts, leading to a small but positive improvement in inflows to these countries.[b]

The 10 major recipients of FDI among African LDCs in 2006 were (in declining order): Sudan, Equatorial Guinea, Chad, the United Republic of Tanzania, Ethiopia, Zambia, Uganda, Burundi, Madagascar and Mali. FDI grew particularly fast (by 50 per cent or more) in Burundi, Djibouti, Guinea-Bissau, Somalia, Madagascar, Ethiopia, Cape Verde, Gambia and Sudan. CNOOC (China), Ophir Energy (South Africa), Soma Petroleum (Canada), Range Resources and Woodside (both Australia) were among the TNCs that contributed to FDI in natural resource exploration in these countries.

In contrast, Angola and Liberia registered negative FDI inflows in 2005 and 2006. In Angola, this was because of acquisitions by the State-owned oil company, Sonangol, of ongoing oil exploitation and refinery projects owned by foreign TNCs. In Liberia, while the negative inflows of $82 million in 2006 were reduced from the previous year's negative level of $479 million, investor confidence is recovering at a slow pace following the end of a series of civil wars and the establishment of a democratically elected government in that country. Inflows stagnated in Lesotho, mainly due to a slowdown in the textile industry and the withdrawal of a number of TNCs involved in that industry.

FDI inflows to the five subregions of Africa in 2006 were uneven, reflecting the influence of different factors, particularly the availability of natural resources, as discussed below.

North Africa[10] North African countries received record FDI inflows (partly from Asian TNCs) that were fairly diversified. All countries in the subregion, except Morocco (where flows remained relatively large), received increased inflows, most of which were concentrated in agriculture, communications, construction, manufacturing[11] and tourism: they were driven partly by investments for expansion and privatisations. As a result, FDI flows to the subregion surged to a record level of $23 billion in 2006, accounting for 66 per cent of inflows to Africa. Egypt attracted an exceptional of inflows, amounting to 43 per cent of the total to the subregiorin,[12] but the share of investments in oil and gas activities, though still large, declined from 60 per cent in 2005 to 21 per cent in 2006. In the Libyan Arab Jamahiriya, FDI inflows rose by 67 per cent over those of 2005, to reach $1.7 billion, the highest level since the end of international sanctions impose on that country. In Tunisia, inflows more than quadrupled, mainly as a result of privatisations in the telecommunications industry.[13] Algeria, Sudan and Tunisia also received more FDI in the petroleum and telecommunications industries, mainly from China, India, Kuwait and Malaysia. In contrast to other North African countries, FDI inflows to Morocco declined due to fewer privatisation sales.

West Africa.[14] FDI inflows to West Africa rose to $7 billion in 2006, following larger investments in all sectors by European and Asian TNCs. The subregion's share in FDI inflows to Africa rose to 19 per cent from 17 per cent in 2005. Nigeria was the main destination in West Africa, accounting for 80 per cent of the FDI to the subregion, dominated by FDI in its oil industry, mostly from China. In Ghana, inflows tripled to $435 million, largely as a result of investment by two United States firms: Newmont Gold Company and Alcoa (in an aluminium company, Valco). Most of the other inflows into the subregion went to the services sector. Cape Verde saw a major disinvestment, with the Government re-acquiring a majority stake in the country's electricity and water utility, Empresa Pública de Electricidade Água de Cabo Verde, thereby reversing a controversial privatisation. On the other hand, FDI in tourism in the country experienced strong growth.[15]

Central Africa.[16] In Central Africa, Asian TNCs made significant investments in many sectors, nudging FDI inflows up to $4 billion in 2006. The subregion accounted for 11 per cent of Africa's total inflows, most of it going to the primary and services sectors, including infrastructure. Equatorial Guinea, Chad, Congo and Cameroon (in that order) were the destinations. A large part of the increase in investment to the subregion reflected greater spending by TNCs on oil and mining exploration. In Cameroon, investments by Total (France) and Pecten Cameroon were the major cause of the surge in its FDI inflows.[17]

East Africa.[18] East African countries recovered from a decline in their FDI inflows as a result of new oil exploration activities in non-traditional producer countries and privatisations. FDI inflows to the subregion rose to about $2 billion in 2006 compared with $1 billion the previous year. However this subregion still ranks low in FDI inflows to Africa. Four countries (Djibouti, Ethiopia, Kenya and Madagascar) that had registered a decline in their inward FDI in 2005 saw increased inflows in 2006. The United Republic of Tanzania had the highest inflows in the subregion, amounting to $377 million in 2006 (most of it due to investment for expansion in the mining industry). FDI into Uganda rose by 19 per cent, partly as a result of investments from Australia (e.g. by Hardman Resources) in the oil industry and from Egypt, India, Kenya, South Africa and the United States in services and agro-processing. In Kenya, FDI increased due to large privatisation sales in the telecommunications industry and investments in railways. The recovery of FDI to Ethiopia in 2006 was a result of increased oil exploration activities in the Ogaden region.

Southern Africa.[19] A significant decline in FDI inflows, particularly to the two principal host countries (Angola and South Africa) in the subregion led to negative inflows amounting to $195 million in 2006. This contrasted with the high growth experienced in 2005 when inflows reached $6 billion. Although South Africa experienced negative FDI inflows, caused by the sale of a foreign equity stake in a domestic gold-mining company to a local firm, there were a number of cross-border M&A deals in the country. For instance, Vodafone (United Kingdom) paid $2.9 billion to rise its stake in Vodacom of South Africa, Tata (India) bought a 26 per cent stake in InfraCo (a telecommunications company), valued at $60 million, and some other Asian TNCs (such as Istithmar, the investment arm of the Government of Dubai) bought V&A Waterfront (South Africa) for more than $1 billion.[20] In Angola, Sonangol's takeover of major oil-related projects from foreign companies, such as the Lobito oil refinery, also resulted in an overall negative FDI inflow, though some foreign investments took place in banking, telecommunications and mining.

(ii) Outward FDI hit new heights

FDI outflows from Africa hit record levels in 2006, to reach $8 billion, nearly four times those of 2005, and more than twice the previous peak in 1997.[21] Investors from South Africa accounted for four-fifths of these. Other source countries, including Morocco, Liberia, Nigeria, Egypt and the Libyan Arab Jamahiriya, in that order, recorded their highest level of outflows. A large proportion of FDI by South African TNCs in 2006 was in natural resource exploration and exploitation. For example, AngloGold Ashanti invested in a gold-mining expansion project in Brazil (in Cuiaba) and in underground gold extraction development in Australia (at Sunrise Dam): and Ophir energy invested in offshore oil exploration in the United Republic of Tanzania. AngloGold also established an alliance worth $58 million with Trans-Siberian Gold of the Russian Federation.[22]

A number of African TNCs in services (many of them from South Africa) also expanded abroad, including into Europe. Outward FDI in telecommunications involved, for example, Orascom (Egypt), MTN (South Africa), Maroc Telecom (Morocco), Naguib Sawiris (Egypt) and Telkom (South Africa).[23] Significant cross-border acquisitions by African firms took place in industries as diverse as health-care services, printing and media, and construction.

Sectoral Trends: Primary Sector's Share Rise

There was a surge of FDI flows to Africa in the primary sector, mainly in oil and gas. In addition, the growing services sector, particularly transport, storage and communications, continued to attract FDI, as reflected by the data on cross-border M&As in 2006. However, it grew at a lower rate than the primary sector.

Inflows into the manufacturing sector continued to grow in North African countries at a slow but stable rate, while in sub-Saharan Africa, no significant manufacturing FDI took place. Conversely, disinvestments occurred in textile processing. Limited production capabilities continue to be a major factor behind the relatively low FDI inflows in manufacturing and the difficulties faced by African countries in seizing the opportunities offered by preferential market access initiatives such as AGOA, Everything but Arms (EBA) and the Cotonou Agreement between the European Commission (EC) and the African Caribbean and Pacific group of countries.

Policy Developments

The rapid growth of inflows to Africa partly reflects the steps taken by countries of this region to open up their economies to foreign investment. UNCTAD's annual survey on changes to national laws and regulations shows that in 2006, 40 African countries introduced 57 new measures affecting FDI, of which 49 encouraged inward FDI.

Of these measures, 14 were related to sectoral liberalization, more specifically:

- Botswana, Burkina Faso, Burundi, Cape Verde, Ghana, Kenya and Namibia allowed partial or full -foreign ownership of their telecommunications industries;
- Congo, Egypt and Nigeria wholly or partially opened up their banking industries;
- Ethiopia approved concessions to its railway company and Mauritius opened its legal professional services industry to FDI;
- Morocco permitted foreigners to own vast areas of land; and
- Swaziland opened up to FDI in insurance.

A number of African countries introduced measures aimed at improving the admission and/ or establishment processes applied to foreign investors. For example. Burkina Faso created a one-stop shop for new businesses; Kenya strengthened its Investment Promotion Agency (IPA); several countries eased or improved registration and fiscal procedures for various business start-ups.[24] For example, Nigeria cut the average property registration time from 274 to 80 days.

Many countries introduced various other measures lo promote foreign investment. These mainly involved lax reductions (Algeria, Egypt, Ghana, Lesotho, Mozambique, Tunisia, Ugainda and the United Republic of Tanzania), the establishment of specialized investment zones or parks (Botswana, Eritrea, Morocco, he United Republic of Tanzania and Zambia, or the setting up of advisory councils for investment promotion (Ethiopia).

In some countries, however, governments adopted policies that were less favourable to foreign investment. For example, in Algeria, Egypt, Equatorial Guinea and Zambia, governments raised various taxes or royalties that may affect foreign investment. Algeria ended majority foreign ownership in its oil and gas industries; Lesotho extended State monopoly over its fixed-line telephone services for a further 12 months; Swaziland closed its retail sector to foreign investors, and Zimbabwe prohibited money transfer operations by foreign or domestic agencies and main banking institutions. In the Libyan Arab Jamahiriya, new measures were adopted, requiring foreign investors to give priority to Libyan nationals in the manufacturing and agricultural sectors, and in construction, electricity, transport and communications in the services sector, as well as to provide training to locals and ensure equal payments between Libyan and foreign staff.

TABLE 13

Africa: distribution of cross-border M&As, by sector and main industry, 2005-2006

(Millions of dollars)

Sector/industry	*Sales*		*Purchases*	
	2005	*2006*	*2005*	*2006*
Total industry	10509	17569	15505	11208
Primary	908	4788	249	356
Mining, quarrying and petroleum	908	4788	249	356
Mining and quarrying	873	524	237	335
Petroleum	34	4265	12	21
Secondary	1676	2017	35	159
Food, beverages and tobacco	17	1 136	3	-
Chemicals and chemical products	12	3	-	120
Stone, clay, glass, and concrete products	967	-	29	-
Metals and metal products	12	783	3	-
Machinery	545	-	-	39
Electrical and electronic equipment	-	8	-	-
Motor vehicles and other transport equipment	3	13	-	-
Services	7925	10783	15 221	10893
Electricity, gas, and water distribution	58	307	-	-
Hotels and restaurants	32	10	-	-
Trade	312	1 001	47	87
Transport, storage and communications	1534	8321	1 307	698
Finance	5398	1 086	13787	9315
Health and social services	587	-	-	-

Source: UNCTAD cross-border M&A database.

At the international level, the region's development partners under the umbrella of the fourth Africa-Asia Business Forum (AABF) and the Tokyo International Conference for Africa's Development (TICAD) implemented measures to boost the region's FDI inflows. The Forum sought to boost the expansion of investments by Asian firms including small-and medium-sized enterprises (SMEs), in Africa.

However, changing regulatory frameworks and improving the business climate may not be enough to attract greater FDI into manufacturing and to benefit from such investments. In countries, with small domestic markets, FDI in manufacturing depends particularly on export markets and on the international competitiveness of African products in terms of unit factor costs relative to other countries. Natural resources are attractive assets for export-oriented production, but they may not provide a sufficient basis for sustainable economic growth. Moreover, natural resources provide rents only for as long as the resources last and are in demand; without technological and skills upgrading and development of downstream industries resource-exporting countries may eventually face stagnant prices and the risk of specializing in products that may become outdated. Accordingly, it is important for host countries to adopt policies that help improve their local capacities, and in particular their labour skills and technological capabilities.

Prospects: Moderate Growth Expected in 2007

Prospects for FDI inflows into Africa in 2007 and beyond are expected to remain positive albeit moderately due to high commodity prices particularly of oil. UNCTAI's World investment Prospects Survey[25] shows that only 20 per cent of the investors interviewed planned to increase investment in Africa between 2007 and 2009 with no significant differences by subregion (Figure 11.5). Returns on capital in the region are expected to remain strong. While FDI in oil and gas and other minerals is likely to remain robust in the medium term, in manufacturing it is likely to fall further, due to tough international competition in garment exports and to the removal of trade preferences. But in the long-term it should revive as new initiatives, such as the African Investment Incentive Act (AIIA) by the United States Government, are implemented.[26]

BOX 2

A renewed push for Asian FDI in Africa

In 2006, TNCs from developing Asia accounted for over half of the cross-border M&As to Africa, worth close to $9 billion, up from $0.1 billion in 2005 (Table 12). This followed previous but slower growth in Asian FDI to Africa, which averaged $1.2 billion annually during the period 2002-2004, Singapore, India and Malaysia are the top Asian sources of FDI to the region, with a combined investment stock estimated at $3.5 billion (*i.e.* of cumulative approved flows from 1996 to 2004), followed by China, the Republic of Korea and Taiwan Province of China. Malaysia's FDI was the most diversified, by country and by industry, while about 3 per cent of China's total outward FDI stock was spread over 500 FDI projects in 48 African countries. Moreover, FDI from China to Africa has been increasing rapidly in recent years.

As part of efforts by the Government of Japan to boost trade and investment flows between the two regions, the fourth Africa-Asia Business Forum (AABF IV) took place in Dares Salaam, United Republic of Tanzania in February 2007. The forum aims at increasing trade opportunities available to Asian TNCs in Africa taking into account the various trade agreements in place, such as AGOA and various new economic programmes for Africa's development (e.g. the New Partnership for Africa's Development (NEPAD)). It also aims to encourage the transcontinental exchange of knowledge and expertise and foster stable and sustainable economic growth and development between the regions within a South-South framework. The sectors targeted by AABF IV are: agro-industry and food processing, building materials, construction and engineering, information and communication technologies, medical equipment and pharmaceuticals, and textiles, garments and leather products.

Participation in AABF IV was open to businesses from African and Asian countries.

Source: UNCTAD, based on information from AABF, 2007.

FDI inflows into Africa in 2007 are likely to remain unevenly distributed by sector/industry and subregion and country, especially because most new investments will be in oil, gas and natural resources which are geographically concentrated. In North Africa, prospects for the region as a whole are bright under initiatives being negotiated or concluded with the EU, with significant new investments expected in Algeria and the Libyan Arab Jamahiriya. In West Africa, Central Africa and Southern Africa FDI inflows will also be concentrated in a few countries, for example, in oil exploration in Nigeria, in mining and associated activities in South Africa, and in oil and related infrastructure development in Equatorial Guinea. FDI inflows into countries with few natural resources are likely to remain slow, including in almost the entire East African subregion, though even here there will he relatively higher flows to countries such as Mauritius because of privatisations and other M&A activity.

Prospects are also good for larger FDI outflows from Egypt, Morocco, Nigeria and South Africa, as TNCs from these countries (in particular in mining and services) are set to continue expanding abroad.

Asia and Oceania

FDI inflows to Asia and Oceania reached a record of $260 billion, marking the fourth consecutive year of growth and representing more than two-thirds of inflows to developing countries. Outward flows from this region grew by 50 per cent, to $117 billion. Six out of the seven developing country TNCs listed in the world's top 100 non-financial TNCs are from this region. This section examines South, East and South-East Asia, West Asia and Oceania.

North and Central Asia—Oil and Gas Fuel Spectacular Growth

As oil prices soared, so did the gross domestic products of the oil and gas exporters nn North and Central Asia, transforming it into one of the world's fastest growing regions. Heading the pack was the world's fastest growing country, Azerbaijan, which is estimated to have grown at the spectacular rate of 34.5 per cent in 2006. The other major oil and gas exporters in the subregion also posted rapid expansions: Kazakhstan grew by an estimated 10.5 per cent, the Russian Federation by 6.7 per cent and Turkmenistan by 14 per cent.

As the hydrocarbon sector grew, so did tic demand for services and investment. In the Russian Federation, fixed capital expenditure grew by 13.5 per cent in 2006 (year-on-year). There was also more demand for services. Retail trade grew by 13.5 per cent in Azerbaijan, 13.0 per cent in the Russian Federation in 2006, and 23.4 per cent in Turkmenistan during the first half of 2006.

Another year of sustained high economic growth performance

Growth was also strong elsewhere in the subregion:

- Armenia grew by 13.4 per cent, owing mainly to a construction boom.
- Georgia's economic expansion continued, with 7.0 per cent growth.
- Uzbekistan continued its strong economic performance, growing by an estimated 7.3 per cent in 2006.
- Tajikistan's GDP is expected to have increased by 7.0 per cent.
- Kyrgyzstan is expected to have expanded by a modest 2.7 per cent owing to positive trends in agriculture, construction and trade—reversing the decline in 2005.

High and Rising Inflation Widespread

Monetary policy was generally targeted at stabilising currencies and containing inflation, which was generally high and rising. For non-oil exporting countries, such as Georgia and Tajikistan, rising oil prices and lax monetary policy in the first half of the year contributed to an increase in inflation. For oil and gas exporters, the substantial increase in export revenues contributed to inflation, white at the same time pushing currencies higher against the dollar. Higher oil prices, the rapid growth in the oil sector and rising real exchange rates for the region's oil exporters raised concerns about the possible occurrence of "Dutch disease" (Box 3).

Export revenues contributed to inflation

The exception was Armenia, where consumer price inflation rose by a modest 2.9 per cent in 2006. One reason has been the willingness of the authorities to allow the national currency, the dram, to appreciate significantly. Since the end of 2003, the value of the dram increased by more than 40 per cent in United States dollar terms, owing mainly to a substantial increase in reinitrance flows into the economy. Although the appreciation of the dram kept prices down, it hurts local exporters and Armenian citizens dependent on external remittances for daily expenses.

BOX 3

Is there evidence of "Dutch disease" in North and Central Asia?

Economic progress in the oil-exporting countries of North and Central Asia has been very impressive over the past five years, mainly driven by high oil prices since 2001. However, there are concerns regarding the forces behind the economic success, especially in Azerbaijan, Kazakhstan and the Russian Federation.

High economic growth and record current account surpluses are presenting challenges for subregional Governments on how they should handle rising inflation, resulting from huge foreign currency inflows, which in turn increased money supply and led to an appreciation of national currencies in real terms. As this could cause a decline in non-oil sector exports, concern has been voiced that these economies are affected by "Dutch disease".

In general. "Dutch disease" creates unbalanced growth in the booming hydrocarbon export sector, at the expense of the tradable goods sector. Non-tradable sectors, such as retail trade, restaurants, hotels and construction, have also flourished as a result of additional spending of oil wealth. The prices of non-tradable goods are expected to rise and the real exchange rate is expected to appreciate. The resultant real appreciation of currency will affect the competitiveness of the tradable goods sectors, particularly exports.

In the Russian Federation, the increase in oil prices has led to a surge in trade and current account surpluses. High inflation has resulted in a real effective appreciation of the rouble by more than 50 per cent between 2000 and 2006, leading to reduced profit margins in the industrial sector. However, the structure of the economy has not changed over time. The share of industry and services in GDP remained relatively unchanged between 2000-2005, and the

Contd..

Contd..box 3

strongest industrial sector growth has been registered in the construction sector, whose share in GDP increased from 6.6 per cent in 2000 to 7.4 per cent in 2004. Manufactured and agricultural exports remained relatively competitive in 2000-2005. However, the share of manufactured exports in total merchandise exports declined to 24.1 per cent in 2005 from 30 per cent in 2000.

Azerbaijan's current account was in a slight deficit in 2001 but turned around to a 1.3 per cent of GDP surplus in 2005 owing to large inflows of oil export revenue. The national currency, the manat, appreciated 7.2 per cent in real terms in 2006, as compared with 2005. The Government allowed the exchange rate to appreciate in nominal terms against the United States dollar in order to restrain the expansion of the money supply and keep inflation under control. As a result, the real effective exchange rate remained below its level in 2000. The share of the industrial sector in Azerbaijan's economy increased from about 40 per cent of GDP in 2000 to more than 60 per cent in 2005, and industry has been the main contributor to the country's economic growth. Azerbaijan's export revenues grew by about 2.5 times between 2000-2005 owing to Increased demand for crude oil and refined products. Oil products remained the country's largest export and accounted for 85.1 per cent of total export revenues in 2000 and 76.8 per cent in 2005. Manufactured goods accounted for 7 per cent of merchandise exports in 2000 and 12.4 per cent in 2005.

High inflation in Kazakhstan from 2000 to 2004 forced the Government to shift its priority from focusing on exchange rate policy to maintaining price stability. The real effective exchange rate appreciated significantly during this period. High oil prices in the meantime led to a doubling of merchandise export revenues between 2000 and 2004. Greater reliance on hydrocarbon resources has adversely affected the structure of the economy of Kazakhstan and has exacerbated the differences between the oil and non-oil sectors. Between 2000 and 2005, the contribution of agricultural and industrial sectors to GDP fell by 2 and 1 percentage points, respectively. The construction sector benefited from the effects of rapid oil sector growth. Its share in GDP increased from 5.3 per cent in 2000 to 6.2 per cent in 2004. In the exports sector, oil remained the country's principal export, its share in total export revenues increased from 52 per cent in 2000 to 64.7 per cent in 2004. And the share of manufactured exports in total merchandise exports fell from 31.8 per cent in 2000 to 24.2 per cent in 2004, reflecting the impact of oil-led currency appreciation on this sector.

All three Governments undertook tight monetary and fiscal policies along with other macroeconomic measures to address symptoms of "Dutch disease". Relevant measures have been undertaken to keep macroeconomic fundamentals within permissible limits and create stabilisation funds to sterilise a large part of oil revenue. The State Oil Fund of Azerbaijan (SOFAZ) set aside a share of the oil profits for long-term investment in public infrastructure and social welfare projects. Through the Fund, the Government is expected to develop the economy, particularly the non-oil sector, build up the country's infrastructure and reduce poverty, as well as improve the country's business climate. The Russian Federation's stabilization

Contd...

Contd..box 3

fund was expected to reach more than $90 billion by the end of 2006 in order to meet the Government's commitments to the pension fund and pay its outstanding debt to the Paris Club of leading creditor countries ahead of schedule. The National Oil Fund of Kazakhstan had assets in excess of $14 billion by the end of 2006 and used sane of them to reduce its foreign debt.

The above analysis on the economic situation of the net oil-exporting countries in North and Central Asia shows that there is some evidence of "Dutch disease" in Azerbaijan, Kazakhstan and the Russian Federation. However, Azerbaijan seems to have successfully avoided "Dutch disease" through its tight monetary policy and effective sterilisation of hard-currency inflows into the stabilization fund. The Russian Federation shows some signs of "Dutch disease". However, the country has the largest and most diversified economy of all the countries in the subregion, and is therefore much less dependent on oil exports. Kazakhstan seems to rely more heavily on the export of hydrocarbon resources than other countries in the subregion and derives a large portion of its GDP from oil and gas revenues. It is, therefore, likely that "Dutch disease" will represent a more serious issue for the country's economy.

Current Account Surpluses for Oil Exporters—Workers' Remittances Boost External Revenues for Others

Again, rising oil and gas revenues dominated the current accounts of the major hydrocarbon exporters. Azerbaijan is expected to record a surplus of 11.2 per cent of GDP.

Higher revenues from oil and gas contributed to current account surpluses

In Kazakhstan, where income payments abroad kept the 2005 current account in deficit, higher oil prices increased the trade surplus from $7.9 billion recorded in the first nine months of 2005 to $11.0 billion during the corresponding period in 2006. As a result of better exports, the current account was estimated to have moved into surplus in 2006.

The Russian Federation expected a current account surplus of 10 per cent of GDP in 2006. owing mainly to a rise in the foreign trade surplus.

Turkmenistan was expected to keep its current account in surplus, with export earnings up by 9.6 per cent, to $4.9 billon Uzbekistan expected a current account surplus of to 0.7 per cent of GDP owing to a large trade surplus and an increase in workers' remittances from abroad. Armenia, Georgia, Kyroyzstan and Tajikistan were also helped by remittances from workers abroad.

Foreign Direct Investment Flows

Foreign Direct Investment (FDI) is an important contributor to the balance of payments in North and Central Asian economies, most of it flowing into hydrocarbons. Azerbaijan received $4.5 billion in FDI in 2005, while oil and gas in Kazakhstan attracted over one half of gross FDI inflows in the first quarter of 2006.

There has been a large inflow of FDI into oil-producing countries

Foreign direct investment in the Russian Federation reached more than $20 billion in the first nine months of 2006 alone, reflecting new opportunities for entrepreneurs active in special economic zones, concessions and other government business development initiatives. However, it is expected that regulations restricting foreign investment in strategic enterprises will be prepared in the course of 2007. Capital inflows were significantly weaker on the non-oil exporting economies.

Foreign Debt Burden Eases

In August 2006, the Russian Federation paid off the final instalment of its $23 billion debt to the Paris Club of creditor countries. An agreement with the Paris Club enabled it to repay its foreign debt ahead of time, saving around $7.7 billion in debt service.

External debt ratios show marked improvement

Kyrgyzstan's external debt of about $2 billion in 2006 was equivalent to 90 per cent of its GDP It was expected to apply to IMF and the World Bank for assistance under the enhanced heavily indebted poor countries (HIPC) initiative and reduce its foreign debt by $1 billion in 2006. Tajikistan improved its -GDP ratio from 90 per cent in 2000 to 32 per cent in September of 2006 after bilateral restructuring agreements with the IMF the Russian Federation, Pakistan and the Islamic Republic of Iran. The World Bank was expected to write off more than $300 million of Tajikistan's debt in 2006. The gross external debt of Georgia amounted to $1.7 billion by mid-2006, equivalent to about 23 per cent of GDR.

TABLE 14

Summary of external accounts for North and Central Asian economies, 2005-2006

(per cent)

	Exports/GDP		*Imports/GDP*		*Current account balance/GDP*	
	2005	*2006*	*2005*	*2006*	*2005*	*2006*
Armenia	19.4	17.5	36.1	37.7	-3.9	-5.6
Azerbaijan	34.8	64.0	33.7	26.0	1.3	11.2
Georgia	..	..	..	..	-11.7	-10.0
Kazakhstan	50.1	83.0	31.2	48.2	-0.9	0.2
Russian Federation	38.6	51.8	57.2	85.8	-8.4	-12.8
Tajikistan	31.9	..	18.0	..	10.9	10.0
Turkmenistane	..	..	..	..	-0.8	2.6
Uzbekistan	..	..	..	..	10.1	10.7

Contd...

Contd...table 14

	Growth rate (per cent)					
	Exports			Imports		
	2004	2005	2006	2004	2005	2006
Armenia	6.0	36.2	-1.1	5.8	33.2	19.7
Azerbaijan	42.6	104.4	94.1	31.5	21.4	17.2
Georgia	31.4	34.8	20.7	36.7	33.8	56.3
Kazakhstan	55.7	37.4	39.0	44.6	30.1	32.0
Kyrgyzstan	24.2	33.3	16.3	24.9	98.7	47.0
Russian Federation	34.8	32.9	28.7	28.0	28.7	36.2
Tajikistan	14.8	15.9	55.8	56.1	97.0	28.9
Turkmenistan	6.6	27.6	9.6	32.2	9.6	5.3
Uzbekistan	32.4	14.9	11.8	27.2	13.1	15.3

Source: ESCAP based on national sources. International Monetary Fund, International Finanacial Statistics. (CD-ROM) (Washington D.C. IMF, 2006).

Medium-term Prospects are Strong

Prospects in North and Central Asia remain strong and growth should continue in 2007-2008. But because it is a major commodity-exporting region, those prospects depend on trends in global commodity prices. The Russian Federation's performance (the subregion's largest trading partner and an important investor in the economies of the region) will also be important.

Strong growth momentum is to be maintained

Strong domestic demand and increased oil and gas production should enable the Russian Federation to continue its expansion in 2007-2008. Annual GDP growth rates could average more than 5 per cent. Inflationary pressures could accelerate due to a surge in fiscal expenditure, increased inflows of foreign exchange and domestic demand. Because growth has so far largely been due to the modernisation of older factories, further institutional reforms are necessary to attract new investment to sustain growth.

Robust growth is expected to continue in other oil-exporting countries. As discussed in box 3. "Dutch disease" could pose some challenges.

- Azerbaijan is forecast to grow by 30 per cent in 2007, its main policy challenge will be to maintain macro-economic stability.
- Kazakhstan is expected to achieve 10 per cent GDP growth in 2007. The sharp rise in GDP and the steady increase in the inflation rate both suggest that the economy may be "overheating".
- Turkmenistan's annual GDP growth is forecast at around 8 per cent in 2007-2008, and inflation has already risen to double digits. To ease inflationary pressure and reduce risks of a downturn in fuel prices, it may be prudent to pursue a moderate fiscal policy and a tough monetary policy.

- GDP growth in Armenia is expected to remain at 8 per cent in 2007.
- Tajikistan is expected to grow by 7 per cent in 2007.
- Kyrgyzstan expects the investment climate to improve and GDP growth to increase to 6 per cent in 2007. As the economy stabilizes and growth picks up, inflation could rise, boosted by rising inflows of workers' remittances.
- Uzbekistan's average annual GDP growth in 2007-2008 is expected to be higher than in 2006. owing to favourable trends in global commodity prices.

REFERENCES

1. Data on gas production in the Perssian Gulf are based on BP, 2006.
2. UNCTAD, New York, 2007.
3. Data on greenfield projects in this Chapter come from OCO Consulting. LOCOmonitor database (www.locomonitor.com).
4. Data on international reserves from the IMF's *International Financial Statistics.*
5. Based on 29 countries; *source:* IMF, *Balance of Payments Statistics.*
6 In addition to major oil producers such as Nigeria, Algeria, the Libyan Arab Jamahiriya, Angola and Sudan, mineral-producing countries such as Kenya, Mauritius, Lesotho, Swaziland, the United Republic of Tanzania, Uganda, and Zambia that had started to receive FDI in manufacturing, especially textile processing and export-oriented activities, also received larger inflows into resource exploration activities.
7. Zambia is the world's fourth largest copper producer, with most of the production undertaken by TNCs. See also "Zambian producers suffer as copper bonanza sends exchange rate soaring". *Financial Times,* 26 September 2006.
8. Under this Act, the United States Government has been offering trade preferences since 2000 to promote trade and investment in Africa. The expiration of this Act has been extended until 2015.
9. In 2005-2006, Lesotho witnessed an 8.3% contraction in manufacturing, which was strongly influenced by the removal of quotas after the expiry of the Multi Fibre Arrangement (MFA) on exports from low-cost Asian producers and the continued strength of the South African rand (Lesotho's mloti is pegged to the rand). *Source:* "Lesotho economy: Manufacturing sector performance to improve", *EIU Viewswire,* 28 June 2006. For Swaziland, see for instance, *Africa Renewal* (previously *Africa Recovery*), Vol. 20, No. 1, April 2006.
10. For example, France's Crédit Agricole acquired Egyptian American Bank (later renamed the new bank Crédit Agricole-Egypt) (Source: "Credit Agricole Egypt's Adrien Phares on his bank's acquisition of EAB", *Business Today,* 16 August 2006). In Nigeria, CNOOC (China) acquired NNPC OML-130 for $3 billion, and in Sudan, inflows surged partly as a result of the sale of Mobitel to MTC Kuwait for $ 1.33 billion.
11. This subregion comprises Algeria, Egypt, the Libyan Arab Jamahiriya, Morocco, Sudan and Tunisia.
12. The North African countries received FDI in the manufacturing sector from TNCs engaged in the production of cosmetics, water storage tanks, auto valves, irrigation pumps, minibus assembly lines, utility vehicles and pick-up trucks, paints, pharmaceuticals and chemical production. *Source:* PricewaterhouseCoopers (www.pwc.com).
13. *Source:* Central Bank of Egypt. For instance, pharmaceutical giant AstraZeneca invested in a plant to manufacture medicines (for cardiovascular disease, psychiatric disorders and cancer) in Egypt in 2006 ("AstraZeneca opens first manufacturing plant in the Middle East", in-Pharma Technologist.com (www.inpharmatechnologist.com).

14. Tunisia sold 35% of Tunisie Telecom (TT) to a consortium comprising Dubai Technology and Media Free Zone, and Dubai Investment Group for $2.3 billion.
15. The subregion comprises Benin, Burkina Faso, Cape Verde, Côte d'Ivoire, Gambia, Ghana, Guinea, Guinea-Bissau, Liberia, Mali, Mauritania, Niger, Nigeria, Saint Helena, Senegal, Sierra Leone and Togo.
16. *Source:* "Ernie Els to design course in Cape Verde Islands", *Golf Today Travel.* 12 September 2006 (http://www.golftoday. co.uk/travel/press_releases/els_cape_yerde.html).
17. The subregion comprises: Burundi, Cameroon, the Central African Republic, Chad, Congo, the Democratic Republic of the Congo, Equatorial Guinea, Gabon, Rwanda and Sao Tome and Principe.
18. Pecten is part of the Shell Group ("Pecten Cameroon Company". *MBendi*, 7 October 2006 (www.mbendi.com).
19. The subregion comprises Comoros, Djibouti, Eritrea, Ethiopia, Kenya Madagascar, Mauritius, Seychelles, Somalia, Uganda and the United Republic of Tanzania.
20. The suhregion comprises Angola, Botswana. Lesotho, Malawi, Mozambique, Namibia, South Africa. Swaziland. Zambia and Zimbabwe.
21. *Sources*: "Vodafone raises South Africa stake to 50%", *Computer Business Review Online.* 7 December 2006 (http:// www.cbronline.com/article_news.asp?guid=78F3F6 ID-8188-461 D-BD07-458659500C6A); "India's Tata group acquiring 26 PCT stake in S.African telecom", *AFX News Limited,* 22 August 2006 (http://www.forbes.com/business feeds afx/2006/08/22/ afx2963999.html); and "Dubai-led group gets Cape V&A for R7bn", *Business Day* 9 October 2006. (http://www. businessday.co.za/articles/ dailymailer.asp.\?ID=BD4A2 75648).
22. www.unctad.org/fdistatistics.
23. *Source:* "South Africa: Scrambling for Africa", *AllAfrica,* 22 November 2006 (http://allafrica.com stories/2 006072403 85. html); "AngloGold in $58 million Russian mining alliance", *BusinessDay,* 7 April 2006; "SA firm wins new oil rights in Tanzania", *All Africa, 1* May 2006 (www.allafrica.com); and "AngloGold in $58 million Russian mining alliance", *BusinessDay, 1* April 2006.
24. Orascom (Egypt) bought a 19.3% stake in Hong Kong-based Hutchison; Telkom acquired part of Portugal Telecom, including its operations in several African countries such as Angola and Morocco; MTN bought into Lebanon's Investcom; Maroc Télécom acquired a majority stake in Burundi's Office national des telecommunications (Onatel): and Naguib Sawiris of Egypt purchased Wind Telecomuncazioni SpA of Italy.
25. Angola eased procedures for the entry of foreigners into the country; Kenya scrapped or simplified various types of operational licences, set up a Business Regulatory Reform Unit to bring standards up to international best practices and introduced a 24-hour service at the port of Mombasa and Mauritania eliminated various restrictions on foreign-exchange operations.
26. Under AGOA, Africa-based clothing exporters were able to import fabric from the cheapest available suppliers while still enjoying duty-free access to the United States market. When this concession expires in 2007, some of the foreign-owned clothing firms in eligible African countries may well decide to relocate elsewhere. In December 2006, the United States Congress passed AHA under the AGOA to help avert the diversion of FDI and the loss of thousands of jobs in the region. The new Act supplements and extends the provisions of AGOA to help producers in sub-Saharan Africa better withstand greater competitive pressures from China following the expiry of MFA in 2005.

3

China's Strategy for Energy Security: Challenges and Prospects

During the last two decades between 1980 and 2000, China experienced sustained growth in its consumption of energy.

Phenomenal Rise in Primary Energy Consumption

The government of China announced revisions of its Gross Domestic Product (GDP) figures for the years from 1993 to 2004 and of its energy consumption data for the years from 1999 to 2004. The GDP revisions stem from surveys indicating that the contribution of the tertiary sector has been underestimated since the mid 1990s. These revisions seem to address the longstanding concerns about the quality of GDP data and the underestimation of energy consumption during the late 1990s and early 2000s. Most observers of China's energy sector doubted the previously reported stagnation of energy consumption during the late years of the 9th Five-Year Plan (1996-2000) (about 1,300 mtce, with an average elasticity that was slightly negative). Instead, they imputed the low numbers to underestimation or underreporting of coal consumption during those plan years.

The revised data in Table 15 show that between 1980 and 2000 China's primary energy consumption more than doubled, rising from about 603 mtce to 1,386 mtce.[1] At the same time, GDP more than quadrupled, resulting in a 0.43 elasticity of energy demand—that is energy demand growth divided by GDP growth (hereafter *energy/GDP elasticity*). The lower elasticity in the 1980s and 1990s, to a large extent, reflected a successful shift away from the highly wasteful energy path of China's economy before the economic reforms that began in the late 1970s and the structural change in the economy that increased the share of less energy-intensive sectors in GDP.

Table 15 presents the impacts of recent GDP and energy consumption revisions on the elasticity of energy demand to GDP[2] and on energy intensity.[3] It shows that although the revisions slightly affect past analyses of energy/GDP elasticity and energy intensity, they do not change past conclusions about these trends during the 10th Five-Year Plan (2001-05)—namely, that energy consumption is accelerating, that energy/GDP elasticity is rising, and that it may continue to do so in the absence of corrective policy measures.

TABLE 15

Primary energy production and consumption, 1980-2000

	Production				*Consumption*			
	1980		*2000*		*1980*		*2000*	
Energy sources	*mtce*	*%*	*mtce*	*%*	*mtce*	*%*	*mtce*	*%*
Coal	442.4	69.4	928.8	72.0	435.2	72.2	938.0	67.7
Oil	151.7	23.8	233.5	18.1	124.8	20.7	321.4	23.2
Natural gas	19.1	3.0	36.1	2.8	18.7	3.1	33.3	2.4
Primary power"	24.2	3.8	91.6	7.1	24.1	4.0	92.8	6.7
Total	637.4	100.0	1,290.0	100.0	602.8	100.0	1,385.5	100.0

Source: China National Bureau of Statistics 2006 (abstract).

a. *Primary power* refers to hydropower, nuclear power, and renewable energy power generation. The conversion of hydropower and nuclear power to coal equivalents uses the average efficiency of thermal power plants in the same year. China began generating nuclear power In 1992, and In 2002, nuclear power accounted for 0.7 per cent of total primary energy consumption.

Final Energy Consumption Pattern

The definition of *final energy consumption* in the Chinese statistical system differs from the internationally accepted definition in two ways:

- It includes energy consumed in transformation uses—mainly electricity generation and petroleum refining.
- Its breakdowns by economic sector and fuel type are infected by some deficient accounting practices.

The most obvious example of such practices is that fuel consumption of cars owned by individuals or companies is not accounted for in the transportation sector but is included in the residential or the industrial sectors. For this report, adjustments have been made to estimate final energy consumption in line with accepted international definitions.

Table 16 presents the final energy consumption between 1980 and 2000 according to both the Chinese and the international definitions. In all cases, electricity is converted to million tons of coal equivalent on the basis of calorific value, not production equivalence value. From 1980 to 2000, final energy consumption grew 3.1 per cent on average (about twice the world average) by the international definition, but only 2.7 per cent on average by the Chinese definition. The difference seems to be consistent with the improved efficiencies achieved in transformation uses during the period.

The table shows also that the relative shares of the industrial, agricultural, and the residential and commercial (which are combined in Chinese definitions) sectors declined, although industry remained the largest consumer. The transportation sector more than doubled its share from 8 per cent to 16.3 per cent (after adjustment) and emerged as one of the key drivers of China's final energy consumption growth during the period. This trend was not well captured by the Chinese statistical system.

The structure of China's final energy consumption for 2000 shows a dramatic transformation over two decades: The share of coal, after adjustment, fell from 69 to 46 per cent, while the shares of oil and electricity, respectively, increased from 18 to 26 per cent and from about 6 per cent to more than 15 per cent. This transformation reflects patterns in the world's major industrial countries. With rising personal incomes and a more sophisticated economy, the relative shares of oil and electricity tend to increase: people can afford cars, air conditioners, and domestic appliances; commercial air travel takes off; factories use more electrically powered equipment; and a greater proportion of freight is moved by road. In line with these changes, the relative shares of the transportation and residential and commercial (buildings and appliances) sectors tend to increase. The shares of the residential and commercial and, more importantly, the transportation sectors in China are still low compared with more industrial countries. In 2000, they accounted respectively for about 20 per cent and 16 per cent of total energy consumption; compare these figures with 27 and 25 per cent, respectively, in Japan. The shares of oil, gas, and electricity will therefore continue to rise if China follows the urbanisation and transportation models of the more industrial countries.

TABLE 16

Final energy consumption by economic sector and fuel, 1980-2000

Economic sector	*Chinese definition*		*International definition*		*Japan (2000)*		*Chinese definition*		*International definition*		*Japan (2000)*
	mtce	*%*	*mtce*	*%*	*%*	*Fuel type*	*mtce*	*%*	*mtce*	*%*	*%*
1980											
Agriculture	34.7	6.0	31.1	6.9	48.3	Coal	335.6	58.3	311.6	69.0	11.0
Industry	392.1	68.3	277.0	61.2		Oil	89.5	15.6	82.1	18.2	59.0
Transportation	29.0	5.0	36.0	8.0	24.6	Gas	23.3	4.1	19.1	4.2	6.7
Residential	119.3	20.7	107.3	23.9	14.5	Electricity	116.1	20.2	28.3	6.3	22.2
Commercial					12.6	Others	10.6	1.8	10.5	2.3	1.1
Total	575.1	100.0	451.4	100.0	100.0	Total	575.1	100.0	451.6	100.0	100.0
2000											
Agriculture	42.9	4.4	40.2	4.9	48.3	Coal	421.6	43.4	382.1	46.2	11.0
Industry	664.8	68.5	489.2	59.2		Oil	267.9	27.6	213.2	25.8	59.0
Transportation	89.8	9.2	134.8	16.3	24.6	Gas	78.3	8.1	66.7	8.1	6.7
Residential	173.7	17.9	162.5	19.6	14.5	Electricity	154.1	15.9	128.3	15.5	22.2
Commercial					12.6	Others	49.2	5.0	36.4	4.4	1.1
Total	971.1	100.0	826.7	100.0	100.0	Total	971.1	100.0	826.7	100.0	100.0

Source: DRC and ERI, based on data from the China National Bureau of Statistics.

Review of the Energy Statistics System

This quick review of the evolution of energy consumption at the primary and final user levels points to a seriously weakened system for tracking energy statistics. The need to rethink and overhaul the system to improve its reliability and effectiveness is urgent, because major planning and policy decisions are based on it. There is a need for clear definitions and categorisation of energy consumption to avoid arbitrary decisions and interpretation during data collection and reporting. Many of the Chinese experts have expressed, doubt the reliability of the system, stressed its deficiencies, and drew attention to the troubling appearance of some false statistical data, especially on coal consumption in the late 1990s and early 2000s.

This overhaul is also needed to align the system with internationally accepted standards, given China's increased integration with global energy markets. The issuance of the Implementation Decree for the Statistics Law on December 16, 2005, was a major step in addressing these problems. However, more remains to be done.

High Growth Forecast for 2000 to 2020

In the early 2000s, several major national and international institutions prepared energy projections for China for the period from 2000 to 2020. These projections assumed that the lower rate of energy consumption relative to that of GDP during the preceding 20-year period would continue.

Study uses the DRC and ERI's projections in their assessment of China's energy future because those projections were designed explicitly to help the government of China explore the issues, options, and uncertainties in shaping a sustainable development path. The DRC and ERI consulted extensively with national and international experts in energy technology and policy during the preparation of the projections and had access to detailed local information. Furthermore, the projections cover the range of energy consumption forecast in the studies by the International Energy Agency (IEA) and the US. Department of Energy (U.S. DOE), as well as other sources.

The focus of the DRC and ERI's study was to explore policy options that China could implement to meet the same economic objective of quadrupling per capita GDP (from US$940 to US$3,760 in constant 2000 dollars) by 2020 with much less energy input per unit of output and greatly reduced pollution from energy production and use. These options would require more stringent energy efficiency and environmental policies and the deployment of new technologies. Table 17 summarises the key differences in policies under the ordinary efforts scenario (business as usual) compared with those under scenarios with greater concern for energy sustainability.

TABLE 17

Key policy elements affecting the projections of the DRC and ERI's scenarios for 2020

Elements of a sustainable energy policy	*Ordinary efforts scenario*	*Promoting sustainability scenario*	*Green growth scenario*
Improvement in energy efficiency	Minimal priority	Moderate priority	High priority with a comprehensive system of financial incentives in place
Better environmental controls	Some use of desulfurisation technology in power plants but not in the majority of plants by 2020	More stringent vehicle emissions standards in big cities; all power plants to have desulfurisation equipment by 2020	More stringent environmental regulations and enforcement
Promotion of renewable energy and other clean energy sources	No explicit policy for development	Moderate promotion	Extensive promotion of renewable energy and gas substitution for fossil fuels
Key new technologies	None	None	Some application of integrated coal gasification combined cycle technology for electricity generation

Source: DRC 2000.

Table 18 summarises the energy projections of the DRC in collaboration with the ERI, along with those of the IEA and the U.S. DOE.[5] The DRC and ERI projections show that China's energy consumption would likely grow at 3.3 to 4.8 per cent between 2000 and 2020, depending on the level of effort devoted to further improvements in energy efficiency and related choices of technology and modes of living. This growth would result in China's primary energy consumption in 2020 ranging between 2,430 and 3,300 mtce, or from 1.8 to 2.4 times the consumption level of 2000. Applying these growth rates to the revised energy consumption for 2000 leads to energy consumption of between 1,992 and 2,300 mtce in 2010 and of between 2,561 and 3,676 mtce in 2020.

All the DRC and ERI's scenarios showed that the relative shares of the transportation sector and the residential and commercial sectors in the final energy consumption would increase significantly [see Table 19, noting that the final energy consumption in the DRC and ERI's study is estimated using the Chinese definition]. In particular, consumption by the transportation sector would increase substantially, from 9 per cent of final energy consumption in 2000 to about 20 per cent in 2020 (this share is higher if the international definition is applied). This increasing share of the transportation sector is a feature of the economic development and urbanisation path that most industrial countries have followed. For example, in 2000, the share of energy used in the transportation sector amounted to about 16 per cent of China's final energy consumption, after revision to meet the international definition. This share is substantially lower than the shares observed in industrial countries: 39 per cent in North American members of the Organisation for Economic Co-operation and Development (OECD), 37 per cent for European members, and 28 per cent for Pacific members of the OECD.[6]

TABLE 18

Projections of China's Primary Energy Consumption, 2000-2020

Consumption and growth rates	*DRC and ERI study scenarios*			*U.S. DOE study scenarios*			*IEA studies*	
	Ordinary efforts	*Promoting sustainability*	*Green growth*	*High*	*Reference*	*Low*	*2002*	*2004*
Consumption level (mtce)								
2010	2,150	2,080	1,870	2,090	1,970	1,840	1,950	2,480
2020	3,300	2,900	2,470	3,220	2,790	2,430	2,560	3,170
Average annual growth (%)								
2000-10[a]	5.2 (4.5)	4.8 (4.1)	3.7(3.0)	4.9 (4.2)	4.2 (3.6)	3.5 (2.9)	4.1 (3.5)	6.4 (6.0)
2010-20	4.4	3.4	2.8	4.4	3.5	2.8	2.8	4.6
2000-20[a]	4.8 (4.4)	4.1 (3.8)	3.3 (2.9)	4.6 (4.3)	3.9(3.6)	3.2 (2.8)	3.5 (3.1)	4.6 (4.2)

Source: Data from DRC, ERI, and U.S. DOE

Note: Figures are rounded for simplicity in presentation.

a. The growth rates in parentheses are based on the revised energy consumption of 1,385.5 mtce in 2000.

China still has substantial room for growth in this sector. Furthermore, all scenarios showed that freight would continue to dominate the transportation sector. Variations among the three scenarios in the projections of the sector's energy consumption were attributable primarily to assumptions about efficiency improvements in freight transport. These improvements are expected to result not only from improved technologies for trucks but also from a modal shift, placing relatively more freight on railways and waterways than on roads. Finally, all three scenarios showed rapidly rising ownership of private automobiles. Such high levels of energy consumption raise a major concern about energy sustainability.

Table 18 also shows that by 2020, with the appropriate policies and incentives (that is, the green growth scenario of the DRC and ERI's study), China could reduce its primary energy consumption by 25 per cent relative to the ordinary efforts scenario. The promoting sustainability scenario, which represents a more moderate commitment of the government to improving energy sustainability, would result in a decrease in energy consumption by only 12 per cent over the ordinary efforts scenario.

Recent Signs of an Unsustainable Energy Growth Path

Energy consumption during the 10th Five-Year Plan is higher than envisaged in all forecasts. Considering the revised energy consumption figures, the average elasticity of energy to GDP during the 10th Five-Year Plan was slightly higher than one, more than twice the average elasticity during the three preceding five-year plans. At the same time, the energy intensity of China's economy—after a long period of steady decline—shows signs of stagnation and even slight increase. To reflect these developments, the IEA in 2004 revised its projections for China's energy consumption growth through 2020, from 4.1 to 6.4 per cent. However, even this upward revision seems, in light of the 10th Five-Year Plan trend, to still underestimate the potential consumption growth [see Tables 18 and 19].

TABLE 19

Final Energy Consumption by Sector and Fuel, 2000-2020

	2000		2020[a]			2000		2020[a]	
Sector	*mtce*	*%*	*mtce*	*%*	*Fuel*	*mtce*	*%*	*mtce*	*%*
Agriculture	42.9	4.4	59-80	3.1-3.2	Coal	382.1	46.2	559-836	29.3-33.7
Industry	664.8	68.5	998-1,345	53.4-54.2	Oil	213.2	25.8	605-827	31.7-33.3
Transportation	89.8	9.2	385-503	20.2-20.2	Gas	78.3	8.1	159-157	6.3-8.4
Residential and commercial	173.7	17.9	463-555	24.4-23.2	Power	154.1	15.9	434-487	22.8-19.6
					Others	42.9	5.0	148-177	7.1-7.8
Total	971.1	100.0	1,905-2,483	100.0	Total	870.6	102.0	1,905-2,484	100.0

Source: DRC 2000.

Note: The final energy consumption in the DRC and ERI's study is presented only according to the Chinese definition.

a. Low end of range represents the amount or share under the green growth scenario. High end of range represents the amount under the ordinary efforts scenario.

Table 20 shows that following a rapid economic recovery from Asia's financial crisis during the late 1990s, China's primary energy consumption rose from about 1,386 mtce in 2000 to about 2,225 mtce in 2005, a growth rate averaging nearly 10 per cent. This rate is more than two times that of the high economic growth period between 1980 and 2000. Energy growth accelerated during the 10th Five-Year Plan from about 3 per cent in 2001, to some 6 per cent in 2002, to about 15 per cent in 2003, to 16 per cent in 2004. That peak was followed by slightly reduced but still strong growth of 9 per cent in 2005. Between 2001 and 2004, for the first time in two decades, the rate of primary energy growth outpaced the rate of economic growth. Electricity consumption statistics, which are more reliable than energy consumption statistics, confirm these trends.

The more rapid growth of energy consumption during the 10th Five-Year Plan has caused concern in China and has attracted attention around the world. Energy demand is growing at higher-than-expected rates, certainly well beyond the objectives of the plan. Power shortages have plagued the high-growth belt in China and have triggered huge investments in power generation: 51 gigawatts of capacity in 2004, 66 gigawatts in 2005, and more than 200 gigawatts under construction in 2006. Most of this additional generation capacity has and will continue to come from medium-sized, relatively inefficient, polluting conventional coal-fired plants. In addition, oil imports during the 10th Five-Year Plan were well beyond most, if not all, forecasts.

TABLE 20

China's Primary Energy Production and Consumption, 2000-2005

Indicator	*2000*	*2001*	*2002*	*2003*	*2004*	*2005*
Total primary energy production (mtce)	1,290.0	1,374.5	1,438.1	1,6384	1,873.4	2,063.0
Shares of production by source (%)						
Coal	72.0	71.9	72.3	75.1	76.0	76.3
Crude oil	18.1	17.0	16.6	14.8	13.4	12.6
Natural gas	2.8	2.9	3.0	2.8	2.9	3.2
Hydropower and nuclear	7.1	8.2	8.1	7.3	7.7	7.9
Total primary energy consumption (mtce)	1,385.5	1,432.0	1,518.0	1,749.9	2,032.3	2,224.7
Shares of consumption by fuel (%)						
Coal	67.7	66.7	66.3	68.4	68.0	68.7
Oil	23.2	22.9	23.4	22.2	22.3	21.2
Gas	2.4	2.6	2,6	2.6	2.6	2.8
Hydropower and nuclear	6.7	7.8	7.7	6.8	7.1	7.3

Source: China National Bureau of Statistics 2006 (abstract).

The energy and electricity elasticities increased suddenly from an average of about 0.4 and 0.8, respectively, over two decades to more than 1.0 and 1.4 during the 10th Five-Year Plan. This increase suggests that China is heading toward a more energy-intensive path than even the ordinary efforts scenario forecasts. It indicates the need to establish a strong policy foundation for slower and cleaner energy growth if China is to build a sustainable future. Furthermore, international experience suggests that the role of energy as a factor of production in China could increase in the future and could contribute to even greater energy growth than anticipated.

A study by the IEA assessed the contribution of energy to the economic growth of several developing countries that experienced high GDP growth in the 1980s and 1990s. In all the countries included in the study except China, the combination of capital, labour, and energy made a greater contribution to economic growth than did productivity increases.[7] The overall conclusion was that energy plays the leading role in the factors of production for countries in an intermediate stage of development. The study noted that at this stage energy-intensive industries are often the key drivers of economic growth but that as an economy matures, these industries become proportionately less important and countries develop more energy-efficient technologies that contribute to productivity increases.

There is some concern that China may not remain the exception that the IEA study indicates. China currently has a much lower per capita income level than some other countries in the study (Brazil, the Republic of Korea, and Turkey). If it were to continue following the model of industrialisation of most developing countries (and industrial countries at earlier stages), energy intensity would likely increase with the growth of per capita income. Furthermore, China's most energy-intensive industries (chemicals, ferrous metals, oil refining, and the like) will likely raise their output substantially in the future. Instead of waiting for the economy to mature, China could chart a new course incorporating a strong emphasis on energy efficiency and cutting-edge technology. It could, thus, try to avoid the adverse impacts—in terms of pollution and oil import dependency—of the energy-intensive path of industrial countries that most developing countries are now following.

China's increased dependence on imported oil since the early 1990s is already a security concern, and that dependence will worsen if recent energy growth trends persist (see Table 21). During the first decade of high growth (the 1980s), China was able to maintain quasi autarky in energy supply. However, by 1993, the country had become a net oil importer, and by 1995, its dependence on oil imports had increased to about 5.3 per cent. This level of dependence was no cause for alarm. However, just five years later, in 2000, the growing demand of the economy had propelled China's dependence on oil imports to nearly 33 per cent. Moreover, net oil imports grew at 14.2 per cent on an average annual basis in those five years, to reach 143.6 million tons in 2005. At this level of dependence on foreign oil supplies, the country's energy security became a major concern for decision makers.

All projections of energy consumption compared with energy supply estimates indicate that China inevitably will become even more dependent on oil imports, even though its remaining exploitable oil reserves are significant. According to DRC estimates, these reserves amount to about 2.4 billion tons. Estimates of annual domestic oil output show production peaking at about 200 million tons in 2015 and thereafter ranging between 180 million and 200 million tons through 2020. In contrast, the DRC and ERI's projections indicate that by 2020 China's oil demand will be double or triple that amount, from 450 million to 610 million tons, in the low and high scenarios. As a result, the country's incremental oil demand between 2000 and 2020 would range from about 12 per cent to about 28 per cent of the incremental global oil demand projected by the IEA.[8]

TABLE 21

China's Oil Consumption and Trade, 1990-2005

Consumption or trade position	*1990*	*1995*	*2000*	*2001*	*2002*	*2003*	*2004*	*2005*
Consumption (million tons)	114.7	160.7	225.0	229.5	248.6	271.9	317.2	330.1
Imports (million tons)	6.9	31.5	94.6	88.5	99.6	129.6	170.6	168.5
Exports (million tons)	30.3	23.0	20.7	19.1	19.5	23.6	19.0	24.9
Net Imports (million tons)	(23.4)	8.5	73.9	69.4	80.1	106.0	151.6	143.6
Dependency on imports (%)	—	5.3	32.8	30.2	32.2	39.0	47.8	43.5

Source: Consumption data from China National Bureau of Statistics 2006 (abstract); import and export data provided by the General Administration of Customs of China.

Note: — = not available.

Even if the current ambitious plans for synthetic fuel production[9] were to materialise, the contribution of these fuels to meeting oil demand would not likely amount to more than 20 million tons in 2020, less than 5 per cent of the lowest estimate of oil consumption by that year. Therefore, China would increasingly rely on oil imports: the share of imports could rise dramatically, to between 50 and 60 per cent of oil consumption by 2020. Furthermore, if recent trends continue, following the path taken by advanced market economies at earlier stages of industrialisation (that is, if energy/GDP elasticity remains greater than 1.0), oil import requirements will exceed the highest current projections. The consequent pressure on world oil markets and the cost to China's economy would be enormous.

The major industrial countries also have experienced high dependency on oil imports, but some have managed to keep imports from increasing for several decades. For example, between 1973 and 2003, Japan maintained its oil consumption at about 250 million metric tons; during the same period, France actually reduced its oil consumption by about 23 per cent, from about 120 million to 93 million metric tons. However, not all countries have been able to constrain imports. The United States, which has a more energy-intensive economy than either France or Japan, experienced an increase in both oil consumption and oil imports during the same period: oil consumption increased by about 8 per cent, and the share of imports jumped from about 36 per cent to nearly 64 per cent because of declining production.

Despite the current high tension in oil markets, it is likely that global and regional markets would again adjust to meet the increasing demand, including China's high incremental imports. There is no consensus among experts about future equilibrium prices; however, it is likely that China would face tighter markets than industrial countries experienced in the past, even during the oil shocks of the early 1970s and early 1980s.

China's coal production could meet current and even higher consumption levels than projected for 2020, but those levels would not likely be environmentally sustainable. Energy projections show that coal would continue to account for more than 60 per cent of primary energy consumption in 2020. Experts consider that the coal supply shortages and related reductions in electricity supply that occurred in recent years were a temporary phenomenon and not likely to present a long-term problem, particularly if transportation bottlenecks continue to be relieved. As Box 4 indicates, massive reserves mean that China is likely to be able to meet coal demand through 2020 even if this demand turns out to be higher than envisaged.

BOX 4

China's Coal Production Prospects during 2020

Under the DRC and ERI scenarios, even the scenario of high energy consumption would not result in an overall supply constraint for China. The country is currently the world's largest coal producer and second largest coal exporter. However, during recent years, especially from 2003 to 2005, coal supply seemed to lag the tremendous growth of demand. Power shortages during recent years resulted from the disruption of coal supplies, and Chinese producers failed

Contd...box 4

in 2004 to honour contracts for export to power plants in the Republic of Korea. But, analyses by the DRC and ERI indicate that these disruptions are short-term bottlenecks and do not signal the decline of the coal industry in China.

China's coal reserves are abundant, according to most experts—despite the lack of agreement on their extent, owing to differences in definitions. The DRC and ERI estimate the country's exploitable coal reserves at more than 180 billion tons. On the one hand, those reserves could sustain the coal supply for about 65 years even if production were to rise to 2.8 billion tons—the maximum annual possible production, according to some Chinese experts. On the other, the development plans of the major players in the coal industry indicate that annual production could grow to more than 3 billion tons by 2020. However, some international experts contest these optimistic projections. More pessimistic projections indicate production deficits of 250 million tons in 2010 and 700 million tons in 2020, Beyond 2020, however, China could face constraints in coal supply if it were unable to Improve efficiency in both the "production and end use of coal as well as to promote fuel diversification more aggressively. In addition some Chinese experts recognize other constraints on coal production, including the availability of water resources and the unsustainable environmental impacts of coal use.

The government of China is addressing the transport and coal-handling bottlenecks that have disrupted supply, especially to the fast-growing eastern coastal regions. Measures to remove these constraints have included, in the late 1990s and early 2000s, an increase in double-track railway length from 24 to 38 per cent of the total length of the system and an increase in electrified lines from 13 to 29 per cent of the total length of the system. In the coming years, investments by and on behalf of coal producers are likely to further improve the situation. Moreover, there are plans for an increase in the number of port installations for handling coal. These installations handled about 276 million tons of coal in 2003. Current expansion plans project an increase in handling capability to about 380 million tons in 2010.

China's relative level of dependence on coal is not unprecedented. Coal accounted for about half of global energy consumption in 1950. As recently as 1965, it still met about 40 per cent of global needs, 53 per cent of the former Soviet Union's, about 60 per cent of the United Kingdom's, and some 64 per cent of Germany's primary energy needs (BP Global 2006).

After 2020, however, China could face coal supply shortages, unless greater energy efficiency is achieved by effective, promptly initiated measures and unless there is further diversification of the fuel mix, particularly to include increased use of gas and renewable energy for power generation. However, the atmospheric concentrations of major pollutants from coal production and use have reached or are approaching unsustainable levels. Unless major efforts are made to improve energy efficiency and deploy clean-coal technologies on a large scale, those concentrations will continue to rise roughly in step with growing consumption. Delay in addressing these fast-growing environmental problems could lead to irreversible damage to the atmospheric, agricultural, and forest environments. Urgency is the characteristic lacking in energy and environmental policy.

The present concentrations of levels of nitrogen oxides and sulfur dioxide have reached or even, in some cases, exceeded the caps that the government has set for these pollutants. In addition, the projections of pollution associated with the DRC and ERI's energy scenarios are all higher than the targets the government envisages for 2020. Even under the most optimistic scenario (green growth), sulphur dioxide emissions would be 100 per cent higher—and nitrogen oxides emissions would be 50 per cent higher—than the environmental caps under consideration

The Urgency for Policy Action

The need for policy action is indeed urgent. Current trends cannot be sustained, and the window of opportunity will not be open much longer.

Recent Trends in Energy Consumption are Unsustainable

If China were to continue following the path of industrial and middle-income countries, its energy consumption would have to grow more rapidly than is currently envisaged by any reputable forecasters. Consumption would soon reach unsustainable levels, essentially because of the great size of the country's population and its economy. For example, if China were to attain the level of per capita energy consumption of Germany or Japan, its energy use would be equal to or slightly more than half of current world energy consumption. Without significantly greater reliance on cleaner technologies, such consumption volumes would have serious negative impacts on the environment, largely because of China's dependence on "dirty" coal. Such volumes would also put strong pressures on future regional and global oil (and probably gas) markets. Clearly then, present consumption trends are unsustainable.

In this connection, the higher energy intensity observed during the 10th Five-Year Plan is a major cause for concern. International data show that the economies of the more industrial countries tend to lock themselves into a narrow range of energy intensity for decades after making major development choices. For example, Fig 21 shows that after the first energy crisis it took more than 30 years for the leading industrial countries to significantly reduce their energy intensity—mainly because large investments in equipment and processes have long life cycles and ingrained behavioral consumption patterns are often difficult to change. Furthermore, a large part of the reductions in energy intensity that were achieved probably stemmed from the deindustrialisation of Western Europe and the United States, the related migration of some energy-intensive industries, and the continuing growth of the service sectors. However, China is in a position to take advantage of the most advanced technologies to leapfrog some stages in the growth of mature industrial countries, thereby achieving its full economic development with relatively less energy consumption and associated environmental impacts.

In summary, current trends are unsustainable, but China has a window of opportunity to break out of its highly energy-intensive growth path, to avoid the energy trajectories followed by the advanced industrial countries, and to adopt a path that is fundamentally more energy efficient and therefore environmentally sustainable. Such a path is in line with the government's policy objectives. However, shifting to this path demands urgent and coordinated action by China at the national and international levels. If China were to miss this opportunity, it could lock into an energy-intensive development path that could be costly for the country and for the rest of the world as well.

In China, the focus of concern about higher energy requirements is on their increasing cost to the economy: in 2005, energy costs in China amounted to 13 per cent of GDP, compared with about 7 per cent in the United States and slightly more than 3 per cent in Japan.[10] This high cost could affect the competitiveness of China's economy in the long term. Chinese decision-makers are also concerned about the security of supply, the volatility of global oil and gas markets, and the negative impacts of extensive use of coal on the local environment. Around the world, the focus is on the surge in China's oil imports and the resulting increased pressure on future oil supplies and prices, as well as the associated rise in greenhouse gas emissions and their impacts on climate change.

Window of Opportunity is Closing Rapidly

The successes of China's past policies in reducing power shortages and transforming the energy sector are well recognised. However, the recent trends are an early warning that the planning approach and current policies may have reached their limits and will not address the new challenges facing the sector. The planning approach is still fragmented, piecemeal, and strongly based on centralized command and control. In contrast, the energy sector is growing at a fast pace, driven by decentralised choices in an increasingly market-oriented economy. Sector operations are also growing in complexity because of greater integration with regional and global energy markets. Furthermore, there is a disconnect between the usual planning horizon (5 to 15 years) and the lengthy lead times required for structural changes owing to the long economic life of assets (30 to 40 years).

China faces a daunting development challenge. But, there is an emerging consensus that the country's current unprecedented attention to energy and its increasingly damaging environmental impacts provide a unique opportunity to focus more strongly on sustainable development and innovative and workable solutions to meet the country's fast-growing energy needs. Such solutions are likely to require increased bilateral and multilateral cooperation to stabilise regional and international energy markets, taking full advantage of cutting-edge technologies to mitigate the environmental impacts of extensive coal use.

There is an urgent need for decisive actions to bring the energy sector back on a sustainable track. China has more than two decades of experience in piloting and assessing policy options. The time for action has arrived. China now stands at a crossroads. It faces major environmental challenges that require innovative thinking and strong political commitment to devise policies that will enable it to continue its unprecedented economic growth with less and cleaner energy. Meeting this challenge will also require more comprehensive international cooperation for technology transfer, if China is to meet environmental objectives in line with its national interests and those of the global community.[11]

CHINA'S GROWING SENSE OF INSECURITY

The growing sense of insecurity is global. Energy supplies can become insecure, because of

- **Geological factors.** Factors such as depletion rates may cause physical limits on fuel supply, so that volume is no longer adequate to meet demand. An example is the Canadian east coast offshore gas fields that were brought to market in 2000 and that have produced much below expectations.
- **Political, military, and diplomatic factors.** Such factors can restrict energy supply, make it prohibitively expensive, or make it physically unreliable. Such factors affected most Iranian oil supplies during the labour strikes of 1978, the revolution of 1979, and the prolonged war with Iraq in the early 1980s.
- **Infrastructure bottlenecks.** Because of such bottlenecks, energy flows may not reach consumers. Energy supplies may no longer be competitive by international standards, as happened to most Western European coal industries in the latter part of the 20th century.

These generic causes of insecurity and their results, together with China's special concerns, are presented in Figure 6.

FIGURE 6

Energy Insecurity: Generic Causes, Effects, and China's Special Concerns

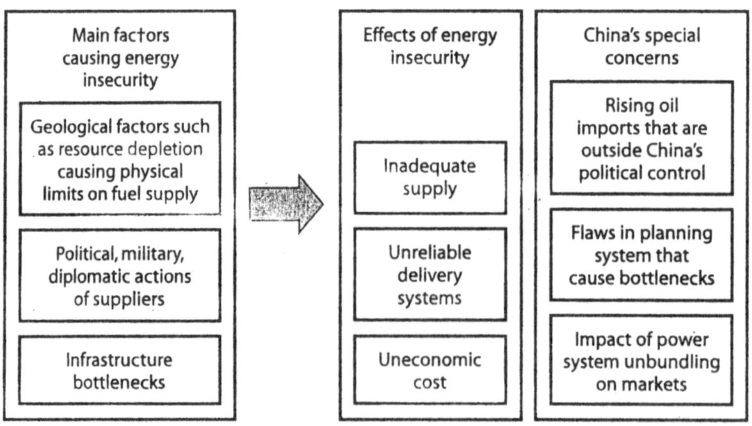

Key International Energy Insecurity Concerns and Their Causes

Since the middle of the last century, the two main global security concerns have been the possible disruption of oil imports—and to a lesser extent imports of gas or coal—and sudden price hikes, usually triggered by oil market events, which can threaten economic stability and competitiveness. For electric power systems, the "California syndrome"—or the association of power system failures with deregulation and competitive markets—has become a major concern. The September 11, 2001, attacks in the United States have raised concerns about the vulnerability of critical infrastructure such as oil and gas pipelines, power plants, oil refineries, and Liquefied Natural Gas (LNG) terminals. The disruption of crude oil, oil products, and natural gas and electricity supply in the United States caused by Hurricane Katrina in September 2005 has focused attention on natural disasters and extreme weather events as a source of energy insecurity.

In addition to its military and political implications, energy insecurity can be costly in economic terms. Increased dependence on energy imports can raise foreign exchange requirements. The disruption of energy supply can stunt economic growth.[12] Furthermore, the need for security-enhancing measures to avoid such threats to economic growth can put a heavier burden on a country's budget.[13]

Oil imports. For the past half-century or more, international energy supply security concerns have focused on oil imports. To a large extent, this focus reflects the growing import dependence of many industrial countries, the concentration of imports from a relatively small number of suppliers, and the fact that on seven occasions those supplies have been significantly disrupted. Despite these disruptions, global oil markets have a good record over a long period of time in dealing effectively with both short- and long-term potential supply-demand imbalances, essentially through the price mechanism. Internationally competitive global trading countries with adequate foreign exchange have always been able to purchase all the oil they need at current market prices. An additional consideration in the first decade of the 21st century is the debate about peak global oil production, which may be bringing another element of uncertainty into policy discussions and long-term market behaviour.

The risks surrounding petroleum imports are threefold:

1. Major exporting countries (for example, Saudi Arabia) or associations of such countries (for example, the Organization of Arab Petroleum Exporting Countries) could change their policies and constrain either total supply or the supply to particular markets.
2. Supply constraints could result from insufficient investments in exploration, field development, and transportation infrastructures. This scenario could occur either because National Oil Companies (NOCs) have inadequate investment funds or because governments restrict investments by International Oil Companies (IOCs) in some of the world's best areas for petroleum prospects (for example, the Islamic Republic of Iran, Kuwait, or Mexico).
3. *Force majeure* events could occur, such as civil disorder (strikes in Nigeria and the República Bolivariana de Venezuela); military actions (the Iran-Iraq War of 1981 to 1984); terrorist activity (so far, there has been only limited and local impact); and natural disasters (hurricanes in the Gulf of Mexico). These events could disrupt or interrupt oil or energy flows at regional or global levels. The perception is that since September 11, 2001, geopolitical uncertainties have been aggravated.

Gas imports. The rapidly developing international gas trade has been less subject to impairments than has oil trade—both of pipeline gas and of LNG. As major producer-exporters, Algeria, Canada, and Russia have been reliable suppliers for many decades. As consumer-importers, France, Germany, Italy, and (to a lesser extent) the United States have relied heavily on imported supplies to support strong domestic gas industries. Japan and the Republic of Korea have each confidently developed a large gas industry and related electricity generation capacity, almost wholly on the basis of imports. Turkey is following a similar path.

Where technical failures have occurred, such as accidental damage to LNG plants overseas, the industry has been able to quickly find alternative sources. International price disputes have arisen in the past—for example, between Canada and the United States, between France and Algeria, and between the Netherlands and other countries of the European Union (EU). However, since the 1980s, greater reliance on market-based pricing and better contracting practices have reduced the incidence of such disputes. Where international gas purchases involve long-term take-or-pay contracts, as is the case with most LNG trade, a valuable interdependence between sellers and buyers is created and contributes to security of supply.

The January 2006 dispute that resulted in a four-day disruption of supplies from Russia to Ukraine raised EU fears about the security of gas for Europe and led to a meeting of Group of Eight ministers in Moscow. Gas trade among the former Soviet countries is of a state-to-state nature. The causes of the dispute are complex, and some are longstanding. Prices are not market based. Other factors included Ukraine's payment arrears, the alleged diversion of gas destined for the European Union, and the rejection of an agreement for partial Russian ownership and for refurbishment of pipelines from Russia transiting Ukraine to Western Europe.[14]

Domestic energy sources. If domestic energy sources are not developed on an economic basis, they may not be secure, even though they are entirely under the control of the government. For example, the old, deep-mined coal industries that supported Western Europe's early industrial supremacy proved unable to meet the energy needs of a modern economy in terms of volume, quality, and price. Also in 1984/85, a one-year miners' strike in the United Kingdom caused the country's most serious peacetime energy crisis. More recently, strikes by petroleum transport workers and blockades to protest high prices for oil products have threatened the continuity of oil supplies to European consumers.

Technical failures may also impair the supply of domestic energy. Examples are accidents at a gas-processing plant in Australia and an LNG plant in Algeria and the failure of gas-producing fields in Canada. Furthermore technical, financial, environmental, and regulatory issues are currently creating obstacles to needed gas development across North America, resulting in high prices and faltering consumption.[15]

A number of costly blackouts have occurred in the large, interconnected, but separately operated North American electricity systems. The most recent one, in August 2003, affected millions of customers and entailed significant economic losses. In the developing world, supply disruptions have occurred mainly because of insufficient generation capacity and weak transmission and distribution systems. These problems have been caused mainly by lack of investment but also by flaws in the planning, approval, or execution of projects. Countries affected include Argentina, Brazil, China, and India. Impairment of fuel supply for power generation can also disrupt electricity supply, as recently occurred in the southeast coastal regions of China.

Because domestic energy supplies are entirely within the nation's political control, as is the case for coal in China, they must in principle be regarded as more secure than imported supplies if they are developed on a sound economic basis and in harmony with global and regional markets. However, policy and regulatory steps need to be taken to avoid security risks. Such steps include subjecting these sources to market forces to ensure that they are internationally competitive, monitoring reserves and resources of fossil fuels related to long-term supply adequacy, addressing social issues that may affect supply, ensuring that investments are adequate to prevent infrastructure bottlenecks, and securing critical infrastructure against failures, however caused. A recent study sponsored by the World Bank, carried out in close coordination with the National Development and Reform Commission (NDRC), outlined a reform strategy in response to concerns about the future of China's coal development (See Box 5).

Multidimensional Nature of Energy Security

Insecurity of energy supply relates to the nation's economy and society because consumption of commercial energy in its various forms is of enormous and pervasive importance. Security has a time dimension: harm can be caused by electricity disruptions that last a few days or by oil supply disruptions that endure for many months. It has geographic dimensions: disruptions may originate thousands of kilometres from the point of interrupted consumption or may arise very close to the consumption point. Supply can be disrupted by accident, sabotage, strikes or other social phenomena, terrorism, overseas wars and political actions, and exceptional climatic events. Mechanisms to address insecurity are therefore multiple: improved training for energy system operators, technical repair capabilities, secure storage of some energy forms, and so on. China's growing sense of insecurity stems from three factors:

1. Rising oil imports have placed nearly half of China's oil supply outside its political and military control, a situation dramatically different from that experienced only a decade ago when net import requirements were negligible.
2. Flaws in the planning system and transportation bottlenecks have threatened the integrity of energy (mainly power) supply, causing alternating cycles of oversupply and shortage.
3. The government's decision to deregulate its power industry has triggered concerns (the California syndrome) about the integrity of the power system.

BOX 5

World Bank's Involvement in China's Coal Subsector

Coal: An Indispensable Source of Energy

China is the world's largest producer and consumer of coal and depends critically on coal to sustain its growing economy. With production and use approaching close to 2 billion tons per year, coal dominates the national energy market. China's coal subsector is not only the world's largest but also the most dangerous in terms of mine safety and the most polluting in terms of coal-fired boiler emissions. Coal is China's least costly source of energy. Despite official promotion of renewables and energy efficiency, coal demand will increase in the foreseeable future because of sustained economic growth and limited hydrocarbon reserves. Coal subsector reforms lag reforms in the rest of the economy. The development of small state-owned coal mines is unsustainable, and China is starting to look to the private sector to replace diminishing reserves and productive capacity, China is at a critical juncture for addressing a number of key challenges related to its large and growing coal industry.

Work to Date: An Emerging Reform Agenda

In response to concerns about the future of China's coal development, the World Bank sponsored a study funded by its Energy Sector Management Assistance Programme to identify key issues and establish a constructive dialogue with the government of China through NDRC. This work included a review by a team of domestic and international experts of the institutional and regulatory framework governing the licensing and operation of coal sector enterprises in China. Coal industry practices were examined in two of the more important provinces, and two mine case studies were produced to demonstrate potential improvements. The findings were discussed at two workshops hosted by NDRC in 2003. These workshops were attended by a broad spectrum of stakeholders, and general consensus was reached on the formulation of a coal industry reform strategy to be sponsored by the World Bank. The strategy had these objectives:

- Rationalise productive capacity and encourage private investment.
- Enhance occupational health and safety.
- Improve environmental protection.

In July 2004, the World Bank issued a final report that consolidated this work (see World Bank 2004).

World Bank Support: A Potential Comparative Advantage

In many countries, the World Bank has supported efforts to introduce modern mining legislation, improve the investment climate, build institutional capacity to enforce laws, mitigate the social and environmental impacts of mining, and promote new investment and private sector development. Encouragement of positive social and economic impacts for local communities has been a growing component of World Bank interventions, one reinforced by the findings of

Contd...

Contd...box 5

the International Finance Corporation's Extractive Industries Review. The World Bank's comparative advantage and expertise in these areas could benefit China's hew policy direction and coal subsector reforms. Preliminary discussions with NDRC suggest that these efforts could be directed toward improving China's coal industry by doing three things:

- **'Improving the management of coal resources.** The legal and regulatory framework could be modernized along the lines identified in World Bank (2004), and interministerial coordination could be improved.
- **Reducing barriers to private investment.** Private sector access to geological and mining data could be improved, with mineral rights granted on an equitable and centralised basis, with security of tenure and increased operational autonomy.
- **Enhancing institutional capacity.** Institutional capacity could be strengthened at all levels of government to deal with critical issues such as environmental protection and restoration of land for reuse, closure of uneconomical and damaging coal mines, and regional economic diversification to reduce dependence on coal mining and increase support for coal mine closures.

Source: World Bank 2004.

Options for Securing Oil and Gas Supply

Long-term energy security requires vision and an integrated policy to support that vision. This section reviews measures widely used in the past, mainly by industrial countries, to secure oil and gas supplies. It includes a brief commentary and evaluation of what China is doing. China ought to consider these measures, evaluate them, and select the ones most appropriate to meet its needs.

Fostering the Development of National Oil and Gas Resources and Implementing the Renewable Energy Promotion Law of 2005

The development of national resources that can pass the test of international competitiveness and implementation of the Renewable Energy Promotion Law (REPL) of 2005 with more reliance on market forces is a foundational policy measure for securing long-term energy supply. Most countries with a heavy dependence on energy imports have focused primarily on policies to encourage domestic energy development. The most successful policies have targeted the development of resources that are economically and environmentally viable. Typically, new laws and amended policies have opened markets to attract capital and technology to energy businesses. They have provided incentives and created markets for the development of renewable energy resources and designed research and development and industrial strategies in new and renewable energy fields. According to the DRC's estimate, if China were to adopt this course of action as part of its general energy strategy, the share of domestic-source primary energy could still be as high as 80 per cent in 2020, compared with about 90 per cent in 2000.

China's oil and gas regime needs to be opened up. Comparative analyses show that the attractiveness of China's petroleum regimes are just average, compared with a worldwide rating of about 280 fiscal systems. Further changes are required to improve China's international competitiveness in several areas: the conditions for access to undeveloped resources, the fiscal terms for the development of such resources, and the conditions for the participation of domestic and international investors in exploration and development. Policy changes in these areas would result in more rapid development of domestic oil and gas and a consequent relative reduction in the nation's long-term import needs. Some examples of energy development incentives are given in Box 6.

China is encouraging a strategic transition of the oil and gas industry from the traditional areas in the northeast to Xinjiang and to offshore regions. Increased competition among the three major NOCs and improved access terms for IOCs, along with a general opening of energy markets, could help channel additional sources of capital and technology for the optimal development of China's oil and gas resources. However, long-term planning and supportive policies are clearly lacking in these areas.

China announced a very ambitious program for the development of renewable energy during the June 2004 Bonn Conference on Renewable Energy.[16] In addition, in late February 2005, China enacted the REPL and launched a competitive concession programme to speed up the development of its sizable wind power resources. Then, at the Beijing International Renewable Energy Conference in November 2005, China announced an even stronger commitment to renewable energy, setting a target of doubling the current use of renewable energy to 15 per cent of the country's energy balance by 2015. The World Bank and the Global Environment Facility are assisting China in this area through the China Renewable Energy Scale-Up Program [CRESP] announced in June 2005.[17]

Securing Imports through Diplomatic and Trade Relationships

Industrial countries have traditionally tried, though not always successfully, to attract foreign energy suppliers for the development of strong, secure trade relationships for energy (especially oil). France, Japan, and the United Kingdom seem to have been the most active in the Middle East, offering advanced technological and industrial assistance along with diplomatic support. Similarly, the United States tends to focus its energy trade relationships on the Middle East for oil imports and on Canada for gas and, increasingly, oil imports. U.S. companies play key technological assistance roles in some Middle East oil states.

The obvious focuses for China's development of these relationships are, for oil, with the Middle East—especially Saudi Arabia, which will continue to be a major oil supplier—and for gas, with Russia, the most important gas exporter. The importance of the emerging focus by China on Saudi Arabia for oil supply and on Russia for gas supply is clear from Table 22.

BOX 6

Examples of Domestic Energy Development Incentives in Other Industrial Countries

Oil Sands

In Canada, development is encouraged by very low rates of taxation for oil sands compared with conventional oil.

Marginal Conventional Oilfields

In the United Kingdom, the government grants tax relief' on a case-by-case basis, to encourage investments that will help produce additional oil from partly depleted fields.

Natural Gas

In Canada, the federal government has subsidised the development of lateral natural gas pipelines and the expansion of distribution systems in order to reduce oil dependency, especially in remote areas.

Renewable Sources for Electricity Generation

In Texas, in the United States, a 1999 electricity restructuring law required 2,000 megawatts of nonhydrological renewable electric energy to be available by 2009. Already in February 2006, some 2,378 megawatts of wind energy alone were on line, according to the Texas Renewable Energy Industries Association, and Texas has overtaken California as the leading wind energy state of the United States.

Wind Power

Following the energy crisis of 1973 to 1974, the United States became the world's largest producer of wind energy. However, since the early 1990s, Denmark and Germany have taken the lead in this area. Both countries have market-based energy policies with a high degree of freedom to invest in, sell, and buy energy without government interference. Tax incentives encourage both investment in wind power and consumption of electricity derived from it. For example, Germany has an eco-tax on all formsof traditional energy and uses the revenues to foster renewables. Currently, Germany has some 15,000 megawatts of wind power generation capacity installed. Denmark provides income tax incentives for investors in wind energy and is second in the world in terms of installed capacity from that source.

TABLE 22

Oil and Gas Reserves in the Middle East and Russian Federation

	Oil			*Gas*		
Country	*Reserves (billion barrels)*	*Share of world reserves (%)*	*Reserves/ production (years)*	*Reserves (trillion cubic feet)*	*Share of the world reserves (%)*	*Reserves/ production (years)*
Saudi Arabia	262	25.0	86	n.a.	n.a.	n.a.
Russian Fed.	n.a.	n.a.	n.a.	1,660	27.0	81
China	24	2,3	19	64	1.0	17

Source: Study team based on data from BP Global 2005. *Note:* n.a. = not applicable.

China appears to be making vigorous efforts to use its diplomatic influence and trading strengths to improve relations with oil-exporting countries and thus to secure access to investment opportunities and trade flows. This effort is characteristic of the normal global competition between buyers of raw materials, in which China is now taking part. This sort of competition has existed for decades between other industrial countries such as those of the EU and Japan. It can take place in ways that do not conflict with the ongoing consultation and cooperation that is necessary between oil importers in organisations such as the International Energy Agency (IEA) and the Asia Pacific Economic Cooperation (APEC).

Building Relationships with the IOCs

Energy is the world's biggest business and the domain of its largest corporations. Among the IOCs, ExxonMobil is the world's largest private corporation. Among the NOCs, Saudi Aramco is the world's largest oil company, with reserves some 20 times greater than those of ExxonMobil. Close relations with these and similar companies can help an importing country access international oil supplies. Indeed, many industrial countries have relied very successfully on the IOCs to secure all their import needs. IOCs can have a useful (import) role in China, and their involvement could be considered along with that of Chinese NOCs to enhance security of supply. Relationships with the IOCs would also provide access to state-of-the-art technology and management practices across the whole range of oil and gas industry activities.

The IOCs are unequalled in their relationships with producing countries; their ownership of equity crude oil; and their control of transportation infrastructure (shipping, pipelines), which gives them great global flexibility in their oil supply operations. They are involved in all segments of the oil and gas business, from exploration and production to retail distribution. They are managerially strong and are experienced in risk-hedging techniques, both areas in which the Chinese NOCs may be relatively weak. However, they currently control only 10 per cent of the world's oil and gas reserves. Of the top 20 owners of oil and gas reserves in 2004,14 were NOCs. State monopolies are the 10 largest owners of such reserves. ExxonMobil and the Shell Group rank 12th and 13th. BP and Chevron-Texaco are 16th and 19th.

Defining a Role for the NOCs

NOCs now are out of fashion in most industrial energy-consuming countries that dabbled with the concept in the past half-century. For example, the U.K. government long ago gave up its share in BP. The later British National Oil Company, which the government created to explore and develop in the North Sea, has been privatised. Petro-Canada has been almost completely privatised, the government retaining only about 14 per cent of the share capital. In France, the former state company Elf is now part of the large, private TotalFinalElf group. The Spanish state company Repsol was successfully privatized, and then it absorbed the privatised Argentine oil monopoly Yacimientos Petrolíferos Fiscales and, as a result, has become a significant international player, particularly in Latin America. Japanese policy-makers appear to be disillusioned with their investments in the Japan National Oil Company. In fact, among the IEA members, only the Italian state company Eni appears to be a significant NOC player.

The Chinese NOCs, with government support and encouragement, have pursued oil and gas production and export investments in many countries. However, a rapid examination of these activities suggests that these investments are made ad hoc. Some of the bilateral deals seem to have been initiated and conducted without proper analysis and due diligence, perhaps guided by an overreaction to emerging oil security concerns. Moreover, as a consequence of their listings on international markets, the Chinese NOCs appear to be facing the dilemma of either pursuing strictly commercial investment strategies or taking into consideration broader objectives of energy security for China. The role of the NOCs in supporting China's energy security objectives seems not yet to have been defined.

The NOCs can contribute significantly to China's oil and energy security by providing access to adequate and secure oil and gas supplies. However, the partially listed companies are increasingly coming under investor scrutiny. A perception that they give precedence to China's national interest over their shareholders' interest could hurt their market standings. Therefore, the government should define and publicize the role of the NOCs in enhancing the country's energy security. If they are required to take on operations that are suboptimal from the standpoint of maximising returns to shareholders, the NOCs should receive adequate and transparent compensation. NOCs also are beginning to face scrutiny over business and environmental practices, including investments in countries at high political risk. This scrutiny will intensify with their increasing international visibility and should be taken into account in devising their global investment strategies and business behaviour. One aspect of current NOC activity directed at improving supply security—the repatriation of equity oil—is highlighted in Box 7.

Clarifying the Security Roles of Foreign Oil Companies

It is timely for the government to similarly clarify the roles that it expects foreign oil companies, both private and state owned, to play in the Chinese market. In particular, there should be clear definition of conditions for market entry and exit and for partnership with Chinese NOCs and other local operators in such areas as importing and storage (including strategic storage), exploration and development, refining and processing, and distribution and marketing. All policy and regulatory conditions should be transparent and be applied in a non-discriminatory manner. Opening markets to enable IOCs and other foreign investors to play a greater role in oil supply and domestic resource development could be a positive signal to the international community, making it easier for Chinese NOCs to engage in similar activities abroad. China's NOCs should at the same time consider strategies for interacting profitably with and learning from foreign oil companies, both NOCs and IOCs, as well as strategies for better integration in global and regional oil markets. All major players recognise and seem to welcome China's increasing role in the oil market and, to a lesser extent, in gas markets. The investments of Chinese NOCs in the development and marketing of new reserves are perceived as a stabilizing factor in future oil and gas markets. More transparency would certainly improve the business orientation of Chinese NOCs and ease their entry into the global market, where they could be world-class players.

BOX 7

Repatriating Equity Oil: Is There a Better Way to Provide Security?

One aspect of the current activities of China's NOCs calls for a specific comment. It appears to be their policy—and possibly that of the government—that their equity (or "owned") crude oil that is found and developed abroad be repatriated to China for refining, almost regardless of its location or quality. The outstanding case is oil production by the China National Petroleum Corporation in Sudan: it is exported to China for refining rather than to the closer south European market.

Argument for Repatriation

This flow of oil is under Chinese control from the point of loading in Sudan to the distribution of the final refined product. Hence, the oil is more secure than any foreign barrels purchased on the international market.

Argument against Repatriation

There may be an added cost to China's NOCs—and therefore to the Chinese economy—resulting from the longer distances involved and the need to dedicate refineries or refinery units to processing so-called difficult grades of crude oil. It is the practice of IOCs to maximise the value of their oil production by selling at the highest available price and to minimise the costs of their refinery feed streams by purchasing at the lowest: available price, regardless of the nationality or ownership of the seller or buyer in each case.

Alternatives

One possibility is to examine whether it might make more sense to sell Sudanese oil to southern Europe and buy other barrels for China's needs. Another is to consider exchanging the Sudanese oil for oil from a closer source, making the supply of the Sudanese barrels to the exchange partner contingent on receiving the exchange barrels in China. That comment is made while recognising that there may be technical or trade obstacles, now or in the future, to delivering Sudanese oil to certain markets.

Establishing Policies to Enhance Short-term Oil Supply

International experience clearly indicates that the accumulation of oil stocks above normal commercial levels is an important and worthwhile component of an integrated approach to improving the security of China's oil supply. There are several key issues to address in any stockpiling programme. First, where, how, by whom, in what amount, and in what form should the stocks be held? Second, how should the costs of stockpiling be met? Third, and perhaps most important, under what circumstances will the government release the oil stocks? In most industrial countries, these issues are a matter of public policy.

Contribution of normal commercial stocks: The oil industry holds commercial oil stocks to deal with fluctuations in demand and to protect against technical failures and operational delays that could affect the continuity of supply for customers. Typically, oil companies attach much importance to keeping their customers supplied. They are also used to working cooperatively to assist each other in the event of technical failures. However, like many other manufacturing and distribution businesses, oil companies around the world have been progressively reducing their inventories to control costs. They do not plan their inventories taking into account supply emergencies caused by geopolitical events. To help address such contingencies, either governments themselves hold reserves in strategic storage or they mandate that the oil companies maintain minimum stock requirements. Some governments adopt both measures.

Strategic oil storage: In the late 1990s, the government of China announced its intention to keep crude oil reserves equivalent to 60 days worth of net imports and 30 days worth of oil products consumption by 2020. China National Petroleum Corporation (CNPC) has begun work on strategic oil storage. Industry analysts have assumed that a portion of the large increases in China. Oil imports in recent years have been for strategic storage purposes.[18] There is no question that accumulating stocks over and above minimum commercial requirements is the most important and valuable step that China can take to avoid negative economic and social impacts of short-term oil supply disruptions. Several oil-importing countries maintain strategic reserves as one element of civilian oil supply security policies; examples include Germany, Japan, Switzerland, and the United States. Reportedly, India has approved an oil supply security plan modelled on the U.S. Strategic Petroleum Reserve.

Current high steel prices[19] have made storage in steel containers—tanks or barges—more expensive. The cost of this storage may be a charge on the general budget as in the United States, or the cost could be recovered by a security tax on oil consumption. Strategic petroleum reserves are attractive to policy-makers because they are known quantities that are available at any one time in given locations under their control. Moreover, policy-makers control the rate at which withdrawals from these stocks can take place in order to achieve policy goals. For example, the U.S. Congress approved the U.S. Strategic Petroleum Reserve in 1975, in the aftermath of the oil crisis of 1973 to 1974; it currently covers about 59 days worth of imports.[20] Japan's strategic petroleum reserve is a minimum of 50 million cubic meters, equivalent to about 55 days of consumption at 2006 rates. Table 27 ranks strategic oil storage and other key measures for short-term oil supply security in terms of their difficulty and relative cost.

A strategic petroleum reserve clearly gives the government the greatest degree of control over the location, levels, quality, physical security, and use of an emergency oil inventory. However, developing a strategic petroleum reserve is an expensive proposition, especially with crude oil prices in the second half of 2006 fluctuating in the US$60 to US$75 per barrel range. A policy decision would be required as to how the costs of a reserve could be met. For example, they could be paid out of general government revenues, as in the United States, or they could be recovered from oil users by a levy on consumption.

TABLE 23

Assessment of Relative Difficulty, Cost, and Degree of Control of Key Measures for Short-term Oil Supply Security

Key measures for short-term oil supply security	*Relative level of difficulty*	*Relative cost to government*	*Degree of government control*
Strategic petroleum reserve	Low	High	High
Mandated minimum commercial stocks	Low	Low	Medium
Spare domestic oil production capacity	Medium	High	Medium

Mandated minimum, commercial stocks: Many countries have laws and regulations that require their oil companies to maintain stocks at certain minimum levels relative to consumption. For example, consistent with the EU directive on stocks, most EU member countries require their industries to maintain minimum stocks. These stocks correspond to 90 days worth of the average internal consumption in the preceding year of the three main categories of oil products. Countries that are in a net export position, such as Denmark and the United Kingdom, do not have the same obligation. The United States does not mandate minimum commercial stocks, but the U.S. Strategic Petroleum Reserve plus commercial stocks are currently equivalent to about 118 days worth of imports. Japan requires companies to hold commercial stocks equivalent to 70 days worth of consumption, over and above the volumes held in Japan's reserve.

Generally, oil companies are authorised to recover from consumers the costs of mandated minimum commercial stocks. If governments apply stockholding requirements equally to all companies and if the companies experience roughly equal cost increases as a result, they are likely, in a market economy, to be able to recover these costs through the selling prices of oil products. The attraction to policy makers of mandated minimum commercial stocks is that there is no budgetary cost, and yet, at least in theory, these stocks can be drawn down only at the direction of the government.

Stocks owned by oil exporters and held in oil-importing countries: Exporters also have a strong interest in avoiding supply disruption in their important markets. Saudi Arabia reportedly maintains a huge storage capacity near Europe and in the United States, in order to ensure timely and cost-efficient delivery of supplies to those markets. There do not appear to be publicly available data about the current quantities, qualities, and locations of the stocks. Also, Saudi Arabia reportedly has sought storage capacity in the Asia-Pacific region but has been unsuccessful because so far no government in the region has allowed Saudi Arabia to set up facilities. There may, therefore, be a mutually beneficial opportunity for a Chinese initiative in this area.

Maintenance of spare domestic oil production capability: This option is costly because, to be effective, it requires the creation of redundancies at many stages of the domestic oil supply chain—the capacity of wells, processing plants, pipelines, and possibly refineries processing crude oil. A review of international experience shows that many countries have not considered it a worthwhile option because of the substantial investment and maintenance necessary. It is mentioned here only because at some stages in the development of the upstream industry such linked spare capacity may exist that could be called on in an emergency.

Two cases illustrate this measure. The first case occurred twice in Texas, United States, during the Suez crisis of 1956 to 1957 and the Suez crisis of 1967. The regulator, the Texas Railroad Commission, gave approval for additional volumes to be produced in the domestic market, which reduced import needs and allowed the diversion of available foreign oil, such as that from the República Bolivariana de Venezuela, to Europe. The second case is Canada's response to the emergency circumstances of 1973 and 1974. Canada's developed wellhead and crude oil pipeline capacities were greater than those of the plants processing associated gas. Therefore, the regulator was prepared to consider permitting the flaring of associated gas in order to bring this spare wellhead crude oil capacity into production.

It is unlikely that there is significant unused oil production capacity in China's domestic oil industry under any normal circumstances. However, it is important to evaluate what, if any, potential may exist in emergency conditions and to keep track of the development of that potential. An assessment should be made as to whether China's production companies could, in an emergency situation, increase production from existing oil wells, where surface facilities such as gas processing or pipelines do not match the developed wellhead capacity. Increasing production might involve, for example, flaring associated gas or transporting extra oil production by what would normally be regarded as non-economic methods, such as long-distance transport by rail or truck. The assessment should be updated from time to time.

Provision of military protection for crude oil traffic in the chokepoints of international tanker transportation. Disruption of tanker traffic in the narrow Hormuz, Malacca, and Sunda straits could affect the reliability or cost of China's oil supply. An interruption of commercial access to the Malacca and Sunda straits would significantly increase the amount and cost of shipping capacity needed to supply Middle East oil to points east of those straits.[21] If this situation were to occur when the international tanker markets were already stressed, it could be very difficult for the industry to compensate for the shortfall in crude oil supply.

Major nations having an interest in the security of global oil supply— and China is certainly one of them—could cooperate in devising measures to ensure that illegal activities in these narrow waters do not disrupt petroleum supplies.[22] Information on these matters is generally not public, and its evaluation is beyond the scope of this report.

Building Flexibility into the Oil-refining Industry

Oil refineries are the critical interface between crude oil supply and the oil products needs of consumers. Typically, refineries are built and operated to handle a predetermined range of crude oil types. That range may be narrow, especially if the refineries are associated with petrochemicals and manufacture of lubricants. Generally, capital costs are lower for refineries that are designed to handle a narrow range of crude oils (in terms of, for example, sulphur content and specific gravity) than for plants that can process a wide variety of feedstocks, including high-sulphur ("sour") heavy crude oils. However, it happens in times of crisis that unusual grades of crude oil may be available when traditional sources are not. In these circumstances, refinery flexibility can be a valuable asset from the standpoint of ensuring the continuity and security of oil products supply.

To the extent that the Organisation of Petroleum Exporting Countries (OPEC) has spare production capacity, it is often in the form of heavy and relatively sour crude oils. For example, in normal circumstances, Saudi Arabia maximizes the production of its Arab Light grade of oil. In emergencies, when larger volumes are necessary, it usually maximises production of the Arab Heavy grade. Refiners who are able to handle this grade of crude and even less desirable grades of oil clearly have an advantage over refiners with less flexible equipment.

A lack of adequate refining capacity to handle heavier and more sulphurous crude oils appears to be an ongoing issue in China's downstream subsector. Several refineries are being upgraded to handle heavier and sourer grades of oil. These programmes should be accelerated, because they will provide access to a wider array of supply sources. They can also result in much improved profitability for refineries that do undertake the investments needed to process heavy sour crude oils. The rise in international crude oil prices in the past five years has been particularly pronounced for grades of oil with high specific gravity and low sulphur. The market price differentials of these grades compared with those of higher specific gravity and more sour crude oils have greatly increased. As a result, the profit margins available to refiners of the more abundant, poorer-quality crude oils have been very large.

One major project undertaken by China in this field is the joint venture between Saudi Aramco, ExxonMobil, and Sinopec to expand and rehabilitate the Quanzhou oil refinery in Fujian province, to be able to process heavier sour Saudi crude oil, among other grades. This initiative should be followed through and extended, and policy-makers could consider linking further incentives and encouragement to build even greater flexibility into the refining industry's processing capability. Greater technical flexibility would enable refineries to seek out poorer-quality crude oils that may be more readily available in an emergency to meet the market's needs.

Maintaining or Developing Fuel-switching Capabilities in Large Consuming Industries

Fuel-switching capabilities often exist in large energy-consuming industrial plants in countries that have deregulated energy commodity markets. For example, this capability often exists in thermal generating stations in areas where different fuels—coal, fuel oil, and natural gas—are available. Many owners of such plants have found it worthwhile to make the additional investment in order to be able to play the market for different fuels. Fuel-switching capability is usually considered for commercial reasons, but it could be encouraged and used to secure supply in emergency cases.

One geographic area where fuel switching for power generation has been important is in the New England area of the United States, where switching is used for electric power generation. Where such equipment exists, it can usefully add to the security of oil supply by enabling the release of oil or gas to other consumers who do not have such capability. However, it may be costly to build some types of fuel-switching capability into a plant, especially because fuel suppliers may have to make related investments. For example, it may require investments in gas pipelines that remain underused at times. The economic case for investment in such capacity requires careful consideration if the switching capability is specifically for security reasons.

Such options have not been considered or even explored in China, probably because of the strict controls on prices and fuel supply and because project approvals depend on initial capital cost, without consideration of risk mitigation and operational flexibility measures. However, if power subsector reform progresses as envisaged and if consumers have direct access to energy providers, international experience shows that they will consider such options to secure access to different segments of the energy market, thus increasing their bargaining power with energy suppliers.

Setting up Emergency Allocation Schemes

It is prudent for governments to have priority allocation schemes in times of scarce supply. These schemes are simpler and cheaper to operate than rationing programmes. Their purpose is to ensure that vital services—police and fire services, ambulances, and hospitals and clinics—have adequate oil supplies in the event of modest shortfalls. A second level of priority might be industrial and commercial transportation needs. At the lowest level might be fuel for discretionary travel requirements. Canada developed an allocation system in the 1970s and revised it in the early 1980s under the authority of its Energy Supplies Allocation Board. Although Canada has since mothballed the system, it could be readied for use at relatively short notice.

No information is available on what China may be doing about emergency allocation programs. The international consensus seems to be that an emergency allocation system is a desirable element of national measures to deal with temporary oil or gas shortages. Allocation systems can minimise economic losses and disruption to vital social and emergency networks and are relatively easy and inexpensive to create.

Establishing Rationing Systems for Oil Products

A rationing system, which would require that consumers present both cash and rights in order to acquire oil products in an emergency, is a complex and controversial project in modern industrial societies. No doubt, it could be managed more easily now, using information technology, than it could be in the era of ration coupons. Nevertheless, it may be too complex a project to embark on after an emergency has already occurred.

In developing a comprehensive energy policy framework, the government needs to decide whether it is worth designing a rationing system for oil products to be held in reserve for emergency use. An alternate, and probably more suitable, approach is to rely on the price mechanism for rationing, combined with a limited allocation program that ensures priority for the fuel needs of emergency services.

Engaging in International Cooperation for Short-term Oil Security

China is now recognised as a major player in world oil markets, and its influence is increasing in natural gas markets. Most industrial countries and major industry players in the market see the need to engage, rather than antagonise, China. This attitude is reflected in the way in which the IEA, the world's leading energy consumer group, and Saudi Arabia, the major producer in OPEC, are both engaging the government of China to address global issues related to energy production and consumption. Political will on all sides should focus on mutually beneficial cooperation that can help bring stability to oil and gas markets. The following paragraphs briefly address areas of actual and potential global, regional, and bilateral cooperation.

Global multilateralism: The International Energy Agency: The oil market is a global one. Any major disruption of supplies that is significantly greater than the worldwide industry's spare production capacity, that lasts for a substantial period of time, and that exceeds the industry's immediate capacity to draw down stocks will therefore have global impacts on oil volumes and prices. In today's interdependent world, no trading country is likely to avoid the risk of economic harm, no matter how well prepared it may be in terms of strategic stocks. Also, countermeasures to deal with the causes and effects of oil disruption, such as price spikes, are much more effective if taken collectively. The Organisation for Economic Co-operation and Development has recognised these two factors, which underlie the creation, in November 1974, of the IEA[23] out of a desire "to promote secure oil supplies on reasonable and equitable terms".[24]

The member countries of the IEA commit to hold emergency oil stocks equivalent to 90 days worth of net oil imports. They also agree to take effective cooperative measures to meet any oil supply emergency (see Box 8). At the same time, over the long term, members strive to reduce their vulnerability to an oil supply disruption. The means to attain this objective include increased energy efficiency; conservation; and development of coal, natural gas, nuclear power, and renewable energy sources, with a strong emphasis on technology.[25]

Formal consultation of a general nature between China and the IEA began in 1994. A memorandum of policy understandings was signed in 1996. The IEA continues to pursue technical contacts and dialogue with those responsible for China's energy policy. The IEA and China have maintained a liaison on security matters and emergency response, particularly since 2002.

BOX 8

The IEA's Approach to Short-term Oil Emergencies

The IEA maintains two approaches to dealing with short-term international oil emergencies. The first, created in 1974, is the Emergency Oil Sharing System (EOSS). The EOSS is based on predefined triggers that activate the system and uses prescribed arithmetic approaches to determine how scarce supplies of imported oil should be allocated among members of the

IEA. There have been several paper exercises of the EOSS, and it has been triggered once, for a short time and on a very small scale. Currently, the system is regarded as too mechanistic and inflexible for use in the event of a major international supply crisis.

The second approach, the Coordinated Emergency Response Measures (CERM), was developed in 1984 to take account of lessons learned during the Iranian revolution and the Iran-Iraq War. The CERM approach includes demand restraint, surge production, fuel switching, and equitable allocation of scarce Supplies among member countries. These measures now take priority over the more narrowly based EOSS provided for in the International Energy Program agreement. When the CERM approach was reviewed in 1994, IEA ministers expressed the view that coordinated stock draws can be a rapid and effective means of restoring interrupted supply, particularly in the early stages of a disruption, but that effective decisions on the stock draw cannot be made in advance of the disruption.

The IEA's Standing Group on Emergency Questions provides an international forum for discussing emergency issues, for planning to deal with them, and for : exchanging information. This Joint Oil Data Initiative—which involves governments, IOCs, and NOCs from IEA and non-IEA countries, OPEC other producers, and consumers and regional associations—provides information exchange on a broader scale. The point is that everyone becomes more secure.

Source: Based on information from the IEA Information Centre.

Consultation and cooperation with the other industrial countries—bilaterally and, particularly, in the IEA context—is clearly important and valuable for all parties. China does not need to be a member of IEA for this activity to be effective in helping meet the country's supply security objectives. The same is likely true even in the event of a global supply emergency, when coordinated actions with international organisations can be achieved without formal membership. However, regional markets could face localised disruption or security issues that require specific measures. East Asia—and more generally Asia—contributes the lion's share in the growth of world energy demand, particularly in the oil and gas markets. The common interests of the East Asian countries require intensified regional cooperation to reduce the cost of energy security and take advantage of their proximity to regions well endowed with supplies.

The industrial countries, individually and through the IEA, attach high value to international energy and oil cooperation for two principal reasons. First, they generally subscribe to the view that markets can work effectively for energy and for oil as for other commodities and that barriers to efficient energy trade should be removed to enable the optimal functioning of markets. Second, they have had favorable experience with such cooperation; for example, in 1990 and 1991 during the Iraq-Kuwait War. The IOCs understandably take a similar view. The Shell Group has recently tried to quantify the outcomes, in terms of global economic growth, of market-oriented versus alternative approaches to dealing with energy security, while addressing social justice and efficiency objectives (these are what Shell calls a "trilemma"). Its conclusion is that global economic growth would be highest where energy security is achieved by heightened investment, consumer countries strike win-win deals with producers, and energy prices include the cost of environmental effects. This work is summarized in Box 9.

Regional multilateralism: Asia Pacific Economic Cooperation: APEC, a younger, less structured organisation than IEA, is a group of circum-Pacific countries, which includes such energy heavyweights as Canada, China, Indonesia, Japan, Mexico, and the United States.[26] Energy issues, including security of supply, have attracted much attention, from the ministerial level down to subcommittees. So far, specific joint actions to improve security have not been agreed on, possibly because key members—Australia, Canada, Japan, and the United States, for example—see global multilateralism as the most effective means to address supply security. They are therefore already heavily involved in the IEA and might see APEC activity as possibly diluting the IEA's key role here.

Regional Multilateralism: Association of Southeast Asian Nations: China is not a member of the Association of Southeast Asian Nations (ASEAN) but has from time to time taken part in its activities.[27] For example, China, together with Japan and the Republic of Korea, which are also non-members, attended a joint ASEAN energy ministers' meeting in June 2004. ASEAN ministers welcomed China's initiative to establish a national oil stockpile programme, looked forward to the technical assistance of Japan and the Republic of Korea on stockpiling matters, pledged concerted efforts to address regional oil market issues, and promised to address issues in natural gas development. Ministers also said they would pursue dialogues and partnerships outside the region, particularly with Middle Eastern oil-producing countries. These issues are all areas of interest and importance to China.

BOX 9

The Shell Group's Latest Energy Security Scenarios

Scenarios are "stories of equally plausible futures". They help governments and corporations make strategic decisions that will be sound for all plausible futures. The Shell Group of companies developed scenario planning in the 1970s. In June 2005, Shell launched new global scenarios that look forward to 2025. The search for energy security remains a key consideration, in Shell's view, which is summarised in the following points.

- Security covers physical supplies threatened by international insecurity and depletion of supply sources.
- Insecurity can arise from lack of investment in existing energy sources, new energy sources and infrastructure.
- Approaches to addressing energy security are affected by different attitudes to globalisation:
  - — In *low-trust globalisation,* security is achieved by proactive policies that diversify supply and reduce vulnerability to external shocks, but OPEC supports high prices and restricts investment (global growth: 3.1 per cent).
  - — In *open doors,* security is achieved by increased investment, win-win deals between consumers and producers, and energy prices that internalise environmental effects (global growth: 3.8 per cent).
  - — In *flags* (nationalism), security becomes a routine part of diplomatic and military relations; consumers trade secure markets for secure supplies (no growth estimate).

Source: Schwartz 1996

Regional Multilateralism: Northeast Asia Energy Cooperation: There may be a valuable opportunity for regional multilateralism of a different sort in northeast Asia among countries such as China, Japan, the Democratic People's Republic of Korea, the Republic of Korea, Mongolia, and Russia. Such cooperation could, for example, harness the markets, technology, and capabilities for capital accumulation of China, Japan, and the Republic of Korea to the development of Russia's Siberian and Pacific energy sources. It would involve technology transfer, investment in energy development, transit arrangements with Mongolia and eventually the Democratic People's Republic of Korea, transportation infrastructure, and consequent trade flows. This security-enhancing cooperation is, of course, different in kind than the policy measures and joint actions in emergency circumstances that have been developed by the IEA. A successful international legal framework for investment and trade in energy, resulting in enhanced confidence, has been developed under the Energy Charter Treaty.[28] The treaty has been ratified by Japan, Mongolia is a full contracting party, and China and the Republic of Korea have observer status. One upshot of the January 2006 Russia-Ukraine gas dispute, which entailed transit pipeline issues, was a request that Russia should ratify the treaty, something that the Russian government has promised to examine.

Bilateral international relations: It is clearly important for China to continue developing and enhancing strong bilateral relations with energy-exporting nations. Bilateral relations are important not only in the Middle East, from which China presently obtains about half its imports, but also in Russia (Siberia), the Central Asian countries (Kazakhstan and Turkmenistan), the Caucasus (Azerbaijan), and Africa (CNPC is the operator and major owner of the largest oil-producing business in Sudan). To judge from the level and frequency of contacts, Latin American countries such as Brazil, Mexico, and the República Bolivariana de Venezuela are all becoming important partners in China's international energy policy. Diplomatic initiatives are often followed by investments by China's NOCs. In this context, CNPC now operates in 32 countries. Not surprisingly, Chinese interests in such areas as Russia, Central Asia, Africa, and the Middle East come up against powerful economic competition.

Bilateral relations are also important with other Asian importing countries, such as India and Pakistan. A reasonable goal for this relationship is not simply to make the supply of energy more secure but to manage, with other Asian giants, the geopolitical implications of China's large and growing energy needs.

Options for Securing Electricity Supply

Despite the tremendous growth of installed electricity capacity in China and the expansion of the transmission system since the early 1980s, the reliability of electricity services in China remains low compared with systems in the industrial countries and even some developing countries. Though difficult to quantify, the economic losses that resulted from power shortages in the 1980s and from 2003 to 2006 are significant, especially in the high-growth regions of the country. For example, it is estimated that economic losses caused by power shortages in Zhejiang amounted to about Y (yuan) 100 billion in 2004.

In March 2002, the State Council issued a decree separating generation plants from transmission and distribution systems. The result, in the absence of well-functioning markets, is a greater disconnect between the development of generation capacity and the development of transmission networks. The events in the United States of September 11, 2001, brought policy-makers' attention to security issues related to intentional damages to generation and transmission installations, beyond the vandalism and pilfering of equipment that often takes place in developing countries.

Securing electricity supply requires increasing the reliability of the electricity industry in China, through more effective and coordinated planning beyond the requirements of the five-year plan for generation, transmission, and distribution. In addition, China needs to improve operation and maintenance procedures as well as develop measures to limit intentional damage to equipment and ensure rapid restoration in case of deliberate attempts to destroy them.[29]

Improving Planning and Maintenance Procedures

Despite some highly visible blackouts, the reliability of electricity services in industrial countries improved significantly during the past decades. Reliability improvements stemmed mainly from technological progress, better interconnection of the systems, increasingly sophisticated forecasting and system planning methodologies, and greater focus on preventive maintenance. However, in recent years, utilities in industrial countries have begun to face serious challenges from customers, such as information technology firms and services providers, whose equipment is particularly sensitive to the quality and continuity of electricity services. These challenges clearly indicate the need to tailor reliability criteria to the specific conditions of the system and the needs of clients.

Improving the reliability of electricity services in China requires improved planning procedures at the generation, transmission, and distribution levels. It also requires increased reliance on preventive maintenance and more flexibility in the project approval process, to allow utilities to better respond to clients' needs for more reliable electricity supply. In China, electricity generation planning suffers from a greater focus on supply than on demand, ad hoc and project-based approval procedures, and a lack of economically and technically justified criteria. Project approval rarely is based on comprehensive, long-term system development studies. Forecasts focus on energy (kilowatt-hours) rather than on loads (kilowatts) and are usually limited to the time horizons of the five-year plans, with no possibility of adjustment during the plan period. These forecasts are based on normative electricity consumption per unit of product for the main industrial sectors, which still account for more than 70 per cent of total consumption.

The planning process does not take into account structural changes of load curves, and the result often is less than optimal investment in peaking capacity. Engineering criteria rarely result from cost-benefit analyses and are not adapted to the specific conditions of the systems. As a result, power systems experience successive boom and bust periods and chronic power shortages. The recent adoption of better planning processes at the utility level has not brought about the expected improvements in reliability. Most provinces have experienced power shortages because of inadequate and short-sighted forecasting, combined with unchanged project approval procedures.

Reliability issues in China are compounded by underdeveloped or inadequately designed transmission systems, mainly because of weaknesses in the planning procedures or the existence of price controls. In China, transmission and distribution systems are developed on an ad hoc basis because they are funded mainly through connection fees. Utilities tend to minimise funding from their own resources or borrowing because strict price controls do not allow them to pass full costs to end users.

The separation of generation from transmission and distribution in China has further deteriorated the power system's planning environment because of the lack of cooperation between generators and network companies. If not addressed through proper regulation, the situation could deteriorate even further. Recent experience in the United States indicates that with the increased deregulation during the 1990s, the development of transmission capacity lagged the growth of generation capacity. One reason for this disconnect was the reluctance of the owners of generation capacity "to reveal their plans for new construction and retirement of existing units any sooner than they have to."

The development of competitive markets in the United States during the 1990s prompted the Federal Energy Regulatory Commission to emphasise the importance of transmission planning on a regional basis. This emphasis led to the creation of regional transmission organizations, with planning (including expansion planning) as one of their eight minimum required functions.[30] However, traditional approaches to planning proved difficult to change because of the vested interests and resistance of the incumbent utilities and the state regulators who traditionally supervised the electric supply industry.

Inadequate planning is likely to be more costly for China because of the rapid growth of the power subsector. To prevent deterioration of the reliability of electricity supply during the transition period from command and control to more market-oriented management of the power industry, China urgently needs to review planning procedures at the generation, transmission, and distribution levels. Although it will take time to reform the project approval process, investment decisions for the five-year plans need to be based on a longer-term vision of the development of the sector. In particular, these plans should integrate structural changes of the load curves, demand-side alternatives to building new capacity, and technological innovation, in order to meet the demand at the least cost and in an environmentally acceptable manner. Reliability criteria should be based on the specific conditions of the different grids and on consumer willingness to pay the costs to meet them. This activity requires the involvement of and coordination among all parties concerned, including utilities at national, regional, and provincial levels. This coordination should include institutes and agencies involved in the development of engineering and reliability standards as well as the planning, environmental, and regulatory agencies.

Better maintenance procedures and increased reliance on preventive maintenance are essential to the dependability of the systems. The coordination of maintenance schedules and procedures also could contribute to increasing the reliability of supply. Furthermore, utilities should devise plans for rapid restoration of service in case of equipment failure. These plans, including emergency allocation schemes, need to be discussed with the authorities concerned to enable them to understand the system constraints and avoid undue interference in case of local interruptions of service. Assistance and mutual support among separate grids need to be discussed and agreed on to avoid domino effects and minimise supply interruptions in case of major blackouts. Most of these measures already exist; they need to be coordinated and codified to improve the reliability of China's power supply.

Improving the Security of Power Systems

As discussed earlier, the need to ensure the physical security of power installations has emerged since the September 11, 2001, attacks in the United States. "Electric service has become a necessity not only in the lives of individuals, but also in the operation of public services; e.g., water supply, sewage disposal, communications, transportation, health activities". Many industrial countries have developed protection measures for the most sensitive installations, such as nuclear power plants. The United States and other countries are considering further security measures to reduce the vulnerability of power systems to attack. These measures include extending protection to installations that are critical to the integrity of the system, sectionalising transmission systems into separate entities to avoid domino effects and extensive blackouts in case of failure or damage to parts of the system, and reducing the visibility of power installations.

It is clear that protection of the installations, changes in the design of power systems, and development of measures to minimise restoration time will increase the construction and operating costs of power systems. Experience in countries affected by political disturbances indicates that substantial increases in project costs have resulted with the transfer of security operation for installations (not specifically power or energy) to investors and project operators. "The usual economic considerations may have to be strained to new limits, and in some instances ignored".

What is true for energy supply systems in general is also true for the electricity industry: security of supply can be improved by demand-side options that make the best use of available capacity, by geographic and fuel-type diversity of supply, and by improved system planning. These means to improve the security of power systems are simply provided for reference purposes. They could more properly be considered aspects of integrated resource planning, power system design, and electricity demand management.

As for oil products, emergency electricity allocation schemes should be considered—to determine priority allocations in times of scarce supply and to prevent collapse of the system and ensure that vital services have adequate electricity supply.

Choosing the Right Mix and Amount of Energy Supply Security Measures

Policy-makers will have to decide, for each source of energy, what is likely to be the most effective mix of measures to enhance the security of supply. Some options to choose from have been provided in this chapter (see Box 10). Each set of mixes will need to be reviewed from time to time as national and international circumstances change.

Policy-makers will also have to decide what amount of security they should aim to buy on behalf of consumers. For example, the likelihood is that a useful degree of security against a short-term partial oil import disruption can be achieved by a relatively small investment in such measures as stockpiling and emergency allocation. To achieve a similar degree of security against the extreme and unlikely case of total, long-term disruption of oil imports would require huge investments. Beyond a point, security investments may yield diminishing returns and at the same time face declining acceptance in the society and a decreasing ability of the economy to pay for security measures.

It is not possible to arrive at a quantitative measurement of security of energy supply. Instead, against the background of assessments of the changing risks to energy security, trade-offs will have to be made between security costs and benefits. The result of successful trade-offs will be the establishment of a comfort zone within which the value of enhanced security approximates the cost of providing it and the relationship of these two variables is stable.[31]

BOX 10

Strengthening China's Energy Security: China's Special Concern

Rising oil imports mean that China's oil supply will be out of China's political control. Policy measures are necessary to strengthen China's energy security.

Measures to Strengthen Long-term Energy Security

China should foster national energy resources development with an emphasis on clean energy (natural gas and renewables) and on more reliance on market forces. These measures will help strengthen the country's energy security in the long term:

- Encourage development of national oil and gas resources through improving access to undeveloped resources, rationalising fiscal terms for their development, and clarifying the role of national and international oil companies.
- Secure imports through diplomatic and trade relationships (with the Middle East for oil and with Russia for gas).

Measures to Strengthen Short-term Oil Security

China also needs to strengthen its oil security in the short-term. It can do so through these measures:

- Maintain oil stocks above minimun commercial requirements by developing a strategic petroleum reserve, mandating minimum commercial stocks, maintaining spare domestic oil production capacity (an assessment of domestic industry's capacity is needed), and providing military protection for oil traffic in the chokepoints of international tanker lanes.
- Build flexibility into the oil refining industry.

Contd...

Contd...box 10

- Maintain or develop fuel-switching capabilities in large consuming industries.
- Set up emergency allocation schemes.
- Establish rationing systems for oil products.
- Increase international cooperation at global-regional, and bilateral levels.

At present, flaws in the power planning system are causing bottlenecks. Deregulation of the power industry will lead to California syndrome concerns.

Options for Better Security of Electric Power Supply

Several alternatives exist for better security of electricity:

- Improve planning and maintenance procedures.
- Integrate resource planning and implement demand-side management.
- Improve physical security of power systems by identifying and protecting critical infrastructure.

Overall Approach to Strengthening Security

An overall approach to strengthening security should begin with these steps:

- Assess the full range of security policy measures.
- Select the most cost-effective mix for the conditions of the time.
- Revisit the chosen mix of measures as national and international circumstances change.

REFERENCES

1. This study focuses on commercial energy. However, biomass played and will continue to play an important role in China.
2. *Elasticity of energy demand* is the rate of energy growth divided by the rate of economic growth. It is a simple, easily measured, but very rough reflection of the relationship of energy to economic growth. It should be stressed that understanding the relationship between energy and economic growth requires more detailed and disaggregated analyses.
3. *Energy intensity* is the amount of energy input to produce a unit of economic output. At the macro-level discussed in this study, it is expressed in terms of grams (tons) of coal equivalent of primary energy per yuan (per Y 1,000) of GDP (constant).
4. Projections published more recently are in the same range. For example, Li (2003) projects 2020 energy consumption of 2,800 mtce under a business-as-usual scenario.
5. The DRC and ERI projections and the U.S. DOE projections were prepared in 1999 and 2000. The IEA projections are more recent but do not have comparable scenarios; IEA's 2002 reference scenario projections of energy consumption were revised upward in 2004.
6. Unless otherwise noted, comparisons in the study are based on IEA (2002, 2004). Comparisons are useful, but they should be considered only as approximations because of the different energy accounting systems used by China (and other countries) and the IEA.
7. A study by the IEA (2004) concluded "In every country studied, except China, the combination of capital, labour, and energy contributed more to economic growth than did productivity increases."

However, questions were raised about China's productivity improvement, the largest in the group: "There are doubts about the accuracy of China's official GDP data. Many studies have concluded that the official statistics understate GDP and overstate growth rates" (IEA 2004).

8. In the reference scenario in IEA (2004), China's incremental consumption between 2000 and 2020 accounts for 18.5 per cent of global incremental consumption.

9. Some Chinese experts observe that synthetic fuel production could be as high as 70 million tons by 2020. The study team considers these estimates highly overstated.

10. Report of the DRC and ERI.

11. This study focuses on China, but international cooperation should also include, India, the other Asian giant.

12. Economic growth in the industrial countries (those of Western Europe, as well as Japan and the United States) was significantly impaired by the energy crises of 1973 to 1974 and 1979 to 1980. Countries were affected by energy shortages, supply uncertainties, inflation resulting from energy price spikes, and arguably by governments' mismanagement of their national energy economies.

13. One assessment by Taylor and Van Doren 2005 finds that the cost of the nearly 700 million barrels in the U.S. Strategic Petroleum Reserve over its 30-year life, allowing for inflation and a modest return on investment, has been US$41 billion to US$51 billion—between US$65 and US$80 on a per barrel basis. The oil currently in storage had a purchase cost much less than the present world price. Yet on many occasions, the oil stored has cost much more than the spot price for the corresponding grade.

14 There have been many public comments on the dispute. One of them is by the well-regarded Oxford Institute for Energy Studies.

15. From 1985 onward, natural gas consumption in the United States recovered from the depressed levels of the era of excessive regulation, but it has been flat for several years.

16. The Bonn Conference on Renewable Energy gave rise to an international policy declaration on renewable energy, an international action programme, and a set of policy recommendations addressed to governments. See http://www.renewables2004.de/en/2004/outcome.asp.

17. The announcement of the scale-up programme can be found at / http://web.worldbank.org/WB SITE/EXTERNAL/COUNTRIES/EASTASIAPACIFICEXT/EXTEAPREGTOPENVIRONMENT/0,contentMDK:20545709~menuPK:502932~pagePK:34004173~piPK:34003707~theSitePK:502886,00.html. Details in Chinese are at http://www.worldbank.org.cn/Chinese/Projects/projects.htm.

18. *The Wall Street Journal* on March 7, 2006, reported remarks by Mr. Ma Kai of NDRC to the effect that, although the first of four strategic oil storage facilities had been completed, fill operations were going to be deferred to the end of 2006 in view of the current high price of international oil supplies.

19. Global steel prices have, however, been declining since the summer of 2005.

20. The reserve is under the authority of the president of the United States. In September 2005, President Bush authorised the release of U.S. Strategic Petroleum Reserve crude oil to help overcome shortages caused by damage to production facilities during Hurricane Katrina. The volumes actually released appear to have been small— about 11 million barrels out of a total reserve of some 688 million.

21. It should be noted that the Suez Canal is another potential choke-point. No significant flow of oil to China comes through the canal. However, the canal is of global significance and therefore of importance to China's security of oil supply, because an interruption of oil flow through Suez Canal would create a worldwide tanker shortage that would affect China.

22. A paper published by the South Asia Analysis Group (Kuppuswamy 2004) states "The security of the Straits of Malacca is an international issue, and safe passage has to be guaranteed under international law. Hence it is not correct to say that only the littoral states have the right to deal with issues concerning the security of this waterway."
23. The IEA is the institutional vehicle for implementation of the 1974 Agreement on an International Energy Programme. The Emergency Oil-Sharing System is embedded in the International Energy Programme.
24. This quote is from the Preamble to the Agreement on an International Energy Programme, dated November 18, 1974. The full text of the agreement can be found at http://www.iea.org/Textbase/about/IEP.PDF.
25. The basic IEA position on energy policy is contained in the document "Shared Goals," which was agreed to in June 1993 by the IEA ministers. The document states, "Improved energy efficiency can promote both environmental protection and energy security in a cost-effective manner" and goes on to relate achievement of these objectives to "Continued research, development, and market deployment of new and improved energy technologies" that can "make a critical contribution to achieving the objectives outlined." Although the document is now 13 years old, it still forms the basis of the IEA's collective energy policies.
26. APEC's research arm, the Asia Pacific Energy Research Center, has provided background advice to APEC ministers in a report titled "Energy Security Initiative: Emergency Oil Stocks as an Option to Respond to Oil Supply Disruptions". The report concluded that emergency oil stocks can contribute usefully to supply security and recommended that emergency oil stocks be separated from commercial ones, that the costs of emergency stocks be internalised in oil products prices (rather than subsidised), and that APEC members coordinate policy. APEC has not yet made any specific policy decisions on oil supply security measures. APEC's Energy Working Group is researching alternative ways to plan for regional emergencies or natural disasters such as the 2004 tsunami.
27. ASEAN member countries are Brunei, Cambodia, Indonesia, the Lao People's Democratic Republic, Malaysia, Myanmar, the Philippines, Singapore, Thailand, and Vietnam.
28. http://www.encharter.org.
29. In this section, a differentiation is made between the reliability of electricity supply and the security of electricity supply. "Reliability encompasses contingencies resulting from flaws in design and human errors; security tends to negate damage and destruction of property and injury or death to humans deliberately caused by other humans."
30. The eight minimum functions of regional transmission organisations, as prescribed by the Federal Energy Regulatory Commission, are transmission tariff administration and design; congestion management; parallel path flow; ancillary services provider of last resort; administration of open access same-time information systems; market monitoring; planning, including of expansions; and interregional coordination.
31. The European Union provides an example of change over time in the security comfort zone for oil supply. For 30 years (1968-98), it was satisfied with a requirement that member countries hold stocks equivalent to 65 days worth of consumption of the major oil products. In 1998, this stockholding requirement was increased to 90 days. Currently, an increase to 120 days is being considered.

4

India's Energy Policy: Requirements and Constraints

India's Energy Requirements

By the world standards, India's current level of energy consumption is very low. For the year 2004-05, the total annual energy consumption for India is estimated at 572 Mtoe (million tons oil equivalent) and the per capita consumption at 531 kgoe (kilograms oil. equivalent). However, with a targeted GDP growth rate of 7 to 8 per cent, and an estimated energy elasticity of 0.80, the energy requirements of the country are expected to grow at 5.6-6.4 per cent per annum over the next few years. This implies a four-fold increase in India's energy requirement over the next 25 years and, hence, the country faces significant challenges in meeting this.

India is well-endowed with coal. However, it is poorly endowed with oil assets and has to depend on crude imports to meet a major share of its needs (around 71 per cent).[1]

India's composition of energy sources and usage

The pie-graph reflects only primary energy sources that are commercially exploited. The following diagram depicts the estimated reserves for various energy sources:

Different demand-side and supply-side scenarios have been developed by India's Planning Commission to meet the future energy requirements. These scenarios look at energy efficiency as well as supply side option:

- Fully exploiting India's hydro potential of 150,000 MW from current level of 32,326 MW
- Scaling up nuclear generation by successfully developing the Fast Breeder Reactor (FBR) technology (which uses uranium as fuel) and developing Advance Heavy Water Reactor for utilising thorium (of which India has abundant reserves).

The usage of such sources of energy is estimated at around 143 Mtoe per annum or approximately 44 per cent of total primary energy use (*Source:* Planning Commission, Government of India).

Future Energy Requirements and Supply Options

Coal is expected to continue to be the dominant energy resource. However, India would have to actively develop non-coal sources given that at a growth rate of 5 per cent in coal production, India's extractable coal reserves would get exhausted in 458 years.

Therefore, from a long-term perspective and in view of growing environmental concerns from use of coal, the country needs to look at developing alternate sources such as nuclear energy.

India has vast reserves of the nuclear fuel thorium but the technology is not yet fully developed for its commercial use.

India's oil assets are meagre but recent discoveries hold promise for India's gas reserves and coal bed methane.

Renewable energy currently contributes small fraction and it is expected to grow very rapidly especially in areas like wind and solar power. In the short-term, renewable energy would play an important role of supplementing the total energy requirement.

Over the longer term, its importance would be more strategic so that the efficient use of energy in industry, lighting, household appliances etc. can lower India's energy needs by 142 Mtoe in 2031-32 (or 7.5 per cent of the total energy requirement).

- **Increase in rail road share of freight:** Currently, road transport carries a major portion of freight traffic. If the share of railways in freight increases from the current level of 32 per cent to 50 per cent by 2031-32, it would contribute towards an energy saving of 34 Mtoe in 2031-32 (or 1.8 per cent of the total energy requirement).
- **Increase in transportation efficiency:** Use of mass transport system in cities, better utilisation of motor vehicles (such as vehicle pooling) and increase in fuel efficiency of motor vehicles (possible to the extent of 50 per cent with, current technology) can save about 81 Mtoe of energy by 2031-32 (or 4.3 per cent of the total energy requirement).
- **Efficiencies in thermal power generation:** Currently, the efficiencies of thermal generation in India stand at 30.5 per cent. An increase to 38-40 per cent through use of super critical boiler technologies could lead to a savings of 111 Mtoe in 2031-32 (or 5.8 per cent of the total energy requirement).

Together the energy efficiency measures can save 351 Mtoe of energy or around 19 per cent of India's energy requirements by 2031-32. The supply side options include:

Exploration of Oil and gas and using it for electricity generation -either through indigenous exploration or through pipeline import and LNG.

- Development of renewable energy sources, including solar power through cost-effective photovoltaic technology, fuel wood, bio-diesel and wind energy.

Key Imperatives for India

To meet its large and growing energy needs, there are certain key imperatives for the Indian energy sector:

Private sector investment needs to complement the public sector: Reliability of energy supply and its cost will be key determinants of both, economic growth and social uplift. Achieving this will require significant investment of capital as well as of capabilities.

The private sector will necessarily need to complement the public sector in both areas. The Government policies continue to lay emphasis on enabling a higher level of private sector participation.

Sectoral reforms are aimed at attracting private investment and efficiency, through different forms of competitive markets. A large part of the power sector, for example, will become contestable by 2008, opening up a USD 5 bn market. Overall, the investment needed in the Indian energy sector is to the tune of USD 120 to 150 bn over the next five years. To encourage private investment, clarity and stability in policy framework is essential as will be performance.

Encourage market mechanisms with credible and independent track records: The benefits of market mechanisms in bringing in production and resource allocation efficiencies are needed.

Market mechanisms will also encourage investments as it will tend to minimise the regulatory risks. However, the market mechanisms have to be introduced gradually as supply side situation improves.

Currently, with the huge deficit in energy products, market mechanisms are likely to get abused if not managed to some degree by an independent regulatory oversight.

Reduce vulnerability to price and supply shocks: The Indian energy basket is weighted towards coal (51 per cent) and oil (36 per cent). From a long-term energy security perspective, it is necessary to diversify the energy basket. For example, if the known coal reserves are expected to exhaust in about 40 years, it would be a challenge to replace 51 per cent of the energy basket. Diversification would mean increasing the share of natural gas, nuclear and hydro energy apart from a strategic thrust towards renewable energy.

The other issue is vulnerability to price shocks. Vulnerability to price shocks are addressed by diversifying the fuel basket, enhancing domestic production of energy and in initiatives such as taking equity positions in energy resources abroad.

We are seeing a positive trend in all these areas. Nuclear, natural gas and hydro power are getting the required impetus. Domestic production is being enhanced with initiatives on private participation.

Bringing in efficiency and enhancing capacity in energy transport infrastructure: In India, there is a high degree of inter-regional disparity in terms of energy sources and the growth centres.

Significant initiatives are underway to enable investment in ports and railway infrastructure to move coal, pipelines and storage network for oil and gas, and transmission network for electricity.

Enhanced transmission capacity will also enable holistic exploitation of the Himalayan hydro resources in Himachal Pradesh, Uttaranchal and the North Eastern states, as also in Nepal and Bhutan.

For this purpose, private participation in energy transport sector is actively being promoted. Private investment in ports, dedicated freight corridors, pipelines and power transmission has already begun to take place.

Tariff reform and power sector reform: This is one of the most difficult and important area as far as the energy sector is concerned.

Prices of electricity and some of the other energy products are highly distorted thereby promoting inefficient end-use and sometimes even inefficient energy choices. For example, power, kerosene and domestic gas are highly subsidised for the BPL families. There have been various policy measures to address this and to some degree of success.

However, the challenge is in implementation and bringing in the required political will to address this issue. Power sector reform on the distribution front is another key area where progress has been slow.

Provide Government Support for Energy Efficiency

The Government needs to create a policy framework that provides incentives for energy efficiency. This could, for example, mean providing incentives in urban areas for mass transport systems and promoting R&D in energy efficiency.

The environment should encourage energy efficiency companies to come up and operate profitably. In parallel, India is also emerging as an active market in terms of Clean Development Mechanism (CDM) projects being conceptualised and registered with the Executive Board (EB).

The growing awareness of the CDM benefits would make this an important area for investments. CDM should also give the necessary fillip for energy efficiency measures.

Coal is expected to continue to be the dominant energy resource. However, India would have to actively develop non-coal sources given that at a growth rate of 5 per cent in coal production, India's extractable coal reserves would get exhausted in 458 years.

India's Energy Facts

The Indian energy sector requires investments to the tune of USD 120-150 billion over the next five years.[2] Thirty-eight coal fields with mineable coal reserves in excess of 2,800 million tonnes have been identified and are in the process of being allocated for captive mining. Six rounds of competitive bidding under the Government policy, named New Exploration Licensing

Policy (NELP), have already been done, around 185 blocks were awarded and reserves estimated at 700 MMT2 of oil and gas have been discovered.

Discoveries of gas to the tune of 700 bcm in the last decade have meant that gas reserves hold promise in India. India has one of the largest reserves of the nuclear fuel—thorium. India is endowed with a hydroelectric potential of about 150,000 MW. The current installed capacity of renewable energy is around 92204 MW, constituting about 7.3 per cent of India's total installed generation capacity. A study conducted for the Asian Development Bank estimated an immediate energy saving potential of 54.500 million kWh and peak saving of 9,240 MW. This has an investment potential of USD 3 billion. The private sector participation is expected to be in projects requiring a capital outlay of around USD 4.5 billion.

India: Sixth Consumer of Energy in the World

India boasts a growing economy, and is increasingly a significant consumer of oil and natural gas

The Indian economy continues to show impressive growth. The country's real gross domestic product (GDP) grew at an impressive rate of 9.1 per cent during the first half of fiscal 2006 (April-September 2006), after growing by 8.7 per cent in fiscal 2005.

Together with the country's impressive growth, India has also become a significant consumer of energy resources. According to EIA estimates, India was the fifth largest consumer of oil in the world during 2006.

Oil

India is a growing net importer of oil. According to Oil and Gas Journal (OGJ), India had 5.6 billion barrels of proven oil reserves as of January 2007, the second-largest amount in the Asia-Pacific region (behind China).

India's crude oil reserves tend to be light and sweet, with specific gravity varying from 38° API in the offshore Mumbai (Bombay) High field to 32° API at other onshore basins. Much of India's crude oil reserves are located off the western coast (Mumbai High) and in the northeast of the country, although substantial undeveloped reserves are located in the offshore Bay of Bengal and in Rajasthan state.

The combination of rising oil consumption and fairly stable production levels leaves India increasingly dependent on imports to meet consumption needs. In 2006, the country produced an average of 846,000 barrels per day (bbl/d) of total oil liquids, of which 77 per cent, or 648,000 bbl/d, was crude oil.

During 2006, India consumed an estimated 2.63 million bbl/d of oil. EIA estimates that India registered oil demand growth of 100,000 bbl/d during 2006. EIA forecasts suggest the country will experience similar gains during 2007 and 2008.

Sector Organisation

India's oil sector is dominated by state-owned enterprises, although the government has taken steps in recent years to deregulate the hydrocarbons industry and encourage greater foreign involvement.

India's state-owned Oil and Natural Gas Corporation (ONGC) is the largest oil company, and also the country's largest company overall by market capitalisation. ONGC is the dominant player in India's upstream sector, accounting for roughly three-fourths of the country's oil output during 2006, according to Indian government estimates.

As a net importer of oil, the Indian government has introduced policies aimed at increasing domestic oil production and oil exploration activities. As a part of this effort, the Ministry of Petroleum and Natural Gas drafted the New Exploration Licensing Policy (NELP) in 2000, which for the first time permits foreign companies to hold 100 per cent equity ownership in oil and natural gas projects. However, to date, only a handful of oilfields are being operated by foreign firms.

India's downstream sector is also dominated by state-owned entities, although private companies have increased their market share in recent years.

The Indian Oil Corporation (IOC) is the largest state-owned company in the downstream sector, operating 10 of India's 17 refineries and controlling about three-quarters of the domestic oil transportation network. Reliance Industries, a private Indian firm, opened India's first privately-owned refinery in 1999, and has gained a considerable market share in India's oil sector.

Exploration and Production

The Indian government has held several licensing rounds under the NELP framework in an effort to promote exploration and production (E&P) activities and boost domestic oil production. To help meet growing oil demand, India has promoted various E&P projects over the last several years in an effort to boost domestic oil production.

The primary mechanism through which the Indian government has promoted new E&P projects has been the NELP framework. Between 2000 and 2005, the government awarded 110 oil and natural gas concessions in five separate licensing rounds. The sixth bidding round (known as NELP-VI) recently concluded, with 52 exploration blocks awarded. As in previous rounds, ONGC and other Indian National Oil Companies (NOCs) fared very well. ONGC secured a total of 25 exploration blocks, often in consortia with other Indian NOCs.

The privately-owned Reliance Industries secured seven deepwater blocks in the Krishna-Godavari and Mahanadi basins, which are considered to be some of India's most promising offshore hydrocarbon basins. The government is expected to formally sign Production Sharing Contracts (PSCs) for the 52 blocks in early 2007.

Notably absent on the list of bidders for the NELP-VI are international oil majors. The Indian government was keen to attract oil majors to utilise their vast deepwater experience and other technical expertise. Some industry publications suggest that the Indian government will now move to an open acreage system, in which domestic and international oil companies can apply for available E&P projects at any time, rather than licensing rounds.

Overseas Exploration and Production

In recent years, Indian NOCs have looked to acquire equity stakes in E&P projects overseas. The most active company is ONGC Videsh Ltd., the overseas investment arm of ONGC. As of January 2007, ONGC Videsh holds interests in 25 oil and natural gas projects in 15 countries, spanning Africa, Asia, Latin America, and the Middle East. One of ONGC Videsh's most high profile investments is its share in the Greater Nile Petroleum Operating Company (GNPOC), which has engaged in E&P work in Sudan since 1997.

ONGC Videsh acquired a 25 per cent equity stake in the company in 2003, with the balance held by the China National Petroleum Company (CNPC, 40 per cent), Petronas (30 per cent), and the Sudan National Oil Company (Sudapet, 5 per cent). The GNPOC acreage in Sudan holds proved crude oil reserves of more than one million barrels, and current production levels from the 8 main GNPOC fields exceeds 300,000 bbl/d. In addition to the upstream activities, the GNPOC companies operate a 935-mile crude oil pipeline that pumps oil to Port Sudan for export.

ONGC Videsh also holds a 20 per cent stake in the ExxonMobil-led consortium that operates the Sakhalin-1 project in Russia. According to company estimates, the oilfields associated with Sakhalin-1 hold recoverable crude oil reserves of 2.3 billion barrels.

Production at Sakhalin-1 started in October 2005, and is expected to reach 250,000 bbl/d in early 2007. Oil from the Sakhalin-1 project will be piped westward to the DeKastri terminal on the Russian mainland for export, while some crude oil will also be pumped into Russia's domestic pipeline system for local consumption.

Downstream/Refining

According to OGJ, India had 2.25 million bbl/d of refining capacity at 17 facilities as of January 2007. Only one refinery, Reliance Petroleum's plant at Jamnagar, is wholly owned by a private company. The Jamnagar facility is Reliance Petroleum's only current refinery, but it is India's largest, with a capacity of 660,000 bbl/d.

Reliance Petroleum is currently constructing a second facility at the Jamnagar site, which is expected to have a capacity of 580,000 bbl/d when completed in 2008. When finished, Jamnagar will be the largest refining complex in the world. IOC is the largest state-owned player in India's refining sector, with 620,000 bbl/d of refining capacity at 7 plants. The company announced expansion plans in October 2006 that call for doubling its refining capacity by 2012.

Refined Fuel Subsidies

Beginning in 2002, the Indian government introduced some measures aimed at deregulation in the downstream oil sector. Private refiners may now directly market some of their own petroleum products to their customers. Additionally, the government phased out the Administered Price Mechanism (APM) on oil products in 2002, replacing it with the new Market Determined Price Mechanism (MDPM).

However, while the MDPM is notionally benchmarked to international oil prices, the Indian government continues to heavily subsidise domestic fuel prices for consumers. The combination of high international crude oil prices and low domestic fuel rates has led some new refinery proposals to have an overt export focus, such as Reliance Petroleum's second Jamnagar facility.

In February 2006, the Indian government Issued a one-time relief subsidy of $1.3 billion to domestic refiners that faced financial difficulties due to capped fuel prices. In June 2006, the government also pushed through a small domestic fuel price increase, although rates remain well below competitive international levels.

Strategic Petroleum Reserve

Indian officials have declared that the country intends to develop a Strategic Petroleum Reserve (SPR). To date, plans have been approved for the construction of storage tanks with 36.7 million barrels of crude oil storage capacity, with several sites near Mangalore on the east coast being considered. Construction at the planned storage sites is expected to begin in early 2007. To date, the government has not reached a decision on when to fill the country's SPR tanks, or how large to build the reserves. The SPR project is being led by the Indian Strategic Petroleum Reserve Corporation Ltd., which is part of Oil Industry Development Board, a state-controlled organisation that manages loans and grants to the oil industry.

Natural Gas

Despite major new natural gas discoveries in recent years, India is considering large-scale imports via pipelines and LNG terminals to help meet growing demand. According to OGJ, India had 38 trillion cubic feet (Tcf) of proven natural gas reserves as of January 2007.

The bulk of India's natural gas production comes from the western offshore regions, especially the Mumbai High complex. The onshore fields in Assam, Andhra Pradesh, and Gujarat states are also major producers of natural gas. According to EIA data, India produced 996 Billion Cubic Feet (Bcf) of natural gas in 2004.

India imports small amounts of natural gas. In 2004, India consumed 1,089 Bcf of natural gas, the first year in which the country showed net natural gas imports. During 2004, India imported 93 Bcf of Liquefied Natural Gas (LNG) from Qatar.

Sector Organisation

As in the oil sector, India's state-owned companies account for the bulk of natural gas production. ONGC and Oil India Ltd. (OIL) are the largest companies by production volume, while some foreign companies participate in upstream developments in joint-ventures and Production Sharing Contracts (PSCs).

Reliance Industries, a privately-owned Indian company, will also have a greater role in the natural gas sector in the coming years, as a result of a large natural gas find in 2002 in the Krishna Godavari basin.

The Gas Authority of India Ltd. (GAIL) holds an effective monopoly on natural gas transmission and distribution activities. In December 2006, the Minister of Petroleum and Natural Gas issued a new policy that allows foreign investors, private domestic companies, and national oil companies to hold 100 per cent equity stakes in pipeline projects.

While GAIL's monopoly in natural gas transmission and distribution is not guaranteed by statute, it will continue to be the leading player in the sector because of its existing natural gas infrastructure (in 2004, GAIL piped 88 per cent of the natural gas consumed in India).

Exploration and Production

There have been several large natural gas finds in India over the last five years, predominantly in the offshore Bay of Bengal.

In December 2006, ONGC announced that it had found an estimated 21 to 22 Tcf of natural gas in place at the KG-DOWN-98/2 block off the coast of Andhra Pradesh in the Krishna Godavari basin. On the same day, ONGC announced another find in the Mahanadi basin off the coast of Orissa state, with an estimated 3 to 4 Tcf in place. Neither of these finds has been certified, but could potentially raise India's natural gas reserve levels significantly.

The discoveries also fit into the recent trend of large upstream developments in the Bay of Bengal, especially in the Krishna Godavari basin. State-owned Gujarat State Petroleum Corporation (GSPC) holds an estimated 20 Tcf of natural gas reserves in place at the KG-OSN-2001/3 block in the Krishna Godavari area. Reliance Industries recently secured government approval for the commercial development of the D-6 block in the Krishna Godavari basin, which holds 9 Tcf of recoverable natural gas reserves (14.5 Tcf total reserves in place). Under the development plan for the D-6 block, Reliance and its equity partner Niko Resources will spend $5.2 billion to bring the first natural gas to the market in 2009. At its peak, the D-6 block is expected to supply 2.8 Bcf/d of natural gas, which would more than double the country's current production level.

Despite these large natural gas finds, most analysts expect natural gas demand in India to outstrip new supply in the years ahead. Indian natural gas consumption has risen faster than any other fuel over the last five years.

ONGC has worked to maximise its recovery rate at the Mumbai High structure, which supplies the bulk of the country's natural gas at present. BG International and Reliance Industries are also jointly working to expand production at the Tapti, Panna, and Mukti fields in the Mumbai High basin. The companies currently produce 300 million cubic feet per day (MMcf/d) at these three fields, although they have not announced a target production level for the expanded project plans.

Natural Gas Imports

Analysts expect that India's natural gas import demand will increase in the coming years. To help meet this growing demand, a number of import schemes including both LNG and pipeline projects have either been implemented or considered.

Iran-Pakistan-India (IPI) Pipeline

India has considered various proposals for international pipeline connections with other countries. One such scheme is the Iran-Pakistan-India (IPI) Pipeline, which has been under discussion since 1994. The plan calls for a roughly 1,700-mile, 2.8-Bcf/d pipeline to run from the South Pars fields in Iran to the Indian state of Gujarat.

While Iran is keen to export its abundant natural gas resources and India is in search of projects to meet its growing domestic demand, a variety of economic and political issues have delayed a project agreement. Indian officials have made it clear that any import pipeline crossing Pakistan would need to be accompanied by a security guarantee from officials in Islamabad. Apart from security concerns, tripartite talks in December 2006 fell apart over natural gas pricing disputes. Both Indian and Pakistani officials refused Iran's proposed price of $8.00 per million Btu (MMBtu), stating that they would not pay more than $4.25/MMBtu (see the Iran and Pakistan Country Analysis Briefs for more information).

Turkmenistan-Afghanistan-Pakistan-India (TAPI) Pipeline

India has worked to join onto the Turkmenistan-Afghanistan-Pakistan Pipeline (TAP, and sometimes referred to as the Trans-Afghan Pipeline). The TAP project consists of a planned 1,050-mile pipeline originating in Turkmenistan's Dauletabad-Donmex natural gas fields and transporting the fuel to markets in Afghanistan, Pakistan, and possibly India. India was invited to join the TAP project in February 2006, and is expected to announce its formal entry into the scheme in late January 2007, at which point it would be known as the TAPI project. Initial plans for the TAPI call for the line to have a capacity between 2-3 Bcf/d at an estimated cost of $3.3 billion.

While India has publicly promoted this scheme in view of slow with Iran, the TAPI project faces a variety of hurdles. India has concerns about the security of the proposed line, which would traverse unstable regions in Afghanistan and Pakistan. Furthermore, a recent review of the TAPI project raised doubts that Turkmen natural gas supplies are adequate to meet its proposed export commitments.

Imports from Myanmar

A third international pipeline proposal envisions India importing natural gas from Myanmar. In March 2006, the governments of India and Myanmar signed a natural gas supply deal, although a specific pipeline route has yet to be determined. Initially, the two countries planned to build a pipeline that would cross Bangladesh. However, after indecision from Bangladeshi authorities over the plans, India and Myanmar have studied the possibility of building a pipeline that would terminate in the eastern Indian state of Tripura and not cross Bangladeshi soil.

Domestic Transmission System

While there are various proposals under discussion for natural gas import schemes into India, there are concerns that India's limited domestic transmission network will constrain natural gas consumption. Currently, much of GAIL's domestic transmission system is concentrated in the country's natural gas production centres, and there is little interconnection between regions. GAIL has announced an ambitious long-term plan to increase its transmission network from roughly 1,900 miles to 6,200 miles to establish a National Gas Grid. However, there are only a handful of actual expansion projects planned for the next few years.

Liquefied Natural Gas

Currently, India has two LNG import terminals, with several others that are planned or proposed. India started receiving LNG shipments in January 2004 with the start-up of the Dahej terminal in Gujarat state.

According to EIA data, India imported 93 Bcf of LNG in 2004, reaching 222 Bcf in 2005. Petronet LNG, a consortium of state-owned Indian companies and international investors, owns and operates the Dahej LNG facility.

The Dahej terminal has a capacity to handle 5 million metric tons per year (MMt/y, or about 975 Bcf/y) of LNG imports. Petronet LNG is also building a second LNG receiving terminal at Kochi, which is expected to have a capacity of 2.5 MMt/y (488 Bcf/y) when completed in 2009. India's second LNG terminal started operations in April 2005 near Surat in Gujarat state. The facility is owned by Hazira LNG, a joint venture of Shell and Total. The facility has an initial throughput capacity of 2.5 MMt/y, with the option of expanding that to 5 MMt/y in the future.

There are several other planned or proposed LNG facilities in India. A 5-MMt/y LNG processing plant in Dabhol was originally scheduled to come online in 2001, but was subsequently delayed after former owner Enron declared bankruptcy. In 2005, the Ratnagiri Gas and Power Company purchased the Dabhol Power Company in an effort to revive the project. The Dabhol site is currently operating a power plant and an LNG regasification unit, but the LNG receiving terminal is not scheduled to begin operations until 2009.

Several other companies are studying possible LNG import sites throughout India. However, these plans will largely depend on which, if any, natural gas import pipelines are completed.

An Overview of Economic and Energy Situation of India

Location Southern Asia, bordering the Arabian Sea and the Bay of Bengal, between Burma and Pakistan.

Independence 15 August 1947 (from UK)

Population (July 2006 est.) 1,095,351,995

Economic Overview

Inflation Rate (2006E) 5.6 per cent

Gross Domestic Product (2006E) $889.3 billion

Real GDP Growth Rate (2006E) 8.5 per cent

Unemployment Rate (2006E) 12.2 per cent

External Debt (2006E) $156.8 billion

Exports (2006E) $196.3 billion

Exports—Commodities textile goods, gems and jewellerry, engineering goods, chemicals, leather manufactures

Exports—Partners (2005E) US 16.7 per cent, UAE 8.5 per cent, China 6.6 per cent, Singapore 5.3 per cent, UK 4.9 per cent, Hong Kong 4.4 per cent

Imports (2006E) $205.6 billion

Imports—Commodities crude oil, machinery, gems, fertilizers, chemicals

Imports—Partners (2005E) China 7.3 per cent, US 5.6 per cent, Switzerland 4.7 per cent

Current Account Balance (2006E)—$13.3 billion

Energy Overview

Minister of Petroleum and Natural Gas Shri Murli Deora

Proven Oil Reserves (January 1, 2007E) 5.6 billion barrels

Oil Production (2006E) 846,000 barrels per day, of which 77 per cent was crude oil.

Oil Consumption (2006E) 2.63 million barrels per day

Crude Oil Distillation Capacity (January 1, 2007E) 2.25 million barrels per day

Proven Natural Gas Reserves (January 1, 2007E) 38 trillion cubic feet

Natural Gas Production (2004E) 996 billion cubic feet

Natural Gas Consumption (2004E) 1,089 billion cubic feet

Recoverable Coal Reserves (2003E) 101,903 million short tons

Coal Production (2004E) 443.7 million short tons

Coal Consumption (2004E) 478.2 million short tons

Electricity Installed Capacity (2004E) 131.4 gigawatts

Electricity Production (2004E) 630.6 billion kilowatt hours

Electricity Consumption (2004E) 587.9 billion kilowatt hours

Total Energy Consumption (2004E) 15.4 quadrillion Btus*, of which Coal (53 per cent), Oil (33 per cent), Natural Gas (8 per cent), Hydroelectricity (5 per cent), Nuclear (1 per cent), Other Renewables (0 per cent)

Total Per Capita Energy Consumption ((Million Btu)E) 14.5 million Btus

Energy Intensity (2004E) 4,205.2 Btu per $2000-PPP**

Environmental Overview

Energy-Related Carbon Dioxide Emissions (2004E) 1,112.8 million metric tons, of which Coal (67 per cent), Oil (27 per cent), Natural Gas (6 per cent)

Per-Capita, Energy-Related Carbon Dioxide Emissions ((Metric Tons of Carbon Dioxide)E) 1 metric tons

Carbon Dioxide Intensity (2004E) 0.3 Metric tons per thousand $2000-PPP**

Environmental Issues: deforestation; soil erosion; overgrazing; desertification; air pollution from industrial effluents and vehicle emissions; water pollution from raw sewage and runoff of agricultural pesticides; tap water is not potable throughout the country; huge and growing population is overstraining natural resources

Major Environmental Agreements Antarctic-Environmental Protocol, Antarctic-Marine Living Resources, Antarctic Treaty, Biodiversity, Climate Change, Climate Change—Kyoto Protocol, Desertification, Endangered Species, Environmental Modification, Hazardous Wastes, Law of the Sea, Ozone Layer Protection, Ship Pollution, Tropical Timber 83, Tropical Timber 94, Wetlands, Whaling.

Oil and Gas Industry

Organization Petroleum: Oil and Natural Gas Corporation (ONGC); Oil India Ltd. (OIL); Indian Oil Corporation (IOC); Reliance Industries (private). Natural Gas: Gas Authority of India Ltd. (GAIL) Major Oil/Gas Ports Oil—Bombay, Cochin, Haldia, Kandla, Madras, Vizag; LNG—Hazira, Dahej. Foreign Company Involvement BG International, BP, Cairn Energy, Marubeni, Niko Resources, Petronas, Shell

Major Refineries (capacity, bbl/d) Reliance Petroleum: Jamnagar (660,000). IOC: Koyali (185,100), Mathura (156,000), Panipat (120,000). Mangalore Refinery and Petrochemicals Ltd: Mangalore (180,000). Hindustan Petroleum Corporation: Visakhapatnam (164,250), Mahul (132,000). Kochi Refineries Ltd: Ambalamugal (152,000). Chennai Petroleum Corporation: Madras (130,660). Bharat Petroleum Company Ltd: Mahul (120,000).

---

*The total energy consumption statistic includes petroleum, dry natural gas, coal, net hydro, nuclear, geothermal, solar, wind, wood and waste electric power. The renewable energy consumption statistic is based on International Energy Agency (IEA) data and includes hydropower, solar, wind, tide, geothermal, solid biomass and animal products, biomass gas and liquids, industrial and municipal wastes. Sectoral shares of energy consumption and carbon emissions are also based on IEA data.

**GDP figures from OECD estimates based on Purchasing Power Parity (PPP) exchange rates.

Source: EIA

India's Energy Security Challenge

Like China, India is a growing giant facing the critical challenge of meeting a rapidly increasing demand for energy. With over a billion people, a fifth of the world population, India ranks sixth in the world in terms of energy demand. Its economy is projected to grow 7-8 % over the next two decades, and in its wake will be a substantial increase in demand for oil to fuel land, sea, and air transportation.[4]

While India has significant reserves of coal, it is relatively poor in oil and gas resources. Its oil reserves amount to 5.9 billion barrels. (0.5 per cent of global reserves) with total proven, probable, and possible reserves of close to 11 billion barrels. The majority of India's oil reserves are located in fields offshore Bombay and onshore in Assam. Due to stagnating domestic crude production, India imports approximately 70 per cent of its oil, much of it from the Middle East. Its dependence is growing rapidly. The World Energy Outlook, published by the International Energy Agency (IEA), projects that India's dependence on oil imports will grow to 91.6 per cent by the year 2020.

Concerned about its growing reliance on oil from the Persian Gulf—65 per cent of its energy is imported from the region - India is following in the footsteps of other major oil importing economies, and seeking oil outside the Gulf. Indian firms' investment in overseas oilfields is projected to reach $3 billion within a few years. Of particular interest is Africa, especially Sudan, where India has invested $750 million in oil, and Nigeria, with which India reached a deal in November 2003 enabling it to purchase about 44 million barrels of crude oil per year on a long-term basis. Additionally, India recently finalised a contract in Syria for the exploration, development and production of petroleum with a Syrian company. Sakhalin, in Russia, and Vietnam and Myanmar in Southeast Asia are also potential suppliers to the Indian market.

But, the most attractive oil domain outside the Persian Gulf is the Caspian Basin, where India is trying to befriend the region's leaders and, if possible, gain a foothold. To support energy security interests in Central Asia, India has already stationed troops in Tajikistan, provided it with $40 million aid package and undertook to refurbish an air base near the Tajik capital Dushanbe. India is also pursuing relations with Kazakhstan, Azerbaijan and Iran.

India policy of source diversification has problematic implications. First, many of the countries with which India is dealing are known for severe violations of human rights, sponsorship of terrorist activities, and general misuse of oil revenues. Further enrichment of oil supplying countries like Sudan, Syria and Iran is not in the interest of India, a country which itself is a prime target of Islamist terrorism. Second, the exploration of overseas oilfields, especially in the area of the South China Sea, could bring India in direct competition with fellow Asian countries like China and Malaysia. Most importantly, this policy contributes to accelerating global depletion of non-Middle East oil reserves, and will lead India and the rest of the world to a point in which dependence on the region would be far stronger.

In addition to its struggle to secure supply, India is becoming increasingly aware of the fact that its economy is highly vulnerable to supply disruptions. Till recently, India did not have an energy security policy or contingency plans to fall back on in case of crisis. Nor is it a member of any organisation like the International Energy Agency, which was born in the aftermath of the

1973 oil crisis to protect members from any future disruptions in the energy market. To minimise the impact of global fluctuations, India is building a strategic crude oil reserve facility on its southern and eastern coasts. Other policies implemented by the government are:

- Increased fuel efficiency through a cut in state subsidies on all petroleum products, except some household necessities such as kerosene and cooking gas which receive the up to 40 per cent subsidy to benefit the poor.
- Shift to natural gas and LNG: India will be a major importer of natural gas and LNG over the next few decades. The cheapest way to supply India with gas would be through pipelines from Central Asia and the Middle East, through Pakistan, but due to tense relations with Pakistan the two countries have not been cooperating on energy schemes and such pipelines are politically infeasible. On the eastern coast, imports of small amount of natural gas from Bangladesh may be feasible. However, Bangladesh's internal party politics does not allow it to take a decision in favour of New Delhi. Consequently, India is focusing on costlier LNG imports especially from Oman and Qatar. This would require construction of LNG terminals which pose security risks and are attractive targets for terrorists.
- Increased domestic production: In the past five years, the government introduced a new exploration licensing policy aimed to promote investment in the exploration and production of domestic oil and gas. It is premature to determine how much oil can be generated domestically and for how long, but privatisation of the oil sector, removal of bureaucratic obstacles and improved business climate could improve India's energy security.
- Increased utilisation of clean coal technology: The country is the third largest coal producer and holder of 7 per cent of global reserves of coal. Coal provides 56 per cent of India's commercial energy supply. Application of the coal gasification combined cycle process is an emerging technology for clean and efficient coal fuelled generation.
- Shift to next generation fuels and increased use of renewable sources of energy: India is probably the only country in the world with a full-fledged ministry dedicated to the production of energy from renewable energy sources. The Indian government is promoting the use of ethanol made from sugarcane and bio-diesel extracted from trees that are common in many parts of India, such as the Jetropha, Karanja and Mahua. Additionally, India is emerging as a growing market for solar, wind and hydroelectric power. According to a report by the American Wind Energy Association India currently ranks fifth in the global wind energy production.

India's Policy for Sustainable Energy

The time is still far when India as a whole can be called a self-sustaining country in terms of energy; be it thermal, natural gas, hydro or nuclear energy, but a start has been made with the Central and the state governments coming forward with a better focussed approach to tap this awesome potential.

In order to fuel a rapidly growing economy, the Indian energy sector requires investments to the tune of USD 120-150 billion over the next five years. The imperative for private sector investment is strong in order to complement the public sector in meeting this investment requirement and to bring the required capabilities and technologies to enhance energy resource extraction, and close the demand supply gap.

The Government of India has recognised the need for private participation and policies to promote private investment are being implemented.[5] Private participation in coal mining for captive use, in oil and gas exploration and the power sector is already seeing significant progress. It is also expected that private participation in nuclear energy would be allowed as and when the Indo-US Nuclear deal comes through. Along with private participation, there is a move to bring in market mechanisms in the energy sector under an independent regulatory body. Progress has been made in sectors such as power, oil and gas, where private participation is already significant.

A gradual approach is important till the supply side position improves and more players enter the sector so that markets can work effectively and power cost become cheaper and self-sustaining. In parallel, the Government is making efforts to broaden the supply base both internally and externally.

It is intended to diversify the fuel basket by increasing percentile shares of natural gas, hydro and even nuclear energy. At the same time, both Government and private sector companies are looking to acquire equity in energy assets abroad and we have seen recent examples in the oil, gas and coal sectors. Energy transport infrastructure such as ports, railways, pipelines and power transmission networks need significant investment and streamlining.

The policy now allows private participation in all these areas and some private sector activity is already underway. Tariff reform in the energy sector and distribution reform in the power sector are two important steps that need to be successfully carried out. Tariff reform to phase out subsidies or to target them effectively and distribution reforms to bring greater efficiency in the power sector are vital. Steps have been taken in these directions with mixed results. Going forward, this is an important area that needs management and a long-term perspective.

Coal: India has vast reserves of coal and participation of the private sector in captive mining, across different user industries, is an immediate opportunity for investment. Thirty-eight coal fields with mineable coal reserves in excess of 2,800 million tonnes have been identified and are in the process of being allocated for captive mining. This may imply a total capital requirement of around USD 1.5-2 billion. Investment activity in other parts of the coal value chain such as in coal washeries has also been seen in recent times.

Nuclear: The envisaged growth of nuclear power in India is possible, provided robust technologies are developed for both the front-end and the back-end of the fuel cycle. India has one of the largest reserves of the nuclear fuel—thorium. However, the nuclear energy programme will continue to be uranium based until commercial production based on thorium becomes feasible. There is a persisting need for developing techniques for economic and efficient extraction of uranium from lean sources.

Oil: The Government's policy of allowing full private participation in upstream exploration and production has already attracted a number of private investors. Six rounds of competitive bidding under the Government policy, named New Exploration Licensing Policy (NELP), have already been done, around 185 blocks were awarded and reserves estimated at 700 MMT2 of oil and gas have been discovered. The sixth round of bidding (NELP-VI) for 65 blocks was successfully completed 2006. In addition, India offers a lot of potential in the refining sector due to the strategic advantages of low cost and location; and is already a net exporter of products. The downstream marketing sector is also now open to private participation.

Renewable: India has a vast potential for renewable energy sources, especially in areas such as solar power, biomass and wind power. The current installed capacity of renewable energy is around 92204 MW, constituting about 7.3 per cent of India's total installed generation capacity. India is already the fourth largest in the world in terms of wind energy installations and we are seeing significant investment activity in this area. Technological breakthrough for cost-effective photovoltaic technology could generate a quantum leap in the renewable energy sector since India is well endowed with solar insolation.

Gas: Discoveries to the tune of 700 bcm in the last decade meant that gas reserves hold promise in India. The potential for Coal Bed Methane appears to be promising and will probably exceed the free natural gas reserves. While in the near term, potential for LNG may be limited due to inability of key sectors such as power to absorb high international prices, in the longer term there would be place for LNG as the share of natural gas in India's energy mix increases. On the demand side, an emerging area is auto-CNG and piped gas which have together accounted for about 7 per cent of the total gas demand in the last five years. In the next few years, at least 30 cities have been identified for city-wide gas coverage by private and public sector players. The draft gas pipeline policy gives support to the development of a national gas grid meant to create gas market across the country.

Hydro: India is endowed with a hydroelectric potential of about 150,000 MW. However, only 17 per cent of the hydroelectric potential has been harnessed so far; with another 5 per cent under various stages of development. Private participation in the hydro sector will be important to meet the target of an additional 45,000 MW of hydro capacity within the next ten years. Various policy measures are being contemplated which seek to address issues such as mitigating geological risks, resettlement and rehabilitation of project affected persons through Public Private Partnership initiatives and incentives for performance. The revised hydro policy was under discussion by the Government of India with respective states.

Ministry of Power Governing the Electrical Growth

The Ministry of Power (MoP) started functioning independently with effect from 2nd July, 1992. Earlier it was known as the Ministry of Energy comprising the Departments of Power,

Coal and Non-conventional Energy Sources. The Ministry of Power (MoP) is mainly responsible for evolving general policy in the field of energy. The main items of work dealt with by the Ministry of Power are to develop the general Policy in the electrical power sector and address issues relating to energy policy and coordination thereof.

The MoP also addresses ail matters relating to hydro-electric power (except small/mini/ micro hydel projects of and below 25 MW capacity) and thermal power and transmission and distribution system network; provides research, development and technical assistance relating to hydro electric and thermal power, transmission system network and distribution systems in the States/UTs; all matters relating to Central Electricity Authority, Central Electricity Board, the Central Electricity Regulatory Commission; and Rural Electrification Corporation.

Power schemes and issues relating to power supply/development schemes/programmes/ decentralised and distributed generation in the States and Union Territories; as well as address matters relating to Undertaking and Organizations like the Damodar Valley Corporation, Bhakra Beas Management Board, NTPC Limited, National Hydroelectric Power Corporation Limited, Rural Electrification Corporation Limited, North Eastern Electric Power Corporation Limited, Power Grid Corporation of India Limited, Power Finance Corporation Limited, Tehri Hydro Development Corporation, Jal Vidyul Nigam Limited and Central Power Recarch Institute.

- 100 per cent 11 kV feeder metering completed in 23 States and 4 more States have achieved more than 90 per cent metering.
- 100 per cent consumer metering has been completed in 8 States and 12 other States have achieved more than 90 per cent metering.
- Rajiv Gandhi Grameen Vidyutikaran Yojna (RGGVY) for Rural Electricity Infrastructure and Household Electrification has been made operational.

The Central Government has launched a new scheme 'Rajiv Gandhi Grameen Vidyutikaran Yojna' for Rural Electricity Infrastructure and Household Electrification' on 4th April, 2005 for the attainment of the National Common Minimum Programme (NCMP) goal for providing access to electricity to all households in the country in five years. The scheme is being implemented through Rural Electrification Corporation (REC).

Under the scheme 90 per cent capital subsidy would be provided on overall cost of the project for provision of:

- Rural Electricity Distribution Backbone (REDB) with at least one 33/ 11 kV (or 66/11 kV) substation in each block.

Installed, Reformed and Accelerated

The All India installed capacity of electric power generation stations under utilities was 124287.17 MW as on 31.3.2006 consisting of 82410.54 MW thermal, 32325.77 MW hydro, 3369 MW nuclear and 6190.86 MW from Renewable Energy Sources (RES) which has increased to 128182.47 MW as on 31st January 2007 consisting of 84149.84 MW thermal, 33941.77MW hydro, 3900 MW nuclear and 6190.86 MW from RES. A Capacity addition of 41,110 MW has been targeted for the 10th Five Year Plan.

Distribution Reforms

The Ministry of Power look various initiatives towards reforms and other policy measures for helping the state power utilities. Some of the major initiatives were establishment of regulatory mechanism at central and slate level, restructuring of the state power utilities, metering of feeders and consumers, energy accounting and auditing, securitization of outstanding dues of CPSUs.

Accelerated Power Development and Reforms Programme

Ministry of Power launched Accelerated Power Development and Reforms Programme (APDRP) in the year 2002-03 with an outlay of Rs. 40,000 crore as additional central plan assistance to states during 10th Five Year Plan.

The programme objectives were to reduce AT&C losses, bring about commercial viability in the power sector, reduce outages, interruptions, increase consumer satisfaction and debt servicing.

In all technical and economic matters, Ministry of Power is assisted by the Central Electricity Authority (CEA). The CEA advises the Ministry of Power on all technical and economic matters. The Electricity Act 2003, mandates the Central Government to prepare an Electricity Policy in consultation with State Governments and the CEA. The Policy aims at accelerated development of the power sector, providing supply of electricity to all areas and protecting interests of consumers and other stakeholders keeping in view the availability of energy resources technology available to exploit these resources, economics of generation using different resources and energy security issues. Salient features of the Policy include:

- Access to electricity Available for all hourseholds in next five years.
- Availability of power: Demand to be fully met by 2012. Energy and peaking shortages to be overcome and spinning reserve to be available.
- Supply of reliable and quality power of specified standards in an efficient manner and at reasonable rates.
- Per capita availability of electricity to be increased to over 1000 units by 2012.
- Minimum lifeline consumption of 1 unit/hoursehold/day as a merit good by year 2012.
- Financial turnaround and commercial viability of electricity sector.
- Protection of consumers' interests.

Status of Power Reforms

- All States have signed Memorandum of Understanding, Memorandum of Agreement and Tripartite Agreements.

- All the States except Nagaland and Arunachal Pradesh have constituted notified State Electricity Regulatory Commission (SERCs) and 21 SERCs have issued tariff orders.
- Thirteen States restructured corporatised State Electricity Boards and one State, *i.e.* Tripura corporatised their Electricity Department. Delhi (2002) and Orissa (1999).
- Village Electrification Infrastructure (VEI) with at least one distribution transformer in each village/habitation.
- Decentralised Distribution Generation (DDG) Systems where grid supply is not feasible or cost effective.

Since April, 2005, till 23rd February 2007, 30,562 villages have been electrified under RGGVY.

Eclectic Initiatives

Generation Performance

There has been significant improvement in the growth in actual generation over the last few years. As compared to an annual growth rate of about 3.1 per cent at the end of 9th Plan and initial years of 10th Plan, the growth in generation during 2006-07 and 2007-08 (upto September, 2007) was of the order of 7.3 per cent and 7.6 per cent respectively.

The electricity generation target for the year 2007-08 has been fixed at 710 BU comprising 572.194 BU thermal; 109.450 BU hydro; 22.713 BU nuclear; and 5,643 BU import from Bhutan.

100,000 MW Thermal Initiative

To accelerate hydro power development, a 50,000 MW hydro electric initiative was launched by Hon'ble Prime Minister of India on May 24, 2003. Keeping in view the huge power generation capacity requirement, MoP/CEA has proposed 1,00,000 MW environment-friendly thermal initiative.

CEA has identified shelf of sites for thermal power projects totalling more than 1,00,000 MW capacity. Large sites are being identified through studies by Central Mines Planning and Design Institute and National Remote Sensing Agency using remote sensing. Projects totalling to about 46,000 MW to be taken up during the 11th Plan. Need for capacity addition during 12th Plan to be firmed up by the end of the 11th Plan.

Setting up of Ultra Mega Power Projects

The Ministry of Power has launched an initiative for development of coal-based Ultra Mega Power Projects (UMPPs) in India, each with a capacity of 4000 MW or above. These projects will be awarded to developers on the basis of tariff-based competitive bidding. To facilitate tie-ups of inputs and clearances project specific Shell companies have been set up as wholly owned subsidiaries of the Power Finance Corporation Ltd. These companies will under-take preliminary studies and obtain necessary clearances including water, land, fuel, power tie-up and such like prior award of the project to the successful bidder.

Initially five sites were identified by CEA in five different states for the proposed Ultra Mega Power Projects. These include two pithead sites—one each in Madhya Pradesh and Chhattisgarh and three coastal sites in Gujarat, Karnataka and Maharashtra. Subsequently on the request of the Government of Andhra Pradesh and Orissa, two sites one each in Orissa (pithead) and Andhra Pradesh (coastal) were identified for setting up of Ultra Mega Power Projects. Sites are also being identified in Jharkhand (pithead) and Tamil Nadu (coastal) based on requests from the State Governments. It is proposed to set up pithead projects as integrated proposals with corresponding captive coal mines.

On the request of the Ministry of Power, the Ministry of Coal has already allocated captive coal mining block for Sasan UMPP in Madhya Pradesh and earmarked a captive coal mining block for Orissa UMPP. For the coastal projects imported coal shall be used.

Electrifying the Rural

Rural Electrification Programme

Rural electrification has been regarded as a vital programme for the development of rural areas since the first plan as per the suggestions of Gandhiji. In 1947, only 1500 villages were electrified in India. The per capita consumption was 14 units.

The initial focus was electrification for irrigation to enhance agricultural produce which was reflected in the definition of village electrification accepted till 1997 that 'a village was deemed to be electrified if electricity is being used within its revenue area for any purpose whatsoever'. In February 2004, the definition was made even more encompassing as also target-specific. A village would be declared electrified if:

- Basic infrastructure such as distribution transformer and distribution lines are provided in the inhabited locality as well as the *dalit basti*/hamlet where it exists. For electrification through Non-conventional Energy Sources a distribution transformer may not be necessary.
- Electricity is provided to public places like schools, panchayat offices, health centres, dispensaries, community centres and such like.
- The number of households electrified was to have been at least 10 per cent of the total number of households in the village.

The Government of India from time to time had launched the following programmes for electrification:

Rural Electrification under Minimum Needs Programme (MNP)

This was started in 5th Five Year Plan with rural electrification as one of the components of the programme. Under this programme funds were provided as Central assistance to the states in the form of partly grant, partly loans and partly subsidies. The scheme was discontinued from 2004 onwards and has been subsequently merged with the new scheme, Rajiv Gandhi Grameen Vidyutikaran Yojana.

Kutir Jyoti Scheme

This programme was launched in 1988-89 to provide single point light connections to households of rural families below the poverty line including Harijans and Adivasi families. This scheme has been now merged with RGGVY and ITMA.

Accelerated Rural Electrification Programme (AREP)

The scheme was introduced in the year 2003-04 under which interest subsidy of 4 per cent was to be provided on loans availed by State Governments/Power Utilities from Financial Institutions for carrying out rural electrification programme.

Accelerated Electrification of One Lakh Villages and One Crore Households

This was introduced in 2004-05 by merging the interest subsidy scheme—AREP and Kutir Jyoti Programme. Under this scheme, there was a provision for providing 40 per cent capital subsidy for rural electrification projects and the balance as loan assistance on soft terms from REC. The scheme has now been merged with the new scheme RGGVY under present dispensation.

Status of Rural Electrification under RGGVY

All the states except Delhi and Goa have signed Agreements under RGGVY. GPSUs are implementing the scheme in 134 districts.

Projects for 316 districts have been sanctioned at the cost of Rs. 11,514.22 crore covering 69,534 unelectrified villages and 27,50,784 BPL households. Since April 2005, till 23rd February, 2007, 30,562 unelectrified villages in Rajasthan, Uttar Pradesh, Uttaranchal, Karnataka, Bihar and West Bengal have been electrified. In 2006-07, 20,743 unelectrified villages have been electrified as on 23rd February 2007.

Status of Power Sector Reforms

- All the states except Nagaland and Arunachal Pradesh have constituted/notified State Electricity Regulatory Commissions (SERCs).
- Twenty-one SERCs have issued tariff orders.
- Consumer Grievance Redressal Forums (CGRFs) have been constituted in 16 States by the distribution licensees for redressal of grievances of consumers. Ombudsmen have been appointed in 15 States to look into the non-redressal of grievances by the CGRFs and suitable penal provisions and penal settlement.
- 26 States have notified rural areas for taking up composite schemes of generation and distribution without licences.
- 27 States have constituted District Committees for coordinating rural electrification, reviewing the quality of power supply and promoting energy efficiency.

- 15 States have set up Special Courts for expeditious disposal of theft-related cases.
- Six States have established Special Police Stations.

Reorganisation of the State Electricity Boards

Before the enactment of the Electricity Act, 2003, various States had enacted State Electricity Reforms Acts, which facilitated the reorganisation of their State Electricity Boards (SEB).

So far, 13 states have reorganised their SEBs. Orissa, Haryana, Andhra Pradesh, Karnataka, Uttar Pradesh, Uttaranchal, Rajasthan, Delhi, Gujarat and Madhya Pradesh have done so under their State Electricity Reforms Acts. Assam, Maharashtra and West Bengal have reorganised their SEBs under the provisions of the Electricity Act, 2003.

Guidelines for Procurement of Electricity

In compliance with Section 63 of the Electricity Act, 2003, the Central Government has notified guidelines for procurement of power by Distribution Licensees through competitive bidding. The Central Government has also issued the standard bid document containing REQ. RFP and mode! PPA for long term procurement of power from projects having specified site and location.

Securitisation of outstanding dues

An Expert Group under the Chairmanship of Montek Singh Ahluwalia, the then Member (Energy), Planning Commission, recommended a scheme for one-time settlement of dues payable by State Electricity Boards (SEBs) to Central Public Sector Undertakings (CPSUs) and the Railways. The recommendations were accepted by the Government of India. All the 28 State Governments signed the Tripartite Agreement (TPA), envisaged under the scheme.

Collection Efficiency

The scheme has resulted in improvement in collection of the dues of the power sector CPSUs. The details of collection efficiency (in percentage) is shown in the table 24 given below.

TABLE 24

CPSU	*2001-02*	*2002-03*	*2003-04*	*2004-05*	*2005-06*	*2006-07 (Apr-Sept 07)*
NTPC	76.74	92.34	100.00	100.00	100.00	100.00
NHPC	69.03	94.44	97.06	100.00	100.00	100.00
PGCIL	88.92	95.16	98.30	99.70	100.00	100.00
NEEPCO	74.78	71.49	87.50	95.23	97.00	89.06
DVC	99.07	91.92	90.64	95.88	96.19	9573
SJVNL	-	-	100.00	100.00	100.00	100.00
THDC	-	-	-	-	-	92.46

Source: The Indian Express, New Delhi, 29th January, 2008.

Promising Prominence

India is endowed with very large viable and economically exploitable hydroelectric potential which is estimated to be about 150,000 MW (84,000 MW at 60 per cent load factor). The current hydel installed capacity in India is about 33,941 MW.

The Government of India has undertaken several initiatives to increase the share of hydel energy in the overall energy mix and the Prime Minister's 50,000 MW Hydroelectric initiative is one of the major steps undertaken by the Ministry of Power in this regard.

Key Issues

Government of India is addressing various issues relating to the development of hydro power. Private sector participation is also being encouraged in a big way. However, key issues still remain; with the major ones being:

- **Funding:** Hydro projects involve high initial costs with one of the lowest lifetime cost of power generation. To meet the funding requirements, the Government has decided that all Central Sector projects will be provided budgetary support. It is also proposed to levy a 'power development cess' in the country to fund hydro projects.
- **Geological risks:** Hydro projects present geological surprises when construction starts and this leads to an increase in project cost; ultimately culminating in additional risks to the investors.
- **Long delays in obtaining clearances:** Projects are delayed because of the large time taken in acquiring land, difficulty in obtaining clearances and issues related to rehabilitation and resettlement. To resolve these, it is proposed that new projects should initially be taken up by government-owned companies for activities such as—conducting investigations, updation of DPRs. obtaining the necessary clearances and execution of pre-construction work.

  Alter the completion of these stages, the projects could be offered to the private sector for execution either on a 'stand alone' basis or for joint venture participation with the state-owned companies.
- **Delays due to disputes between the states:** In case of hydro projects involving dro projects were well recognised as attractive and viable, they could not be taken up for implementation for these very reasons.
- **Simplified procedure for transfer of clearances:** The immediate requirement would be to transfer the clearances already accorded to non-starling hydro projects in the State to the Central Sector or to Independent Power Projects (IPPs) or to JVs between IPPs and the Central Sector.

Policy and Regulatory Framework

Some of the key policy initiatives undertaken by the Government for faster development of hydro potential sector are:

- **Estimates on completion cost (geological risks):** A realistic estimate of completion cost has to take into account the geological and hydrological risks, cost escalation and natural occurrences of landslides, rock falls, etc. The developer will be allowed to submit his proposal for enhanced costs to the Government.
- **Promoting hydro projects with joint ventures:** With a view to bring in additional private investment in the hydro sector, there has been emphasis on schemes through joint ventures between the public and domestic/foreign private enterprises. Relaxation in certain rules pertaining to mandatory sharing of power with neighbouring states is provided in the case of joint venture projects.
- **Support for acquisition, R&R, catchment area development:** The acquisition of forest and private land involves Government procedures and difficult negotiations with the land owners. As per the policy adopted by the State Government, it is now the responsibility of the State Government to acquire the land (whether be it government-owned, private or forest) for the project and also negotiate at its own terms with the land owners. In case any cost is incurred by the developer, it would be considered as 'cost to the project' and allowed to be considered for tariff determination.
- **Preparation of DPRs:** With the objective of reducing time & cost overrun of hydro projects (which have largely taken place on account of poor and hasty investigation and non-availability of proper infrastructure), the Government introduced a 3-stage process for development of new hydro electric projects in the Central Sector. The three Stages are:

  Stage-I: Survey investigation and preparation of pre-feasibility report

  Stage-II: Detailed investigation, preparation of DPR and pre-construction.

  Stage-III: Private sectors perticipetion-hydropower projects.
- The Ministry of Power had come out with a set of guidelines for the development of Large Hydropower Projects (*i.e.* over 100 MW) by private sector through competitive tariff-based bidding. With an aim of developing the large potential of the yet-to-be-developed hydel power in states like Uttarakhand, Himachal Pradesh and the North Eastern parts of the country, the guidelines envisaged supply of surplus power to the deficit states; with host states securing benefits such as 12 per cent free power.
- Given the reservations expressed over the applicability of the tariff-based competitive bidding process to hydro power, the government is planning to come out with a new hydel power policy for allocation and development of hydel projects by the private sector. The new policy would aim to attract private players and is likely to exclude stales from following a tariff-based bidding process for hydro power projects.

Opportunities for India

Only about 17 per cent of the vast hydel potential of 150,000 MW has been tapped so far. Countries like Norway, Canada and Brazil have all been utilising more than 30 per cent of their hydro potential; while, on the other hand, India and China have lagged far behind. India ranks fifth in terms of exploitable hydro-potential in the world. As per an assessment made by Central Electricity Authority (CEA), India is endowed with economically exploitable hydro-power potential to the tune of 148,700 MW.

The Basin-wise Assessed Potential

Under the Prime Minister's 50,000 MW hydro electric initiative, the Central Electricity Authority (CEA) has already completed the preparation of the pre-feasibilily report for 162 schemes covering an installed capacity of 47,930 MW. Most of this untapped potential lies in the North and the North-Eastern states of the country. In addition, 56 number of pumped storage projects have also been identified with a probable installed capacity, India is endowed with hydro-potential of about 250,000 MW. However, only 17 per cent of the hydroelectric potential has been harnessed so far and another 5 per cent is under various stages of development. While private participation is currently low at 3 per cent, private participation in future will be important to meet the ambitious target of 50,000 MW capacity addition in the next ten years.

Small Hydro Opportunity

Small and mini hydel projects have the potential to provide energy in remote and hilly areas where extension of the grid system is considered uneconomical. Realising this fact, the Government of India is encouraging development of small and mini hydro power projects in the country. India has 420 small hydro power projects of upto 25 MW station capacity, with an aggregate capacity of over 1,423 MW. Over 187 projects in this range with an aggregate capacity of 521 MW are under construction.

Potential

An estimated potential of about 15,000 MW of small hydro power projects exists in India. The Ministry of Non-Conventional and Renewable Energy has created a database of potential sites of small hydro and 4096 potential sites (with an aggregate capacity of 10,071 MW) of upto 25 MW capacity have been identified.

MNRE Incentives in Small Hydro Sector

In order to accelerate development of small hydro power, MNRE is giving incentives for—survey and investigation, detailed project report preparation, interest subsidy for commercial projects, capital subsidy for SHP projects in the North-Eastern region, renovation and modernisation of old SHP stations and development of water mills.

India's Initiatives for Integrated Energy Policy

The issue of India's energy security was adequality highlighted address by Murli Deora, Minister of Petroleum and Natural Gas, Government of India, on the occasion of Annual General Meeting of US Energy Association at Washington, DC on April 4, 2006.

The Minister said "It gives me great pleasure to be present here on the occasion of the Annual General Meeting of the US Energy Association and share my views with the distinguished audience on the energy security of India". First, let me congratulate USEA for its pioneering role and for carrying forward the mission of the World Energy Council to promote sustainable supply and use of energy for the greatest benefit of all. Today let me share with you the energy security concerns of India to fuel its targeted economic growth with utmost regard to preserve the environment.

India, cradling a sixth of the world's population is the sixth largest consumer of energy. The structural adjustments initiated in the country's policy making in the 1990s initiated a process of visible economic change in India. With the National Common Minimum Programme and its various policies for stimulating and sustaining growth, India is poised to achieve a sustained GDP growth rate of 8 per cent this year and possibly even higher in future.

With this rapid pace of growth, India at 520 kg of oil equivalent consumes only a third of the world's average annual per capita energy. The country's total primary energy requirements, which are close to 360 million tons of oil equivalent per annum, are projected to go up to 1.6 billion tons of oil equivalent by 2030.

Nearly the entire need of our commercial energy is met by fossil fuels, namely coal and hydrocarbons. Oil and gas currently account for nearly 45 per cent of the primary commercial energy requirements of the country and their share is likely to remain high in future, with gas providing for a larger share.

Our focus to give top priority to our energy security concerns can be seen from a statement made recently by our Prime Minister Dr Manmohan Singh before the Indian Parliament in the context of the historic agreement between India and the US on civil nuclear cooperation. He stated that:

> "The search for an integrated policy with an appropriate mix of energy supplies is central to the achievement of our broader economic or social objectives. Energy is the lifeblood of our economy. Without sufficient and predictable access, our aspirations in the social sector cannot be realised.
>
> "Inadequate power has a deleterious effect in building modern infrastructure. It has a direct impact on the optimal usage of increasingly scarce water resources. Power shortage is thus not just a handicap in one sector but a drag on the entire economy.
>
> "I believe the needs of the people of India must become the central agenda for international cooperation. It is precisely this approach that has guided our growing partnership with the United States".

We are in the process of drafting an integrated energy policy to provide a road map to augment and meet our growing energy need in an environmentally sustainable manner.

It is projected that the demand for oil and gas in India, during 2005 to 2025, will grow steadily at a rate of 4.3 per cent and 7.3 per cent respectively. At current levels, domestic production meets only 25 per cent of the country's oil needs which are at around 2.6 million barrels per day.

This demand is expected to increase to 7.5 mbpd (million barrels per day) when India may need to import almost 85 per cent of its oil requirements unless new major exploratory successes are reported in our now unexplored basins. We expect the demand for natural gas during the same period to increase from 150 million standard cubic meters per day to about 390 mscmd.

India has grafted a multi-pronged strategy to counter the challenge of fuelling India's economic growth. This strategy includes a conscious shift to promote larger public-private participation in oil and gas. Our policy has been carefully evolved to create a level playing field for all the participants in the sector. With the recent passage of the Petroleum and Natural Gas Regulatory Board Bill in our Parliament, agencies to regulate and monitor the mid-stream and downstream sectors of oil and gas are being put in place. For the upstream, the director general of hydrocarbons fulfils the technical regulatory functions.

Our new exploration licensing policy has been successful in opening up new and hitherto unexplored sedimentary basins for exploration and has enabled us to add a sizeable quantum of oil and gas reserves. The global perception of India's hydrocarbon endowment is rapidly changing with more investments and modern technology pouring into India. Our policy dispensation today provides for unhindered flow of investment into the entire hydrocarbon value chain, including exploration and production, refining, pipeline infrastructure and marketing.

While the prices of crude oil and petroleum products have been extremely volatile in the international markets, our policy has been calibrated with extreme care to enable the economically weaker sections access their basic energy requirements. This has been done through a carefully evolved equitable sharing of burden of high prices by all stakeholders, namely government, oil companies and consumers.

Energy efficiency and energy conservation are the two vital areas of energy management. The energy intensity in the Indian economy has registered a considerable decline over the past 15 years or so making our industrial sector globally more competitive... we are not complacent. Newer and better ways of energy use are being continuously employed in our economic activity. This is particularly important in the context of globalisation.

Another important component of our oil and gas security is to acquire equity oil and gas assets outside India. Indian companies have succeeded in getting a significant foothold and are currently operating in 14 countries with a production of about 100,000 barrels per day of oil and oil equivalent gas in Sakhalin-1, Sudan and Vietnam. Our emphasis is to further expand overseas activities and secure a significant portion of our domestic requirement through equity oil and gas route. In addition to accelerating efforts at home and through international participation, India sees enhancement in its energy security through building energy corridors for supply of oil and gas across, and within its borders. Coming to the renewable sources of energy, India, as you are aware, is among the select list of countries with a large installed capacity of wind power. Environmental concerns demand that we enhance the share of renewable energy sources as expeditiously as possible.

Those of you who have been visiting Delhi and Mumbai over the past few years will be able to notice the considerable reduction in emissions in these metropolitan cities of late. We have achieved this through converting a large proportion of our fleet of vehicles from the emission-spewing gasoline and diesel to environmentally clean CNG (compressed natural gas). We are planning to expand CNG and piped natural gas facility to more cities and towns in the next few years, with the twin objectives of better environment and better economy.

It would be prudent for developing economies to start using new technologies for enhancing their energy security. This will not only enable efficient and more productive use of their resources but would also help the world in proving many technologies viable through higher and larger commercial usage.

Technologies in the field of gas hydrates, coal gasification, gas to liquids, coal-bed methane, ultra deep exploration and production are lesser known in the developing world. Time has now come for the world to collectively share the responsibility for sustainable development and elevation in the quality of life of the masses. India is exploring the possibility of meeting its energy requirements from various sources of energy—through fossil fuels, thermal power, hydro-electric, nuclear power or renewables. In this regard, US and India have initiated the Indo-US energy dialogue, which would provide a meaningful exchange of information and a forum to help us plan and implement our agenda for energy security.

The recent conclusion of agreement between US and India during the visit of the American President George W. Bush on civil nuclear energy cooperation marks a turning point in the ever-increasing cooperation and mutual understanding between the two countries. India has always been engaged in peaceful nuclear energy programme to meet its growing energy demand. This measure will help India add to its power generation capacity. This cooperation in civil nuclear programme, I am sure, will expand to other areas too.

Our cooperation should cover the entire energy spectrum from oil and gas to clean coal, coal-bed methane, gas hydrates, wind and solar power. India has already agreed to participate in the FutureGen programme for zero emission thermal power plants and integrated ocean drilling programme for gas hydrates. I would urge that India and the US partner and initiate an institutional process of ensuring global energy security and lay the foundation of a new beginning to realise the vision of a secure, sustainable, equitable, efficient and productive global energy market.

USEA and Indian institutions could cooperate and share knowledge, information and expertise in the energy sector. An effective arrangement could be worked out within the framework of the Indo-US energy dialogue to achieve this and to strive towards the laudable goals of ensuring for our citizens access to energy in an economical and an environmentally sustainable manner in years to come. I once again thank the USEA for giving me an opportunity to share this platform and wish them all success in promoting the vision of WEC (World Energy Council) on energy.

India Plans $250 M Energy Security Fund

India's planning to set up a $250 million autonomous National Energy Security Fund. The fund, which will exclude nuclear energy, is expected to be raised with the help of government-controlled upstream and downstream energy companies. The government has said it will levy a 0.2 per cent tax on the oil and gas companies to achieve the energy security target. Indian Prime Minister Manmohan Singh's energy coordination committee recommended the creation of an energy security fund. The recommendation of the committee has been referred to the Finance Ministry and the Planning Commission for implementation. The fund will be used for research and development projects in the energy sector; gas hydrate and coal gasification programmes would be a priority.

The committee, in its recent meeting, expressed concern over the gas shortage and recommended new power plants be given the go-ahead only when long-term gas supply contracts were secured. The committee has also recommended adoption of a give-or-pay and take-and-give contracts where both buyer and seller have agreed to trade on a contracted amount of gas. The committee said in case either party does not supply or buy the contracted amount, they still pay the other party the money for the entire contracted amount. It has also said the gas price needs to be regulated and the administered price of gas needs to be allocated to priority sectors such as fertiliser plants and power plants.

India sets up new energy security office in Foreign Ministry

India has decided to set up an energy security office in its Foreign Ministry, in an indication of how the country's energy needs are increasingly being tied to diplomatic policy.

The move is intended to help Indian companies acquire energy resources overseas and sensitize Indian diplomatic missions in identifying such opportunities.

The office will also promote the transfer of new energy technologies to India and support the international activities of government ministries and departments dealing with energy issues. India's rapid economic expansion currently close to 9 per cent per year could be halted, if the country doesn't move quickly to secure energy supplies for the future. India's domestic supplies are limited and, therefore, it must acquire enough energy resources overseas.

Indian companies, however, have been far less successful than their Chinese competitors in doing so, largely because of inadequate diplomatic involvement. "The possibility of bilateral cooperation in the areas of oil, natural gas, petrochemicals, hydrocarbons, non-conventional energy, and joint ventures are also constantly being explored with various countries".

State-run ONGC Videsh Ltd., the overseas arm of India's main petroleum exploration company, Oil and Natural Gas Corporation has so far committed about US$5 billion (3.7 billion) in investment in oil and gas resources abroad. Oil-rich Nigeria and Russia account for much of the investment.

Possibilities of cooperation in non-conventional energy are also being explored, citing the completion of a civilian nuclear deal with the United States. That deal is intended to help lift an international ban on nuclear trade with India. The government also has signed agreements with Brazil for cooperation in bio-fuel and with Thailand for cooperation in renewable energy.

India on African Safari, Hunting Oil

Mahatma Gandhi once said that "commerce between India and Africa will be of ideas and services, not of manufactured goods against raw materials after the fashion of western exploiters." However, according to Zambian opposition MP Guy Scott, "People are saying, 'The Whites were bad, the Indians were worse, but the Chinese are worst of all."

China's increasing influence in Africa has attracted great attention in recent years. But, Asia's other rising power, India, is also becoming more active on this front, as its economic links are moving beyond its traditional partners in the British Commonwealth. Indeed, India's non-oil trade with West Africa currently stands at more than $3 billion and is rising fast, accounting for 1.2 per cent of the country's total foreign trade.

India's economic activity in Africa goes far beyond its ever popular Bollywood movies. Indian investment in Côte d'Ivoire is expected to grow to $1 billion by 2011, which represents 10 per cent of total Indian foreign investment in the last decade. India's state-run Oil and Natural Gas Corporation (ONGC Videsh) produces Sudanese oil, and over the next two years Indian diplomatic missions will open in Mali, Gabon, Niger, and Burkina Faso. Until 2003, the Indian Foreign Ministry had a single Africa division; it now has three: West and Central Africa, East and Southern Africa, and West Asia and North Africa.

A study by the Federation of Indian Chambers of Commerce and Industry identified five main sectors that can act as "engines of growth" to boost Indo-Africa trade: pharmaceuticals and the health sector, information technology, water management, food processing, and education.

Nigeria is India's largest trading partner in Africa. Bilateral annual trade turnover exceeds $3 billion, with oil constituting more than 96 per cent of Indian imports from Nigeria. India maintains a three-pronged strategy: term contract for crude purchase, participation in the upstream sector, and refineries.

This puts India in direct competition with the West and other Asian countries to secure West African resources. But, India's quest for energy in West Africa is not a core component of the government's energy policy; rather, it is part of its effort to diversify energy sources by offering infrastructure investments, in addition to cash bonus payments when contracts are signed.

Seventeen of the 45 blocks are being reserved for unknown companies that will be given a first right of refusal on acreage in exchange for promises to invest heavily in projects not directly related to oil production, such as new power plants and refineries. These negotiations have been ongoing, and India's ONGC, in alliance with Mittal Energy, part of the Mittal companies run by Indian billionaire Lakshmi Mittal, is tipped to get the right of first refusal for a number of blocks.

During a Nigerian mini-bid round in 2006, ONGC-Mittal was offered the right of first refusal for three blocks. ONGC-Mittal Energy is keen to secure blocks with proven reserves, but also is less concerned about the fine detail of the infrastructure packages than their Asian competitors. The creation of ONGC-Mittal in late 2005 seems to have been intended to cut through bureaucratic processes, learn from the private sector, and strengthen bids as an infrastructure provider.

In 2005, the Indian Cabinet's Committee on Economic Affairs prevented, on due diligence grounds and at the last moment, the overseas arm of ONGC Videsh from entering into a $2 billion deal for a stake in a Nigerian oil block. But the 2007 licensing round appears to have been rushed through to raise cash during the dying days of the Obasanjo administration, and it would serve India's government well to watch this process closely, too.

Other parts of the Mittal dynasty have also raised eyebrows in West Africa. In late 2005, Mittal Steel, the world's largest steel company, signed a $900 million deal with Liberia's

Transitional Government to mine iron ore, which many claim allowed Mittal to opt out of human rights and environmental law. The elected government of President Ellen Johnson-Sirleaf in 2006 reviewed the deal, and the Liberian Senate is currently scrutinising it.

India's business engagement in Africa attracts mixed opinion. Mahatma Gandhi once said that "commerce between India and Africa will be of ideas and services, not of manufactured goods against raw materials after the fashion of western exploiters." However, according to Zambian opposition MP Guy Scott, "People are saying, The Whites were bad, the Indians were worse, but the Chinese are worst of all."

India should not regard Africa as simply a source of natural resources. Instead, it needs to invest in the region's human capital and share Indian know-how. Many Indian goods have much greater suitability for African than Western markets. Sales of Tata cars, for instance, are booming in many African countries.

But, shared know-how should move beyond economic links. India's democracy in a post-colonial setting has relevant lessons for Africa. India also offers important experience in agricultural expansion, clean water management, and confronting the growing threat of climate change.

Whatever role India ultimately plays in Africa, perhaps its most important contribution could be to introduce competition. India's government needs to carefully watch how its companies and others rise to this challenge.

REFERENCES

1. "Energising India" *The Indian Express,* New Delhi, 29 January 2008.
2. Ibid.
3. htt:/www. energypublisher.com
4. htt:/www.iags.org
5. "Energising India", op.cit.
6. htt:/www.rediff.com
7. htt:/www. earthtimes.org
8. htt:/www. iht.com
9. htt:/www.sundaytimes.lk

5

Sino-Indian Energy Cooperation in Sudan: Opportunities and Obstacles

Africa is frequently viewed as a loser in the process of economic globalisation. Writers have emphasized that Africa is of little relevance 'because no important economic interests are greatly affected.[1] But, Africa's oil and gas is one of the few outstanding exceptions to the perceived insignificance of Africa. The United States will soon depend on Africa for a quarter of its total crude oil imports, and Africa already accounts for more than a quarter of China's oil imports today. According to the BP chief executive John Browne, 'Unless geologists succeed in finding new and so far unidentified provinces, as consumers we will all be dependent on supplies from just three areas—West Africa, Russia and, most important of all, the five states around the Mideast Gulf'.[2] Crude oil is one of the world's most important strategic resources, and Africa has attracted a lot of attention among corporate and political decision-makers because of growing global oil demand.

Indeed, it has been suggested that Africa is experiencing a 'New Scramble' thanks primarily to its oil and gas wealth, with the United States and the People's Republic of China actively competing for access to Africa's resources. But, is the term 'New Scramble' fitting to describe what is currently unfolding in Africa? This study aims to scrutinise the claim that Africa is facing a New Scramble, analysing the nature of the economic and political changes at work, the importance of Africa's oil, and the likely effects of the new oil rush.[3]

The study starts with an overview of the phenomenon labelled by some as the 'New Scramble'. The main body of the paper evaluates the existence of a New Scramble from three subject perspectives: history, international relations, and business studies. Finally, by analysing the likely impact on the economies of oil-producing states, it considers whether we should dismay or rejoice over the 'New Scramble for Africa'. It concludes that the existence of a New Scramble or a US-Chinese race for Africa should be treated with some caution and that the use of terms such as 'scramble' and 'race' is perhaps misleading, while the economic impact of oil investments is likely to be bleak.

New Scramble for African Energy

In 2004, *The Economist* magazine loosely used the term 'A New Scramble' in an article about China's business links with Africa.[4] Elsewhere, the term 'New Scramble' had been used to refer to the expanding-interests of the United States in Africa.[5] A preoccupation with China and the United States reflects discussions in the corridors of power in Washington and Beijing about a new Sino-American rivalry in Africa, coming only less than a decade after talk of a developing US-French rivalry in Africa.[6]

There is evidence of greater involvement of the United States and China in Africa," in terms of both commercial interests and political engagement. The recent expansion of Chinese interests has caught particular attention.[7] China is currently Africa's third most important trading partner, ahead of the United Kingdom and behind the United States and France.[8] Foreign Direct Investment (FDI) to Africa from China reached US$900 million in 2004. In April 2006, China National Offshore Oil Corporation (CNOOC) announced that it had completed a US$2.3 billion deal to buy a 45 per cent interest in an offshore oil-mining concession in Nigeria.[9] By 2004, 28.7 per cent of Chinese crude oil imports already derived from African oil-producing countries.[10] Indeed, according to the *Economic Observer*,[11] Angola has overtaken Saudi Arabia in terms of the quantity of crude oil supplied to China in the first six months of 2006.[12] More than 800 Chinese companies are reportedly operating in 49 African countries, and Chinese trade with Africa was said to surpass US$50 billion in 2006—a five-fold increase from five years ago.[13]

American investments in Africa have not risen at the same exponential rates over the past decade, but they are still enormous. According to the US Department of Commerce, US direct investment to Sub-Saharan Africa in 2004 amounted to US$13.5 billion, 23.4 per cent more than in 2003—and oil-producing countries (Equatorial Guinea, Gabon, Angola, Chad, and Nigeria) were the top five recipients. At the same time, oil imports (crude and non-crude) continued to dominate imports from Sub-Saharan Africa with US$40.1 billion in oil imports in 2005, accounting for 79.8 per cent of all US purchases in the continent.[14] African oil imports to the United States have been steadily rising and already account for some 20 per cent of total US imports; indeed, the United States already imports more oil from Africa than from the whole Persian Gulf.[15] According to a recent report by the Council on Foreign Relations, the region's importance to the United States is not only because of the scale of US investment, its share of US imports, and the US citizens who help explore and produce those volumes, but also because the Gulf of Guinea countries produce high-quality low-sulphur oil that is highly valued by the US market.[16]

In this study, we concentrate mainly on the United States and the People's Republic of China, but one should note that the current pursuit of African oil riches extends to actors from other countries including emerging economies such as Malaysia, South Korea, Brazil, and India. In March 2006, the president of South Korea, Roh Moo-hyun, visited three resource-rich African countries, which according to a South Korean minister had a clear rationale: 'Closer cooperation with Africa's oil producers will help South Korea diversify its petroleum import sources'.[17] Brazil's president Lula da Silva has made a number of trips to Africa which are thought to help in selling Brazilian goods and services to oil-rich African countries and boosting Brazilian access to African oil. The prospect for oil in Sào Tomé e Principe has seen the Brazilian authorities opening their first embassy on the island in 2003. In addition, Brazil has opened an oil-backed loan credit line with Angola for US$580 million for the next three years paid with 20,000 barrels of oil a day.[18] Malaysia and India are also making significant investments in African oil-producing countries. In 2005, India offered lines of credit worth up to US$1 billion for infrastructure projects to West African petro-states (in the words of a senior Indian oil ministry official) 'in exchange of oil exploration rights'.[19] But does all of that newfound interest in Africa amount to a New Scramble?

A Historical Perspective of the Quest for African Energy

From a historical perspective, the first 'Scramble for Africa's oil' arguably started just prior to and after decolonisation.[20] Algeria—Which had extracted small amounts of oil from 1918—began producing significant quantities of oil when Algeria's Edjeleh and Hassi Messaoud oil fields began production in 1957.[21] Also in 1957, the first tanker load of crude oil was exported from Gabon,[22] and Nigeria started producing oil in December of that year,[23] while Libya started producing oil in 1961.[24] Africa's oil output increased more than 20-fold between 1960 and 1970 (Table 25). International events such as the Yom Kippur war in 1973 and the Iranian revolution in 1979 further underlined Africa's importance as an oil-producing region.

TABLE 25

Changing Profile of African and World Oil Ouput
(million metric tonnes) (1950-2005)

	African output	*World output*	*Africa as per cent of total world output*	*Africa's main oil-producing country*
1950	2.6	522.1	0.5	Egypt
1953	2.9	659.4	0.4	Egypt
1955	2.0	774.0	0.2	Egypt
1957	2.7	887.4	0.3	Egypt
1960	13.8	1,056.9	1.3	Algeria
1961	23.7	1,125.4	2.1	Algeria
1962	38.9	1,220.8	3.2	Algeria
1963	57.1	1,309.4	4.4	Algeria
1964	82.4	1,409.6	5.8	Libya
1965	106.5	1,566.3	6.8	Libya
1966	135.4	1,700.6	8.0	Libya
1967	149.1	1,824.7	8.2	Libya
1968	191.0	1,990.9	9.6	Libya
1969	242.7	2,141.2	11.3	Libya
1970	292.3	2,355.2	12.4	Libya
1971	273.8	2,492.7	11.0	Libya
1972	275.1	2,636.6	10.4	Libya

Contd...

Contd...table 25

1973	287.1	2,866.6	10.0	Libya
1974	264.9	2,87.5.2	9.2	Nigeria
1975	242.5	2,734.4	8.7	Nigeria
1976	289.0	2,969.0	9.7	Nigeria
1977	303.4	3,073.3	9.9	Libya
1978	298.0	3,103.1	9.6	Libya
1979	326.4	3,233.1	10.1	Nigeria
1980	300.6	3,087.9	9.7	Nigeria
1981	239.4	2,910.0	8.2	Nigeria
1982	230.5	2,795.6	8.2	Nigeria
1983	233.3	2,759.2	8.5	Nigeria
1984	248.8	2,814.6	8.8	Nigeria
1985	260.9	2,792.1	9.3	Nigeria
1986	260.6	2,936.0	8.9	Nigeria
1987	260.2	2,947.2	8.8	Nigeria
1988	274.9	3,069.1	9.0	Nigeria
1989	296.7	3,102.9	9.6	Nigeria
1990	320.9	3,170.6	10.1	Nigeria
1991	328.3	3,160.4	10.4	Nigeria
1992	335.3	3,189.7	10.5	Nigeria
1993	332.0	3,188.4	10.4	Nigeria
1994	333.9	3,236.9	10.3	Nigeria
1995	339.3	3,280.9	10.3	Nigeria
1996	355.9	3,375.9	10.5	Nigeria
1997	370.4	3,480.9	10.6	Nigeria
1998	363.9	3,547.6	10.3	Nigeria
1999	361.2	3,479.3	10.4	Nigeria
2000	373.0	3,613.8	10.3	Nigeria
2001	375.2	3,593.7	10.4	Nigeria
2002	379.6	3,572.0	10.6	Nigeria
2003	399.6	3,705.8	10.8	Nigeria
2004	441.0	3,865.3	11.4	Nigeria
2005	467.1	3,895.0	12.0	Nigeria

Source: 1950-64 data from Jonathan Baker, "Oil and African Development', *Journal of Modern African Studies* 15 (1977), pp. 175-212; 1965-2005 data from *BP Statistical Review of World Energy* (BP, London, 2006).

Indeed, the first oil-driven 'Scramble' was arguably of much greater significance than the current one. It led to major political, economic, and social transformations in some of the key oil-producing states in Africa, including Libya, Algeria, and—above all—Africa's most populous country of Nigeria. From a level of 20,000 barrels per day in 1960, Nigeria's daily oil production rose to over 2 million barrels in 1973; Nigeria's oil production today is only slightly higher than that achieved in the 1970s.[25] This rise in crude oil output was reflected in oil's share of Nigeria's total exports (an increase from 10.75 to 83.14 per cent between 1963 and 1973) and oil's contribution to Nigeria's total government revenue (an increase from 26.3 to 82.1 per cent between 1970 and 1974).[26] Compared with the deep transformations that took place in the 1960s and 1970s, the impact of today's 'Scramble' in countries such as Nigeria and Angola will be relatively insignificant.

More fundamentally, the use of the term 'New Scramble' is historically misleading, in that the original term 'Scramble for Africa' in the 1880s and 1890s signified a very different process. This period witnessed European nations including Britain, France, Germany, and Belgium turn Africa into colonies following 'a formal partition of Africa at the Berlin conference between 1884 and 1885. The Berlin conference provided those European nations with the legitimacy to govern Africa politically, militarily, and economically according to their spheres of control.[27] Hence, access to natural resources such as oil in the colonies was dictated by the colonial power that provided the human expertise, capital, and technology to ignite the oil boom that followed. Key characteristics of the nineteenth century Scramble are missing from the current expansion of interests in Africa. For instance, there are no clear spheres of interest or spheres of control today.[28] Foreign investment was neither particularly important before the Berlin Conference in 1884 nor important in the immediate period afterwards, in contrast to the current expansion that is driven by foreign investment. But, above all, the role of Africans in the nineteenth century Scramble was very different, in that the process was driven and dictated by European colonial interests, whereas today African leaders act in the role of decision-makers.

If judged by the original meaning of the term 'scramble' in the 1880s and 1890s, Africa's oil boom in the 1960s had much more of a colonial imprint than the oil rush we are witnessing today. The development of oil resources in African colonies was pursued for strategic and economic interests of the colonial powers, and private and public firms of the colonial powers developed the oil sector. In Anglophone Africa, a Shell-BP venture was given an effective monopoly for oil exploration and production in Nigeria and a 1914 colonial ordinance stipulated that only British oil companies were permitted to obtain oil licences in Nigeria, allowing Shell-BP to establish an effective domination of the country's oil production.[29] In Francophone Africa, French oil interests dominated the oil industry at independence in Algeria and Gabon; the new Algerian government was even made to sign a guarantee that French oil companies would receive preferential treatment in the granting of oil concessions for six years after the country's independence.[30] The situation was perhaps less clear-cut in many other African countries, but it is less than a coincidence that, for instance, the Italian oil company Agip had become by far the largest foreign oil-producing firm in Italy's former colony Libya.[31]

In contrast to the first oil boom around the time of decolonisation, today's oil boom has few marks of neo-colonialism, as American, Chinese, and other firms compete against each other to gain endorsement among African governments, who remain firmly in charge of decision-making. It is African governments, not external actors, who dictate terms for foreign investors today. As discussed above, from a historical perspective, the claim of a 'New Scramble' can hardly be supported.

New Scramble: An International Perspective

In a world, where both developed and developing countries require huge quantities of oil resources, Africa has once again become strategic for major actors in the international system. Strategic considerations related to Africa are, of course, influenced by global processes and rivalries, with China's great power status having recently received particular attention. There is a growing body of realist literature, which debates whether the rise of China as a world power entails an attempt to counterbalance US unpolarity in world affairs and whether this will lead to a more or less stable and peaceful world.[32] While we shall not recount those arguments here, it is apparent that there has been a major shift in China's relationship with the outside world in the last decade, and China has emerged as an active player in international affairs, as evidenced by the number of bilateral agreements, the number of trade and security accords, and China's participation in key multilateral organisations.[33] There is little doubt that access to natural resources is an important consideration in China's new active role in the international system.

There is also little doubt that the interest in Africa's oil and gas resources has spurned a rivalry between international actors in Africa, notably the American and Chinese governments.[34] The US government launched its National Energy Plan in May 2001. Authored by Vice-President Dick Cheney and also known as the 'Cheney Report', the plan set out US energy requirements over the next 25 years. To achieve it, the report encourages the White House to make oil imports 'a priority of our [US] trade and foreign policy'; it calls on the president and other top officials to find ways to meet America's growing oil requirements. In late 2002, the US president George W. Bush took an unprecedented step, welcoming 11 African heads of state—most of them oil-rich states—to the White House, while other top US officials including the US Secretary of State Colin Powell visited Nigeria, Angola, and Gabon. In May 2004, Angola's president dos Santos was welcomed at the White House by President Bush, and the visit culminated with the Angolan authorities extending Chevron's operatorship of block 0 for a further 30 years. These were just some of the key milestones in the new strategic US relationship with Africa.

The US interests in Africa are complex, and many issues such as terrorism are high on the agenda. Africa is littered with fragile states. Upcoming and existing oil-producing countries in Africa such as Mauritania, Sào Tomé e Principe, and Equatorial Guinea have been marred by coup attempts. In addition, the failure to share the revenues generated by natural resources such as oil in an equitable manner has created disenchanted and disillusioned young populations, which may provide a fertile ground for religious fundamentalism and a haven for terrorists. Therefore, Washington views it as in its interest to prevent Africa—particularly oil-producing countries—from inheriting the Middle Eastern scenario of constant political instability. Indeed, commentators have claimed that the US base in Djibouti plays the dual role of monitoring extremism in the region whilst protecting its oil interests. The Bush Administration's Pan-Sahel Initiative (PSI) and the regional establishment of associated basing rights are said to have been designed to secure US national security interests—namely oil.[35] Furthermore, the US Department of Defence has begun searching for possible sites for forward operating bases like those in

Kyrgyzstan and Uzbekistan. The attractive candidates for such facilities are Senegal, Ghana, Mali, Uganda, Kenya, and Sào Tomé e Principe, with the latter being close to the major West African oil-producing countries. Although officials tend to talk mainly about terrorism when explaining the need for such facilities, they have told Greg Jaffe of the *Wall Street Journal* that 'a key mission for US forces [in Africa] would be to ensure that Nigeria's oil fields, which in the future could account for as much as 25 per cent of all US oil imports, are secure'.[36]

The US initiatives were mirrored by China's new strategic relationship with Africa. In 2000, China established the China-Africa Cooperation Forum, which meets every three years, and amongst other things, it aims to promote economic cooperation between Africa and China. Nearly 80 foreign ministers and ministers of international economic cooperation from 45 African countries attended the first forum held in Beijing. In 2004, the Chinese president Jiang Zemin visited Tunisia, Libya, and Nigeria; the first visit to Nigeria by a Chinese head of state for 31 years. In February 2005, Zeng Peiyan, China's deputy prime minister, visited Angola and signed nine agreements on mineral resources and infrastructure, petroleum exploration and prospecting, and economic and technical assistance. In early 2006, Chinaese president visited Nigeria. During the visit, President Hu Jintao secured four oil licences from Nigeria in a deal worth US$4 billion in investment.[37] China has also cancelled around US$10 billion in bilateral debt from African countries.[38]

For China, energy security is a primary motive for its involvement in Africa, but it has been shown that it is not the only one. Beijing's engagement with Africa is thought to have two components: diplomatic and economic. Diplomatically, China seeks African support for its status as a key power in world affairs as well as to dimmish Taiwan's chances of diplomatic recognition in Africa.[39] Economically, China's rapid economic boom requires African raw materials (particularly oil) and a market for its goods. According to the US Energy Information Administration, China accounted for 40 per cent of total growth in global demand for oil in the last four years.[40] In 2003, China ranked second just after the United States and ahead of Japan in oil consumption, and Beijing estimates its consumption will amount to 450 million tons in 2020, 60 per cent of which would be imports." It seems that the United States and China are competing to secure access for the oil riches of Africa. Therefore, it was a somewhat different motive that brought together the world's two most powerful states to get actively involved on the African continent. But oil and gas resources were undoubtedly a key motive.

Both the American and the Chinese governments were important in paving the way for American and Chinese oil interests in expanding in Africa. The US government used diplomatic instruments (e.g. re-opening its embassy in Equatorial Guinea and invitations to Washington), economic incentives (e.g. financial facilities offered by the US Export-Import Bank for doing business in Nigeria), and military aid (the largest portion of US military aid to Africa was aimed at Nigeria and Angola).[42] While the US government assisted private US firms in obtaining oil concessions for oil exploration and production, the Chinese government focused instead on securing oil supplies through bilateral agreements. As the most notable example, Sinopec—a

Chinese state-owned oil company—acquired oil concessions in Angola's Blocks 3 and 18 on the back of a US$2 billion oil-backed credit from China's Eximbank in 2004 to rebuild the country's railways, government buildings, schools, hospitals, and roads.[43] Indeed, Block 3 once belonged to France's Total, which the Angolan authorities declined to renew to Total in favour of Sinopec. Sonangol has also recently agreed with Sinopec on a joint venture to build a new refinery on the south coast of Angola, a project that international oil companies deemed economically unviable.[44] The Angolan example demonstrates how China has adopted an aid-for-oil strategy that has resulted in increasing supplies of oil from African countries.

While foreign governments continue to intervene to safeguard their strategic interests in Africa, the US-Chinese rivalry provides a marked contrast to the externally driven Scramble of the 1880s. Indeed, the appearance of new economic powers in world affairs such as China has marginalised the Western driven economic model based on externally imposed conditional ties on issues ranging from the respect of human rights and good governance, to liberal economic reform, in exchange for financial assistance. Energy hungry nations such as India, Brazil, South Korea, Malaysia, and China have proven more supportive and have provided loans, debt relief, scholarships, training, and provision of military hardware without political or economic conditionalities, in exchange for a foothold in the oil business. In turn, incumbent African leaders have identified Chinese unconditional financial resources, cheap products, and know-how as an important tool to fend off pressure for political and economic reform from international organizations such as the International Monetary Fund (IMF) and Western governments. As one American diplomat put it: "We [the United States] were not prepared to provide the Angolan authorities with much needed financial assistance to rebuild the country—so the Angolans had no choice but to turn to the Chinese for that assistance in exchange for oil".

It is perhaps an obvious statement to point out that the source of the new strategic alternatives for African countries is oil wealth, which gives relatively low, especially if African offshore operations are compared with those in the North Sea or the Gulf of Mexico." Just as importantly, a key attraction of Africa for oil companies is the high success rate in drilling operations, that is, the number of successful oil- and gas-well discoveries divided by the total number of drillings. As a key geological advantage, the quality of African oil tends to be high; African crude oil tends to be of relatively high API gravity (which stands for the American Petroleum Institute standard) and low sulphur content (which is sought after), with a few notable exceptions such as Egyptian crude.[45]

In addition to the relatively low operational costs and quality of the oil, Africa has transport advantages; this is both economically advantageous and strategically significant. In comparison with crude oil from the Middle East, crude oil from West and North Africa is closer to the markets of Europe and the United States, so an oil tanker journey from Nigeria or Angola is at least several days shorter, and the buyer can therefore save money on the payment of tanker charter and insurance. Furthermore, North Africa has a key advantage of supplying oil and gas via pipelines to Europe, and there are currently plans for expanding and building new pipelines from Libya and Algeria to Spain and Italy, as well as a pipeline from Egypt through Turkey to Europe planned for 2011. The most ambitious plan is to build the 4,300-kilometre long Trans-Sahara pipeline from Nigeria through Algeria to Europe (rumoured to require an investment of US$10 billion), for which a feasibility study has recently been completed.[46]

To sum up, while any generalisations are difficult and there are undoubtedly exceptions, African oil and gas resources offer clear commercial advantages to international oil firms. This helps to understand why African oil production over the next decade will be expanded at a quicker pace than the world average. But can we argue that there is a Scramble for Africa from a business perspective?

If a scramble for Africa has taken place, one would expect that companies engaged in African operations have both increased in quantity and have a more diverse make-up. One measure of this commercial engagement is the number of oil companies that hold oil and gas licences in a given country. In the largest petro-state—Nigeria—the current number of companies with an Oil Mining Licence (OML) and an Oil Prospecting Licence (OPL) is 77 (as of September 2006), of which 45 are indigenous Nigerian firms. To put this into context, in 1966 and 1986, 8 and 12 oil companies respectively had OMLs or OPLs in Nigeria. By 1998, and still before the current influx of Chinese and other emerging market firms, their number had already risen to over 50.[47]

In terms of the composition of companies, there is a more readily visible diversity, given the influx of Chinese, Indian, Brazilian, and other companies—from both the public and the private sectors. In Nigeria, for instance, valuable oil licences have been awarded to Brazil's Petrobras, the CNOOC, India's Oil and Natural Gas Corporation (ONGC), the Korean National Oil Corporation, as well as smaller Western oil companies and indigenous Nigerian firms. Senior executives of Western firms privately express their concerns about the influx of new players, and they see them as a potential threat to their position. One of the most often heard complaints of Western managers is that the new Asian firms often pay little attention to social and environmental concerns. As one senior-executive of a British oil firm told us, 'at the moment, there is a skewed playing field' where Western firms may spend more money on social and environmental improvements than their non-Western counterparts, while they may be excluded from certain areas altogether such as from the Sudanese oil sector.[48]

On various occasions, the new players have encroached on territories previously in the domain of the giant multinationals such as Exxon, Shell, and BP. In Angola, the authorities declined to new an oil concession to Total in favour of Sinopec, as we previously mentioned. During the second licensing round in Libya in 2005, European and Asian companies received almost all of the oil licences with just one exception; winners included companies from Japan, Russia, Turkey, Indonesia, India, and China.[49] During the 2005 licensing round in Nigeria, the government awarded two deep onshore oil concessions to the Korea National Oil Corporation, and the Economist Intelligence Unit commented that 'the list of auction winners was notable for the near absence of the six Western oil multinationals that operate the joint venture companies that produce almost all of Nigeria's oil output'.[50] Therefore, by the measure of the diversity of companies entering Africa, one can indeed speak of a Scramble.

However, while the entry of emerging market firms is in itself an important and underresearched phenomenon, one should caution against overemphasizing their impact. With the notable exception of Brazil's Petrobras, which is recognised as one of the world's most experienced oil firms in offshore petroleum technology, the other oil firms from emerging markets are relatively inexperienced market players. As argued by an international oil company executive:

> The Chinese have not yet got hold of the necessary technology and human expertise to challenge Western firms over the monopoly of African oil. In addition, international oil companies will only invest in an oil and gas field if it is of commercial significance in order to justify the investment required for such operations. On the other hand, the Chinese do not have those concerns while bidding for oil and gas licences because they are government funded companies.

The above quotation implies that the Chinese may end up paying inflated prices for oil licences, but they threaten Western interests, to a large extent, in onshore areas and in the so-called marginal oilfields where less technical expertise is required—not in the most sought after deep offshore areas. Indeed, in a number of cases such as Gabon, the new entrants have focused on marginal fields, which have been either abandoned by major oil companies or considered commercially unviable by the established larger multinational firms. Furthermore, as mentioned earlier, the Chinese commercial engagement in the oil sector focuses on supply contracts and buying shares in existing oil fields; with the notable exception of the Sudan, the Chinese state-owned firms do not yet operate any significant oil-and-gas-producing fields of their own.[51] Deep offshore oil fields in the Gulf of Guinea are considered the greatest and most profitable prize in Africa; here, the dominant companies are Exxon, Shell, BP, and a handful of others, while most other companies lack the financial and—above all—the technical capability to seriously rival them. Therefore, the new players do not necessarily directly threaten the position of the established Western firms with regard to the most attractive business opportunities. The claim of an unfolding 'Scramble' or 'US-Chinese rivalry' needs to be treated with some caution.

At this point, it is pertinent to point out that competition between Western firms for oil and gas concessions in Africa has surely existed for decades. New actors such as Italy's Agip in the 1960s, which was then prepared to offer more favourable deals to African governments, have sometimes caused major concern to the established players. But beyond a number of re-negotiated deals and the excitement of the moment, one needs to wait until there are discernible shifts in the overall situation. The impact of Chinese and other emerging market oil firms on the ground is still relatively small. For instance, over 95 per cent of the oil produced in Africa's largest petro-state, Nigeria, is generated by only five companies: Shell, Exxon, Chevron, Total, and Agip; this situation is unlikely to change soon either in Nigeria or in some other key petro-states. If a major shift is going to happen in future, it will take years to materialise.

While China has become one of Africa's main trading partners, its foreign investment is still lagging behind. According to the United Nations Conference on Trade and Development

(UNCTAD), 'notwithstanding growing interest among Asian investors, most of Africa's FDI inflows originate mainly from developed countries (Western Europe, the United States) and South Africa'. The top five investors to Africa are France, the Netherlands, South Africa, the United Kingdom, and the United States, which accounted for 'more than half of total inflows to Africa' in 2003 and 2004.[52] The Chinese impact will be felt to a much greater extent over the coming years, but the currently available data do not yet point to a shift in investment.

African Energy and the Prospects of African Economies

Investment in Africa's natural resources offers one of the very few ways for the continent to attract any significant private investment. According to UNCTAD figures, five major oil-producing countries—Angola, Egypt, Equatorial Guinea, Sudan, and Nigeria—accounted for almost half of all FDI inflows to Africa in 2004 (see Table 26 for a list of major oil-producing countries). The share of oil and gas in the total FDI was 93 per cent in Angola, 64 per cent in Egypt, 94 per cent in Equatorial Guinea, and 90 per cent in Nigeria.[53] The oil and gas sector in the Gulf of Guinea alone was forecast in 2004 to attract US$30-40 billion in investment this decade.[54] As one senior official of the US State Department observed few years ago, African oil is the 'only game in town'.

TABLE 26

Africa's Major Oil-producing Countries (1,000 barrels per day)
(1996-2005)

	1996	*1997*	*1998*	*1999*	*2000*	*2001*	*2002*	*2003*	*2004*	*2005*
Nigeria	2,145	2,316	2,167	2,066	2,155	2,274	2,103	2,263	2,502	2,580
Algeria	1,386	1,421	1,461	1,515	1,578	1,562	1,680	1,852	1,946	2,015
Libya	1,452	1,489	1,480	1,425	1,469	1,421	1,374	1,486	1,607	1,702
Angola	716	741	731	745	746	742	905	885	986	1,242
Egypt	894	873	857	827	781	758	751	749	721	696
Sudan	5	9	12	63	174	211	233	255	325	379
Equatorial Guinea	17	62	85	96	117	173	210	234	329	355
Congo (Brazzaville)	200	225	264	293	275	271	258	243	240	253
Gabon	365	364	337	340	327	301	295	240	235	234
Chad	-	24	168	-	-	-	-	-	-	173
Tunisia	89	81	83	84	78	71	75	68	72	74
Cameroon	110	124	105	95	88	81	75	68	62	58
Other Africa	62	64	63	56	56	53	63	71	75	72
Total Africa	7,441	7,768	7,644	7,606	7,844	7,918	8,022	8,438	9,266	9,835

Source: BP Statistical Review of World Energy (2006).

The oil sector investment could potentially stimulate the economic development of oil-producing countries through its employment and supply chains as well as through its contribution to public finances. Indeed, oil-producing states from Kuwait to Gabon appear richer than many comparable non-oil-producing states. Perhaps nowhere else in Africa was the impact of an oil boom more visible than in Libya. When Libya became independent in 1951, the country was amongst the poorest in the world, with a GNP per capita of some US$35. Only about 1 per cent of the country was arable in an economy reliant on agriculture, 90 per cent of Libyans were illiterate, and an industrial sector was almost non-existent.[55] Libya was an 'unviable state' in the sense that its fledgling domestic economy failed to generate nearly enough revenue to sustain even the low-living standards at the time.[56] The country became essentially reliant on foreign aid. However, with the start of oil production after 1960, the country's GNP per capita jumped from over US$250 in 1960 to over US$2,000 in 1969 and over US$5,600 in 1974.[57] From being the poorest state in North Africa, Libya rose to being a serious economic and political player.

Despite major ideological differences between firmly socialist countries such as Algeria and firmly capitalist countries such as Nigeria, the economic policies of the major petro-states showed similarity. Nationalisation or partial nationalisation in the 1970s was seen as a means of indigenising the oil sector and transferring technology, while oil revenues were to be channelled into industrialisation initiatives to shake off the heritage of 'neo-colonial' trading relationships with Western states. But, these strategies failed in Nigeria, Algeria, and elsewhere, as industrialisation was mainly based on subsidies for ultimately inefficient import-substituting industries.

One of the false promises of oil relates to employment generation. The oil industry is highly capital-intensive; it means that large amounts of capital and equipment but few workers are required to run production operations and the sector generates relatively little local employment. For instance, the oil and gas sector in Algeria provides over 95 per cent of the country's export revenues but employs perhaps some 135,000 people. In comparison, Algeria's agricultural sector and construction sector employed 1.5 and 1.1 million people by the late 1990s, respectively.[58] But Algeria is Africa's giant in the oil industry with a well-developed oil refining and petrochemicals sector. Other oil producers such as Angola and new petro-states such as Chad and Equatorial Guinea have even fewer local workers and are unlikely to achieve the Algerian levels of employment in the hydrocarbon sector in the near future. For instance, Angola's oil sector employs 19,000 Angolans; after half a century of oil production in Angola, only 50 per cent of engineers are Angolans, which is still a higher share than in new petro-states such as Equatorial Guinea.[59]

Given its failures to jump-start industrialisation or provide employment, the key economic impact of oil is the inflow of hard currency proceeds into an economy. But oil revenues have had many negative economic consequences. As has often been recited, many petro-states have previously suffered from the phenomenon known as the 'resource curse'. Despite being well endowed with natural resources, petro-states have experienced economic underdevelopment and political mismanagement, a finding strongly supported by many quantitative and qualitative studies and accepted by World Bank and IMF economists.[60] Quantitative studies show that states with a high share of natural resource exports have had lower economic growth rates than states without these resources. The causes of this lower growth include a phenomenon known as Dutch Disease: large inflows of foreign exchange make exports of agricultural and manufacturing goods more expensive and draw resources from non-mineral sectors, thereby stifling the development of those sectors. Natural resource exports are also said to undermine good governance and political accountability to society, not least through the neglect of non-mineral tax revenues, the relaxation of government accountability standards, and the growth of a dependency mentality. We shall not recount those arguments here, as they are well known and can be found elsewhere.[61]

A small number of resource-rich developing countries—in particular, Botswana, Chile, and Malaysia—have not only been able to beat the 'resource curse' but have achieved high economic growth through skilful government policies, but they were mining—not oil-producing—countries.[62] African petro-states failed to establish stabilization funds, foster effective institutions or other measures to cope with some of the adverse economic consequences of oil wealth and to provide for future generations when oil riches run out. The greed of decision-makers and pressures from interest groups and the public ensured that such measures had little prospect of success. Ironically, a reserve fund was established in one of Africa's most repressive regimes—Equatorial Guinea.[63] Establishing such funds was more difficult in countries with more decentralized political power and with greater likelihood of change in government where many actors competed for the spoils of oil riches, particularly under democratic regimes. In those countries, government proposals for conserving oil revenues tended to meet with considerable resistance. When Nigeria's government proposed to put a US$1.98 billion windfall from 2000 into a reserve account (known as the 'rainy day' fund), the representatives of the 36 federal states revolted and forced the government to share the oil revenues.[64] Similarly, when Algeria's president Bouteflika proposed that, in the wake of Sonatrach's record US$20 billion in export revenues in 2000, oil and gas revenues should be channelled to a newly established stabilisation fund, many interest groups lobbied against the proposal and deflected government policy.[65]

The most far-reaching attempt to avoid the pitfalls of the 'resource curse' in an African petto-state was the World Bank-imposed revenue management system in Chad. However, as Scott Pegg demonstrated in a previous issue of *African Affairs*, 'its record to date is far from impressive'.[66] Even though parts of the World Bank programme yielded some economic and social benefits, the Chadian policy experiment is unlikely to be repeated in any of the established petro-states. In Chad, external funders had relatively high bargaining power before the start of oil production, as the country needed their support. Following the inflow of oil revenues, this leverage quickly declined and the World Bank experiment did not extend to new Chadian oil fields while the Chadian government has recently forced the World Bank into a U-turn. In 2006, Chad's agreement with the World Bank was re-negotiated and greatly watered down and the 'future generation fund' aimed for long-term social development was scrapped, as President Idriss Deby demanded more access to the country's oil revenues to purchase weapons for use against rebels.[67] In established petro-states, the World Bank has had even less leverage than in Chad, and alternative sources of support from China and elsewhere further reduce that leverage. In summary, oil sector investment is unlikely to generate economic prosperity short of radical solutions.

One cannot dispute the increased international importance of Africa, which can be attributed to the increasing demand for its natural resources and the interest from 'new' players such as China and India. China's rise as one of Africa's principal commercial partners is also of immense importance. But, efforts have been made to provide a nuanced view of what has been sometimes labelled the New Scramble for Africa. The conclusions we reached were somewhat different from what we expected before investigating this topic in greater depth. On the basis of our analysis of the historical, international relations, and business perspectives, we conclude that the existence of a 'New Scramble' or a US-Chinese race should be treated with some caution and the use of terms such as 'scramble' and 'race' is perhaps misleading. The existence of a Scramble can at best be framed in narrow terms as an increased international interest in African oil resources focused largely on the Gulf of Guinea, entailing greater private investment and diplomatic engagement from a larger than before number of external actors.

From a historical perspective, today's interest in Africa is markedly different from what has been termed the Scramble for Africa in the late nineteenth century; indeed, we believe that the expansion of the oil industry in the 1960s was more akin to a Scramble than the phenomenon we witness today. A crucial contrast is that African' tend to be in the driving seat today, and future research should pay greater attention to the strategies that Africans use in channelling external sources of investment and political support instead of focusing on American or Chinese policies and strategies.

From an international relations perspective, there are most grounds to detect the effects of the increased external interest in Africa. The Chinese loans and investments in particular have opened new policy options to African leaders. Dos Santos in Angola or Obiang in Equatorial Guinea no longer have to rely on the support of either the Western governments or the Bretton Woods institutions alone. One can therefore speak of a qualitative shift in external relations, but once again it may be advisable not to overestimate it. Oil-producing states such as Angola and Equatorial Guinea have already previously side-stepped the Bretton Woods institutions thanks to the oil boom, as they were able to obtain finance through oil revenue receipts from Western firms or oil-backed loans from Western banks without any strings attached.[68] Just like all other external support, the significance of Chinese loans and investments needs to be seen in the overall context of the bargaining power of African states; booming Angola has more bargaining power than Gabon where policy options are restricted because of declining oil production.[69] The divide between states that experience an oil boom and states that experience an oil sector decline is of greater significance than the presence of specific external actors.

From a business perspective, one should also caution against overvaluing the significance of US-Chinese rivalry or, more generally, a commercial race for Africa's resources. Western managers are surely concerned, and various valuable commercial concessions have been allocated to Chinese firms at the expense of established Western rivals. However, for the most part, the new entrants do not pose a direct threat to the established companies in many areas, given their divergent focus and skills. It is possible that this may change in future, especially if new actors such as China's Sinopec are able to accumulate more expertise in oil exploration and production in deep offshore areas. For the time being, the visibility of Chinese investments in Africa does not necessarily translate into direct competition. This applies as much to the oil sector as to many other sectors, for instance, tourism in Sierra Leone.[70]

Beside of the question of the existence of a Scramble or a race for Africa, what is perhaps most important is what effect the increased investments will have on African economies and ordinary Africans. As we briefly outlined above, past lessons from oil-producing states do not encourage optimism. Oil and gas investment has many proven negative economic and social effects, which often outweigh the benefits. Whatever we call them, the new investments in the African oil and gas sector may not necessarily be good news for ordinary Africans.

ENERGY PROFILE OF SUDAN

Sudan is becoming a significant world oil producer, proven oil reserves of five billion barrels as of January 2007 up from an estimated 563 million barrels of proven oil reserves in 2006.

Sudan is developing its significant hydrocarbon resources. The country's oil exports, which have increased sharply since the completion of a major oil-export pipeline in 1999, account for 70 per cent of total export revenues. Additional growth in Sudan's hydrocarbon sector will likely occur with a refurbished infrastructure, which has seen little improvement since the beginning of the country's civil conflicts in 1955.

As of January 2007, according to the Sudanese Minister of State for Energy and Mines Sudan is considering joining the Organization of Petroleum Exporting Countries (OPEC) in the future.

In January 2005, the Sudanese government in Khartoum and the Sudan People's Liberation Army (SPLA) in the south signed the Comprehensive Peace Agreement (CPA), which ended 21-year of civil war. Prior to the signing, several important issues were agreed upon by the two parties including the sharing of oil revenues (50:50). Also in 2005, President Bashir formed a border commission tasked with defining the border between northern and southern Sudan, in accordance to the CPA.

Much of Sudan's Oil Producing Region Lies in the Disputed Border Area

In 2004, Sudan's energy consumption mix was dominated by oil (93 per cent), with the remainder coming from hydroelectricity (7 per cent). Natural gas, coal, nuclear and other renewables are currently not part of the country's energy consumption mix. Between 1984-2004, the share of oil in Sudan's energy mix increased from 86 per cent to 93 per cent. Hydro-electricity consumption experienced a decrease, during the same time period, from 14 per cent to 7 per cent.

Oil

Sudan is becoming a significant world oil producer. According to Oil and Gas Journal (OGJ), Sudan contained proven oil reserves of five billion barrels as of January 2007 up from an estimated 563 million barrels of proven oil reserves in 2006. The majority of proven reserves are located in the south in the Muglad and Melut basins.

Due to civil conflict, oil exploration has mostly been limited to the central and south-central regions of the country. It is estimated that vast potential reserves are held in northwest Sudan, the Blue Nile basin, and the Red Sea area in eastern Sudan.

Sector Organisation

The Sudan National Petroleum Corporation (Sudapet) is active in Sudan's oil exploration and production. However, due to its limited technical and financial resources, Sudapet often develops joint ventures with foreign companies in oil projects. Foreign companies involved in Sudan's oil sector are primarily from Asia. They are led by the China National Petroleum Corporation (CNPC), India's Oil and Natural Gas Corporation (ONGC) and Malaysia's Petronas.

In October 2005, Sudan established the National Petroleum Commission (NPC) to bolster the development of the country's oil resources. To accomplish its mission, NPC allocates new oil contracts, and it ensures an equal sharing of oil revenues between the national government in Khartoum and the Government of South Sudan (GoSS).

In addition, NPC is responsible for resolving duplicate oil contract issues in which the GoSS has allocated contracts overlapping contracts previously granted by Khartoum. NPC is currently scrutinising duplicate contracts given to Total and White Nile Ltd. over Block B and the White Nile Petroleum Operation Company (WNPOC) and Ascom Group of Moldavia over Block 5b. President Bashir is believed to co-chair the NPC with Vice-President Salva Kiir, who also heads the GoSS.

Exploration and Production

Oil production has risen steadily since the July 1999 completion of an export pipeline that runs from central Sudan to the Port of Sudan. In 2006, crude oil production averaged 414,000 barrels per day (bbl/d), up from 363,000 bbl/d in 2005.

According to Angelina Tany, Minister of State for Mines and Energy, Sudan plans to be producing one million bbl/d of crude oil by the end of 2008.

Greater Nile Oil Project

In 1996, Canadian independent Arakis Energy (Arakis) began development of the Heglig and Unity fields (Blocks 1, 2, and 4), which contain estimated recoverable reserves of 600 million-1.2 billion barrels of oil. Because the fields are not located near the Red Sea coast, Arakis entered into a consortium with the Greater Nile Petroleum Operating Company (GNPOC) to raise investment for a 994-mile pipeline from the fields to the Suakim oil terminal near Port Sudan.

In September 1999, the first cargo of crude departed the export terminal. Although GNPOC originally constructed the pipeline with throughput of 150,000 bbl/d, its has since been increased to 300,000 bbl/d, while maximum capacity is estimated at 450,000 bbl/d. As of January 2007, combined production from Blocks 1, 2, and 4 was estimated at 260,000 bbl/d. The GNPOC joint venture is operated by CNPC (40 per cent), with partners Petronas (30 per cent), ONGC (25 per cent) and Sudapet (5 per cent).

Blocks 3 and 7

In June 2004, Petrodar, a consortium of CNPC (41 per cent), Petronas (40 per cent), Sudapet (8 per cent), Gulf Oil Petroleum (6 per cent), and the Al-Thani Corporation (5 per cent) awarded a $239 million contract to Malaysia's Ranhill International and Sudan's Petroneeds Services International for development work on Blocks 3 and 7.

The blocks contain the Adar Yale and Palogue oil fields, with estimated recoverable reserves of 460 million barrels. As of January 2007, Blocks 3 and 7 combined produced an estimated 165,000 bbl/d of oil. The fields could reach peak production of 200,000 bbl/d by late 2007. In November 2005, CNPC brought online the Petrodar pipeline linking the two blocks to Port Sudan. The pipeline has current throughput of 150,000 bbl/d and maximum capacity of 500,000 bbl/d. The project also includes a 300,000 bbl/d central processing facility at Al-Jabalayan and production facilities at Palogue.

Block 5a

In April 2005, the Sudanese government signed an agreement with WNPOC for the development of the Thar Jath and Mala fields on Block 5A. First oil from the block came online in June 2006 at an initial rate of 38,000 bbl/d. As of March 2007, the field was still producing at 38,000 bbl/d, while full capacity is estimated at 60,000 bbl/d.

Oil from the field flows through a 110-mile pipeline to Port Sudan. WNPOC is a consortium of companies, which include Petronas (68.875 per cent and operator), ONGC (23.125 per cent) and Sudapet (8 per cent).

Block 6

In November 2004, CNPC brought online its Fula field on Block 6 at a rate of 10,000 bbl/d. Current output on the block is 40,000 bbl/d, but is expected to eventually reach 80,000 bbl/d. CNPC has constructed a pipeline that links the Fula field to the Khartoum refinery.

Exploration and development of Sudan's oil resources has been controversial. International human rights organisations have accused the Sudanese government of financing human rights abuses with oil revenues, including the mass displacement of civilians near the oil fields. Factional fighting in the South and rebel attacks on oil infrastructure have kept oil production and exploration from reaching full potential to date.

In October 2004, for example, the Sudanese government prevented a militia attempt to sabotage the country's main oil export pipeline. However, the 2005 Comprehensive Peace Agreement (CPA) between the northern government in Khartoum and the GoSS could facilitate additional investment in both production facilities and new exploration initiatives in Sudan.

In January 2005, after the official signing of the CPA, IOCS including Total, Marathon Oil Corporation, and the Kuwait Foreign Petroleum Exploration Company (KFPEC) renewed their exploration rights in southern Sudan.

Exports

In 2006, Sudan consumed 94,000 bbl/d and exported approximately 320,000 bbl/d of crude oil, with the majority of crude destined for Asian markets. According official trade statistics as reported to the Global Trade, Sudan shipped 124,000 bbl/d of its crude exports to Japan in 2006. China also imported a significant portion of Sudanese crude exports in 2006 averaging 99,000 bbl/d. Additional importers of Sudanese crude Include South Korea, Indonesia, and India.

According to the International Crude Oil Market Handbook, Sudan's "Nile" export crude blend is considered sweet and light, having a gravity of 33 degrees API and a low sulphur content of 0.045 per cent.

Refining and Downstream

According to OGJ, Sudan's refineries in Khartoum and Port Sudan had total combined refining capacity of 121,700 bbl/d as of January 2007.

In July 2006, CNPC announced the completion of the Khartoum refinery expansion project, which doubled the refinery's capacity from 50,000 bb/d to 100,000 bbl/d. The Khartoum refinery processes Nile blend crude, which has a low sulfur content and high fuel-yield. The additional refinery capacity from the expansion should help alleviate the short supply of refined products available in Sudan, while giving the country some additional export capacity.

The Port Sudan facility is located near the Red Sea and is Sudan's smallest refinery, with capacity of 21,700 bbl/d. In September 2005, a contract was awarded to Petronas to build a new refinery at Port Sudan. The refinery will be designed to process Dar blend crude, which has high-acid content and is found in Sudan's Melut basin. The refinery will have capacity of 100,000 bbl/d and could be operational in 2009. Petronas is joined with the Sudanese Ministry of Energy and Mining in a 50:50 partnership in the project.

Electricity

Sudan generates the majority of electricity by conventional thermal sources. In 2004, Sudan had 760 megawatts (MW) of electricity generation capacity. Sudan generated 3.8 billion kilowatthours (Bkwh) of electricity in 2004, and consumed 3.6 Bkwh.

The majority of electricity in Sudan is generated by conventional thermal sources (76 per cent), with the remainder coming from hydroelectricity (24 per cent). The country's main hydroelectricity generating facility is the 280-MW Roseires dam located on the Blue Nile River basin, approximately 315 miles southeast of Khartoum. The facility has frequently been attacked by rebel groups, and low water levels often cause its capacity to fall to 100 MW.

Sector Organisation

State-owned National Electricity Corporation (NEC) is responsible for electricity generation, transmission and distribution in Sudan. NEC transmits electricity through two interconnected electrical grids, the Blue Nile Grid and the Western grid, which cover only a small portion of the country. Regions not covered by the grid often rely on small diesel-fired generators for power. Only 30 per cent of the population currently has access to electricity, but the government hopes to increase that figure to 90 per cent in coming years.

An Overview of Sudanese Economy and Energy

Location Northern Africa, bordering the Red Sea, between Egypt and Eritrea

Independence 1 January 1956 (from Egypt and UK)

Population (2006E) 41,236,378

Economic Overview

Currency/Exchange Rate (4/13/07) 1 Sudanese Dinar (SDD) = 0.0043 USD

Inflation Rate (2005E): 8.5 per cent; (2006E): 7.2 per cent

Gross Domestic Product (2006E) $36.5 Billion

Real GDP Growth Rate (2005E): 7.9 per cent; (2006E): 9.0 per cent

External Debt (2006E) $29.7 Billion

Exports (2006E) $5.9 Billion

Exports— oil and petroleum products; cotton, sesame, livestock, groundnuts, gum arabic, sugar

Exports— Partners (2005E) China 71.1 per cent, Japan 12 per cent, Saudi Arabia 2.8 per cent

Imports (2006E) $7.6 Billion

Imports— foodstuffs, manufactured goods, refinery and transport equipment, medicines and chemicals, textiles, wheat

Imports—Partners (2005E) China 20.7 per cent, Saudi Arabia 9.4 per cent, UAE 5.9 per cent, Egypt 5.5 per cent, Japan 5.1 per cent, India 4.8 per cent

Current Account Balance (2006E) $3.9 Billion

Energy Overview

Proven Oil Reserves (January 1, 2007E) 5 billion barrels

Oil Production (2006E) 414 thousand barrels per day

Oil Consumption (2006E) 94 thousand barrels per day

Crude Oil Refining Capacity (2007E) 121.7 thousand barrels per day

Proven Natural Gas Reserves (January 1, 2007E) 3 trillion cubic feet

Natural Gas Production (2004E) None

Natural Gas Consumption (2004E) None

Recoverable Coal Reserves (2003E) None

Coal Production (2004E) None

Coal Consumption (2004E) None

Electricity Installed Capacity (2004E) 0.8 gigawatts

Electricity Production (2004E) 3.8 billion kilowatt hours

Electricity Consumption (2004E) 3.6 billion kilowatt hours

Total Energy Consumption (2004E) 0.1 quadrillion Btus*, of which Oil (93 per cent), Hydroelectricity (7 per cent), Natural Gas (0 per cent), Coal (0 per cent), Nuclear (0 per cent), Other Renewables (0 per cent)

Total Per Capita Energy Consumption ((Million Btu)E) 3.8 million Btus

Energy Intensity (2004E) 2,651.4 Btu per $2000-PPP**

Environmental Overview

Energy-related Carbon Dioxide Emissions (2004E) 9.8 million metric tons, of which Oil (100 per cent),

Natural Gas (0 per cent), Coal (0 per cent)

Per-Capita, Energy-related Carbon Dioxide Emissions ((Metric Tons of Carbon Dioxide)E) 0.3 metric tons

Carbon Dioxide Intensity (2004E) 0.2 Metric tons per thousand $2000-PPP**

Environmental Issues: inadequate supplies of potable water; wildlife populations threatened by excessive hunting; soil erosion; desertification; periodic drought

Major Environmental Agreements party to: Biodiversity, Climate Change, Climate Change—Kyoto

Protocol, Desertification, Endangered Species, Law of the Sea, Ozone Layer Protection signed, but not ratified: none of the selected agreements

Oil and Gas Industry

Major Oil Ports: Port Sudan

Foreign Company Involvement: China National Petroleum Corporation (CNPC), India's Oil and Natural Gas Corporation (ONGC) and Malaysia's Petronas, Total SA, Marathon Oil Corporation, and the Kuwait Foreign Petroleum Company

Major Oil Fields: Adar Yale, Fula, Heglig, Mala, Palogue, Thar Jath, and Unity

Major Pipelines: 994-mile pipeline from Heglig and Unity fields to the Suakin oil terminal—870-mile pipeline linking Melut Basin to oil export terminal near Port Sudan and a 110-mile pipeline linking the Thar Jath and Mala fields to Port Sudan.

Major-Refineries Khartoum (100,000 bbl/d), Port Sudan Refinery (21,700).

*The total energy consumption statistic includes petroleum, dry natural gas, coal, net hydro, nuclear, geothermal, solar, wind, wood and waste electric power. The renewable energy consumption statistic is based on International Energy Agency (IEA) data and includes hydropower, solar, wind, tide, geothermal, solid biomass and animal products, biomass gas and liquids, industrial and municipal wastes. Sectoral shares of energy consumption and carbon emissions are also based on IEA data.

**GDP figures from OECD estimates based on purchasing power parity (PPP) exchange rates.

Sources: EIA

Sudan Energy Profile

Data	*2006*				*2007*
	Sudan	*Africa*	*World*	*Rank*	*Sudan*
Petroleum (thousand barrels per day)					
Total Oil Production	380	10405	84597	33	470F
Crude Oil Production	378	9697	73539	32	NA
Consumption	80	3018	84846	83	NA
Net Exports/Imports (-)	301	7387	–	21	NA
Refinery Capacity	122	3230	85345	74	122
Proved Reserves (billion barrels)	1	103	1293	45	5
	2005				*2006*
	Sudan	*Africa*	*World*	*Rank*	*Sudan*
Natural Gas (Billion Cubic Feet)					
Production	0	6103	101528	83	0
Consumption	0	2951	103700	101	0
Net Exports/Imports (-)	0	3153	–	–	NA
Proved Reserves	3000	476509	6046062	57	3000
Coal (Million Short Tons)					
Production	0	276	6490	67	NA
Consumption	0	211	6483	111	NA
Net Exports/Imports (-) (Trillion Btu)	0	1668	–	–	0
Electricity (Billion Kilowatthours)					
Net Generation	4	533	17351	116	NA
Net Consumption	3	474	15747	118	NA
Installed Capacity (GWe)	1	107	3872	119	NA

Contd...

Contd...

Total Primary Energy (Quadrillion)					
Production	1	35	460	58	NA
Consumption	0	14	463	104	NA
Energy Intensity (Btu per 2000 U.S. Dollars)	1	107	3872	119	NA
Carbon Dioxide Emissions (Million Metric Tons of CO_2)					
Total from Consumption of Fossil Fuels	10.79	1,043	28,193	99	NA

– = Not applicable; NA = Not available;
F = Forecast value

Source: EIA, International Energy Annual

Politics of Energy Security: The Case Study of Sudan

On March 9, 2003, Talisman Energy, a large Canadian independent,[71] sold its 25 per cent share of the Greater Nile Petroleum Operating Company (GNPOC) in Sudan to a subsidiary of India's national oil company for about $771 million.[72] Tansman had been in Sudan for less than four years, purchasing its 25 per cent stake from Arakis Energy, another Canadian independent, in October 1998.[73]

At first glance the project appears to have been a spectacular success. In August 2000, two years after signing the contract, Talisman announced that it expected its current year's income to be four times that of the previous year and that it now pumped more oil and gas than any other Canadian company.[74] Oil production was consistently described as exceeding expectations: Sudan's 2001 output was up 16 per cent compared to the previous year, production was estimated to reach 300,000 barrels per day (bbls/d) in 2003, and the project's pipeline to the Red Sea reached capacity in 2002.[75]

Talisman's stock price, however, did not reflect these "facts on the ground." While the company's shares sold at a 20 per cent premium (to net asset value) before the investment, it was priced at a 10 to 20 per cent discount during the period Talisman was in Sudan.[76] The share price recovered almost immediately upon announcement of the sale, trading very close to its all time high in June 2002.[77]

What accounts for this difference between investors' perceptions and the company's performance? The answer, in large part, is a sustained effort by activists to link Talisman to the massive violations of human rights that have occurred during Sudan's brutal civil war and the successful campaign by these groups to persuade institutional investors to divest the company's stock.

Talisman left Sudan to escape a political crisis over a subsidiary which never accounted for more than 12 per cent of its operations; the company felt that the benefits gained from Sudanese production were not worth the considerable costs. Talisman CEO Jim Buckee's statement after the sale was announced is to the point: "Talisman's shares have continued to be discounted based on perceived political risk in-country and in North America .... Shareholders have told me that they were tired of continually having to monitor and analyse events relating to Sudan.[78]

Oil has always been a risky business in terms of both geology and politics. Crude oil deposits are often found in locations that are difficult to access, provide inhospitable operating environments, and are in politically unstable or violent countries.

> The first determinant of the oil industry structure is the inherent unpredictability of investments in foreign oil ventures which has always made them highly speculative. Probabilities of large losses have had to be weighed against the possibilities of large gains. The risks that the foreign oil company confronts are technical, economic and political ....
>
> The foreign oil company carries the ever-present political risks that the government of the host country may alter or terminate its concession, impose heavier royalties or taxes, or even nationalise all or part of its investment. Or war, civil disturbances, or economic crises may stop oil production or cause uncompensated loss of its property.[79]

Political risks have always been a factor in international operations: International oil companies were first nationalised in Russia after the Bolshevik revolution.[80] A total of ten countries nationalised oil production before 1970, and during that decade there was widespread nationalisation of operations in producing countries.[81] There have been numerous instances of governments forcing renegotiation of contractual terms, and of oil production and pipeline operations– and oil company personnel—caught in the midst of violent conflicts. Petroleum exploration, development, and production are not for the faint of heart.

Political risk, however, has normally been country-specific. Oil companies were concerned primarily with events within the host country that could compromise ownership rights, operations, or the safety of employees.[82] The root cause of Talisman's difficulties was its operations in Sudan. However, the company was able to manage in-country political risk: Despite the fact that its concession was located in an active war zone and was the target of armed attacks, the oil production and transport business in that country was successful and profitable. The political risks that drove Talisman out of Sudan took form in North America and reflect the increasing complexity of the political environment in which the oil industry, and all multinational firms for that matter, now operate.

The Talisman case is emblematic of changes in the politics of the oil industry and, more generally, of significant changes in the international political system which have taken that system well beyond its state-centric Westphalian origins. The modern international political system was defined by geography (mutually exclusive territorial jurisdiction), state centrism (states as the only actors and the only subjects of public international law), and the absence of any central authority.[83] It was a world of discrete and meaningful borders and sovereign states. The political environment in which the oil industry now operates is changing rapidly and is becoming much more complex.

States are no longer the only significant actors in international politics. International organizations such as the United Nations and civil society advocacy groups or Non-Governmental Organizations (NGOs) now play a major role. Borders and sovereignty are far from inviolate, and the once sharp distinction between domestic and international affairs is becoming blurred. The separate spheres once occupied by public and private authorities (and public and private actors) are becoming interwoven, overlapped, and confused.[84]

The Talisman case illustrates both these changes in international politics and the political risks faced by international firms. Talisman's problems stemmed only indirectly from the risks of doing business in Sudan; rather, they resulted from the interactions of a number of very different political actors located primarily in North America. First, sustained and well-organised efforts by Canadian and international civil society advocacy groups were able to inform a wide swath of the public about the brutal human rights violations in Sudan, link Talisman directly to them, and mobilise campaigns to convince investors to sell.[85] Second, while multinational firms have always gotten caught in jurisdictional disputes and inter-state politics, the web in which Talisman was ensnared is unusually complex, involving both U.S. and Canadian domestic politics and U.S.-Canadian relations.

Third, the concept of state sovereignty is undergoing change, and by the late 1990s there was no question whatsoever that human rights abuses would not be protected by national borders. Kofi Annan,[86] the Secretary-General of the United Nations, stated, "Nothing in the U.N. charter precludes a recognition that there are rights beyond borders.! While the war in Sudan is a domestic affair, albeit with some external involvement, there is a clear recognition that the human rights abuses which occur there, including the slave trade, are an international problem subject to international remediation.[87]

Last, Talisman Energy is a private actor that found itself in a no-man's land between a public and private role. There were a number of attempts to hold Talisman "responsible" for human rights violations in Sudan, including its failure to use its leverage with the government to effect change in that regime's policy.[88] Thus Talisman, a Canadian company, found itself being sued in a court in New York for actions it was accused of taking in an African country.[89]

This study will proceed by first reviewing the troubled and violent post-colonial history of Sudan and then discussing Talisman's entry into that country's oil industry. It then turns to the allegations against Talisman and the efforts mounted by NGOs to attempt to force both the Canadian government and investors to sanction the company for its role in exacerbating human rights violations in Sudan. The study next deals with U.S. domestic politics and U.S. attempts to sanction Sudan, U.S. Canadian interactions, and the Canadian government's position *vis-a-vis* Talisman. It then looks briefly at the question of public authority and the court case against the company. The study concludes with a discussion of the implications of the case for the politics of the oil industry.

Sudan has been racked by civil war for all but eleven of the years since its independence from Great Britain in 1956 (the war actually started in 1955).[90] The "second civil war," which began in 1983, has been characterised by a vicious brutality resulting in two million deaths—the majority civilian—and over four million displaced persons.[91] Sudan, which has been described as a microcosm of the African continent,[92] sits on the divide between primarily Arab and Muslim North Africa and the primarily Black, Christian, and "Animist" area south of the Sahara. The southern provinces are ethnically diverse, containing a large number of tribes and linguistic groups.[93] As will be seen, a focal point of the war has been the Upper West Nile region in which Talisman's operations were located.

The origins of the conflict go back to the "Southern Policy" established under British Colonial rule after World War I, which proscribed the teaching of Arabic and Islam in the three southern provinces and encouraged the use of English and conversions to Christianity.[94] The policy was designed to curtail the north's influence and resulted in the isolation and political and economic marginalisation of the three southern provinces. That isolation has continued to this day and is a primary cause of the current civil war in Sudan.[95]

Sudan's independence, in January 1956, found the country in the midst of a rebellion; that rebellion intensified in 1958 when General Abboud seized power andbegan a campaign to forcibly extend Islam to the south.[96] By 1963, it had taken the form of a "full-fledged civil war.[97] Another coup resulted in General Nimeiri becoming President in 1969.[98] After a foray into Cold War politics and a failed communist coup, Nimeiri began negotiations resulting in the Addis Ababa agreement of 1972, which provided security guarantees and some degree of political and economic autonomy to the south.[99] The agreement ended Sudan's first civil war after seventeen years.[100] While the Addis Ababa agreement held for eleven years, by the late 1970s Nimeiri was under increasing pressure from hardliners to again exert control over the south, and his regime turned from left-authoritarianism to strict Islamism.[101]

The situation in Sudan was complicated by the discovery of oil in the southern provinces during the 1970s, which eventually dramatically altered the balance of power in the country and provided an additional motivation for conflict. Chevron was granted a concession in 1975, started drilling in 1977, and discovered significant reserves of oil in the early 1980s.[102] Stability and peace in Sudan then quickly deteriorated into a resumption of an even more brutal civil war. In 1980, Nimeiri attempted to redraw the boundaries of the Upper Nile province to include the areas where oil had been discovered,[103] and in 1983 he issued an order abrogating the Addis Ababa agreement, returning powers to the central government, eliminating the south's autonomy, and dividing it into three administrative provinces.[104] A few months later, he transformed Sudan into an Islamic state, declaring that *sharia* was to be the law throughout the country.[105] Southerners mobilised around the Sudan People's Liberation Army (SPLA) to rebel, and the war resumed in all its fury.[106]

General Nimeiri's regime lasted until 1985, when it was overthrown by the army after a general strike and popular uprising.[107] Sadiq al Mahdi became Prime Minister,[108] for a time it appeared that peace was once again possible. But General Umar al-Bashir, who took power in a 1989 coup,[109] resumed the war with a vengeance, pursuing the "imposition of God's law" throughout the country.[110] While a settlement now appears possible, during the time Talisman operated in Sudan the country was still in the midst of a very violent and brutal civil war. One observer characterised the fighting as accomplishing very little militarily: "The government controls only key garrison towns in the south; the rest of the region is ruled by the SPLM or one of the many other factions that have evolved over the years.[111] I will return to the state of the war in the late 1990s as part of the story of Talisman's operations in Sudan.

It is important to note that the civil war in Sudan is complex, and, by the late 1990s, it could no longer be characterised as a straight-forward conflict between the Islamic north and Christian, "Animist," and tribal south. While the government's attempt to impose Islam and Islamic law on the entire country continues to fuel the conflict, the longstanding marginalisation of the southern provinces, an attempt by the Government to extend its control over the disputed areas, and a struggle among several groups for control over Sudan's territory and resources are all important reasons for the continued fighting.[112]

During the 1990s, the war evolved from its roots as a largely north-south conflict "into a contest for power that involves groups from across the nation."[113] In addition to the forces of the government in Khartoum and the SPLA, it involves a relatively large number of militias and inter-tribal factions, some of whom change sides as it is advantageous.[114] As Randolph Martin describes it,

> Sudan's low intensity conflict little resembles a war in the traditional sense, with national armies fighting over a contested border. The vast majority of Sudan's casualties are not combatants killed in battle but southern civilians who fall victim to famine and disease ... .[115]

The war involves a massive displacement of civilians, attacks on civilians by a number of different groups, and human slavery as a result of raids by Khartoum-supported *murahaleen* militias on southern tribes.[116] While both sides are guilty of atrocities and attacks on civilian non-combatants, there is general agreement that the primary responsibility for the destitution, death, and destruction in the south lies with the government of Sudan.[117]

Oil and the Entry of Talisman

Oil exploration and development in Sudan began in the early 1960s and accelerated in 1974 when Chevron was granted a concession in which Shell later took a 25 per cent interest.[118] Chevron and Shell eventually spent $1 billion in Sudan, drilling 52 wells, including 34 "suspended wells" capable of completion at a later date.[119] By 1982, Chevron had made a number of significant discoveries, and operations in Sudan appeared to have considerable potential.[120]

However, in February 1984, a rebel group kidnapped and killed three expatriate Chevron employees, and the company suspended its operations and withdrew from Sudan.[121] Chrevron attempted to resume its activities in 1988, but finally left the country in 1990, relinquishing its concessions.[122] State Petroleum then entered into a production-sharing agreement with the government of Sudan in 1993, acquiring a large part of what had been Chevron's concession.[123] One year later, Arakis Energy Corporation, a Canadian independent oil company, undertook a "reverse takeover" of State, becoming the overall owner of the concession.[124] At this point, the project involved exploration, development, and production, and the construction of a pipeline to transport oil to Port Sudan on the Red Sea.

Arakis found it was not able to finance exploration, development, and construction of the pipeline on its own, and in December 1996 it entered into a consortium, the Greater Nile Petroleum Operating Company (GNPOCJ), in which it held a 25 per cent share and was the field operator.[125] The China National Petroleum Company held 40 per cent, Petronas of Malaysia held 30 per cent, and Sudapet, the Sudanese national firm, held 5 per cent.[126] Arakis' concessions were in the conflict area, and the SPLA threatened to attack their operadons.[127] It was alleged that Arakis hired the South African mercenary firm Executive Outcomes to protect its fields.[128]

Arakis encountered significant political and business problems in its struggle to develop its Sudanese operations. During 1997, the Canadian government, concerned about the situation in Sudan, asked Arakis to reconsider its participation in the project.[129] In November, President Clinton signed an executive order freezing all Sudanese assets in the United States and imposing a ban on all financial and trade relations with Sudan.[130] The sanctions prevented any U.S. citizen from doing business in Sudan and ruled out American participation in Sudanese oil.[131]

The major problem, however, was that Arakis was not able to raise the $200 million or more necessary to fund its share of the $1.4 billion project. The project was too large an undertaking for Arakis, which was a relatively small Canadian independent.[132] The company was also hampered by American sanctions, which prevented it from attempting to raise funds in the U.S. bond market.[133] Last, the company went to the markets in the midst of an eight quarter decline in oil prices, from $23 per barrel to a low of $13 in the summer of 1998. As a result of its difficulties, Arakis encouraged offers from other companies.[134]

Talisman Energy originated as a spin-off of the Canadian subsidiary of British Petroleum.[135] In 1998 it was the second largest Canadian independent oil company;[136] that is, it had only "upstream" operations (exploration, development, and production) and did not refine petroleum or own retail outlets. On August 17, 1998, Talisman and Arakis agreed to a friendly takeover: Talisman acquired the outstanding shares of Arakis, and in doing so it acquired the latter's 25 per cent interest in the GNPOC in Sudan.[137] The deal, which was to be completed on October 8, provided a 10-1 exchange of Talisman for Arakis shares and a loan of up to $54 million to Arakis to fund State Petroleum's share of the project's capital requirements.[138]

Only a few days later, Talisman received a rude jolt about the realities of doing business in Sudan when the United States launched a missile attack on the al-Shifa plant in Khartoum, claming it was producing chemical weapons.[139] Talisman CEO Buckee noted that "certainly, not one of the things we had contemplated was a bombing of Khartoum by the Americans.[140] Nevertheless, the takeover took place as planned in October.[141]

Talisman acquired a 25 per cent share of five oil fields under development, with estimated production of 150,000 bbls/day starting in late 1999 (37,500 to Talisman), and the 932 mile pipeline to Port Sudan which had an initial capacity of 150,000 bbls/day.[142] The pipeline and a marine oil terminal were expected to ex-completed by the third quarter of 1999.[143]

Talisman took over Arakis on what were regarded as favourable terms for a number of reasons. First, Arakis was in obvious difficulty, unable to either fund the project satisfactorily or meet its obligations to its partners. Second, the dramatic fall in oil prices reduced the value of all oil companies' stocks. (The slide reversed in the same quarter the takeover was announced.) Third, American sanctions reduced potential competition, as U.S. firms could not participate in the Sudanese oil industry. Last, the fact that Talisman participated only in upstream operations—it did not own refineries or gas stations—appeared to reduce the potential impact of consumer boycotts or other protests related to the human rights situation in Sudan.

Nonetheless, Talisman's share price fell after the agreement, slipping 11 per cent in the first few weeks after the deal was announced. Investors were concerned about dilution of the stock resulting from the additional shares issued to Arakis investors, as well as the very real political risks in Sudan and the controversy surrounding operations in that country because of the brutality of government operations and American sanctions.[144]

Some analysts, however, saw the project as a high risk-high return operation with a great deal of upside potential that made sense for Talisman. Robert Hinkley of Merrill Lynch, for example, discounted the political risk and noted that Talisman's development of Sudan is "going to generate a lot of cash flow, and its going to be a very economic project, with a lot of exploratory upside."[145] There was general agreement that oil exploration was a risky business and that the Sudanese fields and pipeline, which were scheduled to come on-stream within a year, were a good investment for Talisman.[146]

Talisman's CEO, Buckee, discounted the risk and argued that the share price would recover as investors realised the long-term potential in the project.[147] He characterized the security situation as satisfactory, with the site protected by the Sudanese government, and argued that media coverage had overplayed the dangers in that country—that "[A] lot of the stories have been made lurid and exaggerated."[148]

A Tidal Wave of Protest

While Buckee may well have been correct to discount the in-country risk to his operations, the very negative media coverage of the war in Sudan was but a harbinger of things to come. Within a few months of Talisman's takeover of Arakis, a coalition of civil society advocacy groups launched a massive campaign aimed at Canadian and American political authorities, Talisman's shareholders, and institutional investors holding or contemplating purchase of the company's stock.

NGOs such as Amnesty International, the American Anti-Slavery Group, the Canadian Inter-Church Coalition, and many others used the internet very effectively to publicise both the brutal human rights violations occurring as a result of the war in Sudan and what they felt was

Talisman's complicity in the process.[149] Using both electronic and more conventional methods, they lobbied the executives and legislatures in both the U.S. and Canada to take action against both Sudan in general and Talisman in particular, attempted to convince the company's shareholders to force the company to withdraw from the GNPOC, and perhaps most effectively, waged what has been called one of the largest divestment campaigns since the efforts against the apartheid regime in South Africa.[150]

The divestment campaign, which was spearheaded by the American Anti-Slavery Group, was aimed directly at the major institutional investors holding Talisman stock.[151] That organisation, and many others, mobilised activists who brought pressure on investors directly by linking them publicly to the brutality and slave trade in Sudan through their ownership of Talisman stock. They also lobbied legislators in both the U.S. and Canada to bring pressure on investors through their respective regulatory authorities.

At least one financial journalist was sympathetic to these activists' claims. SmartMoney.com ran a story asking if the mutual funds owning Talisman were supporting genocide.[152] The article detailed the charges against the company, noted that most of the mutual funds contacted either would not talk to the reporter or argued that divestment would not be productive, and then provided a list of the ten funds holding the largest amounts of Talisman stock, suggesting that rather than wait for the funds to move readers might want to adjust their own portfolios.[153]

The campaign was successful. During 1999 and 2000, at least six U.S. pension funds sold millions of Talisman shares as a result of activist pressure.[154] TIAA-CREF, the Texas Teachers Retirement Fund, CALPERS (California), the New Jersey Employees Retirement Fund, and the New York City Pension Fund were among those divesting.[155] Advocacy groups also mounted coordinated campaigns against mutual funds holding Talisman stock. For example, a "Fidelity Awareness Week" was declared in March, 2001, during which a large number of protest letters were sent to Fidelity Investments asking them to divest.[156] Similar efforts were directed against Vanguard and other mutual funds.[157] It is difficult to gauge their success: While Fidelity did sell a large block of its Talisman stock, it appears to have bought most of it back.[158] It is reasonable to assume that the activists' campaigns had some discernible effect on purchases and sales of Talisman stock.[159]

As noted above, legislatures in both Canada and the U.S. were also targets of the NGOs' campaign. Their efforts were successful in the United States as the House of Representatives and the Senate passed the Sudan Peace Act in 2002.[160] The original House version would have prevented firms investing in Sudanese oil from raising money in U.S. capital markets or trading on American exchanges absent public disclosure about the nature and extent of its commercial activity in Sudan, the relationship of the commercial activity to any violations of religious freedom and other human rights in Sudan, and the contribution that the proceeds raised in the capital markets in the U.S. would make to the entity's commercial activity in Sudan. That provision was dropped in the final version of the legislation.[161]

While the main purpose is to use the Talisman case to inform a discussion of the dramatic changes in the politics of the oil industry rather than to undertake a detailed analysis of the situation in Sudan, it is important to note that a wide spectrum of observers agree that oil discoveries and production by the GNPOC, combined with the opening of the pipeline, have had a direct effect on the war and have exacerbated human rights violations. The Harker Report, prepared at the request of the Canadian Minister of Foreign Affairs, concluded that oil has become a key factor in the war: "The evidence we gathered, including the testimony of those directly involved directs us to conclude that oil is exacerbating the conflict in Sudan."[162] Similarly, Martin argues that "Nothing has contributed as much to the conflict's sustainability as the opening of Sudan's oil pipeline."[163]

A Center for Strategic and International Studies report on U.S. efforts to end the war concluded that "oil is fundamentally changing Sudan's war."[164] It argued that oil shifted the balance of military power to the government in Khartoum and prompted the regime to focus its military efforts on oil operations, resulting in the "forced mass displacement of civilians."[165]

Petroleum operations affect the war and the civilians caught in the war zone in a number of ways. First, the motivations of the contending parties have been transformed by the discovery of oil. To a significant extent, the war is no longer simply about control of territory, but rather about control of a valuable resource.[166] Second, and perhaps more important, oil has provided a steady stream of significant revenues to a country that was among the poorest in Africa, an "economic basket case."[167]

The start of significant oil production in late 1999 transformed Sudan from a poor oil-importing country to a significant exporter, and both revenues and economic growth have been up sharply since that time. Oil revenues increased by almost 900 per cent in three years, from $61 million in 1999 to almost $600 million in 2001.[168] The dramatic increase in resources available to the government in Khartoum resulted in a very significant increase in military expenditure and the purchase of modern weapons, including helicopter gunships.[169] Sudan can now manufacture its own light arms and munitions and is planning to build its own tanks and artillery.[170]

Third, given the revenues they produce and the impact of those revenues on the balance of power in the country, oil operations including the pipeline are a natural target of rebel groups. The SPLA's operations against Talisman's facilities have resulted in increased government efforts to protect oil production, which includes attacks upon and displacement of civilian groups. As the *Economist* notes, prior to the end of 1999 much of the war effort involved the government in Khartoum arming Arab militia groups and encouraging them to raid the tribes in the south for cattle and slaves.[171] The government now takes direct action to protect oil operations, including displacement of civilians: "Now the government wants the southerners out."[172] Last, there is agreement, including that of the company itself, that Talisman's facilities have been used as a base for military operations against rebel groups and civilians in the south.[173]

The last issue aside, there is disagreement about whether Talisman was directly complicit in human rights violations; there is, however, widespread agreement that its involvement was, at least in part, responsible for an exacerbation of the conflict and an increase in the violations of the rights of civilians in the area, including their displacement.[174] Arguably, Talisman's direct complicity stems from its decision to request protection from a regime with the Khartoum government's history.[175] While Talisman Energy was only one of four partners in the GNPOC, it is clear that its participation was critical to the project's success. It provided funding and, more importantly, technical know-how and a great deal of expertise and experience in exploration and development.[176]

Needless to say, the company disagrees with this assessment. Aside from the issue of whether the intensity and nature of the conflict has been exaggerated by the press, it argues that in the longer run constructive engagement is the best course of action in Sudan.[177] In the company's 2001 Social Responsibility Report, CEO Buckee noted that some people argue that Talisman should leave Sudan. His response was that "many people we speak to believe that the appropriate moral response is to stay and use our corporate resources in a broad and responsible manner to encourage peace, provide economic opportunities and support the communities in which we operate. We share this view...."[178]

A second prong of Talisman's response was to add the International Code of Ethics for Canadian Business to its business code and engage Price Waterhouse Coopers to help verify compliance.[179] Last, the company engaged in extensive community development efforts, including building hospitals, clinics, schools, and wells in their area of operations.[180]

All of that said, it is clear that the activities of the advocacy groups had a significant effect on Talisman's share price and enterprise value. While it is impossible to disentangle the impact of the risk within Sudan, American sanctions, shareholder activism, and the divestment campaign, it is reasonable to assume that the impact of the latter has been significant.

In Table 30,[181] Talisman Energy's enterprise valuation is compared with that of four other comparable Canadian independents: Alberta Energy Corporation (AEC), Canadian Natural Resources, Nexen, and PanCanadian Petroleum. Two metrics are shown, enterprise value/ operational cash flow and enterprise value/earnings before interest, taxes, depreciation, amortization, and exploration (ev/ebitdax). The comparisons of the five-company averages are of interest. Talisman outperforms its competition on both metrics in both 1997 and 1998. (The agreement with Arakis was announced in August 1998.[182]) During 1999 and 2000, the years when the protests and divestment campaigns were in full swing, Talisman underperformed compared to its competition. On the other hand, AEC, one of its primary competitors which had avoided involvement in Sudan, outperformed competitive firms on both metrics in 1999 and 2000. Again, while it is impossible to link the decline in valuation to the divestment campaign with any degree of certainty, it is clear that Talisman's stock price fell despite the success of its oil operations in Sudan. It is reasonable to assume that the decline in valuation of the company reflected the negative publicity and pressure on investors to sell resulting from the efforts of the advocacy groups.

TABLE 27

Corporate Valuation Comparisons

	1997	*1998*	*1999*	*2000*
AEC				
ev/op.cash flow	8.7	13.7	13.5	7.6
ev/EBITDAX	5.7	10.5	8.6	5.7
Talisman				
ev/op.cash flow	8.5	9.0	8.5	3.5
ev/EBITDAX	8.4	14.1	6.7	3.6
CNR				
ev/op.cash flow	7.8	8.3	9.3	3.2
ev/EBITDAX	7.6	6.9	7.6	2.8
Nexen				
ev/op.cash flow	7.3	6.1	8.6	5.0
ev/EBITDAX	6.6	5.5	6.7	3.7
Pan Canadian				
ev/op.cash flow	5.8	7.6	6.9	5.4
ev/EBITDAX	6.4	6.3	6	4.7
avg. ev/op.cash fl.	7.6	8.9	9.4	4.9
avg. ev/EDITDAX	6.9	8.7	7.1	4.1
Talisman				
vs. av ev/op cash fl.	112	101	91	71
vs. av. Ev/EDITDAX	121	163	94	88
AEC				
vs. av ev/op cash fl.	114	153	144	154
vs. av. Ev/EDITDAX	82	121	121	139

American and Canadian Politics

In a message to a summit on Sudan on November 9, 1999, U.S. Secretary of State Madeleine Albright articulated the Clinton Administration's stance toward the regime in that country: "Our policy is to isolate the Government of Sudan; to counter the threat it poses to the United States, its neighbours and its own people; and to press for fundamental change in its policies."[183] She noted that the National Islamic Front had seized power from a democratically elected government, actively supported terrorist organisations, compiled an appalling human rights record, and prolonged a vicious and inhumane war.[184]

The United Nations first condemned Sudan for gross violations of human rights in 1992, and in 1996 the Security Council imposed diplomatic sanctions on the government in Khartoum for its involvement in terrorism.[185] U.S. actions against Sudan began in 1993, when that country was added to the list of states sponsoring terrorism. In April 1996, President Clinton signed the Anti-Terrorism Act, which barred Americans from engaging in financial transactions with governments on the list, including Sudan.[186]

More comprehensive sanctions were enacted in November 1997, when President Clinton's executive order (under the International Emergency Powers Act) froze all Sudanese assets in the United States and imposed a ban on all bank loans, investments, and trade with that country.[187] Clinton cited Sudan's sponsorship of terror, its efforts to destabilise neighbouring countries, and its human rights violations in announcing the sanctions.[188] As noted above, the U.S. sanctions in place in 1997 and 1998 both made it difficult, if not impossible, for Arakis to raise funds in U.S. markets and limited Talisman's competition in bidding for that company as U.S. oil firms were barred from operations in Sudan.

Secretary Albright had very strong feelings about the regime in Sudan; when she was the American ambassador to the United Nations she called the country a "viper's nest of terrorism."[189] During a trip to Africa in October 1999, she met with Sudanese rebels and then, in Nairobi, announced that she planned to talk to the Canadian government about Talisman's involvement in Sudan.[190] She did so shortly thereafter in an apparently strong letter to the Canadian Foreign Affairs Minister, Lloyd Axworthy, urging him to force Talisman to withdraw from Sudan.[191]

As the *Financial Times* noted, "Canadians are not used-to such bad publicity."[192] While Mr. Axworthy's initial response was apparently some degree of anger over U.S. interference in Canadian affairs, within days he had expressed strong reservations about Talisman's involvement in Sudan, called CEO Jim Buckee in for consultations, and launched a very high-profile investigation of the role of oil operations in the civil war.[193] He quickly sent a fact-finding team to Sudan headed by John Harker, a former director of affairs for the Canadian Labour Congress, to investigate Talisman's involvement in the conflict.[194] Axworthy threatened sanctions if the investigation found that oil money was either perpetuating the conflict or contributing to human rights abuses.[195]

The Harker Report concluded that while the war in Sudan was not fundamentally about oil, it had become a key factor—that "oil is exacerbating the conflict in Sudan."[196] It argued that it "is difficult to imagine a cease-fire while oil extraction continues, and almost impossible to do so if revenues keep flowing to GNPOC partners and the GOS [government of Sudan] as currently arranged."[197] Last, while noting that there are limits to the ability of a government to compel ethical behaviour on the part of a corporation, it argued that Talisman's owners had both the opportunity and the responsibility to do so.[198]

The Report stopped short of explicitly recommending that Talisman be sanctioned, and the Canadian government eventually decided not to take action. However, the open nature of the Albright-Axworthy interchange and the very public scolding of Talisman by Mr. Axworthy certainly increased awareness of the issue among the Canadian public at large and provided at least moral support to the advocacy groups opposing Talisman's operations in Sudan. It may also have supported, at least indirectly, some of the shareholder actions regarding operations in Sudan.

Toward the end of its term, the Clinton Administration attempted to move away from its policy of strict isolation of Sudan and attempted to engage the government in Khartoum in an effort to find a negotiated end to the civil war.[199] Relations between the United States and Sudan became much more complex under President Bush, for a number of reasons.

Sudan became more salient in the United States because of pressure from Christian groups who formed some of the administration's core support.[200] These groups tend to see the conflict in straightforward terms—as the oppression of Christians in the south by the Islamic government in the North—and their actions both raised the profile of the Sudanese civil war in the United States and increased pressure on the administration and Congress to further sanction Sudan.[201] Ultimately, both the Senate and the House passed the Sudan Peace Act in 2002, which threatens further sanctions against the Sudanese government if it does not negotiate in good faith to end the conflict. A very controversial provision that would have prevented foreign oil companies with operations in Sudan from accessing U.S. capital markets was dropped as a result of administration pressure.[202]

The situation was further complicated by the September 11, 2001, attacks on the World Trade Center and the advent of the War on Terrorism. Although Sudan was under U.N. and U.S. sanctions because of its support for terrorist organizations (indeed, it provided a haven for Osama bin Laden for a period),[203] it immediately condemned the 9/11 attacks and offered to cooperate in the fight against terrorism, provide unrestricted access to its records, and even hand over some wanted terrorists to American authorities.[204] As a result, U.S. Sudan relations improved considerably, and the U.S. did not object to the lifting of United Nations sanctions later that year.[205]

Coincidentally, the Administration began an effort to bring a negotiated end to the conflict in Sudan, appointing former Senator John Danforth as an "envoy for peace" in early September 2001.[206] (It is of interest that President Bush specifically mentioned that Danforth was "an ordained minister" in his announcement.[207]) While there were considerable setbacks during 2002, including helicopter gunship attacks on a U.N. food distribution center,[208] rebel military successes in the south,[209] and the Khartoum government's negative reaction to passage of the Sudan Peace Act,[210] the Danforth initiative concluded that it was clear that the war was not winnable by either side and that "this is the time for a major push for a compromise settlement."[211] Danforth negotiated a number of agreements between the government and the SPLA/M in the months following his appointment in September 2001.[212]

The Machhakos protocol, negotiated during 2002, provided for the continuation of Islamic law in the north for an additional six years by the SPLA/M in exchange for six years of southern autonomy ending with a referendum on the south's independence.[213] By early 2004, the conflict in southern Sudan had eased to a much lower level of intensity, and a final accord between the warring parties appeared possible.[214]

Talisman under Judicial Investigation for Human Rights Violation

In November 2001, an attorney, who is a board member of the American Anti-Slavery Group filed a $1 billion class-action lawsuit against Talisman, on behalf of the Presbyterian

Church of Sudan and a number of individual plaintiffs, in the U.S. District Court for the Southern District of New York.[215] The suit, which was amended in February 2002 to add the Islamic Government of Sudan as a co-defendant,[216] charges Talisman with violating the human rights of Christian and other non-Muslim minorities in Sudan by conducting a campaign of ethnic cleansing to clear the land for oil exploration.[217]

The case was brought under the Alien Tort Claims Act,[218] which allows foreigners to sue in U.S. courts for acts committed in other countries that violate "the law of nations."[219] In cases to date, courts have held that gross violations of human rights such as summary execution, torture, cruel, inhuman, or degrading treatment, genocide, war crimes, and forced labour, among others, violate the "law of nations."[220] The Talisman case is one of a number of recent suits brought against multinational firms for alleged violations of human rights abroad. The increased use of the Alien Tort Claims Act in American courts is a reflection of the difficulty of sanctioning multinational firms for human rights violations. In this case, as is true generally, the home country (Canada) was unwilling to sanction Talisman for acts committed outside of its jurisdiction, the host country (Sudan) had little interest in doing so, and the reach of international organisations and/or international law does not encompass the acts of a private firm.[221]

Although Talisman sought to have the case dismissed on several grounds, including that it was improperly brought in the United States, in March 2003 a federal district judge ruled that the case was properly brought in the Manhattan federal court.[222] The judge rejected arguments that the case might hinder the foreign relations of the United States, noting that the American government had declared Sudan a sponsor of state terrorism and that President Bush had signed the Sudan Peace Act.[223]

Oil and Politics

There is no doubt that the modern interstate political system is in the throes of change. It is evolving from a system rooted in territorial sovereignty—characterised by discrete and meaningful borders, a clear separation between domestic and international affairs, a marked distinction between the public and private spheres, and states as the only meaningful actors (and only subjects of international law)—to one in which sovereignty and geographic jurisdiction are compromised, borders are less meaningful, the sharp separation between domestic and foreign is diffuse and blurred, multiple actors are politically significant, and the public-private distinction is confused.[224]

All of these changes directly affect the political environment of the oil industry and the political risks faced by oil firms. More generally, we are in the midst of a period of major systemic change and transformation—characterised by very high levels of uncertainty and turmoil—which in itself affects the magnitude and nature of risks faced by multinational firms.

Talisman's CEO, Jim Buckee, has a reputation as a risk-taker. As discussed earlier, upstream oil operations are inherently risky in terms of geology, politics, and security. The irony of this case is that Talisman handled what would conventionally be assumed to be the political risks of its operations well. It operated very successfully in a politically unstable and war-torn environment, increasing output and delivering crude oil through the pipeline in the midst of a violent civil war. While the "political risks" that drove it out of Sudan are a consequence of its operations in that country, they did not arise within its borders.

U.N. Secretary-General Kofi Annan, in the context of Kosovo, argued that strictly traditional notions of sovereignty could no longer do justice to people's aspirations to fundamental freedom.[225] As noted earlier, he said that nothing in the U.N. Charter "precludes a recognition that there are rights beyond borders."[226] It is of interest that none of the actors in the Talisman case argued that Sudan's civil war was a domestic affair or that events within that country's borders should not be subject to outside intervention. While Sudan's support for terrorism certainly played a role in the U.S. sanctions, so did the regime's gross violations of human rights. Sovereignty is no longer an acceptable defence. Human rights have become a significant international issue, and human rights violations within countries are now deemed to be the responsibility of the international community.

The advocacy groups that played a major role in this case are political actors who command significant political power in the international system. In a traditional state-centric international system, all of Talisman's significant political interactions would have been limited to the host and home governments—Sudan and Canada.

Talisman was a means rather than an end for the NGOs. Their objective was to effect change in Sudan—to end the slave trade and protect the human rights of the people in the south. It is of interest here to note how much of the responsibility for human rights—for monitoring, advocating, publicising violations, and even enforcement—has shifted to civil society groups. They, rather than governments, are the significant political actors in this case. While there is no doubt that many of the groups involved were concerned about the morality of Talisman's entry into Sudan, their primary objective was to bring about change in that country's policies. While American sanctions and Canadian pressure certainly played a role, at the end of the day it was the civil society organisations that forced Talisman's withdrawal from Sudan.

Talisman was an attractive target both because of its presumed leverage over the National Islamic Front and because of its vulnerability in North America. While the NGOs had little direct leverage with the Sudanese government, they were able to exert considerable pressure on the company through shareholders and investors. It is also clear that the ability of advocacy groups to coordinate their activities, inform and mobilise public opinion, and bring pressure to bear on target groups has been exponentially increased by the emergence of the internet.

Multinational firms have been caught in interstate politics for a long time, and there is nothing startlingly new about Talisman's problems in that regard. However, the situation in which Talisman found itself was unusually complex and reflects the internationalisation and increased salience of human rights. While Talisman is a Canadian company, events in the United States were crucial to the outcome of this case. Arakis' inability to tap into American capital markets because of the sanctions in place certainly played a role in its demise. Similarly, Talisman's entry was facilitated by the absence of competition from U.S. oil firms.

The complex domestic politics in the United States vis-a-vis Sudan certainly affected the company. The increased power of Christian groups after the Bush Administration took power and the response of the Sudanese government to the 9/11 attacks led in opposite directions and created a climate of uncertainty in American-Sudanese relations. The very high degree of economic integration between the U.S. and Canada was a major factor in Axworthy's rapid decision to respond to Albright's concerns. It is clear that it was the expressed concern of the U.S. government that led ultimately to the Canadian government's decision to mount an investigation of Talisman's operations in Sudan and bring pressure to bear on the company.

One of the characteristics of a system in transition is the presence of asymmetries or incongruities. In the current state of affairs, there is a geographic incongruity between an economy which is global and political authority which is still primarily national and local.[227] One result is incomplete governance: international phenomena and international actors subject to fragmented, geographically-rooted political and regulatory authority.[228]

Thus, while human rights violations have become an international issue, and the monitoring and enforcement of human rights standards a responsibility of the "international community," in practice effective governance is a problem. Sanctions which are imposed unilaterally by one or more national authorities are unlikely to be effective, as compliance will always be an issue.[229] Leaving aside the question of Talisman's culpability for the moment, the company was unlikely to be sanctioned for its role—direct or indirect—in human rights violations by either host or home country. Sudan did not have any interest whatsoever in doing so, and while Talisman is a corporate citizen of Canada, the actions in question occurred far beyond that country's borders. Even if there were agreement on a standard or code of behaviour for multinational firms relative to human rights, it is far from clear who would enforce it.

At this point many of the actions of multinational firms are beyond the reach of either international institutions or public international law. The United Nations Global Compact attempts to bring together companies, U.N. agencies, and civil society groups to support a set of principles dealing with human rights, labour, and the environment, but participation is voluntary and the Compact does not have enforcement capabilities.[230] Even though human rights may be an international problem, there are no international institutions with the power to monitor and enforce corporate violations.

In this case, the incomplete and fragmented governance structures increased both the uncertainty of the political environment in which Talisman operated and the political risks faced by that company. Attempts at "international governance" took the form of the campaign by civil society groups and the court case brought in New York under the Alien Tort Claims Act. While the NGO campaign was successful in terms of its objective of forcing Talisman to withdraw from Sudan. The international oil industry, and multinational firms in general, are left without any clear set of standards or any agreed upon monitoring and enforcement mechanism.

Regardless of what one thinks of Talisman's entry into and operations in Sudan, it is hard to disagree with Buckee's observation that "corporations . . . are increasingly being asked to step into roles that were once the domain of governments or international bodies such as the United Nations. Defining what is properly expected of a company needs to be more clearly articulated and more rigorously debated."[231] Governance is incomplete, and the line separating private actors from public responsibilities has become blurred and diffuse.

During the late 1990s, Sudan was a very difficult and risky operating environment. However, the problems that Talisman faced in Sudan were well within the bounds of the industry's, and that company's, experience and expectations. They were well within the parameters established by an international political system rooted in mutually exclusive territorial jurisdiction, a system—from a multinational company's point of view—comprised sovereign home and host countries with discrete and meaningful borders.

The political problems that drove Talisman from Sudan reflect a much more uncertain, rapidly evolving, and complex global political system—a system characterised by multiple actors, a lack of fixed geographic coordinates, deep transnational integration, complex networked interconnectedness, and incomplete systems of governance. The evolution of the system has affected the magnitude and quality of the political risks faced by oil firms. In a very real sense they are more systemic and less determinate than in the past; they are certainly more difficult to forecast and manage than ever before.

The European Union (EU) Calls on Talisman Energy to Halt Activities in Sudan

The pressure on Talisman just increased by several notches, as the Parliament of the European Union has passed a resolution that will be forwarded to the ACP-EU Council, as well as to Talisman and its Greater Nile partners, and EU governments with oil companies contemplating an entrance into Sudan.

> "The European Parliament] calls on international oil companies working in Sudan, such as Talisman Energy Inc. of Canada, to halt their operations as long as abductions of children and slavery continues and a peaceful solution has not been found to the [Sudan] conflict; calls on EU companies to refrain from oil investments in Sudan and urges the EU Member States to exert their influence to this effect."

The resolution comes in the context of the Parliament's response to the Government of Sudan's ongoing support for one of the most obscenely cruel terrorist groups in the world, the Lord's Resistance Army (LRA), which operates out of northern Uganda, with sanctuary in southern Sudan courtesy of the Khartoum regime (Talisman's business partner). A list of defining atrocities, focussing mainly on the terrible abuse of children, is contained in the full resolution of the EU Parliament (attached below).

The signal to oil companies operating in Sudan, or contemplating an entrance, could not be clearer. It is a direct rebuke of Talisman's absurd and disingenuous rationale for staying, and a decisive warning to those (e.g., TotalFinaElf) who have been mentioned as possible buyers of

Talisman's 25 per cent stake in the Greater Nile project. It is noteworthy that the resolution "urges the EU Member States to exert their influence to this effect [*i.e.*, preventing EU companies from investing in oil development in Sudan]."

There is a larger message here for Talisman and the callously disingenuous Mr. Buckee: your presence in Sudan continues to gain an ever-larger profile, with more and more destructive consequences for share price. Expect to see more such resolutions, and legislative responses, and nationally representative denunciations of Talisman. There will be opprobrium without end!

Buckee once dismissed opposition to the Sudan venture as "background noise." Well, take a look around, Jim: the "background" is everywhere—and shouldering its way ever more insistently to the "foreground" of the world's conscience.

Talisman will be hounded relentlessly—by human rights groups, by advocates from the faith communities, by legislation, by resolutions of Parliament, by ordinary folks—until they withdraw from Sudan.

Divestment pressures continue to grow in direct relation to the visibility of Talisman's morally outrageous complicity with the Government of Sudan, its business partner and "security provider." And as the nature of that savagely destructive "security" becomes more widely known, the link between Talisman and genocidal destruction of the peoples of southern Sudan becomes more obvious.

This will not "blow over"; there is no "riding out the storm." On the contrary, the storm of outrage continues to gather force. It will destroy Talisman in the equity markets if the company does not withdraw from Sudan.

Resolution of the Parliament of the European Union (EU):

On the abduction of children by the Lord's Resistance Army (LRA)

The European Parliament,

Having regard to the Convention on the Rights of the Child, its Optional Protocols, the 1999 ILO Convention concerning the Prohibition and Immediate Action for the Elimination of the Worst Forms of Child Labour, the Rome Statute of the International Criminal Court and the 1977 Additional Protocols to the Geneva Conventions,

Recalling its previous resolutions on child soldiers,

A. Considering that an armed rebellion has been raging in Northern Uganda since 1986, under the present name of the Lordl's Resistance Army (LRA);

B. Considering that the LRA is armed by the Sudanese government army, which also provides it with food and logistical support, as a counter-move for the support of the Ugandan government to the Sudan Peoplel's Liberation Army (SPLA);

C. Considering that, according to UNICEF, the LRA has abducted at least 14,000 children, as young as seven years old, in Northern Uganda, particularly in the districts of Gulu and Kitgum; whereas about 5000 children have since returned or escaped and thousands remain unaccounted for, of which not more than 2000 are reportedly still alive;

D. Considering that these children are taken to camps in South Sudan from where they are sent to fight both the Ugandan government army in the Uganda territory and the SPLA in South Sudan;

E. Considering that the children abducted by the LRA are subjected to extremes of brutality and are forced to conduct a reign of terror against their own people the Acholi population- by killing innocent people or by cutting off limbs, ears and lips, the total number of deaths estimated at over 100,000 and the total number of displaced people at present at over 300,000;

F. Considering that the girls are often submitted to sexual abuse and brutality by the LRA commanders, the best documented case being the girls of Aboke;

G. Considering that thousands of children have already died in captivity, from hunger and disease, during the fighting or beaten and stabbed to death as punishment for those who tried to escape;

H. Whereas a Peace Accord between Uganda and Sudan was signed in Nairobi on 8 December 1999, which included among other things a commitment by the Sudanese government to stop its support to the LRA and guarantee the safe return of the Ugandan abducted children held in rebel camps in Sudan;

Whereas the political will to implement the Peace Accord has been lacking on both sides, both countries have continued to support each other's armed rebels, and very few abducted children have been returned by Sudan;

J. Whereas despite the Nairobi Peace Accord some 300 children have again been abducted by LRA rebels since the beginning of this year, according to UNICEF, of which 143 have escaped;

K. Whereas an amnesty law was approved by the Ugandan Parliament on 6 December 1999, its implementation being seriously delayed; whereas LRA leader Joseph Kony has already rejected the amnesty but some of his soldiers have applied for it;

L. Whereas LRA representatives are allowed to collect funds, make public statements and operate freely from the territory of the EU, and have been travelling unhindered within the EU and between the EU and Sudan;

1. Strongly condemns the continuing abduction of children in Northern Uganda by the LRA and the subsequent use of these children in armed combat, which is a flagrant violation of several UN Conventions and international humanitarian law;

2. Calls on the government of Sudan to stop supporting the Lord's Resistance Army and to cooperate In the immediate and unconditional release of all the abducted children, as stipulated in the Nairobi Peace Accord;

3. Condemns the fact that, in Sudan, the use of child soldiers and the enslavement of children continues, and supports the action plan put forward by UNICEF to eradicating these practices;
4. Calls on the government of Sudan to consider the issue of the abducted children as a humanitarian issue and separate it from the larger political issues in the region;
5. Calls on the government of Sudan to allow free and full access by humanitarian organisations such as ICRC and UNICEF to the LRA camps to ascertain the identities of the abducted children and ensure their safe return to their home communities;
6. Calls on the government of Uganda to continue efforts to find a peaceful solution for the conflict in Northern Uganda and to speed up the implementation of the Amnesty Act despite the rejection of LRA leader Joseph Kony;
7. Calls on all parties involved in the conflict in Sudan to resume talks to find a peaceful solution to the conflict in South Sudan;
8. Calls on international oil companies working in Sudan, such as Talisman Energy Inc. of Canada, to halt their operations as long as abductions of children and slavery continues and a peaceful solution has not been found to the conflict; calls on EU companies to refrain from oil investments in Sudan and urges the EU Member States to exert their influence to this effect;
9. Calls on the Council to assume a more active role in urging the implementation of the Nairobi Peace Accord;
10. Calls on the Commission to support all efforts to rehabilitate and reintegrate the returning children and to support the affected communities in Northern Uganda;
11. Calls on the Council to support initiatives that prohibit the use of child soldiers and urges the ratification of the optional protocol of the UN Convention of the rights of children, setting 18 as the minimum age for recruitment of soldiers;
12. Calls on individual EU Member States to ban LRA operations and travelling of LRA representatives within the EU and between EU Member States and non-EU Nations;
13 Instructs its President to forward this resolution to the Commission, the ACP-EU Council, UNICEF, international oil companies working in Sudan, and the governments of Uganda and Sudan.

Sudan's Energy Sector: Implementing the Wealth-Sharing Agreement

On June 5, 2004, the government of Sudan and the Sudan People's Liberation Movement/ Army (SPLM/A) signed a framework peace agreement in Naivasha, Kenya, endorsing final principles for ending a 21-year civil war that has taken 2 million lives. The accord—the result of a two-year concerted multilateral effort led by Kenya, the United States, Norway, the United Kingdom, and the United Nations—provides for sharing political power and oil revenue between the government and the southern-based rebels, and a future referendum on secession for the south after a six-year interim period. The two parties began talks on details of a cease-fire agreement on June 21 and adjourned in late July without success. The six-month pre-interim period will not begin until a cease-fire agreement has been concluded.

The current crisis in Darfur poses a grave threat to the north-south peace process and must be resolved if the protocols signed in Naivasha and Machakos are to reach the implementation phase. Although this crisis may delay the cease-fire talks and the signing of a final comprehensive agreement, it remains essential that both the Sudanese and the international community begin now to prepare for the priority implementation challenges that lie ahead.

The wealth-sharing protocol, which was agreed upon in January 2004, is pivotal to Sudan's stability in the pre-interim and interim periods, and failure to implement this component of the overall agreement successfully will pose a significant threat to the continuing peace process. The protocol outlines guiding principles for joint management of Sudan's oil revenues and operations but leaves a myriad of details to be resolved during the six-month pre-interim period. The challenges of implementation facing each of the two parties will differ and will need to be tackled with the specific needs of both sides in mind.

On July 15, 2004, CSIS, in collaboration with the U.S. Institute of Peace, held a half-day conference to profile the priorities and challenges faced by Sudan and the international community in implementing the wealth-sharing protocol agreed upon by the government of Sudan and the SPLM/A in January 2004. After presentations from representatives of each of the two negotiating parties, Roger Diwan of PFC Energy presented the current outlook for Sudan's oil sector.

Endre Stiansen, senior researcher at the University of Oslo, Robert D. Ebel, lead economist at the World Bank, and Bruce Ehrnman from the U.S. Department of State outlined the negotiation process that unfolded in Naivasha and examined the next steps required during the pre-interim and interim periods to ensure successful implementation of the agreement. The final panel looked more specifically at issues of revenue and operational management and drew from the comparative experiences of other oil-producing states. Presentations were made by David Goldwyn of Goldwyn International Strategies, lan Gary of Catholic Relief Services, Hesketh Streeter, director of International Affairs at BP, and Robert E. Ebel of the CSIS Energy Program. The following is a summary of the central arguments made by the participants.

The Parties' Perspectives

SPLM/A representative, Steven Wondu, outlined four issues central to the successful implementation of the revenue-sharing components of the protocol. First is the absence of a sufficient tax base in southern Sudan, which will take several years to develop. Wondu stressed that in the meantime, the Government of South Sudan (GOSS) will be under pressure to create a credible tax collection mechanism independent from that applied in the north. Although the protocol specifies the sources of tax revenue for the national, southern, and state tiers of government, these levels overlap and will generate confusion and potential conflict.

Second, serious efforts are needed to develop a robust private sector that will not only generate revenue but also relieve demand for limited government jobs. Government enterprises, by comparison, have proven unreliable sources of revenue in other developing countries. Third, in the short and medium term, oil will remain the sole significant source of domestic revenue. The success of the entire peace agreement will depend on the parties' satisfactory implementation of the oil revenue-sharing provision, yet the formula for oil revenue sharing is complex and can be easily manipulated. The national government and the government of South Sudan will share the net revenue from oil (NRO) on an equal basis, but determining the volume of oil sold and the debit charges in the revenue account will be problematic. It is important that the government of South Sudan trust the system and not suspect foul play, and the best insurance against this is oversight by an independent third party.

The wealth-sharing agreement provides for a Fiscal and Financial Allocation and Monitoring Commission (FAMC) whose terms of reference are limited to the supervision of the distribution, not the determination, of revenue. The commission is a part-time committee, but a full-time secretariat of technical experts drawn from both parties should be mandated to examine the nominal account entries and certify that they are accurate. This would go a long way to allay fears and build confidence.

Lastly, it is important to consider revenue distribution mechanisms and the urgent need for functioning financial institutions. The agreement requires the national government to transfer oil revenue to the GOSS and to oil-producing states promptly. Wondu asserted that to avoid delays and misunderstanding, the oil revenue account should be directly linked to the general governmental fund accounts of the three recipients—the national government, the GOSS, and the states. Yet, none of these arrangements will be possible without a banking system in the south.

Abdel Kabeir, deputy chief of mission at the embassy of Sudan, added that the wealth-sharing agreement is based on the principle that the entire country will benefit from current and potential resources that go beyond oil to include other minerals and forestry products. Because oil is subject to global market swings, and exploration and production can be highly uncertain, Kabeir argued that wealth-sharing should be linked to the national income, rather than to a single sector.

Kabeir stressed the importance of two issues: revenue flows and accountability. From the government's perspective, the agreed mechanism to handle revenue flows is very sound, Kabeir agreed with Wondu on the need for increased confidence, but asserted that the central government will not impede or manipulate income flows to the GOSS. It will be necessary to make use of existing infrastructure and not expend scarce resources on redundant projects. On accountability, the government that will be formed from the Naivasha accord will be equipped with new, clear guidelines on how wealth—both current and future—should be shared. The spirit and comprehensiveness of this agreement dil er fundamentally from past agreements.

Current Status of the Oil Sector in Sudan

As the largest source of revenue, oil will figure prominently in the implementation of an eventual peace accord. It is therefore critical that both parties have an accurate picture of the sector's potential—and limits. Sudan's licensed acreage is currently dominated by Asian national oil companies, most importantly China National Petroleum Corporation (CNPC), Malaysia's Petronas, and India's Oil and Natural Gas Corporation (ONGC). Western companies, which have superior technology and capital, are notably absent due to sanctions, safety concerns, and reputational risk. At present, Sudan's oil sector produces 310,000 barrels per day (b/d), with the majority coming from the Greater Nile Petroleum Operating Company's (GNPOC) Muglad basin fields in southern Sudan.

Increased future production will be driven by exploration, which is dependent on the progress of the peace process and an increase in operator safety. At the moment, Sudan's conflict keeps approximately one-half of the prospective segment of the Muglad basin off-limits to exploration. Once the peace process is successfully concluded, the government is expected to hold a licensing round for northern concession blocks (blocks 11-15) to expedite the return of Western companies.

Future production will follow one of two scenarios: (1) without exploration, production will decline rapidly after 2007; or (2) if there is successful exploration and discoveries are followed by significant capital investment, production could plateau at approximately 450,000 b/d for the next 15 years. This expected increase in production assumes the accuracy of recent CNPC reports of the discovery of several hundred million barrels in the more secure area of blocks 3 and 7 in the Melut basin. Yet, CNPC has a history of inflating reserve and production forecasts. Given current data, it is extremely unlikely that Sudan's production will ever exceed 1 million b/d—the threshold set for the oil stabilization fund.

Negotiations in Naivasha and Machakos

Although multiple implementation challenges remain, the talks on wealth sharing saw a new level of engagement by both negotiating parties and external actors, which proved critical to the success of this phase. First, there was a need for external, technical expertise, which came from the IMF, World Bank, and others. Second, SPLM chairman John Garang and Sudanese vice president Ali Osman Taha spent significant time at the talks and, in one-on-one encounters, broke through certain impasses and reached tough decisions. Third, the delegations themselves began to engage more fluidly with each other as the negotiation process moved forward.

A central problem remaining with the wealth-sharing and other protocols is that they focus on what is shared, but not how the revenue-sharing formulas are actually to be implemented. The parties will not address how wealth is to be shared until they negotiate the final protocol on implementation modalities. The benefit of this sequencing is that it makes an agreement possible when those final compromises are either too technically challenging or too divisive politically. A tremendous amount of work remains during the implementation phase, not the least of which is creation of a new government in the south.

The wealth-sharing protocol addresses four main issues: revenue division (including fiscal transfers between different levels of government); banking and currency; land; and foreign funding. The energy sector itself is not dealt with separately in the agreement, but rather is addressed generally under the revenue division and land issues.

When the parties tackled the division of oil revenue, the debate was informed by three factors: First, oil is the largest source of revenue for the government of Sudan. Second, most of the known oil is located in southern Sudan, and the SPLM wants to use oil revenue as an income base for an independent South Sudan. And third, both parties agree that ownership of oil follows from ownership of land. Both parties, however, have very different interpretations of this third point.

Based on the Land Act of 1970, the government regards all land where oil is currently produced and explored as government land; therefore, all oil belongs to the central government. The SPLM, however, does not recognise the 1970 law, which was formulated in the midst of the first civil war without input from the SPLM. From the SPLM perspective, land (both surface and subsurface) belongs to the local communities. It was clear from the outset of the negotiations in Machakos that the parties would not agree on this point in the near term. A compromise was necessary, and that compromise was that the ownership of subterranean resources, including oil, would remain undecided for the duration of the pre-interim and interim period.

What was agreed was *the formula* for sharing the revenue from this subterranean land. Revenue from oil in southern Sudan is to be split 50-50 between the national government and the GOSS after two deductions: 100 per cent of the net revenue from producing states goes to the government. The government redistributes 2 per cent of the revenue from a particular producer state back to that state government. A second deduction is then made for the Oil Stabilization Account if oil prices rise above an agreed upon threshold price. The wealth-sharing agreement, however, contains very few specifics on the logistics of this stabilisation fund. For instance, a benchmark price has not yet been determined. This formula is applied only to revenue from oil produced in southern Sudan. Revenue from oil produced elsewhere will not go to the government of South Sudan, unless it does so through other allocations (influenced by the work of the Fiscal and Financial Allocation and Monitoring Commission) designed to ensure that revenue is distributed equitably throughout the country.

What does this mean? There are three obvious problems:

1. *Income flows:* How is the new national government going to mobilise revenues? The national government will face an immediate, substantial cut in income when the revenue-sharing agreement is implemented. At the same time, the government of South Sudan will face the inverse problem—a sudden surge in revenues and a lack of institutional and absorptive capacity.

2. *Intergovernmental systems:* How will revenue be distributed in a transparent manner? Institutions necessary for financial transfers, especially at the local level, are lacking. A transparent institutional infrastructure must be built up.

3. *Institutional capacity:* There is not yet a clear plan for the numerous new institutions that will be needed in the new Sudan. We know, for example, that there will be a national petroleum commission, but exactly how will it function? How will it be structured? And, how will it relate to other institutions (e.g., the existing Ministry of Petroleum and Energy)?

Five less obvious problems reside in the text of the wealth-sharing agreement and will have a significant impact on the energy sector. These include:

1. Agreement on the meaning of the text and elaboration on several implementation issues, including the structure of the stabilization fund.
2. An implementation schedule, as well as terms of reference for the various committees agreed upon.
3. Agreement on the status of existing contracts.
4. Agreement on land ownership, which will have a major impact on the energy sector in the long run. (Land commissions are to be set up in the north, south, and all disputed areas.)
5 Determination on what will happen after the six-year interim period. (There is very little on this in the agreement.)

Expansion of revenue sources remains a pressing concern for the national government, which is facing significant pressure to raise revenue in the face of the cuts that will come with implementation of the agreement. The national government is seeking to expand social services throughout the country, but this effort is hampered by a critically weak fiscal base. The broader questions surrounding taxation are just some of those that need to be tackled in the near term. Currently, the tax to GDP ratio is approximately 10 per cent (prior to the impact of the revenue-sharing agreement).

The average is 19 per cent for developing countries, and 30 per cent for developed countries—indicating the extent to which the Sudanese government must mobilize revenues through a reconfiguring of the national tax system, especially state and local taxes. The challenge of mobilising state and local taxes will be particularly important for southern Sudan, which must avoid falling victim to the effects of "Dutch Disease," brought about when oil windfalls push up the real exchange rate of a country's currency and render other exports noncompetitive. It can provoke a rapid, distorted growth of services, transportation, and construction, while simultaneously discouraging agriculture and certain types of industrialisation.

In addition to the need for revenue mobilisation, there is a need for transparent distribution of these revenues. The contested areas of Abyei, Southern Blue Nile, and the Nuba Mountains will pose particular problems. These "Three Areas" technically lie in the north but share cultural and political connections with the SPLM/A. These areas will be autonomous units but will also be part of the intergovernmental transfer system.

Implementing the Wealth-sharing Agreement

As the likely source of economic development in southern Sudan, it is critical that the oil sector be harnessed in a manner that avoids the common pitfalls seen in the other African oil-producing states. Finding a way to make oil production benefit overall stability and economic development is essential in improving the lives of the Sudanese population. Revenue transparency and operational management provide two fundamental challenges to this goal, but experiences in other oil-producing countries offer lessons on policies and practices that help to mitigate related risks.

Challenges for International Oil Companies

In the event of a comprehensive peace accord and implementation of the wealth-sharing agreement, will international oil companies feel secure enough to return, spend serious dollars, and generate wealth for Sudan in the next five years? Without significant changes and clarification, probably not.

The comparative experiences of oil companies in other countries suggest several cautions. Of the international companies, however, the Chinese, Indian, and Malaysian companies are more likely than the Western majors and independents to take risks. First and foremost, companies have a very low tolerance for risking lives. They also have a low tolerance for risking capital in places where they do not already have significant investment in the ground. Moreover, companies are averse to high levels of contract risk; they need clear and sustainable fiscal and legal rules. And last, companies are reluctant to place themselves in the middle of land disputes where countries or internal groups are arguing over who has the right to develop resources. Companies realise that in many cases, litigation and reputation risks are far greater than the potential financial rewards.

In their considerations to invest and operate in Sudan, international oil companies face three central challenges:

1. *Security:* The greatest challenge will be in the undeveloped fields, and as long as the risk of violence remains high, international oil companies will not return. Field development will be expensive and companies will be in remote and unprotected areas. Key considerations will include; Are the companies welcome by local communities? Who will maintain security—local militias or the combined forces of South Sudan and others?

2. *Fiscal and legal regime:* The agreement calls for respect of existing contracts and creation of a conducive policy environment to maximize investment. However, there remain many open and undecided fiscal and legal issues:

   - The agreement also says that parties may sue if they believe their rights have been violated. It is unclear, however, which rights are to be protected, what constitutes a violation, and how and when these suits would be litigated. Those companies with existing operations will likely manage this risk. But for those companies just starting in undeveloped blocks, it is likely that this will need to be resolved before any substantial investment is made.

- The agreement states that every level of government has the right to tax and issue levies. Will these apply to existing contracts? Will there be a national tax regime? A national energy policy limiting local taxes? It is difficult for companies to estimate the return on their investment without knowing the extent of their future tax obligations.
- The agreement calls for communities to be involved in negotiation of new contracts. This is likely to be either a deterrent or at least a severe impediment to new contracts.
- The agreement provides for land claims that can be submitted to the National Land Commission, including just compensation and nonfinancial remedies (return of land). Do these include claims on existing contracts? If so, and if they are submitted, how long will it take to resolve them?
- A final, major contractual risk is *sustainability.* Will legal rights and fiscal terms that apply during the interim period apply if the south secedes? Without an assertion by the SPLM that they will abide by the agreed terms regardless of the referendum result, companies will be very reluctant to invest. A six-year deal is insufficient in a 30-year business.

3. *Administrative capacity:* The southerners in particular are going to need training and access to expertise and necessary information for participation in the National Petroleum Commission, the Land Commission, and various ministries in the national government. They will need training in industry best practices—in transparency, auditing, contracts, and management. Most importantly, they will need to secure unbiased advice and assistance at nonextortionate prices.

Transparency and Accountability

Even if all the other obstacles to peace are overcome, Sudan faces a very difficult road when it comes to turning petroleum wealth into lasting peace and prosperity. Sudan is a very difficult environment in which to achieve transparent and accountable oil revenue management, but it will be a crucial element of any lasting piece. Oil exporters in the Gulf of Guinea have failed to turn their oil booms into broad-based economic development and are instead marked by high levels of corruption, conflict, and economic decay.

Sudan must place an early emphasis on transparency and accountability to avoid falling prey to the all-too-common "resource curse." In the current policy environment, oil dependence hurts development in multiple ways. Oil booms raise expectations and increase appetites for spending. Governments dramatically increase public spending based on unrealistic revenue projections, but the quality of this spending often decreases. The volatility of oil prices, loss of fiscal control, and inflation, hinder growth, equity, and poverty alleviation. Foreign debt tends to grow faster in oil-exporting countries, mortgaging the future, and non-oil productive activities, such as manufacturing and agriculture, are adversely affected (Dutch Disease). Over time, oil revenues decrease reliance on non-oil taxes, and can actually replace previously existing taxation systems—freeing oil-exporting governments from the types of citizen demands for fiscal transparency and accountability that arise when people pay taxes directly to the government.

Without improving their democratic institutions and administrative capacity, it will be difficult for Sudan to use petrodollars to fuel poverty reduction; instead, oil monies are more likely to make matters worse for the poor.

Recommendations

Even with these multiple challenges, it is possible to work within the framework of the agreement to accelerate investment and promote the effective allocation of oil resources. The current crisis in Darfur and web of U.S. sanctions mean that the implementation process will not realistically begin for at least another six months. This time must be used effectively to address some of the most pressing questions, and several recommendations stand out:

To donors and other external actors:

1. The World Bank and others need to *identify and fund a cadre of experts and trainers* to work with GOSS over the next year to train them for leadership in the oil sector at both the state and local level. Donors must ensure that there are *sufficient staff budgets.* Examples from Chad, Cameroon, and others illustrate that without strong and independently funded staffs, these commissions and auditors cannot function.
2. There must be a *strong, coherent donor policy* that insists on transparency, fair and accountable revenue management and allocation, and respect for human rights. Donors need to make clear in advance that there will be no major flows of funds without auditing of expenditures at the state and regional level—under the national government and the GOSS. Donor thresholds must be made clear up front so all parties can prepare to meet them. Donor leverage should be properly sequenced, with significant steps toward the building of good governance taking place prior to oil sector development assistance.

To the government of Sudan and SPLM:

3. The parties need to start now on development of a *national energy policy.* They need to identify the major obstacles to investment and work through a policy that is amenable to all parties and binding at federal, state, and local levels. If parties wait until the institutions are formed, it will be years before a conducive policy environment is formed.
4. The SPLM and others ought to make a statement that they will live by fiscal and legal terms regardless of the outcome of the referendum.

5. The parties need to develop an *infrastructure security policy* to make clear for investors who will provide security and how.
6. Space should be created for *civil society* groups to play a role in the monitoring of oil revenues and expenditures. This participation can be institutionalised through some of the formal mechanisms provided for in the wealth-sharing agreement (the National Petroleum Commission, Fiscal and Financial Allocation and Monitoring Commission, and Land Commissions), which so far, only provide for participation by the government, SPLM, and regional representatives.
7. It is important that transparency be pursued with *contracts* as well as revenue flows. The agreement states that those who have access to existing contracts must sign "confidentiality agreements"—not a good starting point for building a transparent oil sector. Furthermore, it will be important to verify both international oil company payments to the government and government payments to southern Sudan.
8. A policy for dealing with *oil-backed loans* should be established. A significant share of Sudan's future oil revenue is already dedicated to repaying these loans, and a transparent process will be needed to determine the extent to which future wealth is already leveraged. It is in both parties' interests to examine who has the ability and authority to take out such loans, and whether it is best to place a moratorium on them during the interim period.
9. As it currently stands, the wealth-sharing agreement does not address the specific operational modalities of the *Oil Revenue Stabilisation Account* or the *Future Generation Fund.* These stabilisation funds are key to Sudan's economic development and stability and will need to be carefully crafted and negotiated if they are to be effective.
10. The *revenue-sharing formula* itself may prove to be problematic. First, the 2 per cent of revenue that is to go to the producing states/regions (in proportion to each state/region's production) is likely to be inadequate. In Chad, 5 per cent of revenue goes to the producing states, while in Nigeria it is 13 per cent. Second, huge political questions and challenges are likely to surface when defining the various producing regions. The potential for continued local grievances will remain high.
11. Finally, it will be important to control the *expectations of political leaders* and their public rhetoric as much as possible. Some of the potential production and revenue amounts, as well as development assistance requirements, predicted by political leaders have been off the mark and will only exacerbate mistrust among various parties. Quick, visible results from oil revenue spending will be important in building confidence both between the parties and within local communities.

Thus, there are numerous issues that remain to be dealt with if the wealth-sharing agreement is to be implemented successfully. If oil revenue is not managed well, the overall peace process stands to suffer. Appropriate transparency and accountability must be built into the norms and institutions of post-conflict Sudan, and are integral to ensuring that peace between the north and south, as well as within the south itself, is not undermined.

China, India and Africa: New Partners in Energy Security

As G8 leaders pat themselves on the back for debt relief and development assistance to Africa, China and India are doing their part to help develop Africa's economies. The two Asian giants are pouring funds into the continent to find energy for their superheated economies and markets for their products.

Chinese companies are snapping up African oil and gas fields, investing in telecom companies, and funding programmes to boost farm output. The value of China's trade with Africa has jumped from $10 billion in 2000 to nearly $30 billion in 2004. India arrived late but is starting to see gains as well. It is a driving forced hind "the new African Institutes for Science and Technology, which aim to replicate India's technologyled economic growth. In 2004, India extended $500 million in credit to eight West African countries to promote the purchase of Indian information technology. India's state-owned oil firm has invested heavily in Sudan and is exploring options in West Africa. "China is making greater inroads," says Peter Draper of the South African Institute of International Affairs, "but with its historical connections, India will catch up."

Why all the interest in the forgotten continent? A goodie bag of exploitable markets and exploitable resources. China has flooded Africa with cheap textiles, rice, and electronics. India has cornered the market in generic pharmaceuticals used to treat HIV and offers the hardware and software needed to get Africa on the information superhighway. Africa, in turn, is feeding the insatiable Asian thirst for energy: Both India and China have negotiated oil, gas, timber, and coal contracts worth billions of dollars,

The burgeoning business offers African leaders an inside look at China and India's enviable development models, which over the last decade have drawn the attention of the whole world.

Darfur Rebels Vow more Attack on Sudan oilfields

Darfur rebels vowed to launch more assaults on oil installations across Sudan until Khartoum gave in to a string of demands, including compensation for Darfuris and full representation in the national government. "This is only the beginning," said Ahmed Tugud, the chief negotiator of the Justice and Equality Movement. "We will carry out attacks across Sudan and our main target will be oilfields."

JEM said it attacked Sudan's Defra oilfield killing 20 government soldiers and taking two foreign hostages, one Canadian, the other Iraqi. The government denied any such attack.

Ahmed Tugud told Reuters no harm would come to the hostages, saying they were in "secure hands". But he said the insurgent group was not ready to announce what it planned to do with them.

A spokesman for Sudan's Ministry of Energy and Mining denied there had been an attack on Defra, saying: "There is no problem there. Everything is secure."

Sudan is highly sensitive about reports that risk damaging its hugely opaque oil industry, a vital source of revenue for the country.

A spokesman from China's embassy in Khartoum said he could confirm an attack happened in the region and that some people were "abducted by JEM". He added: "We are studying the situation. I can't comment further."

Canada's Foreign Ministry said it was checking reports that one of its citizens had been kidnapped but had no confirmation yet. Tugud said attacks on oilfields would continue until Khartoum agreed to a string of JEM demands, including compensation for the people of Darfur, a Darfuri regional government and full representation in Sudan's national government.

Message to China

The Defra oilfield in Sudan's Kordofan region, neighbouring Darfur, is run by The Greater Nile Petroleum Operating Company (GNPOC) consortium. China's CNPC has the biggest stake in the group, alongside India's ONGC, Malaysia's Petronas and Sudanese state-owned Sudapet.

Tugud said the Defra attack was meant as a message to China, which JEM accuses of arming the Khartoum government. "All the weapons we took from the soldiers were Chinese. The Sudan government is using the oil money it gets from China to buy weapons to kill our people," Tugud said. JEM earlier gave foreign oil companies a week to leave Sudan.

China's interest in African oil has exposed its companies to increasing risk in recent months. Separatist rebels in Ethiopia's remote Somali region killed nine Chinese workers in a raid on an oil installation in April. Chinese oil workers have also been kidnapped in volatile southern Nigeria. Sudan's Ministry of Energy and Mining lists 24 companies with stakes in oil concessions in the country, including Total of France.

The reported attack cast a further shadow over peace talks between Darfur rebel groups and the Sudanese government, due to start in the Libyan city of Sirte.

JEM leaders said they were meeting their counterparts in the Unity faction of the rebel Sudan Liberation Army (SLA-Unity) to decide whether to attend the negotiations brokered by the U.N. and the African Union.

The talks have already been hit by boycotts. Six other SLA factions announced they were pulling out. The founder of the splintered movement Abdel Wahed Mohamed Ahmed al-Nur also says he will not go.

Insurgent groups say they have not been given enough time to prepare negotiating positions or reach common ground with other factions. Many were also angered by the invitations to the talks which, they said, limited the number of representatives from each group and did not include foreign delegates.

China's CNPC Signs Exploration Agreement with Sudan

China's top state-run energy group, China National Petroleum Corp. (CNPC), has signed an agreement with the Sudanese government to prospect for oil and gas in Sudan's northern territory.

Under the agreement, CNPC would have exploration rights to 13 oil blocks located in the northern coast of the Red Sea. The fields have a total acreage of about 3.8 square kilometres.

The deal includes a production-sharing contract. CNPC will partner Indonesia's state oil and gas company Pertamina and Sudan's state-owned Sudapet in the exploration project.

CNPC, a leading energy investor in Sudan and parent of oil and gas firm PetroChina, also holds a 50 per cent stake in the Khartoum refinery—the only oil plant in Africa's largest country.

China now produces roughly 226,000 barrels of oil everyday from three oil-fields in Sudan, or about 3 per cent of China's demand.

Sudan oil minister says energy cooperation with China fruitful

Since the Beijing Summit of the Forum on China-Africa Cooperation held in November 2006, thanks to the joint efforts of China and Sudan, bilateral cooperation has further deepened within the framework of China-Africa cooperation. To date, cooperation between China and Sudan has covered multiple sectors, including energy, human resources development, and contracting of engineering projects. All the projects are progressing smoothly and have produced positive outcomes.

In an interview with the official Chinese news Agency Xinhua, Awad Ahmed Al-Jaz, Sudanese Minister of Energy and Mining, remarked that the energy industry is the most important area of cooperation between China and Sudan and also the most fruitful area of bilateral cooperation.

Al-Jaz stressed that over the past decade, encouraged by both Chinese and Sudanese governments, China National Petroleum Corporation [CNPC] has actively invested in Sudan and made important contributions to Sudan's economic development and social progress. He pointed out: Thanks to the CNPC's strong assistance, Sudan has transformed itself from a crude oil importing country into a crude oil exporting country and has established a complete industrial chain for the oil industry; led by the rapid development of the oil industry, Sudan's overall economy is developing vigorously and entering a phase of economic boom. Attention to human resources development is a salient feature of China-Sudan cooperation. According to the eight-point consensus reached at the Beijing Summit of the Forum on China-Africa Cooperation, China shall strengthen cooperation with Africa in such areas as human resources development and education and actively train and develop talent for Africa.

Al-Jaz expressed the view that the Chinese Government and a batch of Chinese enterprises, represented by the CNPC, have established a unique model of cooperation with the Sudanese Government and enterprises over time. Under this model, the Chinese Government and enterprises not only provide capital, technology, and equipment for Sudan, but also attach great importance to Sudan's human resources development.

During his assignment, it was observed that all the projects that the CNPC has invested in so far around Sudan are actively training and employing local Sudanese employees, to translate into action the consensus of the Beijing Summit of the Forum on China-Africa Cooperation on Human Resources Development. In the CNPC-invested projects, such as oilfields and the Khartoum oil refinery, numerous CNPC-trained local Sudanese employees are working there. They include not only a large number of operatives, but also a batch of mid-level and senior professional managers.

Zhu Junfeng, head of the CNPC Coordination and Leading Group for Sudan Projects and general manager of CNPC International (Nile) Limited emphasised that all the ongoing CNPC projects in Sudan employ a large number of local Sudanese employees and in some projects, over 90 per cent of the staff are local Sudanese. He remarked that training local Sudanese employees not only satisfies the demand of the projects for skilled manpower, but also produces a large number of operatives and managerial talent for Sudan's oil industry. He said: The CNPC's projects in Sudan will strive towards mutually beneficial and win-win outcomes by sharing interests with the people of Sudan.

Hao Hongshe, commercial counsellor with the Economic and Commercial Section of the Chinese embassy in Sudan, said: Besides energy and human resources development, the cooperation between China and Sudan is currently developing in greater depth across a wider scope on a continuous basis. Besides oil projects, a large number of engineering contracting projects are making smooth progress and have produced positive results. With significant economic and social benefits, these projects have a bearing on Sudan's national economy and the livelihood of its people. The El Gaili Power Station project that Harbin Power Engineering Company Limited is building in Sudan is one such project.

El Gaih power station is a large gas and oil-fired power plant planned by the Sudanese Ministry of Energy and Mining and Sudan National Electricity Corporation. This power station was to be built over four phases. For the first phase, the total contract value was $149 million and the installed capacity 200,000 kW. When it went into service in August 2004, its generation capacity accounted for approximately one third of Sudan's national total at the time.

During July 2007, the second phase of the project was entering the completion stage. Lu Hua, manager of Phase II Extension of Sudan El Gaili Power Station of Harbin Power Engineering Company Limited, said: The smooth execution of the El Gaili Power Station project has solved the challenging problem of power shortage that confronted Sudan for many years. The local people lovingly refer to Chinese and Sudanese workers taking part in the project as "bringers of light."

In recent years, the Sudanese oil industry has been developing vigorously, driving the rapid growth of Sudan's national economy. Sudan's overall economic strength is growing steadily and its investment environment is improving gradually. Sudan wishes to see the further promotion of cooperation in such sectors as natural gas, electricity, minerals, communications, and agriculture under the joint endeavour of the Chinese and Sudanese Governments in accordance with the eight-point consensus reached at the Beijing Summit of the Forum on China-Africa Cooperation. He expressed his conviction that with the joint efforts of China and Sudan, the cooperation between the two countries has huge potential and broad prospects.

REFERENCES

1. Susan Strange, *Mad Money*, Manchester University Press, Manchester, 1998.
2. Quoted in 'A serious problem', *Petroleum Economist*, March 2006.
3. The current discussions around the race for African oil resources tend to focus on West Africa and the Gulf of Guinea—notably, the offshore areas of the coasts of Nigeria, Angola, and many other West African states. In this study, we refer to the entire African continent to capture developments elsewhere such as in Libya, which has the largest oil reserves in Africa.
4. 'A new scramble', *The Economist*, 27 November 2004.
5. Pierre Abramovici, 'United States: the New Scramble for Africa', *Review of African Political Economy*, 31, 2004, pp. 685-90.
6. Peter Schraeder, 'Cold War to Cold Peace: explaining U.S.-French competition in Francophone Africa', *Political Science Quarterly*, 115, 3, 2000, pp. 395-419.
7. Howard W. French, 'Commentary—China and Africa', *African Affairs*, 106, 2007, pp. 127-132.
8. Esther Pan, 'China, Africa and Oil', *Council on Foreign Relations*, 2006.
9. 'China's Hu urges more Africa ties', *BBC News online*, 27 April 2006.
10. David Zweig and Bi Jianhai, 'China's global hunt for energy', *Foreign Affairs* 84, 5, September/ October 2005, pp. 25-38.
11. An official Beijing economic journal.
12. Quoted by the Portuguese News Agency (LUSA)—'Angola: Luanda was China's No. 1 crude supplier in first half of year' 23 August 2006.
13. *Xinhua News Agency*, 19 October 2006.
14. United States Department of Commerce: International Trade Administration, 'US-Africa Trade Profile' *Home page* 19 April, 2006.
15. United States Department of Energy, Energy Information Administration 31 August 2006.
16. Anthony Lake, Christine Todd Whitman, Princeton N. Lyman, Ralph Bunche and Stephen Morrison, 'More than humanitarianism: a strategic US approach toward Africa' *Council on Foreign Relations 2006 Report*, 19 April 2006.
17. Sohn Se-joo, an assistant minister at the South Korean Foreign Ministry, *Yonhap News*, 5 April 2006.
18. Angolan Embassy in the UK newsletter. No. 105, May 2005.
19. 'Indian cash eyes West Africa oil', *BBC News Online*, 24 November 2005.

20. In the modern era, the first search for oil in Algeria took place in the late nineteenth century and in Nigeria before the First World War. Production started in Egypt in 1910, and Egypt became the key African oil-producing country. But, Africa's role in the international oil markets was limited until decolonisation.
21. Ali Aissaoui, *Algeria; The Political Economy of Oil and Gas*, Oxford University Press, Oxford, 2001, p. 130.
22. Douglas A. Yates, *The Rentier Stale in Africa: Oil rent dependency and neocolonialism in the Republic of Gallon,* Africa World Press, Trenton NJ, 1996.
23. Jedrzej George Frynas, Matthias Beck and Kamel Mellahi, 'Maintaining corporate dominance after decolonization: the first mover advantage of Shell-BP in Nigeria', *Review of African Political Economy,* 27, 2000, pp. 213-230.
24. Judith Gurney, *Libya: The political economy of oil,* Oxford University Press, Oxford, 1996, p. 91.
25. Jedrzej George Frynas, Oil in *Nigeria: Conflict and litigation between oil companies and village communities,* LIT Verlag/Transaction Publishers, Hamburg/New Brunswick, NJ/London, 2000, p. 17.
26. *Ibid,* p. 24.
27. On the nineteenth century Scramble for Africa, sec e.g. G.N. Sanderson, 'The European partition of Africa', *The Journal of Imperial and Commonwealth History,* 3, 1, 1974, pp. 1-54.
28. One can argue that spheres of influence exist to some extent. For instance. Equatorial Guinea and Sào Tomé e Principe are dominated by US interests, while Gabon and Congo-Brazzaville are largely French-dominated. However, these spheres of interest are not airtight and—as in the cases of Equatorial Guinea and Sào Tomé e Principe — do not have a neo-colonial imprint.
29. Frynas, Beck and Mellahi, 'Maintaining corporate dominance after decolonisation'.
30. Aissaoui, *Algeria: The political economy of oil and gas,* p. 63.
31. Gurney, *Libya: The political economy of oil.*
32. Christopher Layne, 'The unipolar illusion: why new great powers will arise', *International Security* 17, 4, 1993, pp. 5-51; William C. Wolhforth, 'The stability of a unipolar world,' *International Security* 24, 1 1990, pp. 5-41; Zbigniew Brzezinski and John J. Mearsheimer, 'Clash of the titans'. *Foreign Policy,* January/February 2005, pp. 46-49.
33. Evan S. Medciros and M. Taylor Fravel, 'China's New Diplomacy", *Foreign Affairs,* 82, 6, 2003, pp. 22-35.
34. Michael Klare and Daniel Volman, 'The African "oil rush" and American National Security', *Third World Quarterly,* 27, 4, 2006, pp. 609-628.
35. Jeremy Keenan, 'Terror in the Sahara: the implications of US imperialism for North and West Africa', *Review of African Political Economy,* 31, 2004, pp.475-496.
36. Michael Klare, *Blood and Oil: The dangers and consequences of America's growing dependency on imported petroleum (The American Empire Project)* Metropolitan Books Publishers, New York, 2004, p. 144.
37. China's Hu urges more Africa ties', *BBC News online.*
38. Council on Foreign Relations Home Page.
39. Chris Alden, 'China in Africa', *Survival* 47, 3, 2003, p. 151.

40. Council on Foreign Relations.

41. 'Moscow and Beijing, Asia's roaring economies: China's trade safari in Africa', *Le Monde*, 4 February 2004.

42. Total US security aid to Angola and Nigeria stood at some US$300 million in the fiscal years 2002-2004, which was a substantial increase from previous years. See Klare and Volman, The African "oil rush" and American national security'.

43. Following the end of the Civil War, Angola was desperate to organize a donors' conference to gather pledges for aid to help rebuild infrastructure destroyed by the war. The international community link aid pledges to the condition that Angola reached a formal agreement with the International Monetary Fund, particularly because of misgivings regarding the management of the massive revenues generated from oil, while China does not impose conditionality on its loans and aid.

44. 'Forward, with China', *Petroleum Economist*, May 2006.

45. Refineries usually prefer crude oil with a low sulphur content because they must remove the sulphur from the oil. Norman J. Hyne, *Nontechnical Guide to Petroleum Geology, Exploration, Drilling and Production*, PennWell, Tulsa, 1995, p. 14.

46. 'Trans-Sahara pipeline: more than mirage', *Petroleum Economist*, May 2006.

47. Frynas, *Oil in Nigeria*, pp. 35-36. The increase in the number of different companies can be partly attributed to the growth of indigenous firms in Nigeria. Since the early 1990s, successive governments in Nigeria encouraged and mandated the inclusion of local Nigerian partners when new oil licences were awarded. These firms had frequently very limited technological expertise and served neopatrimonial interests.

48. Personal communication with a senior executive of an international oil company (October 2005). Nonetheless, it remains debatable to what extent there are fundamental differences between the "responsible" Western firm and the "irresponsible" Chinese or Malaysian firm. On the one hand, there are doubts about the sincerity of Western firms with regard to Corporate Social Responsibility, and, on the other hand, the nature of the oil business causes a number of severe negative political, economic, and social effects which equally apply to Western and Asian firms. See Scott Pugg, 'World leaders and bottom feeders: divergent strategies toward social responsibility and resource extraction' in Christopher May (ed.), *Global Corporate Power*, Lynne Rienner, Boulder, 2006; Jedrzej George Frynas, 'The false developmental promise of corporate social responsibility: evidence from multinational oil companies', *International Affairs*, 81, 2005, pp. 581-598.

49. This provided a marked contrast to the first licensing round in 2005 when US companies secured most of the oil concessions. Economist Intelligence Unit, *EIU Country Report Libya—January 2006*, London 2006, p. 26.

50. Economist Intelligence Unit, *EIU Country Report Niggeria-November 2005*, London, 2005, p. 26.

51. Furthermore, the Sudanese fields are located inland, and the Chinese firms do not in any way threaten the position of Exxon, BP, and other major firms in the most sought-after offshore areas in the Gulf of Guinea.

52. UNCTAD, *2005 World Investment Report: Transnational corporation and internationalization of R&D*, Geneva, 10 April 2006, pp. 42-3.

53. *Ibid.* The report provided no figures for Sudan.

54. 'West African Nations critical to U.S. Energy Security—Gulf of Guinea provides 14 per cent of U.S. oil supply', *US Department of State*, 20 March 2006.

55. Gurney, *Libya: The political economy of oil*, pp. 2-3 and 195-8.

56. The term 'unviable state' was previously used by one of the authors to characterize the islands of Sào Tomé e Principe (STP) that have been entirely dependent on foreign aid and loans for some time; Jedrzej George Frynas, Geoffrey Wood and Ŗ.M.S. Soares de Oliveira, "Business and politics in Sào Tomé e Principe', *African Affairs:* 102 (2003), pp. 51-80. However, STP is likely to undergo a similar transformation to Libya because of an anticipated oil boom.

57. Gurney, *Libya; The political economy of oil*, p. 193.

58. Aissaoui, *Algeria: The political economy of oil and gas,* p. 291.

59. IPEDEX, 'Mapping Report: National education mapping and training needs in the Angolan petroleum industry 2001-2007' (Confidential report for the Ministry of Petroleum/Norwegian Petroleum Directorate and Angola's Ministry of Education, Luanda, 2003).

60. Alan Gelb *et al., Oil Windfalls: Blessing or curse,* Oxford University Press, New York, 1988; Jeffrey D. Sachs and Andrew M. Warner, 'Natural resources and economic development: the curse of natural resources', *European Economic Review,* 45, 2001, pp. 827-838; Thorvaldur Gylfason, 'Natural resources, education and economic development' *European Economic Review,* 45, 2001, pp. 847-59; Carlos Leite and Jens Weidmann, *Does Mother Nature Corrupt? Natural resources, corruption and economic growth,* International Monetary Fund, Washington, DC, 1999.

61. M.L. Ross, 'The Political Economy of the Resource Curse', *World Politics,* 51, 1999, pp. 297-322.

62. M. Sarraf and M. Jiwanji, *Beating the Resource Curse: The case of Botswana* (The World Bank, Washington, DC, 2001); D.E. Hojman, 'The political economy of Chile's fast growth: an Olsonian interpretation' *Public Choice* 111, ½ (2002), pp. 155-78; R.P. Royan, 'From primary production to resource-based industrialisation in Malaysia' in A. Farooq (ed.). *Development Policies in Natural Resource Economies,* Edward Elgar, Cheltenham, 1999.

63. Economist Intelligence Unit, *EIU Country Profile 2004,* London, 2004, p. 26.

64. Deutsche Presse-Agentur, 21 February 2001.

65. Aissaoui, *Algeria: The political economy of oil and gas,* p. 33.

66. Scott Pegg, 'Can policy intervention beat the resource curse? Evidence from the Chad-Cameroon pipeline project', *African Affairs* 105, 2006, p. 22.

67. 'World Bank set to release Chad's frozen oil funds', 27 April 2006, *Alexander's Oil and Gas Connections,* 31 August 2006.

68. See, Frynas, 'The oil boom in Equatorial Guinea'.

69. In contrast to booming Angola, President Bongo in Gabon is forced to listen to IMF advice in trying to negotiate a re-scheduling of Gabonese debt, despite major Chinese and Brazilian interest in Gabon's iron ore and other minerals and despite efforts to open up marginal oilfield to new entrants. We are grateful to one of the reviewers for pointing this out.

70. In 2005, it was announced that up to US$200 million would be invested in Sierra Leone's hotel infrastructure by a Chinese company called Henan Guoji (this would make it the biggest foreign direct investment in the country), which provides an example where Chinese investments do not encroach on Western interests.

71. An independent oil company is distinguished from the vertically integrated "majors" in the industry in that it typically is both smaller and participates in only a limited portion of the value chain. *See, e.g.*, Alberto Clô, oil economics and policy 44 (2000). Talisman Energy's operations involve exploration, development, and production of oil and natural gas—upstream operations—but not refining or retail distribution. *See* Talisman Energy, *at* http://www.talisman-energy.com.

72. Canadian Press, Talisman Completes Sale of Sudan Oil Interest, Toronto Star, Mar. 13, 2003, at C6.

73. Lily Nguyen, As Talisman Cuts Sudan Ties, Some Weigh Wisdom of Foray, Mail. & mail, March 13, 2003.

74. Tamsin Carlisle, For Canadian Firm, an African Albatross—Oil Driller Talisman Energy Pays a Painful Price for Its Sudan Investment, Wall Street Journal, Aug. 17, 2000, at A19.

75. Energy Information Administration, U.S. dept. of energy, country analysis brief: Sudan, *at* http://www.eia.doe.gov/emeu/cabs/sudan.html (last modified Jan. 13, 2003); *Exploration Hums as Sudan's Oil Output Reaches Pipeline Capacity,* oil & gas J., Aug. 26, 2002, at 45; *Sudan,* oil & gas J., Mar. 18, 2002, at 51.

76. Carlisle, *supra* note 4, at A19; David Olive, *Sudan's Misery Sure to Outlast Sudan,* Toronto Star, June 21, 2002, at E4.

77. Wojtek Dabrowski, Out of Sudan: Talisman's Shares Climb After Reported Oil-Stake Sale, Gazette, Montreal, June 14, 2003, at D10.

78. Press Release, Talisman Energy, Inc., Talisman to Sell Sudan Assets for C$1.2 Billion (Oct. 30, 2002), *available at* http://www2.ccnmatthews. com/3gCNRP/pdf/20021030131n.pdf.

79. Neil H. Jacoby, Multinational Oil: A Study in Industrial Dynamics 16-17, 1974.

80. Stephen J. Kobrin, Diffusion as an Explanation of Oil Nationalization: Or the Domino Effect Rides Again, 29 J. Conflict Resol. 3, 13 (1985).

81. *Ibid.* at 13-14.

82. See Jacoby, *supra* note 9.

83. See Stephen J. Kobrin, Back to the Future: Neomedievalism and the modern Digital World Economy, 51 J. Int'l aff. 361, 363 (1998) [hereinafter Kobrin, *Back to the Future*].

84. *See generally* bringing transnational relations back in: non-state actors, domestic structures and international institutions (Thomas Risse-Kappen ed., 1995) (analyzing the impact of non-state actors on world politics and on the foreign policies of states); Virginia Haufler, *Crossing the Boundary Between Public and Private: International Regimes and Non-State Actors, in* regime theory and international relations 94 (Volker Rittberger ed., 1993) (dicussing the interactions between state and non-state actors); Peter J. Spiro, *Globalization, International Law, and the Academy,* 32 N.Y.U. Journal of International Law and Politics567, 569-72 (2000) (discussing the reconstruction of international society to recognize non-state institutions).

85. Amnesty Anti-slavery Group, Western Capital Aids Genocidal War Effort in Sudan (1999) (documenting the links between Talisman and human rights abuses), *at* http://www.iabolish.com/act/camp/divestment/about/AASGdivestmentreport.htm; Amnesty int'l, Sudan: oil in Sudan: deteriorating human rights (2000) (documenting the links between human rights violations in Sudan and foreign oil companies, including Talisman), *at* http://web.amnesty.org/library/indexENGAFR542001200?open&of=ENG-SDN; Press Release, Am. Anti-Slavery Group, Anti-Slavery Group Hails Texas Teachers for Divesting from "Slave

Stock" (Oct. 30, 1999), *at* http://www.iabolish.com/news/global/old/austinl0-30-99.htm (announcing the first victory in the Anti-Slavery Group's divestment campaign aimed at Talisman); Press Release, Amnesty International, Sudan: Talisman Energy Must Do More to Protect Human Rights (May 1, 2001), *at* http://web.am-nesty.org/library/index/ENGAFR540102001; Press Release, Inter-Church Coalition on Africa, Sudan Urgent Action Updates and Bulletin 1999 #3: Sudan, Oil, Crimes Against Humanity . . . and Canada (Sept. 20, 1999), *at* http://www.web.net/~iccaf/humanrights/sudaninfo/urgact3sudan.htm (calling on citizens to write the Canadian Minister of Foreign Affairs expressing concern about Talisman's actions in the Sudan).

86. Kofi Annan, *Two Concepts of Sovereignty, Economist*, Sept. 18, 1999, at 49.

87. G.A. Res. 51/112, U.N. GAOR, 51st Sess., U.N. Doc. A/RES/ 51/112 (1997); Question of the Violation of Human Rights and Fundamental Freedoms in any Part of the World: Situation of Human Rights in Sudan, Comm'n on Human Rights, Report of the Special Rappoteur, U.N. ESCOR, 59th Session, U.N. Doc. E/CN.4/2003/42 (2003).

88. Georgette Gagnon *et al.*, Deconstructing Engagement: Corporate self-regulation in conflict zones—implications for human rights and canadian public policy 3 *passim* (2003), *available at* http://www.law.utoronto.ca/documents/Mackin/DeconstructingEngagement.pdf; Human Rights watch, Sudan, oil, and Human Rights 385-437 (2003), *available at* http://www.hrw.org/reports/2003/sudanll03/sudanprint.pdf.

89. Presbyterian Church of Sudan v. Talisman Energy, Inc., 244 F. Supp. 2cT289, 303 (S.D.N.Y. 2003).

90. International Crisis Group, God, Oil and Country: changing the logic of war in Sudan 3, 2002.

91. *Ibid.*; Randolph Martin, *Sudan's Perfect War,* 81 Foreign Affairs, 111, 2002.

92. Pablo Idahosa, Business Ethics and Development in Conflict (Zones); The Case of Talisman Oil, 39 J. Bus. Ethics, 227, 230 (2002).

93 *Ibid.* at 230-31.

94. International Crisis Group, *supra* note 21, at 8.

95. Gagnon *et al.*, *supra* note 19, at 15; International crisis group, *supra* note 21, at 6, 8, 13; Idahosa, *supra* note 23, at 230.

96. International Crisis Group, *supra* note 21, at 9.

97. *Ibid.*

98. *Ibid 10.*

99. *Ibid 10-11.*

100. Georgette Gagnon and John Ryle, Report of an Investigation into Oil Development, Conflict and Displacement in Western Upper Nile, Sudan 18 (Canadian Auto Workers Union et al., 2001), *available at* http:// www.iabolish.com/act/camp/divestment/Rylefmal.pdf; International Crisis Group, *supra* note 21, at 11; Sudan Update, Raising the stakes: Oil and Conflict in Sudan 75 (1999), *available at* http://www.sudanupdate.org/REPORTS/ Oil/Oil.pdf .

101. International Crisis Group, *supra* note 21, at 12; Idahosa, *supra* note 23, at 231.

102. John harker, Canadian Department of Foreign Affairs and International Trade, Human Security in Sudan: the Report of a Canadian Assessment Mission 12 (2000). A Lebanese newspaper claimed Chevron's discoveries were larger than reserves in Saudi Arabia. Sudan update, *supra* note 31, at 15-16.

103. Human Rights Watch, *supra* note 19, at 96-97.
104. International Crisis Group, *supra* note 21, at 13.
105. *Ibid*
106. Gagnon and Ryle, *supra* note 31, at 18; Harker, *supra* note 33, at 53; International Crisis Group, *supra* note 21, at 13.
107. International Crisis Group, *supra* note 21, at 14.
108. *Ibid.*
109. *Ibid.*
110. *Ibid* at 14-15. *See* Sudan update, *supra* note 31, at 78; Martin, *supra* note 22, at 113.
111. Martin, *supra* note 22, at 111. The SPLM (Sudan People's Liberation Movement) is the political arm of the SPLA). J. Millard Burr and Robert O. Collins, Requiem for the Sudan: War, Drought, and Disaster Relief on the Nile 13 (1995).
112. In a background paper, Talisman Energy attributed the conflict to "Roots in tribalism, with elements of religion, Marxism, regional conflicts, colonialism and uneven economic development." *Talisman Energy, Sudan.*—The Greater Nile Oil Project: Background Paper 10 (1998).
113. Gagnon *et al.*, *supra* note 19, at 15.
114. Human Rights Watch, *supra* note 19, at 8, 116-19, 133-36, 143-53, 178-86 (2003) (detailing the activities of various militias operating in Sudan throughout the 1990s).
115. Martin, *supra* note 22, at 117.
116. Gagnon et al., *supra* note 19, at 15-16; *see also* Martin, *supra* note 22, at U7-18.
117. Human Rights Watch, *supra note 19, at* 36, 50-59 (2003); Question of the Violation of Human Rights and Fundamental Freedoms in any Part of the World, *supra* note 18.
118. Talisman Focuses Growth Strategy on E&P Outside Canadian Core, Oil & Gas J., May 31, 1999, at 21.
119. Talisman Energy, *supra* note 43, at 4.
120. Harker, *supra* note 33, at 53; Sudan update, *supra* note 31, at 16.
121. Gagnon et al., *supra* note 19, at 18-19.
122. Sudan Update, *supra* note 31, at 18-19.
123. *Industry Briefs,* Oil & Gas Journal, Sept. 20, 1993, at 32; *Plans for First Oil Exploration Revived in Two Sudanese Fields,* Oil & Gas Journal, May 3, 1993, at 48.
124. Arakis Energy Corporation, Notice of Special Meeting of Security Holders to be Held October 7, 1998, Notice of Petition, and Management Information Circular, Concerning an Arrangement Involving Arakis Energy Corporation and Talisman Energy Inc. 31 (Sept. 3, 1998); Sudan update, *supra* note 31, at 84; Stephen Chase, *Talisman Bids for Arakis Energy* (Aug. 18, 1998), *at* http://www.vitrade,com/talisman/980818_globe_and_mail.htm.
125. Sudan Update, *supra* note 31, at 87-88.
126. *Ibid.*
127. *Ibid.* 86.
128. *Ibid.* at 87.

129. *Ibid.* at 89.

130. Exec. Order No. 13,067, 62 Fed. Reg. 59989, Nov. 5, 1997.

131. *Ibid.* Gagnon *et al.*, *supra* note 19, at 19; Sudan update, *supra* note 31, *at* 89-90.

132. Chris Varcoe and Stephen Ewart, *Talisman Buys Arakis,* Calgary Herald, Aug. 18, 1998, at D 1.

133. Jeffrey Jones, Cash Crunch May Force Sale of Canada's Arakis Energy, J. Com. July 9, 1998, at 9A.

134. Claudia Cattaneo, *Talisman Has Resources, Experience to Tackle Sudan,* Financial Post, Aug. 26, 1998, at 25; Jones, *supra* note 64, at 9A.

135. *Canada: The Human Factor,* 66 *Petroleum Economist*, 48, 48, 1999.

136. Cattaneo, *supra* note 65, at 25.

137. *Ibid.*

138. Talisman Energy, *supra* note 43, at 2; *see also* Sudan update, *supra* note 65 at 91-92; Cattaneo, *supra* note 65, at 25.

139. Sudan Update, *supra* note 31, at 58, 91.

140. Jeffrey Jones, Talisman Chief Gets Quick Lesson in Risks of Sudan Oil, J. Com., Aug. 26, 1998, at 7A.

141. Human Rights Watch, *supra* note 19, at 168.

142. Talisman energy, *supra* note 43, at 2-3; Cattaneo, *supra* note 65, at 25; *see also* Sudan update, *supra* note 31, at 41, 45, 55.

143. Cattaneo, *supra* note 65, at 25.

144. Edward Alden, Talisman in $196m Purchase of Arakis, Financial Times, Aug. 18, 1998 at 21; Cattaneo, *supra* note 65, at 25.

145. Cattaneo, *supra* note 65, at 25.

146. *Ibid.*

147. Alden, *supra* note 76, at 21; Chase, *supra* note 55.

148. Alden, *supra* note 76, at 21; *see also* Chase, *supra* note 55.

149. Amnesty Anti-Slavery Group, *supra* note 16; Amnesty International, *supra* note 46; Press Release, Inter-Church Coalition on Africa, Sudan Urgent Action Updates and Bulletin 1999 #3: Sudan, Oil, Crimes Against Humanity . . . and Canada (Sept, 20, 1999), *at* http://www.web.net/~iccaf/ humanrights/ sudaninfo/urgact/Sudan.htm.

150. Michael Scherer, *Gas War* (June 21, 2001), *at* http://www.mother jones.com/news/feature/2001/06/ Sudan.html.

151. Amnesty Anti-Slavery Group, *supra* note 16; Press Release, Amnesty Anti-Slavery Group, American Anti-Slavery Group Urges Fidelity and Vanguard to Dump Talisman Stock (Jul. 23, 1999) *available at* http://www.sudan update.org/REPORTS/Oil/19sum.html; Associated Press, *Group Calls for Stock Boycott to Prevent Slavery* (July 28, 1999), *available at* http://www.anti-slavery.org/pages/updates/ap-oil.html.

152. Lewis Braham, *Are These Funds Bankrolling Genocide? at* http://sbartmoney.com/fundwatch/ index.cfm?story=19990722 (July 22, 1999).

153. *Ibid.*

154. Charles Gillis, *U.S. Pension Fund Dumps Its Stake in Talisman,* post, Dec. 9, 1999, *available at* http:// www.vitrade.corn/talisrnan/ 991209_right_time_to_sell.htm; David B. Ottaway, *Chinese Fought on NYSE Listing: Groups Cite Oil Firm's Role in Sudan,* Washington Post, Jan. 27, 2000, at E1.

155. *Canada: The Human Factor, supra* note 66, at 48; Gillis, *supra* note 86; Ottaway, *supra* note 86, at E1.

156. Elizabeth Neuffer, *Critics Decry Oil Investors' Link to Sudan War,* Bos-Ton Globe, Mar. 26, 2001, at A1.

157. Associated Press, Group Calls for Stock Boycott to Prevent Slavery, *supra* note.83.

158. Scherer, *supra* note 82.

159. *Ibid.*

160. Sudan Peace Act, Pub, L. No. 107-245, 116 Stat. 1504 (2002).

161. *Ibid.;* H.R. 2052, 107th Cong. (1st Sess, 2001), Sec. 8.

162. Harker, *supra* note 33, at 15.

163. *See* Martin, *supra* note 22, at 118.

164. Francis M. Deng & J. Stephen Morrison, Center for Strategic and International Studies, U.S. Policy to end Sudan's War 4 (2001), *available at* http:// csis.org/.africa/sudan.pdf.

165. *Ibid.*

166. International Crisis Group, *supra* note 21, at 99-106.

167. *Ibid.* 101.

168. Gagnon and Ryle, *supra* note 31, at 35; *see also* Energy Information Administration, *supra* note 5.

169. The cost of war per day in 2001 was more than $1 million. International Crisis Group, *supra* note 21, at 102.

170. Martin, *supra* note 22, at 118-19.

171. *War, Famine and Oil in Sudan,* Economist, Apr. 15, 2001, at 41.

172. *Ibid.*

173. Gagnon and Ryle, *supra* note 31, at 42; Harker, *supra* note 33, at 16. In its 2000 Social Responsibility report, Talisman noted that despite their stated position and advocacy efforts there were at least four instances of non-defensive use of their Heglig airstrip in 2000. Talisman Energy, Corporate Social Responsibility 2000 16, *available at* http://www.talisman-energy. com/pdfs/csr2000_report,pdf (last visited Apr. 15, 2004).

174. Gagnon *et al., supra* note 19, at 3 *passim;* Harker, *supra* note 33, at 12-16, 26, 60-66; Human Rights Watch, *supra* note 19, at 385-437.

175. Human Rights Watch, *supra* note 19, at 388-397.

176. Gagnon and Ryle, *supra* note 31, at 6, 27, 40.

177. Talisman Energy Inc., Corporate Social Responsibility, 2001 5, *available at* http://www.talisman-energy.com/pdfs/csr2001.Jreport.pdf (last visited Apr. 15, 2004).

178. *Ibid.*

179. Jacqueline Sheppard and Reg Manhas, *Sudan Experience Offers Corporate-Responsibility Lessons, Opportunities,* Oil and Gas Journal, Nov. 13, 2000, at 70.

180. *Ibid.* at 72-73.

181. Located at the end of the Essay. Compiled by the author, with permission, from data supplied by Evaluate Energy, a research company providing proprietary data to the oil industry.

182. Cattaneo, *supra* note 65, at 25.

183. Secretary of State Madeleine K. Albright, Message from Secretary Albright to the Sudan Summit (Nov. 9, 1999), *available at* http://secre-tary.state.gov/www/statements/1999/991109.html.

184. *Ibid.*

185. S.C. Res. 1054, U.N. SCOR, 51st Sess., 3660th mtg. at 2, U.N. Doc. ES/1054 (1996); Sudan update, *supra* note 31, at 79-80, 86. 108. ted dagne, cong. res. serv., order code IB98043, issue brief for Congress, Sudan: *Humanitarian Crisis, Peace Talks, Terrorism*, and U.S. policy at CRS-9, 2003.

186. Sudan Update, *supra* note 31, at 86.

187. Dagne, *supra* note 118, at CRS-13; Sudan update, *supra* note 31, at 89-90.

188. Dagne, *supra* note 118, at CRS-13.

189. *Ibid.*

190. Madelaine Drohan, *Sudan Play Bad Timing for Talisman,* globe & mail, Oct. 27, 1999.

191. Steven Frank, Crude Pressures: A Canadian Oil Company Operating in Sudan Gets Targeted by Rebels, the U.S. State Department and Its Own Foreign Affairs Ministry, Time Canada, Nov. 22, 1999, at 36 (LEXIS, Magazine Stories, Combined Library); cf. Human Rights Watch, supra note 19, at 414 (discussing U.S. criticism of Canada for not sanctioning Talisman); Gary Park, Canada Appoints Envoy to Investigate Talisman's E&P Project in Sudan, Plait's Oilgram news, Oct. 27, 1999, at 1 (LEXIS, Newsletter Database) (noting that Albright requested Canada match U.S. trade and investment sanctions against Sudan).

192. Graham Bowley, *Talisman May Not Find Good Fortune from Sudan Oil,* Financial Times, Nov. 19, 1999, at 14.

193. *Ibid.;* Peter Foster, Editorial, *Talisman in Ethical No Man's Land,* Financial Post, Nov. 12, 1999, at C1; Drohan, *supra* note 123, at B2.

194. Sheldon Alberts, Ottawa Not Ready to Put Sanctions On Talisman: *Axworthy,* Nat'l Post (Toronto), Nov. 23, 1999, *available at* www.vitrade.com/talisman/991123_ottawa_not_ready_ to_put_sanction.htm; Frank, *supra* note 124, at 36; Andrew Nikifbruk, *Oil Patch Pariah,* Canadian Bus., Dec. 10, 1999, at 69.

195. Alberts, *supra* note 127; *Canada: The Human Factor, supra* note 66, at 48; Foster, *supra* note 126, at Cl; Frank, *supra* note 124, at 36; Nikifbruk, *supra* note 127, at 69.

196. *Ibid.* at 17.

197. *Ibid.* at *18.*

198. *Canada Opts Not to Sanction Talisman Operations in Sudan,* Oil & Gas Journal, Feb. 21, 2000, at 22. At least one journalist argued that Axworthy wanted to sanction Talisman but was prevented from doing so by business pressure on his ministry, which dealt with both foreign affairs and trade. Aileen McCabe, *Canadian Business Interests Trump Human Rights,* Ottawa Citizen, Oct. 26, 2000, at A5.

199. Martin, *supra* note 22, at 123.

200. Mark Turner, U.S. Evangelists Focus on Sudan to Declare a Holy War of Words. Financial Times (U.S. ed.), Apr. 11, 2001, at 18.

201. *Ibid.*

202. Sudan Peace Act, *supra* note 92, at 1507-1508.

203. Dagne, *supra* note 118, at CRS-10; Energy Information Auministration, *supra* note 5; Martin, *supra* note 22, at 124.

204. Ruth West, The Price of a Barrel of Oil? A Few Lives: In Sudan, Western Companies Are Bankrolling a Vicious Civil War, New Statesman, January 14, 2002, at 36.

205. Dagne, *supra* note 118, at CRS-4 to -5.

206 West, *supra* note 138, at 36; *see* Energy Information Auministration, *supra* note 5.

207. Office of the Press Secretary, Danforth to Lead Search for Peace as Special Envoy (Sept. 6, 2001), *at* http://www. whitehouse.gov/news/releases/2001/09/20010906-9; Alan Sipress, *Danforth Tapped far Sudan,* wash. post, Sept. 7, 2001, at A18.

208. Office of the Press Secretary, *supra* note 141.

209. John C. Danforth, Special Envoy for Peace, *Report to the President of the United States on the Outlook for Peace in Sudan,* at 8 (April 26, 2002), *available at* http://www.state.gov/p/af/rls/rpt/10150.htm.

210. Human Rights Watch, *supra* note 19, at 292-95, 506.

211. *Ibid.* 506-507.

212. Danforth, *supra* note 143, at 19.

213. Press Release, Human Rights Watch, Sudan: Danforth Peace Intiative Process (May 15, 2002), *at* http://www.hrw.org/press/2002/05/su-dan0515.htm.

214. William Wallis, *Sudan Peace Talks Reach Critical Point,* Financial Times, Aug. 8, 2003, at 9.

215. *Ibid. Mark Lacey, Rebels, Many in Teens, Disarm in Sudan's South,* New York Times, Jan. 27, 2004, at A10.

216. *Presbyterian Church of Sudan,* 244 F. Supp. 2d 289.

217. Press Release, Abolish, Amended Complaint Filed in Talisman Suit (Feb. 25, 2002), *at* http://www.iabolish.com/news/global/2002/talis-man02-25-02.htm.

218. *Presbyterian Church of Sudan,* 244 F. Supp. 2d at 296, 299; Press Release, iAbolish, *supra* note 151.

219. 28 U.S.C. § 1350 (2000); *Presbyterian Church of Sudan,* 244 F. Supp. 2d at 303; *see also* Filartiga v. Pena-Irala, 630 F. 2d 876 (2d Cir. 1980).

220. 28 U.S.C. § 1350 (2000).

221. *Developments in the Law—International Criminal Law: Corporate Liability for Violations of International Human Rights Law, 114 Harv. L. Rev. 2025, 2037 (2001).*

222. *Ibid.* at 2025.

223. *Presbyterian Church of Sudan,* 244 F. Supp. 2d at 335-341 (seeking dismissal on the basis of "lack of subject matter jurisdiction, lack of personal jurisdiction, lack of plaintiffs' standing, *forum non conveniens,* international comity, act of state doctrine, political question doctrine, failure to join necessary and indispensable parties, and because equity does not require a useless act").

224. Larry Neumeister, *Talisman Can Be Held Liable for Genocide: Judge,* Gazette (Montreal), Mar. 20, 2003, at A14.

225. Stephen J. Kobrin, The Architecture of Globalisation: State Sovereignty in a Networked Global Economy, in Governments, Globalization and International Business 146, 148 *passim* (John H. Dunning ed., 1997); Kobrin, Back to the Future, *supra* note 14, at 362 *passim*.
226. Michael Littlejohns and David Buchan, *Annan Backs 'Rights Beyond Borders,'* Financial Times, Sept. 21, 1999.
227. *Ibid.*
228. Kobrin, Back to the Future, *supra* note 14, at 361 *passim*.
229 *Ibid.* at 369-375.
230. *Ibid.* at 382.
231. United Nations Global Compact, *What is the Global Compact, at* http:// unglobalcompact.org/content/ aboutthegc/overview_about.htm.

• • •

6

Exploring Strategies for Sustainable Energy

Meaning and Scope of Sustainable Energy

Energy sustainability is defined as access to adequate and reliable supplies of environmentally and socially acceptable forms of energy at competitive prices without compromising the energy needs of future generations. In this definition.

- **Access** denotes the ability to purchase energy from domestic and foreign sources on a commercial basis, with no undue impediments imposed by governments, such as quotas on imports or exports.
- **Adequate** means that energy supplies are sufficient to meet the volume of consumers' needs and will remain so long enough to justify investments in particular kinds of energy processing and in transporting, distributing, and using equipment.
- **Reliable** signifies that the systems for delivering any particular energy form are inherently robust or can become so through the technical, commercial, and administrative measures to provide reasonable security against unplanned interruptions.
- **Environmentally and socially acceptable** implies that the production, processing, transportation, and use of energy meet not only current standards of social acceptance and environmental protection but also take into account changes in those standards over time—changes that are likely to make standards more demanding.
- **Competitive price** refers to better integration in the global energy market to allow China to benefit from access to energy at costs that are comparable with or below those of the country's international trading partners.

Essence of Energy Sustainability

The core of the analysis in this study concludes that sustainable development of the energy sector would require a national energy policy that embodies the following four pillars:

Ensure efficient use of energy to keep energy consumption growth lower than economic growth to the greatest extent possible. Industrial countries, even the most efficient ones such as Japan, experienced energy demand/gross domestic product elasticity of 1.0 or more during their industrialisation phases. Given the size of China's economy and growth, such high elasticity could lead to unsustainable development of the sector. Shifting to a less energy-intensive path will require dramatic efficiency improvements in energy conversion and consumption across all economic sectors and areas of personal energy use, particularly energy for mobility and household use, two of the most important drivers of growth in energy consumption.

Make optimum use of the country's sizable energy resources. China's landmass, including offshore areas, undoubtedly contains large energy resources. Some of these are underused, and others have yet to be discovered. Maximum development of these resources, on an internationally competitive basis, will contribute to minimizing energy import needs and related security and financial concerns. Energy policy, therefore, should ensure the progressive opening of these resources to national and international sources of capital and enterprise, as well as the use of the most advanced technologies for their development. Similarly, they should be fully exposed to international market pricing to ensure that, as in other economic sectors, they are developed on a globally competitive basis.

Safeguard the environment from the adverse effects of energy production, conversion, and consumption. Serious environmental harm has resulted from China's present energy system, particularly its extensive coal use. Without fundamental policy changes, rapidly rising coal use and accelerating growth in automotive fuel consumption will lead to an intolerable level of environmental degradation. Policy-makers must call on all of the available tools to support this pillar, including but not limited to the following: pricing-in of externalities, better and higher taxation of fuel consumption, promotion of advanced and clean coal technologies, maximum economic development of renewable energies, and incentives to channel the universal need for personal mobility toward enhanced public transportation.

Make vital energy installations more secure and be better prepared for supply disruptions. China's inevitable accelerating integration into the global energy economy has created the opportunity to diversify the country's energy balance and build into it more "clean" natural gas. In the next two decades, this programme will be one of the most important. At the same time, this diversification poses the challenge of addressing concerns about security of supply, particularly oil imports, and about the vulnerabilities of critical energy infrastructure, such as liquefied natural gas import terminals and nuclear power stations. Enhancing the security of the energy supply calls for a suite of measures ranging from general pricing and taxation policies to highly specific steps such as emergency oil stockpiling and allocation schemes. In particular, as network energies—notably gas and electricity—account for an ever-growing share of national energy consumption, energy infrastructure will become more vulnerable. Special attention needs to be given to enhancing the security of these vital points.

TABLE 28

Selected energy resources and reserves

(million metric tons unless otherwise indicated)

Country or area	*Bituminous coal/Anthracite* Proved amount in place	Proved recoverable reserves	Estimated additional amount in place	*Sub-bituminous coal/ Lignite* Proved amount in place	Proved recoverable reserves	Estimated additional amount in place	*Peat* Proved amount reserves	Proved recoverable
Afghanistan	112	66	400	..	..	..	..	..
Albania	..	...	..	712	..	..	..	155
Algeria	40	40	0	..	..	..	..	..
Angola	..	..	..	..	..	..	..	..
Argentina	..	..	..	195	130	7735	90	*80
Armenia	..	..	..	..	..	..	..	..
Australia	90400	47300	125000	48000	43100	215000	..	..
Austria	1	0	3	343	25	61	..	..
Azerbaijan	..	..	..	..	..	..	..	..
Bahrain	..	..	..	..	..	..	..	..
Bangladesh	1054	..	..	..	..	..	*138	..
Barbados	..	..	..	..	..	..	..	..
Belarus	..	..	..	..	..	..	323	323
Belgium	715	410	1400	..	..	..	..	..
Belize	..	..	..	..	..	..	..	..
Benin	..	..	..	..	..	..	..	..
Bolivia	..	1	..	..	..	..	..	..
Bosnia and Herzegovina	..	..	..	..	..	..	..	..
Brazil	0	..	..	17072	11950	15319	0	0
Brunei Dannsalam	..	..	..	..	..	..	..	..
Bulgaria	48	13	1200	4791	2698	2618	5	5
Burkina Faso	..	..	..	..	..	..	..	..
Burundi	..	..	..	..	..	..	56	56
Cambodia	..	..	..	..	..	..	..	..
Cameroon	..	..	..	..	..	..	..	..
Canada	8625	4509	26045	14355	4114	31990	1092	0
Central African Rep.	..	..	..	4	4	..	..	..
Chad	..	..	..	..	..	..	..	..
Chile	79	31	125	4579	1150	5000	..	..
China	114500	62200	363200	108800	52300	304700	4687	328
Colombia	5449	6368	13173	411	381	3176	..	..
Congo	..	..	..	..	..	..	..	..
Costa Rica	..	..	..	27	..	22	48	..
Côte d'Ivoire	..	..	..	..	..	..	..	..
Croatia	..	6	..	33	33	..	..	..
Cuba	..	..	..	..	..	..	..	..

Contd..

Contd..table 28

Cyprus	..	..	..	..	..	..	..	..
Czech Republic	6401	2613	..	2547	3564	..	..	..
Oem. Rep. of Congo	720	88	..	..	..	..	..	..
Denmark	..	..	..	63	..	0	..	..
Ecuador	..	..	..	30	24	6	..	..
Egypt	25	13	..	27	22	52	..	..
El Salvador	..	..	..	..	..	..	..	..
Equatorial Guinea	..	..	..	..	..	..	..	..
Estonia	..	..	..	..	..	..	2000	2000
Ethiopia	..	..	..	23	11	..	..	..
Faeroe Islands	..	..	..	..	..	..	..	..
Falkland Is. (Malvinas)	..	..	..	..	..	..	0	0
Fiji	..	..	..	..	..	..	..	..
Finland	..	..	..	..	..	..	850	420
France incl. Monaco	593	95	200	124	21	165	..	..
Gabon	..	..	..	..	..	..	..	..
Georgia	..	..	..	..	..	..	..	..
Germany	67000	24000	186000	78000	43000	..	157	96
Ghana	..	..	..	..	..	..	..	..
Greece	..	..	..	5312	3000	0	640	4000
Greenland	..	..	..	183	183	200	..	..
Grenada	..	..	..	..	..	..	..	..
Guatemala	..	..	..	..	..	..	..	..
Guinea	..	..	..	..	..	..	..	..
Guinea-Bissau	..	..	..	..	..	..	..	..
Guyana	..	..	..	..	..	..	..	..
Haiti	..	..	..	13	..	27	..	..
Honduras	..	..	..	21	..	..	..	..
Hungary	1407	596	702	8306	3865	5289	..	..
Iceland	..	..	..	..	..	..	..	..
India	196892	74733	86088	26000	2000	3932	..	..
Indonesia	0	770	0	1331	4450	6299	49000	0
Iran (Islamic Rep. of)	3754	193	..	2295	..	..	..	..
Iraq	..	..	..	..	..	..	..	..
Ireland	19	14	26	12	9	29	154	106
Israel	..	..	..	..	..	..	500	386
Italy and San Marino	..	..	..	75	34	302	..	..
Jamaica	..	..	..	..	..	..	200	32
Japan	8277	785	..	175	17	..	..	..
Jordan	..	..	..	..	..	..	..	..
Kazakhstan	..	3100	..	..	3000	..	.	..
Kenya	..	..	..	..	..	..	..	..

Contd..

Contd..table 28

Korea, Republic	138	82	272	..	..	..	..	..
of Korea.Dem. Ppl's.Rep.	2000	300	2700	300	300	2200	..	..
Kuwait	..	..	..	..	..	..	..	..
Kyrgyzstan	..	..	..	..	812	..	..	..
Lao People's Dem. Rep.	..	..	..	..	..	..	..	..
Latvia	..	..	..	..	..	..	190	94
Lebanon	..	..	..	..	..	..	..	..
Liberia	..	..	..	..	..	..	..	..
Libyan Arab Jamah.	..	..	..	..	..	..	..	..
Lithuania	..	..	..	..	..	..	937	269
Madagascar	1000	..	..	75	..	..	..	..
Malawi	15	2	..	..	..	..	..	..
Malaysia	15	4	78	126		575	0	0
Mali	..	..	..	..	..	3	..	..
Mauritius	..	..	..	..	..	..	..	..
Mexico	1211	1211	1960	732	351	213	..	..
Mongolia	12000	..	..	12000	..	..	..	..
Morocco	16	5	..	42	..	2	..	..
Mozambique	0	240	155	..	..	..	..	..
Myanmar	5	2	120	..	..	80	..	..
Nepal	..	..	..	..	..	..	..	..
Netherlands	1406	497	2750	..	..	..	120	120
New Caledonia	4	2	8	..	..	..	..	..
New Zealand	136	29	642	2583	542	12201	1640	0
Nicaragua	..	..	..	..	..	..	..	..
Niger	0	70	..	..	...	..	..	..
Nigeria	..	21	21	338	169	1000	..	..
Norway. Svlbd. J.Myn.	1	54	1	64	6	100	745	350
Oman	..	..	..	..	..	..	..	..
Pakistan	..	..	..	145	2928	1	..	..
Panama	..	..	..	..	..	..	..	..
Papua New Guinea	..	..	..	..	..	..	..	..
Paraguay	..	..	..	..	..	..	..	..
Peru	0	960	0	..	100	..	..	..
Philippines	40	24	8	343	275	37	..	..
Poland	60185	14309	113300	14184	2196	30700	890	0
Portugal	8	3	0	38	33	0	..	..
Qatar	..	..	..	..	..	..	..	..
Republic of Moldova	..	..	..	..	..	..	..	..
Romania	1	1	1	3199	3610	1976	25	13
Russian Federation	75753	49088	1582479	124823	107922	2358085	17680	11554
Rwanda	..	..	..	..	..	..	..	..
Samoa	..	..	..	..	..	..	..	..

Contd..

Contd..table 28

Saudi Arabia	..	..	..	..	..	..	..	..
Senegal	..	..	..	..	..	..	40	24
Serbia and Montenegro	..	..	..	..	..	..	..	..
	..	..	..	..	..	..	..	..
Sierra Leone	..	..	..	..	..	..	..	..
Slovakia	..	..	..	347	172	..	..	..
Slovenia	..	..	..	414	59	32	..	..
Solomon Islands	..	..	..	..	..	..	..	..
Somalia	..	..	..	..	..	..	..	..
South Africa Customs Un.	128407	55333	205253	30	999	100	47	30
Spain	1700	200	3000	860	460	1260	94	70
Sri Lanka	..	..	..	.	..	..	5	5
Sudan	..	..	..	..	..	..	..	..
Surinam	..	..	..	..	..	..	..	..
Sweden	..	..	..	4	1	20	700	70
Switzrtd Liechtenstein	..	..	..	..	..	..	..	..
Syrian Arab Republic	..	..	..	..	..	..	..	..
Tajikistan	..	..	..	..	..	..	..	..
Thailand	..	..	..	2315	2000	3000	..	..
Timor-Leste	..	..	..	..	..	..	..	..
Togo	..	..	..	..	..	..	..	..
Trinidad and Tobago	..	..	..	..	..	..	..	..
Tunisia	..	..	..	..	..	..	..	..
Turkey	590	449	249	7339	626	110	..	..
Turkmenistan	..	..	..	..	..	..	..	..
Uganda	..	..	..	..	..	..	..	..
Ukraine	21850	16388	5406	23958	17968	5819	2160	684
United Arab Emirates	..	..	..	..	..	..	..	..
United Kingdom	1500000	1500	190000	1000	500	..	0	8
United Rep Tanzania	•304	*200	*1500	..	..	..	..	..
United Slates	246650	111338	456153	208548	145305	665887	26000	13000
Uruguay	..	..	..	..	..	..	..	..
Uzbekistan	..	1000	..	..	3000	..	..	..
Venezuela	1328	479	4528	..	..	0	..	..
Vietnam	312	150	..	..	..	..	..	..
Yemen	..	..	..	..	..	..	..	..
Zambia	0	0	0	69	55	18	..	..
Zimbabwe	1535	734	5820	965	..	..	..	..

Energy Crisis in the Past: Lessons for the Future

For the past half-century, international security concerns about energy supply have tended to focus, first, on oil imports. There has been a second, at least latent concern about the security of imported gas supplies. A third concern relates to the importance of electricity security. Moreover, particularly in recent years, there has been a realization that domestic energy sources may not provide truly secure supplies. Coal imports have not attracted significant attention from a security standpoint.

This study reviews international experience in relation to each of these areas of potential energy-supply security concerns and, when appropriate, includes assessments and implications for China's energy policies.

Concerns about Oil Imports

Concerns about oil imports reflect the international experience since the middle of the 20th century, during which as many as seven significant oil supply disruptions occurred. There are basically three perceived risks surrounding petroleum imports:

Major oil-exporting countries, or the associations that group those countries, will change their policies.

- Market failures could result from insufficient investments in exploration, field development, and transport infrastructure.
- *Force majeure* events could result in potential short-term interruptions.

Table 29 summarises the main oil supply crises that have taken place since the early 1950s.

TABLE 29

Major Global and Regional Oil Supply Crises since 1950

Years	*Event/s*
1951-54	The first post-World War II oil crisis occurs: nationalisation of the Anglo-Iranian Oil Company by Iranian Prime Minister Mohammed Mossadegh. Exports were cut off for about three years, but additional supplies were quickly developed from other Middle Eastern countries, particularly Kuwait.
1956-57	The Suez Crisis involves the blockage of the Suez Canal, the destruction of pipeline pumping stations, and a resulting global tanker shortage. The United States calls on its spare production to meet the deficit.
1967	The six-day Arab-Israeli War causes blockage of the Suez Canal and a global tanker shortage. However, the United States again has sufficient spare capacity to avert a crisis.
1973	The Yom Kippur Arab-Israeli War and the Arab oil embargo cause crude oil prices to rise drastically from US$2.90 per barrel in September to US$11.65 per barrel in December. The United States draws down its spare capacity before the war begins. Physical shortages occur in Europe and North America, partly as a result of clumsy interventions by consuming country governments (for example, the United States) and of foreign exchange shortages (for example, in Turkey)
1979-81	During this period, several events cause a dramatic increase in oil prices: Iranian worker strikes, revolution, the hostage crisis, and war with Iraq. Panic sends official oil prices from US$13 per barrel to US$34 per barrel.

Contd...

Contd...table 29

1990-91	Iraq invades Kuwait, and Coalition forces invade Iraq, resulting in the loss of exports from both countries, a brief spike in oil prices, and then a fallback because there is enough spare capacity in the world supply system to cope with the export loss.
1990-2003	The United Nations imposes a partial embargo on Iraqi oil exports.
December 2002-January	Strikes and demonstrations in the República Bolivariana de Venezuela cause exports to cease.
2003	The invasion of Iraq, led by the United States, causes a brief curtailment of oil exports, followed by their restoration to near pre-war levels. Iraqi production of about 2.0 million barrels a day (exports 1.5 million) in mid 2006 accounts for only about 7 per cent of production by the Organization of Petroleum Exporting Countries.

Potential Policy Changes of Major Countries/Groups

Of the individual oil-producing countries, Saudi Arabia has by far the largest oil reserves, the biggest developed capacity to produce crude oil, and the greatest amount of spare producing capacity to deal with supply shortfalls. Its development and export policies are therefore potentially critical for global supply. Of the intergovernmental energy organizations, only the Organisation of Petroleum Exporting Countries (OPEC) is in a strong position to have an adverse impact on oil supply. Its members account for about three-fourths of the world's reserves, more than 40 per cent of the world's current oil supply, and virtually all of the spare capacity.

Neither Saudi Arabia nor OPEC has signalled any fundamental policy change. Both appear committed to supplying sufficient oil to balance the world's needs. However, structural changes in the industry seem to indicate that this commitment will come at much higher price levels than seemed possible five years ago.

The Organisation of Arab Petroleum Exporting Countries (OAPEC), another intergovernmental organisation, applied selective export embargoes on crude oil exports to Germany, the United Kingdom, and the United States in 1973 and 1974. However, the organisation has renounced the use of the "oil weapon" in support of its members' political aims. OAPEC now devotes its efforts exclusively to commercial and technical cooperation in petroleum matters.

The current situation shows no major policy change, but the concentration of petroleum resources in countries that are members of OPEC gives OPEC the ability to have a substantial impact on the security of global oil supply. OPEC members could limit petroleum production, and reorient bilateral trade relationships.' Reductions of output could cause worldwide price increases (mainly for oil) as prices rise to equilibrate curtailed supply against demand. The duration of the effects could be from short term (six months to a year) to long term (more than five years). The importance is obvious for China to maintain good and close diplomatic and trade relations with individual major exporting countries and with their international organisations.

Market Failure Resulting from the Under-investment in Securing Supply

Oil is such an important source of revenue in most oil-exporting countries that it usually comes under the control of governments through National Oil Companies (NOCs). NOCs do not operate on commercial and profit motives alone. Often they have difficulty accessing investment funds needed to develop the petroleum resources available to them.[2] By contrast, International Oil Companies (IOCs) are typically well financed. They are more likely to be constrained by investment opportunities rather than by lack of funds, at least in the upstream (production) subsector of the industry.

Industry failure to make needed investments may also result from policies of governments around the world that, for environmental or social reasons, limit the industry's access to geologically attractive areas for petroleum exploration. For example, the U.S. government does not allow new exploration off the east and west coasts of the country. There is also an ongoing dispute about providing oil companies access to strongly prospective areas in the Alaska National Wildlife Reserve. Regulatory delays, sometimes reflecting environmental opposition to project development, can affect the construction of petroleum facilities such as Liquefied Natural Gas (LNG) import terminals, pipelines, and oil refineries in industrial countries. In North America, Western Europe, and Japan, it is very difficult and expensive to find sites for large new plants of this sort. Regulatory approvals for site development are also costly and time consuming. For example, in the United States it takes at least two and one-half years to obtain all the permits needed for a new LNG import terminal.

If market failures limit available supply, the flow of oil may be unable to meet demand. In a free market, prices will rise to keep the market in equilibrium. If prices are not allowed this function, however, physical shortages may result. The duration of these effects could be short term to several years. Box 11 reviews the significance of the current oil price spike in the security-of-supply debate.

Expert opinions differ on the future supply and price of oil. Some say that reserves have been increasing, that there is a satisfactory (high) ratio of reserves to production, and that foreseeable supply is sufficient to meet demand to 2020 and beyond. However, others claim that some producing countries and IOCs are overstating their reserves. They also state that member countries of OPEC have not made sufficient investment to turn OPEC reserves into productive capacity; that there are few large, new discoveries being made; that IOCs are having great difficulty replacing their own current production; and that IOCs have achieved only minor production increases in the past decade.

It is widely believed that the global oil industry *may* have entered a new phase in the first years of the 21st century. This phase has two principal features: (a) the demand shock of increasing imports by China and India and the still-growing consumption in the United States and (b) the virtual disappearance of spare production capacity. The principal reflection of this phase is that long-term crude oil futures prices were in the range of US$15 to US$25 per barrel in the 1990s and have now risen to the range of US$60 to US$75 per barrel. Some considerations affecting this new phase are presented in Box G.12. For China, it would clearly be imprudent to plan energy policies that are based on the assumption that the strains on world oil supply will quickly disappear and that prices will fall back to the levels of the 1990s (that is, US$15 to US$25 per barrel). Instead, policy directions should be created that are sustainable at price levels as high as US$50 per barrel for extended periods.

BOX 11

The 2003-06 Oil Price Spike—'How Significant Is It in the Energy Security Debate?

Price Behaviour

International crude oil prices have been rising irregularly for the past three or four years. At times, they have approached US$80 per barrel. These are the highest nominal levels ever seen. However, they are still less in constant dollar terms than they were in the early 1980s, when, for a time, spot prices of Arab light crude oil reached US$40 per barrel, equivalent to more than US$85 per barrel in 2006. Despite current high oil prices, global economic growth has continued, notably in both China and the United States, which are large net importers.

Price Expectations

When international oil prices spiked up to some US$75 per barrel in 2005 and 2006, there was widespread market speculation that the potential existed for prices to "superspike" to US$100 or more per barrel. These speculations were particularly strong in the financial industry and from oil traders. What in fact happened was that by the autumn of 2006 prices had fallen back to around US$60 per barrel.

Observation

There is no quantitative basis for confidently forecasting the development of international oil prices. The present historically high prices and the expectations for prices in excess of US$100 per barrel expressed earlier should not unduly colour Chinese policy-makers' consideration of energy security matters.

Potential for Short-term Interruptions of Oil Supply

For policy-makers, the potential for short-term interruptions of oil supply tends to be the security issue of greatest concern because of the economic output loss and social disruption that can result. Fortunately, interruptions are not frequent. Interruptions or delays in oil flows could occur as a result of a variety of events taking place outside the importer's borders. Because of the integration of global oil and tanker markets, there can be adverse impacts on importers' interests—for example, as a result of price spikes or effects on trading partners' economies—even though there may be no direct impact on their oil import flows.

Interruptions could occur in many circumstances. One possibility is civil disorder in oil-producing areas, such as in Nigeria or the República Bolivariana de Venezuela. Another is a military action affecting major oil exporters, such as the Iran-Iraq War of 1981 to 1984 and the Iraq War of March 2003. Terrorist activities could affect tanker traffic in global oil chokepoints such as the Strait of Hormuz in the Persian/Arabian Gulf and the Strait of Malacca between the Indian and Pacific Oceans (significant incidents have not yet taken place).

BOX 12

Causes of the First 21st Century Oil Shock

Under-investment

"The illusion that oil is in perennial oversupply has led to two decades of under-investment in the oil industry. The world has been living off the legacy spare capacity built up many years ago: (Edward Morse, HETCO, as quoted in *Economist* 2005, 6)

Demand

In 2004, global oil demand grew at 3.9 per cent, the fastest rate in more than 25 years (*Economist* 2005,4). The increases fell back to 1.4 per cent in 2005, still requiring the addition of 1.2 million barrels per day to world demand (IEA 2006). In December 2006, demand growth for the year was estimated at 1.1 per cent or 0.9 million barrels per day, of which China accounted for nearly half while OECD demand fell by a marginal amount (IEA *Monthly Oil Market Report*).

Demand Outlook

The International Energy Agency in December 2006 estimated 2007 global oil demand growth at about 1.7 per cent or 1.43 million barrels per day. China's consumption was expected to grow by 5.4 per cent and contribute about 25 per cent of the world increase, the same proportions as the Agency forecast for the Middle East. No other regions were expected to increase their consumption even half as fast as these two. Oil demand in Europe and in the OECD Pacific region was expected; again to decline marginally. The forecasted global oil demand growth is equivalent to the production of three or four large oilfields (IEA *Monthly Oil Market Report*).

Supply

The demand shock reduced effective OPEC spare capacity in January 2006 to about 1.4 million barrels per day (IEA 2006). The IEA commented earlier that the last time that OPEC spare capacity was not a market issue was from 2000 to 2002, when that capacity was nearly 5.0 million barrels per day. At the end of 2006, as a result of relatively weak demand growth in that year, the IEA assessed effective OPEC spare capacity at 2.4 million barrels per day (IEA *Monthly Oil Market Report*).

Outlook for Spare Capacity

'While it is hoped that increasing investment will raise the level (from 1.3 million) [of spare capacity] overtime, current non-OPEC investment schedules suggest this will not re-enter the comfort zone in the near future" (IEA 2005, 4).

There is also the potential for natural disasters at home or abroad to damage critical oil and gas infrastructure. For example, in August 2005, Hurricane Katrina in the United States resulted in the temporary loss of about 1.2 million barrels per day of oil production (about 20 per cent of the U.S. total) and a large amount of gas production. This loss occurred mainly because almost all offshore producing platforms in the Gulf of Mexico had to be shut down. Some of the platforms were damaged, and production of several hundred thousand barrels per day was still closed in mid 2006. Also, oil-refining operations were curtailed because units were shut down for safety reasons or were rendered inoperable by flooding or the loss of electricity supply.

It should be pointed out that the hurricane also resulted in a reduction of U.S. oil consumption compared with expectations. Katrina was the worst, but not the first, hurricane to disrupt the U.S. oil industry. The experience of August 2005 highlights the importance of preparing for the unexpected in terms of security of oil and energy supply. Proponents of strategic oil storage in the United States and in the other member countries of the International Energy Agency probably never expected that the second emergency draw-down of strategic oil reserves (the first being during the Iraq-Kuwait crisis of 1990 to 1991) would be to deal with the losses caused by disruption of U.S. oil supply attributable to weather events.[3]

The world of the early 21st century has become a more dangerous place from the standpoint of securing uninterrupted supplies of oil in international trade than was the world of the last two decades of the 20th century. Some of the major oil-exporting countries appear to exhibit actual (Nigeria) or potential (Saudi Arabia) political instability. Significant tensions have arisen between the United States and certain exporters (the Islamic Republic of Iran and the República Bolivariana de Venezuela). Some large exporters (the Gulf states) may be militarily vulnerable *vis-à-vis* their larger neighbours. At the same time, the cushion of spare capacity to produce and transport oil that is available worldwide to cope with disruptions is proportionately smaller than in recent memory. Clearly, China must fashion its energy and oil policies with a view to reasonably minimising oil import requirements, drawing its needed imports from a variety of sources, and taking steps nationally and internationally, by itself and cooperatively with other countries, to address the effects—direct and indirect—of any oil supply disruption that it may face.

Gas Supply Concerns

Gas supply is more reliable than oil supply, though concerns do exist.

Adequate Supplies at Competitive Prices

The global natural gas resource may be at least as large as the global conventional oil resource. However, it is developing more slowly, and the rate of gas reserve use is less than half the rate at which oil reserves are being produced. Much gas around the world is *stranded,* which means that there are resource discoveries capable of development but, there are not facilities connecting the supply to markets. The gross supply situation in relation to actual and potential demands appears, on a global scale, to be better for gas than for oil, although the mature North American industry is facing problems, as discussed later.

It is difficult to generalise about gas prices in the same way as oil prices. Gas markets are regional rather than global. However, there seems to be agreement that it is technically possible to supply large volumes of gas in the form of LNG to major consuming areas at costs, including return on investment, in the range US$25 to US$30 per barrel of crude oil equivalent. The prices at which this gas is sold will, of course, depend on conditions in the various markets it serves.

A Good Record of Supply

Gas supplies, domestic and imported, in industrial countries have proven to be very secure, both for pipeline gas from local sources and for imported pipeline gas and LNG. Indeed, gas supply has, perhaps, been more secure than any other energy form. When security failures have happened, they have resulted mainly from technical accidents, supply shortages, and price disputes.

Technical Failures

In the case of interconnected transmission and distribution systems for gas supply, it is nearly always possible to mitigate the impacts of technical failures by cooperation within the industry. Such failures include pipeline rupture resulting from corrosion or mechanical damage or from natural disasters such as floods, earthquakes, or slope instability in mountainous areas. The most challenging technical failures are those in critical system components that take a long time to repair, such as large gas compressors and gas processing plants. An example of such a failure is the serious disruption caused by the Longford, Victoria, Australia, gas-processing plant incident in 1998 (Box 13). Gas supplied by a network of transmission competent suppliers having a good track record is a well-tried way for buyers to secure a reliable supply.

BOX 13

Regional and Liquefied Natural Gas Supply Issues

Australian Gas Supply Interruption, 1998

In 1998, a gas-processing plant explosion cut off all the gas supply to the state of Victoria (population 5 million). The resulting crisis was reported to have cost gas users more than US$1 billion.

Arun, Indonesia, 2002

The ExxonMobil LNG plant and export terminal, Indonesia's largest, was temporarily shut down because of security risks from separatist rebels in that area of Sumatra. Since early 2005, exports from Arun have been cut back below the level of contractual commitments because of continuing production problems the area, despite the end of the insurgency there.

Skikda, Algeria, January 2004

An explosion destroyed three of six liquefaction trains and damaged the remaining three trains. In 2004, LNG production was reduced by 75 per cent. Sonatrach, the owner of the plant, is rehabilitating the damaged trains and replacing the destroyed trains with one large new one, due on stream in 2007.

Contd...

Contd...box 13

LNG Shipping

The Center for Liquefied Natural Gas (2005) claims, "The safety record of LNG ships far exceeds any other sector of the shipping industry."

The Russian Federation-Ukraine, January 2006

As the result of a dispute that appeared to relate to gas pricing, Russian exports to Ukraine were halted for four days and then quickly and completely restored. The root causes of the dispute are complex, and some are longstanding. Thus, prices were not market based, there were large payment arrears, Ukraine was alleged to have diverted gas intended for the European Union (EU) markets, there was a dispute about ownership and refurbishment of transit pipelines, and there were issues about access to Russian gas stored in Ukraine for the EU markets.

Supply Shortfalls

Concerns about the adequacy of gas supply from producing sources are rarely a short-term issue and then only when a single source dominates. Such a situation arose in the early 1970s in the Canadian province of British Columbia. The transmission pipeline system depended heavily on two producing fields. The fields were relatively new and had complex reservoir conditions. Water coning quickly developed as production rose, and a number of highly productive wells had to be abandoned.

The immediate problem was solved by interrupting the supply to customers who did not have firm contracts and by securing alternative supplies to the affected markets. Subsequent exploration successes resulted in the development of new fields with much better producing characteristics, allowing the restoration of supply in two years.

Today, in North America, there are concerns about the adequacy and price of long-term gas supply. These concerns persist even though, gas prices are low relative to crude oil, partly because of short-term demand effects mainly having to do with mild weather. After some 70 years of growth of the modern gas industry, it appears that the developed resource base is no longer capable of meeting demands and that the market will require supplemental supplies. Some technical, financial, environmental, and regulatory issues must be resolved in bringing on new large-volume sources, such as gas from Alaska and the Canadian north, coal-bed methane, and imported LNG. Some recent Canadian views, by government and by industry, as to North American gas supply security are summarised in Box 14.

In the meantime, prices are high by historical standards, and gas consumption appears to be falling slowly. For example, the industrial sector is using less gas. Manufacturers of ammonia and other fertilizers and some energy-intensive metallurgical industries have moved overseas to gas-rich jurisdictions such as Trinidad and Tobago. These developments are troublesome for policy-makers and often result in ill-advised disruption of market functioning. If markets are allowed to work, investors will respond to higher prices and consider supply projects. If regulators promptly permit new investments, a better balance of supply and demand will be restored and prices can be expected to fall back, perhaps to LNG import parity.

Price Disputes

Price disputes in the gas subsector tend to be international rather than national and intergovernmental rather than inter-corporate. Several such disputes arose in the 1970s and 1980s—between Canada and the United States, between Algeria and United States, and within Europe.[4] The disputes arose basically because pricing provisions in the contracts before the energy crisis of the 1970s did not allow gas prices to increase with the rapid rise in commodity value related to soaring oil prices. There were also differences in opinion about the methodology of determining netback prices. A gas dispute between the Russian Federation and Ukraine led to curtailment of supplies to Ukraine in January 2006 (see Box 13). The proximate cause was the fact that prices to Ukraine were very low compared with the prices that Russia obtained for exports to the European Union (EU) and no price-escalation mechanism had been agreed to.

BOX 14

Canadian Perspectives on the Security of Gas Supply

"Canada has an abundance of gas resources and the necessary infrastructure to deliver natural gas to market.

"Our market-oriented energy policy framework has been successful in providing us with a competitively priced, secure source of natural gas supply.

"Mature conventional North American natural gas basins, ever-increasing demand, and higher gas prices are attracting investment.

"New sources of natural gas supply—coal-bed methane, Alaska, the Canadian North, and methane hydrates—will arrive.

"Governments and regulators have a role to play in creating a favourable climate for investments in resources and infrastructure."

—Graham Flack, Associate Assistant Deputy Minister for Energy Policy, Natural Resources Canada

By a Natural Gas Industry Representative

"Current market tightness combines with environmental issues to produce perverse public attitudes respecting support for new supply.

"The public does not obviously share industry's perspective on importance of gas to our long-term energy future.

"Ensuring reliable policy support rests in good measure on reliable public support.

"Industry (and government) needs to articulate why gas passes the test of sustainability (in a multidecade context) and how we are working to ensure the industry's sustainability.

"We need a more systematic approach and need to get governments and other communities working with industry."

—Michael Cleland, President of the Canadian Gas Association

Source: Forum on Continental Energy, Woodrow Wilson Center, Washington, DC, March 21, 2005

Very low gas prices cause resentment in the gas-producing jurisdictions, discourage the development of new supplies, and encourage buyers to increase consumption. The government of Canada used its energy regulator as the instrument to break the pricing provisions of existing export contracts and drive up prices almost in step with rising oil prices. Canadian disappointment with export pricing was one factor that led to a steady decrease in gas exports through the mid 1980s. The government of the Netherlands used diplomacy with its EU partners to achieve more reasonable prices for gas exports. Algeria and France engaged in intensive diplomatic dialogue with ups and downs but managed over time to resolve contentious issues. The dialogue between Sonatrach (Algeria) and El Paso and other importers (the United States) was not successful. The resolution of their differences ultimately took place in the U.S. court system.

A similar situation may exist today in relation to the export of Bolivian gas to Brazil and Argentina. There are clear parallels with the Russia-Ukraine situation. Bolivian export prices, which were determined by government-endorsed contracts, are much below commodity value in consuming areas in relation to today's oil prices. Bolivia is attempting, through discussions between regulators and also at a senior inter-governmental level, to achieve higher prices. It is possible to minimise price disputes and, if they arise, avoid harmful effects on supply by including appropriate pricing provisions in contracts, such as a provision for third-party dispute resolution. International experience strongly indicates that market-based deals negotiated between exporting and importing companies are much less prone to price disputes than are arrangements determined by governments.

Assessment and Implications

The rapid growth in the share of natural gas in energy balances worldwide is a positive factor, improving the security of international and national energy supply; providing a versatile, competitive energy source; and reducing environmental pollution. China, which is sharing in these trends, can make its gas supplies even more secure by diversifying sources to minimise technical risks, ensuring that contracted reserves are reliable, and insisting on freely negotiated contract terms that protect buyers' and sellers' interests in changing market circumstances.

Concerns about Electricity Supply Failures

Concerns about the electricity aspect of supply security arise primarily because of the North American and European blackouts in large, inter-connected but separately operated systems. They have affected large numbers of consumers in recent decades (see Table 32). There were extensive disruptions of power supplies in eastern Canada and the New England area of the United States. One set of failures resulted from the ice storm of the winter of 1997/98, which destroyed a high-voltage transmission line and took out many distribution lines when ice loads greatly exceeded their design parameters.

In 2003, another massive blackout occurred in the northeast United States and Ontario as a result of cascading failures caused initially by a tree falling on a power line. That incident and some other disruptions, such as a blackout in Italy during the summer of 2003, were blamed on the deregulation of the industry. That debate is beyond the scope of this report, but it should be noted that major blackouts occurred in New York and Ontario, Canada, in 1965 and in France in 1978 when utilities in those places were still vertically integrated. Those failures involved private utilities in New York and publicly owned ones in France and Ontario.

In most of the developing countries, supply disruptions occur mainly because of insufficient generation capacity attributable to flaws in the planning, approval, or execution of power projects, such as in China currently, or the lack of funding resources, as in Argentina, Brazil, and India during recent years. Supply disruptions of this kind have sometimes been the catalyst for profound reforms of the power subsectors in many large developing countries. The dimensions of major electricity failures occurring in industrial countries in the past 40 years are summarised in Table 30.

TABLE 30

Some Major Electricity Failures of the Past 40 Years

Date	*Region*	*Megawatts lost*	*Customers affected (million)*
November 1965	New York and Ontario	20,000 (13 hours)	30.0
July 1977	New York	6,000 (26 hours)	9.0
1978	France	11,800 (several hours)	2,0
July 1996	Western United States	28,000 (up to 9 hrs)	
August 10,1996	Western United States	Unknown	7.5
December 1997—January 1998	Ontario and Quebec, Canada, and parts of northeast United States (ice storm damage to transmission and distribution systems)	n.a	1.4
August 14, 2003	Northeast United States and Ontario	60,000-65,000 (30 hours)	50.0

Source: Based on Hilt 2005. *Note:* n.a. = not available.

Concerns may also exist about fuel supply for electricity generation, where the supplying industries have been affected by disruptions caused, for example, by labour disputes or by oil crises. There is no information showing significant impairment of electricity supply in any industrial country as a result of oil supply problems. In the United Kingdom, electricity supply was adequately maintained in 1984 and 1985, despite a coalminers' strike that lasted almost a year. The lack of impairment of electricity supply was attributable to the large coal stocks on hand when the strike began. Nuclear power was able to handle most of the base load, and oil-fired thermal stations absorbed a greater share of demand. This experience highlights the value of energy source diversification in the electricity industry.

A robust electricity supply system is an essential underpinning of a modern industrial state. As China's power system grows in size and complexity, and as reforms are introduced that enable the electricity subsector to capture the efficiencies associated with market behaviours and market pricing, policy will need to be directed to ensuring that investments are optimised in the various components of the industry and that operators maintain the highest standards. In this connection, valuable lessons can be learned from the experience of Europe and North America in avoiding power shortages and outages and in dealing with them when they occur.

Coal Supply: Competitiveness and Environmental Concerns

Although international coal trade is long established and growing quickly, most of the world's coal tends to be used in the country that produces it. However, even the supply of coal drawn entirely from domestic sources may not be secure because of social disturbances or transport bottlenecks. It might also not be secure because of policies that focus on the economy's need for adequate and reliable sources of environmentally acceptable forms of energy at competitive prices.

During the past few years, railway bottlenecks have triggered important coal supply problems in China's coastal provinces. The supply problems have entailed extreme power shortages, especially during the summer. In the case of Western Europe, the old coal industries clearly failed to provide supplies that were adequate and competitively priced. Most of those industries have closed—including those in Belgium, France, Germany (hard coal), the Netherlands, and the United Kingdom—for this reason. There are also many examples of coal industries that did not meet the test of environmental acceptability and contributed disproportionately to problems of human health and loss of amenity associated with poor urban air quality in countries such as China and Turkey.

Dependence on a very large, domestic coal industry can cause energy security problems. Thus, adequacy of supply is not necessarily assured. Reliability may be impaired, for example, by railway transportation bottlenecks. Moreover, domestic supplies in all the markets served may not be internationally competitive, measured, for example, against the prices that Asian competitors pay for coal from Australia or LNG from the Middle East. China's policy-makers therefore need to keep in mind the insecurity implications of excessive dependence on domestic coal.

STRATEGIES FOR CLEAN AND COST-EFFECTIVE ENERGY IN THE 21ST CENTURY

The global community today is working toward a potential *double dividend:* meeting the essential needs of economic growth and fighting poverty, while at the same time leaving a smaller environmental footprint. Strategies to support clean energy and a low-carbon economy are vital to fulfilling this promise.

Affordable and reliable energy services matter today more than ever in the fight against poverty. Most economic activity, even the village and household enterprises in developing countries that are the main source of income for the poor in those countries, would be impossible without energy. The services that hydrocarbons and electricity provide—motive power for industry and agriculture, transportation of people and goods, heating and cooling of workplaces, power for appliances—increase productivity and economic output. Thus economic growth that creates jobs and raises incomes depends on greater access to and more efficient use of energy services and their constituent energy resources. There is a strong correlation between commercial energy consumption and national income: countries with higher income per capita also tend to be those with higher energy consumption per capita.

It also shows a similarly strong correlation across countries between commercial energy consumption and the Human Development Index (HDI). This standard measure, reported annually by the United Nations (UN) Development Programme, is derived from indicators that reflect countries' progress in providing the most basic human needs: a long and healthy life (life expectancy), possession of knowledge (literacy and educational achievement), and a decent standard of living (income, measured in dollars adjusted for international differences in purchasing power).

Yet, the reality today in many of the world's least developed countries is that, the poor often cannot afford to purchase sufficient fuel and electricity to meet their basic cooking and lighting needs, and energy services are often only intermittently available to industry and social services. This lack of reliable energy services constrains the delivery of social services and imposes a huge cost on industry and commercial firms, undermining their competitiveness and therefore their ability to expand and provide employment. The poor performance of the energy sector in many countries is evidenced by poor resource utilisation, low asset yields, and commercial and technical inefficiency, leading to much energy being wasted, as well as financial losses.

The good news is that much can be done at the national and local levels of government to promote the development of sustainable energy. Governments can remove institutional and regulatory barriers that prevent energy companies from delivering modern fuels and electricity to firms and households. They can also help mobilise financial resources for investments in energy infrastructure and services. At the same time, they can and should regulate the environmental performance of energy production and use. Legislators and other policy-makers can take the lead in linking energy planning to national plans for economic and social development and can play a critical role in sustaining political commitment to sound energy sector management and governance.

However, action at the national and lower levels alone is not enough to ensure sustainable energy development. There are also global aspects to the challenge, and these will require international consensus building, coordination, and action. This chapter provides a brief introduction to these aspects from a number of viewpoints:

- Energy security
- Energy and poverty reduction
- Energy and the environment
- Investment for energy development

- Development and deployment of clean-energy technology
- International trade in energy.

Energy Security

For both the developed and the developing countries, energy security means a reliable and affordable supply of energy that makes further economic development possible and supports a high and growing quality of life. For the international community, including the World Bank, energy security means ensuring that countries can sustainably produce and use energy at reasonable cost in order to facilitate economic growth (and, through this, poverty reduction) and directly improve the quality of peoples' lives by broadening access to modern energy services.

Today, world energy demand is growing rapidly. The latest forecast of the International Energy Agency (IEA) shows global energy demand, under current policies, increasing by more than 60 per cent from 2004 to 2030. IEA concludes that the world's primary energy resources are adequate to meet this projected increase in demand: proven reserves of gas, oil, and coal far exceed cumulative projected consumption, and more reserves will be added during the projection period. But developing these resources and ensuring that demand is met will require a huge amount of investment at every point in the energy supply chain. If that investment is not forthcoming or is delayed, shortages, price increases, and price volatility may impede economic growth in both developed and developing countries.

IEA's projections imply increasing interdependence between energy-producing and energy-consuming countries, because a pronounced shift in the geographical sources of incremental oil and natural gas supplies will occur over the next several decades, and because growth in energy demand will be increasingly concentrated in developing countries. International trade in primary energy will have to expand to accommodate the growing mismatch between the location of demand and that of production. As energy markets become increasingly global, integrated, and interdependent, an enhanced policy dialogue between the governments of importing and exporting countries will be essential in addressing long-term energy security risks. All countries—energy producers and consumers, rich and poor—have a vital common interest in ensuring a sustainable supply of the energy needed for a growing global economy.

The attention of the international community toward the issue of energy security has been greatly heightened by the increase in oil prices to record levels in nominal terms since 2002. This poses a risk to all countries, but especially the poorer oil-importing countries, which are the least able to cope. The direct effect on an economy is felt through the worsening of the balance of payments and the subsequent contraction of the economy required to restore balance-of-payments equilibrium. The impact of the shock is proportional to the percentage rise in oil prices times the ratio of net imports of oil and oil products to Gross Domestic Product (GDP)[5] The increase in the oil bill has been particularly severe for a number of countries that combine high energy intensity (that is, high consumption of energy per unit of GDP produced) with a heavy reliance on imported oil. For these countries, even the relatively modest hike in oil prices between 2003 and 2004 implied an increase in their oil bills of between 1.5 and 5 per cent of GDP.

A sustained price increase of $10 per barrel would deliver an economic shock equivalent to a 1.5 per cent loss of GDP, on average, for the world's poorest countries (those with GDP per capita of less than $300). With a sustained price increase of $20 a barrel relative to 2003, the GDP loss for these countries would be 3 per cent. The lowest-income countries experience the largest proportionate loss of GDP, as they are the most dependent on oil imports. Countries have limited options for dealing with high oil prices, especially in the short run. Policies that reduce dependence on oil as a primary fuel and that reduce energy intensity take time to have an effect, but in the long run they can reduce the vulnerability of the economy to oil price shocks.

Energy and Poverty Reduction

Improved energy services will be critical for strategies aimed at achieving the Millennium Development Goals (MDGs). Worldwide, nearly 2.4 billion people use traditional biomass fuels—wood, agricultural residues, and dung—for cooking and heating, and nearly 1.6 billion lack access to electricity. Four out of five people without access to electricity live in rural areas. The average resident of a poor country consumes only 5 per cent of the modern energy services (fossil fuels, electricity, and renewables) that his or her counterparts in the developed countries consume. Modern energy services provide lighting, cooking, heating, refrigeration, transportation, motive power, and telecommunications that are indispensable to increasing productivity, creating enterprises, raising employment and incomes, and providing safe water and sanitation as well as health and education services. Without access to these services, the poor are deprived of opportunities for economic development and improved living standards.

Low-income households are affected most by increases in world oil prices. Households experience the effect of high oil prices directly when they purchase petroleum products (such as kerosene, liquefied petroleum gas, and gasoline) and indirectly when they purchase other goods or services, including transport and water services, whose costs are raised by higher oil prices. Higher oil prices reduce the expenditure of households at all income levels in oil-importing countries, and the poorest may have to cut their spending the most.

Policy-makers have many options for improving the focus of current energy policies on poverty reduction. Among the more important options to consider are the following:

- **Designing scaled-up programmes for energy access**. Scaling up implies the need for programmes that will achieve ambitious rates of access within 10 to 15 years. Three types of access usually need to be addressed: access to cleaner cooking systems, access to electricity, and access to mechanical power. With respect to the first of these, the goal is to increase the use of modern cooking fuels, as well as the adoption of improved cook stoves and an increase in sustainable biomass production. Increasing access to mechanical power plays a critical role in meeting the MDGs though agroprocessing and water pumping. Mechanical agroprocessing increases food production and reduces the labour that women must devote to producing food. Water pumping improves health and nutrition and enables irrigation.

- **Maximizing the development impact of electricity scale-up programmes.** Here the implication is that implementation should be driven by considerations of poverty reduction, including the enhancement of productive enterprises and income generation and delivery of health and education. Scaling up also implies implementing the electrification of homes and institutions, as quickly as possible, for the largest number of people feasible, while balancing affordability to end users with that to the government in terms of the capital subsidies required. Large gains in electrification rates among households and among health, education, and oilier public institutions are feasible through grid extension.

  Many of those unnerved today live in urban or periurban areas within reach of the grid and can be connected through phased programmes of grid extension. In other areas, where grid extension is not cost-effective, independent small grids and solar photovoltaic systems will be necessary for remote institutions and households that can afford such systems. Modern lighting systems for basic needs can be marketed to very poor households. For example, LED (light-emitting diode) lamps manufactured locally and sold by local private operators can provide good-quality lighting at a lower operating cost than kerosene lamps.

- **Ensuring that service providers are capable of delivering ambitious electrification targets.** Successful implementation requires that service providers, including incumbent national utilities, be fully capable of undertaking the necessary planning and execution functions and that they exercise commercial discipline in their operations. Scaling up electricity access implies an expansion in electric power generation. In Sub-Saharan Africa and elsewhere, economies of scale can be achieved by developing large generation and transmission projects that will serve regional needs; small *island* systems are prone to high costs as well as to heightened risk of service interruption.

- **Establishing effective regulatory frameworks and policies for rural and off-grid areas for various types of providers of energy services.** Sound regulatory frameworks would stimulate local community participation, remove barriers and develop the roles of local entrepreneurs in providing energy services under new business models, and mobilise women's groups to find locally tailored solutions for meeting energy needs.

- **Focusing subsidies on the public good component of energy services.** The transfer mechanisms used should be targeted to the poor, predictable, transparent, and fully funded. The prices charged for energy supply and services—supported by appropriate regulatory and tax policies—should remove market distortions that favor highly polluting forms of energy, by taking both the economic and the environmental costs and benefits into account. Many governments subsidise petroleum products, holding prices to consumers below international prices. When such subsidy schemes remain in place for a long time, the drain on the public finances can become very large, to the point where it limits spending on desirable social programmes. In addition, such subsidies distort the economy: low prices provide little incentive for efforts to increase energy efficiency and substitute for oil. Removing subsidies on oil products has proved politically difficult in many countries, especially when oil prices are rising rapidly. It is easiest to reduce subsidies, when international oil prices are falling, by reducing the domestic price by less than the reduction in the is international price until the two prices are at parity.

BOX 15

Energy and the Poor: A Fact Sheet

- Some 1.6 billion people worldwide lack access to network electricity. In the absence of vigorous new policies, 1.4 billion people will still lack electricity access in 2030—only 200 million fewer than today.
- Four out of five people without electricity live in rural areas of the developing world, mainly in South Asia and Sub-Saharan Africa.
- Some 2.4 billion people rely on traditional biomass—wood, agricultural residues, and dung-for cooking and heating. This will increase to 2.6 billion by 2030 with no change in policies.
- Poor people in developing countries spend up to a quarter of their cash income on energy.
- In 2004, the richest 20 per cent of the world's population consumed 58 per cent of total energy usage, whereas the poorest 20 per cent consumed less than 4 per cent.
- The world's 1 billion poorest people use only 0.2 ton of oil-equivalent energy per capita annually, whereas the 1 billion richest—those earning on average over $20,000 a year—use nearly 25 times as much.
- High transaction costs and high unit costs of investment constrain electricity service provision in poor rural areas because of low demand and dispersed populations. The cost of connections can range from $400 to $1,000 for households who may only consume $4 worth of electricity a month.
- Indoor air pollution from solid fuel use is responsible for 1.5 million deaths a year worldwide. These deaths occur disproportionately among women and children.
- Low-grade fuels and poor environmental controls in transport and industry are a leading cause of severe urban air pollution in the fast-growing cities of developing countries. More than 80 per cent of all deaths in developing countries attributable to air pollution-induced lung infections are among children under five.

Country-specific energy strategies to help achieve the MDGs will be vital. It will also be important to work *upstream,* for example, by supporting evaluations of energy-poverty linkages in country poverty assessments, so that long-term national poverty reduction strategies incorporate energy strategies and plans. In this regard, actions in the energy sector should be linked with complementary activities in other areas such as agriculture, health, education, finance, enterprise development, and institution building.

International support for energy programmes, both through bilateral development assistance and from the international financial institutions, will continue to be critical. Often this support will be best applied when it leverages the complementary roles of public and private investments (both local and international) and when it draws on the comparative strengths of different stakeholders to manage different risks through public-private partnerships. Such partnerships make possible a coordinated effort to expand energy services to the poor. Mobilising and coordinating long-term commitments from development partners to scale up energy investments, transfer knowledge, and deploy financing instruments for leveraging private capital and resources will be key, particularly for countries with the largest concentration of the energy-poor, such as those in Sub-Saharan Africa and South Asia.

Energy and Environment

The links between energy and the environment are many and profound, and the environmental impacts of energy use are felt both locally, from indoor pollution from cooking fires to urban air pollution, and globally, through emissions of greenhouse gases by power plants, factories, and automobiles.

Climate Change

Climate change presents an urgent challenge. The Earth's climate is already changing because of human activities, primarily the combustion of fossil fuels, deforestation, and other land management practices, and it is projected to continue to change in the coming decades. The Earth has already warmed by about 0.6°C over the past 100 years, and it is projected to warm by as much as another 5.8°C during the next 100 years in the absence of effective, internationally agreed-upon policies to address climate change.

For governments today, climate change poses one of the greatest challenges of the new millennium, namely, how to achieve and sustain economic growth, with its promise of prosperity for all, while reducing the threat of climate change to human health and ecological systems. In fact, the two are linked: sustaining global prosperity becomes increasingly difficult with a global climate that continues to become warmer and more unstable. But economies cannot grow without increasing energy consumption, and, today, energy production is primarily dependent on the carbon-emitting fuels that result in global warming. How these energy and environmental challenges are addressed in the next two decades will, to a large degree, determine whether future generations enjoy sustainable growth, environmental quality, and national security.

Developing countries and the poor people, who live in them, are the most vulnerable to climate change. Warmer temperatures, more-variable precipitation, and an increased incidence of extreme climatic events will become more common and, when coupled with rising sea levels, will threaten agriculture, water resources, human settlements, human health, and ecological systems, undermining economic development and the achievement of many of the MDGs. Dealing with climate change will require the development and implementation of climate-friendly technologies.

Air Pollution and Its Impacts

Most of the industrialised countries have managed to clean the once heavily polluted air in their cities, despite continued high energy use per capita. In many developing countries, however, local air pollution from energy use remains a major environmental and public health hazard. Exposure to smoke and soot has been estimated to cause as many as 4 million premature deaths each year, as well as 40 million new cases of chronic bronchitis and widespread cases of other respiratory illnesses. Small particulates (airborne particles less than 10 microns in diameter) from fuel combustion are particularly dangerous and are a leading cause of cardiovascular disease, chronic bronchitis, and upper and lower respiratory tract infections.

Lead exposure is another widespread public health hazard in regions that still use leaded fuels. Lead is a treacherous poison: at lower levels of exposure, no obvious symptoms may occur, but children exposed to lead become less able to learn, putting them at a lifelong disadvantage.

In addition to its effects on human health, air pollution from energy use damages ecological systems. Emissions of sulfur dioxide and nitrous oxide per cent react with other chemicals in the atmosphere to form sulfuric acid and nitric acid, which fall back to earth in rainfall. This acid rain has been found to damage crops, forests, rivers, and lakes, sometimes thousands of kilometres from the original source.

The first step in addressing local pollution is to identify and implement those solutions that provide environmental benefits at no additional cost. These win-win opportunities include, improvements in energy efficiency at the user level and a switch from highly polluting to less polluting energy fuels. Energy sector reform that introduces competition between alternative energy forms and between suppliers, and that allows market prices to send the right signals to producers and consumers alike, will promote the shift from polluting to clean energy use.

Reducing local air pollution beyond what can be achieved through these win-win strategies, however, comes at an additional cost. Even so, the financial cost of abatement (for example, to meet improved emission standards in power generation) is usually small compared with the value of the health and environmental damage thereby avoided. It is, therefore, important for policy-makers to take account of these external effects.

There is considerable scope for international action on air pollution issues. The phasing out of lead additives from gasoline is an example: regionwide harmonisation of fuel specifications and fuel pricing can help eliminate fuel smuggling and fuel adulteration. Regional agreement on the timetable for revised fuel specifications permits suppliers to make informed investment decisions about the refinery reconfiguration that will be necessary to supply fuels with the new specifications.

Energy Sector Investment

Converting the world's resources into available supplies on a scale that meets projected demand will require massive investment. IEA estimates that total capital investment of $8.1 trillion, equivalent to an average of $300 billion a year (in 2005 dollars), is needed from 2003 to 2030 to meet the energy needs of the world's developing and transition economies. Of this investment, roughly 73 per cent will be for electricity, 12 per cent for oil, 12 per cent for natural gas, and 3 per cent for coal. Financing will come from three sources: internal cash generation, private financing, and public funding. Developing countries will face great challenges in raising these funds from domestic and international capital markets (public funding is limited and usually cannot be diverted from priority social spending), because their needs are larger relative to the present size of their economies and because the investment risks are bigger. The extent to which the huge investment gap, especially in the electricity sector, can be funded in the future will depend on the pace of policy and regulatory reform, including the measures needed to attract private sector investment in these countries.

Although many of the barriers to increased investment in developing countries relate to their overall investment climate, others are specific to the sector. A survey of international investors revealed that the most significant barriers to investment in the electric power industry in developing countries are weak legal protection for investors, absence of multilateral guarantees, and weak payment discipline on the part of consumers.[6] The study pointed to several priorities for governments seeking to attract and retain international (and domestic) investment in the industry:

- **Ensure adequate cash flow.** Among the highest priorities identified by investors were the need to set prices adequate to cover costs and the need for discipline in payment collection. Investors are unlikely to consider a proposed investment if these conditions are not present.
- **Maintain the stability and enforceability of laws and contracts.** A clear and enforceable legal framework is always important to investors. The rules of the game should not be altered at the government's convenience once investment decisions have been made on the basis of those rules. A government's willingness and ability to honour its commitments are key.
- **Be more responsive to the needs of investors.** Investors identified government unresponsiveness to their needs and timeframes as the most important factor in the failure of investments. They considered the administrative efficiency of the host government one of the top criteria in deciding whether to invest in a country. Better preparation of the proposed transaction before inviting investors to participate can help reduce processing delays and investors' opportunity costs.
- **Minimise government interference.** Investors are most satisfied with their investment experience when they are free to realise returns from their investments without government interference. Investors pointed to their ability to exercise effective operational and management control of their investments as a key factor in successful operations. Investors also give much weight to the independence of regulatory processes from government interference.

Energy Technology: Development and Deployment

Achieving a truly sustainable global energy system will require technological breakthroughs that will radically alter how energy is produced and used. Which new technologies and which new forms of energy will transform today's energy systems remains uncertain. Lack of some immediate and unforeseen technological breakthrough, fossil fuels are expected to remain the backbone of primary energy supply for the next several decades. This underscores the need for high-performance technologies that permit the continued use of existing fossil fuels together with abatement of the resulting greenhouse gas emissions, particularly in electric power generation. Government action can promote faster deployment of the enhanced energy technologies that are available today. The resulting gain in market share will, in turn, make these technologies still more cost effective.

An extensive array of technologies and practices in both energy supply and end use are already available to enhance access to energy; improve energy security, and promote environmental protection at the local, regional, and global levels. No single energy production or end-use technology promises to alter the energy development path of any country. Instead, a broad portfolio of technologies, supported by appropriate policies, will be required to address the challenge of reducing the emissions that cause local and regional air pollution.

These technologies are also required for the transition to a low-carbon economy. The same technologies employed to reduce greenhouse gas emissions normally reduce the emissions of local and regional pollutants as well. A clean-energy, low-carbon economy can be realised through a balanced portfolio of energy production and distribution technologies. On the supply side, the technologies needed include new thermal power plants based on combined-cycle and supercritical boilers; natural gas as a bridging fuel in the transition period until renewable energy technologies become commercially viable; new renewable energy technologies (solar, wind, small and large hydropower, biomass and biofuels, and geothermal sources); and improved nuclear fission technologies. Energy supply technologies are complemented by end-use efficiency technologies in the transportation sector (including efficient gasoline and diesel engines), the buildings sector (insulation, advanced windows, new lighting technology, and efficient space cooling and heating), the industrial sector (cogeneration, waste heat recovery, preheating, new efficient process technologies, efficient motors and drives, and improved control systems), and the agricultural sector (efficient irrigation pumps), as well as in municipal and urban systems (district heating systems and combined heat and power).

Renewable forms of energy today still satisfy only about 3 per cent of the world's primary energy demand. Hydropower is the largest renewable source; *new* renewables, such as solar and wind power, each account for only a small fraction of global energy demand. Several European governments currently favour using renewables to reduce carbon dioxide emissions, and they have set national targets for increasing their use. Several developing countries, such as China and Brazil, also have programmes to promote renewables. Renewables are, on average, more expensive per unit of energy than fossil fuels in supplying large, grid-connected power systems, but as their deployment becomes more widespread, their unit costs will fall. Therefore, new government policies that push for faster deployment of renewables will be important if renewables are to meet a much larger share of world demand than the 4 per cent currently forecast by 2030.[7] Several renewable energy technologies are potentially lowest-cost options for mini-grid applications (village- and district-level networks with loads between 5 and 500 kilowatts that are not connected to a national grid).

Energy Trade

Like trade generally, trade in energy can be mutually beneficial to both suppliers and customers. In various regions of the world, neighbouring countries are seeking to develop their energy trade for a number of reasons:

- **Energy trade can advance regional economic integration.** Regional trade in electric power helps build institutions and relationships that, as part of a wider network of institutions, can help integrate a region economically and politically. Joint development of energy projects can help build closer ties between countries through closer collaboration and increased economic interdependence.

- **Trade can underpin energy security.** Trade can increase the reliability of energy supply by making one country's lower-cost supplies available to other countries. Also, cross-border energy supply often contributes to the diversification of energy sources—a key component of energy security. Stable long-term agreements between countries are necessary for such trade to flourish, however.
- **Trade can exploit economies of scale.** Many national markets, especially in Africa, are too small to justify the investment needed to develop the energy supply opportunities available to them. Merging national markets can provide the needed economies of scale in such cases. As markets mature and competition is introduced, the integration of small neighbouring markets can provide the scale necessary for competition to be effective.

The interconnection of contiguous electric power networks can capture significant economies of scale. The price of electric power generation in grid-based systems can vary enormously from one country to another, depending on the availability of hydroelectric resources, the cost of fuel, and many other factors. Interconnecting transmission networks and integrating power system operations can thus bring significant benefits. In a regionally integrated power system, the direct benefits accruing to each national power sector include reduced operating costs, increased efficiency, lower energy costs, and increased system reliability. Operating costs are lower in an interconnected network because they allow development of the least-cost regional energy resources. Also, by aggregating the demand of contiguous national systems, regional integration creates sufficient demand to justify large investments that would not have been economically feasible at the national level.

International Organisations Active in Promoting Sustainable Energy

A number of international organisations have initiated programmes and activities aimed at ensuring sustainable energy. This section discusses a few of the more prominent.

Food and Agriculture Organization

The work of the Food and Agriculture Organisation (FAO) in the energy sector focuses on bioenergy, agro-energy, wood energy, and climate change. Providing multiple energy services for cooking and heating as well as power for electricity, industry and transportation, and bioenergy can contribute significantly to increased labour productivity and diversification of economic activities in rural areas. FAO works to ensure the delivery of sustainable, equitable, and accessible bioenergy sources and services irrespective of gender, wealth, location, or culture, for sustainable development, energy security, and climate change mitigation.

International Atomic Energy Agency

The mandate of the International Atomic Energy Agency (IAEA) is to build national capabilities in overall energy planning and, in particular, nuclear power for peaceful purposes.

IAEA's Major Programme on Nuclear Power, Fuel Cycle, and Nuclear Science provides three major services: support of power programmes for additional uses of power reactors, catalysing of innovation, and energy analysis and building of planning capabilities.

International Energy Agency

IEA is an intergovernmental body committed to advancing the security of energy supply, economic growth, and environmental sustainability through cooperation on energy policy. IEA acts as energy policy adviser for its 26 member countries in their efforts to ensure reliable, affordable, and clean energy for their citizens. Founded during the oil crisis of 1973-74, IEA had as its initial role the coordination of national measures in times of oil supply emergencies. But in recent decades, as energy markets have changed, so has IEA. Its purview now extends well beyond oil crisis management to broader energy issues, including climate change policies, market reform, collaboration on energy technology, and outreach to the rest of the world.

United Nations Development Programme

The efforts of the UN Development Programme (UNDP) in energy are focused on supporting the achievement of the MDGs, especially the goal of halving, by 2015, the proportion of people living in poverty. Increasing access to sustainable energy services is one of six priority areas in UNDP's energy and environment practice and one of 30 service lines in its development support worldwide. In support of energy-related work, UNDP aims to strengthen national policy frameworks to support energy for poverty reduction and sustainable development; increase access to energy services to support growth and equity; promote clean energy technologies for sustainable development; and augment access to investment financing for sustainable energy.

United Nations Environment Programme

The energy programme of the UN Environment Programme (UNEP) focuses on building human and economic capacity—the technical skills, institutions, and markets to create sustainable development that avoids the huge environmental burdens of past development. Underpinning all UNEP energy activities is the integration of environmental and social factors into energy-related decisions, bringing a longer-term, more comprehensive approach to the sector.

United Nations Framework Convention for Climate Change

The Climate Change Secretariat in Bonn, Germany, is the secretariat to both the United Nations Framework Convention on Climate Change (UNFCCC) and the Kyoto Protocol. A total of 189 parties have ratified the UNFCCC, and 161 parties have ratified the protocol. The UNFCCC entered into force in 1994 and the protocol in 2005. The ultimate objective of both the UNFCCC and the protocol is the stabilisation of greenhouse gas concentrations in the atmosphere at a level that would prevent dangerous anthropogenic interference with the climate system. That level should be achieved within a timeframe sufficient to allow ecosystems to adapt naturally to climate change, ensure that food production is not threatened, and enable economic development to proceed in a sustainable manner.

World Energy Council

The work of the World Energy Council (WEC) spans the entire energy spectrum—coal, oil, natural gas, nuclear, hydropower, and new renewables—and focuses on market restructuring; energy efficiency; energy and the environment; financing of energy systems; energy pricing and subsidies; energy poverty; ethics; benchmarking and standards; use of new technologies; and energy issues in developed, transitional, and developing countries. Every three years, WEC holds a World Energy Congress, which features a major energy erudition, keynote addresses, roundtables, and technical presentations by energy experts.

World Health Organisation

The World Health Organisation (WHO) provides information on the many linkages between climate variability and health and reviews the threats to health posed by human-induced climate change. WHO provides regular updates on the linkages between household energy, indoor air pollution, and health, and it implements projects and programmes to tackle this preventable disease burden and evaluates the impacts of technical solutions on health, socioeconomic conditions, and the environment.

United Nations Department of Economic and Social Affairs

The Department of Economic and Social Affairs of the United Nations Secretariat works in three main interconnected areas:

- To compile, generate, and analyse a wide range of economic, social, and environmental data and information upon which member states of the United Nations can draw to review common problems and take stock of policy options
- To facilitate the negotiations of member states in many intergovernmental bodies on joint courses of action to address ongoing or emerging global challenges
- To advise on ways and means of translating policy frameworks developed in the UN conferences and summits into programmes at the country level and, through technical assistance, help build national capacities.

The World Bank Group and Sustainable Energy Development

The World Bank Group supports government efforts at sustainable energy development in developing countries through financing, advice, and knowledge transfer (Box 15). The International Finance Corporation issues loans and equity, and the Multilateral Investment Guarantee Agency issues guarantees, to support private investment in energy. The International Bank for Reconstruction and Development (IBRD) and the International Development Association (IDA) can issue partial risk guarantees, with sovereign counter-guarantees, to support such investment, particularly where the key risk of a project relates to concerns about government performance or policy reversal. Similarly, IBRD or IDA partial credit guarantees with sovereign counter-guarantees can help catalyse long-term private financing for projects that improve public services. IBRD loans and IDA credits to countries with sovereign guarantees can also be used when private financing cannot be catalysed.

BOX 16

Selected World Bank Group Energy Projects in 2005

- In China, the Renewable Energy Scale-up Project supports that country's commitment to increase the share of renewable energy in electric power generation to 15 per cent by 2020 compared with 7 per cent in 2005.
- In the Lao People's Democratic Republic, the Nam Theun 2 Project will enable the country to export electricity to Thailand. The resulting income can be spent on improving living standards.
- In Nigeria, the National Energy Development Project supports the government's energy sector reform and facilitates the transition of the energy sector to the new market and institutional structure. Investments will be made to upgrade and improve the power transmission system and to reduce losses and improve the reliability of electricity service as well as customer service. The project will increase access to electricity in rural areas and will promote the use of renewable energy.
- In Bulgaria, the Energy Efficiency Project supports a large increase in energy-efficiency-promoting investments through the development of self-sustaining, market-based financing mechanisms. The project has a credit enhancement facility to mitigate investment risk, supports a Bulgaria Energy Efficiency Fund, and provides capacity building and information dissemination services.
- In Peru, the Community Development Carbon Facility supports the 4.1-megawatt Santa Rosa Hydro Project, the first small-scale clean-development mechanism project in the country. The Peru Rural Electrification Project will make investments to supply electricity services to about 160,000 currently unserved rural households, businesses, and public facilities (such as schools and health clinics that serve about 800,000 people), using both conventional grid extension and renewable energy sources.

The World Bank Group works with member countries and multiple other partners on urgent energy development issues, including increasing access to clean fuels and electricity, securing reliable energy supply that underpins economic growth, catalysing investments in the sector, reducing the sector's demand on public finances, and improving governance in the sector.

In the context of the Group of Eight's Gleneagles Communiqué on Climate Change, Clean Energy and Sustainable Development of July 2005, the World Bank Group is preparing an investment framework for clean energy and development, which will complement ongoing Bank activities in energy sector reform, energy investment, implementation of projects of the Global Environment Fund, development of carbon markets, and development and application of methodologies to address climate variability and change.

The Development Committee of the World Bank and the International Monetary Fund, which facilitates intergovernmental consensus building on development issues, endorsed the approach in an April 2006 communiqué and noted that the goal of securing affordable and cost-effective energy supplies to underpin economic growth and poverty reduction need not conflict with the goal of preserving the environment. The Development Committee called on the Bank to review its existing financial instruments and to explore the potential value of new financial instruments to accelerate investment in clean, sustainable, cost-effective, and efficient energy.

Important Web Links on Sustainable Energy

International Atomic Energy Agency	http://www.iaea.org
International Energy Agency	http://www.iea.org
UN Department of Economic and Social Affairs	http://www.un.org/esa/desa
UN Development Programme Energy and environment	http://www.undp.org/energyandenvironment
UN Environment Programme Sustainable energy	http://www.unep.org/themes/energy
UN Framework Convention on Climate Change	http://www.unfccc.int
World Bank	http://www.worldbank.org/energy
World Health Organisation	http://www.who.int

REFERENCES

1. The Repéblica Bolivariana de Venezuela may currently be contemplating such action (in this case, away from the United States and toward China).
2. The Mexican state company PEMEX is currently in that position.
3. The draw-down in connection with the Hurricane Katrina emergency was, however, small: about 11 million barrels out of a total reserve of some 685 million barrels.
4. European disputes arose between the Netherlands and the other European Union countries and between France and Algeria.
5 Robert Bacon, 2005. The Impact of Higher Oil Prices on Low Income Countries and the Poor: Impacts and Policies. *Energy Sector Management Assistance Program Knowledge Exchange Series 1*, World Bank, Washington, DC.
6. Ranjit Lamech and Kazim Saeed, 2003. What International Investors Look for When Investing in Developing Countries. Results from a Survey of International Investors in the Power Sector. *Discussion Paper* 6, World Bank, Washington, DC.
7. International Energy Agency, 2004. *World Energy Outlook,* Paris.

Appendices

I

Symbols

The following symbols and abbreviations have been used in this book

C:H	ratio between carbon and hydrogen
cSt	centistoke
cu m (or m^3)	cubic metre
C_3H_8	chemical symbol for propane gas
C_4H_{10}	chemical symbol for butane gas
°C	degree Celsius
kcal	kilocalorie
kg	kilogramme
kg/cm^2	kilogramme per square centimetre
kWh	kilowatt-hour
LPG	liquefied petroleum gas
mg/g	milligramme per gramme
MJ	megajoule (10^6 joules)
NGL	natural gas liquids
RON	research octane number
t	metric ton
TCE	ton of coal equivalent
TJ	terajoule (10^{12} joules)
TOE	ton of oil equivalent
*	estimate by the Statistics Division of the United Nations Secretariat
..	not applicable
0	less than 0.5 of the unit specified or nil.

• • •

II

Glossary

Solid Fuels

Hard coal: Coal that has a high degree of coalification with a gross calorific value above 23,865 KJ/kg (5,700 kcal/kg) on an ash-free but moist basis, and a mean random reflectance of vitrinite of at least 0.6. Slurries, middlings and other low-grade coal products, which cannot be classified according to the type of coal from which they are obtained, are included under hard coal. There are two sub-categories of hard coal: (i) coking coal and (ii) other bituminous coal and anthracite (also known as steam coal). Coking coal is a hard coal with a quality that allows the production of coke suitable to support a blast furnace charge. Steam coal is coal used for steam raising and space heating purposes and includes all anthracite coals and bituminous coals not classified as coking coal.

Lignite: One of the two sub-categories of brown coal. Brown coal is coal with a low degree of coalification which retained the anatomical structure of the vegetable matter from which it was formed. It has a mean random reflectance of vitrinite of less than 0.6, provided that the gross calorific value (on a moist ash-free basis) is less than 23,865 KJ/kg (5,700 kcal/kg). Brown coal comprises: (i) lignite—non-agglomerating coals with a gross calorific value less than 17,435 KJ/kg (4,165 kcal/kg) and greater than 31 per cent volatile matter on a dry mineral matter free basis and (ii) sub-bituminous coal—non-agglomerating coals with a gross calorific value between 17,435 KJ/kg (4,165 kcal/kg) and 23,865 KJ/kg (5,700 kcal/kg) containing more than 31 per cent volatile matter on a dry mineral matter free basis.

Peat: A solid fuel formed from the partial decomposition of dead vegetation under conditions of high humidity and limited air access (initial stage of coalification). Only peat used as fuel is included. Its principal use is as a household fuel.

Patent fuel (hard coal briquettes): A composition fuel manufactured from coal fines by shaping with the addition of a binding agent such as pitch.

Lignite briquettes: A composition fuel manufactured from lignite. The lignite is crushed, dried and moulded under high pressure into an even-shaped briquette without the addition of binders.

Peat briquettes: A composition fuel manufactured from peat. Raw peat, after crushing and drying, is moulded under high pressure into an even-shaped briquette without the addition of binders.

Coke: The solid residue obtained from coal or lignite by heating it to a high temperature in the absence or near absence of air. It is high in carbon and low in moisture and volatile matter. Several categories are distinguished:

(a) Coke-oven coke: The solid product obtained from carbonisation of coal, principally coking coal, at high temperature. Coke-oven coke is also called metallurgical coke and is used mainly in the iron and steel industry. Semi-coke, the solid product obtained from carbonisation of coal at low temperature, is included with coke-oven coke. It is used mainly as a domestic fuel.

(b) Gas coke: A by-product of coal used for the production of gas works gas in gasworks. Gas coke is mainly used as a domestic fuel.

(c) Brown coal coke: A solid product obtained from carbonization of brown coal briquettes.

Oil shale: A sedimentary rock containing a high proportion of organic matter (kerogen), which can be converted to crude oil or gas by heating.

Bituminous sands: Sands or sandstones containing a high proportion of tarry hydrocarbons, capable of yielding oil through heating or other extractive processes. Heavy oils and tars which are so dense and viscous and lacking in primary energy that they cannot be produced commercially by conventional methods, that is, by natural flow or pumping, are also included.

LIQUID FUELS

Crude oil: A mineral oil consisting of a mixture of hydrocarbons of natural origin, yellow to black in colour, of variable density and viscosity. Data in this category also includes lease or field condensate (separator liquids) which is recovered from gaseous hydrocarbons in lease separation facilities, as well as synthetic crude oil, mineral oils extracted from bituminous minerals such as shales and bituminous sand, and oils from coal liquefaction.

Natural Gas Liquids (NGL): Liquid or liquefied hydrocarbons produced in the manufacture, purification and stabilisation of natural gas. NGLs include, but are not limited to, ethane, propane, butane, pentane, natural gasolene, and plant condensate. NGLs are either distilled with crude oil in refineries, blended with refined petroleum products or used directly depending on their characteristics.

Plant condensate: Liquid hydrocarbons condensed from wet natural gas in natural gas processing plants. It is used as a petroleum refinery input.

Natural gasolene: Light spirit extracted from wet natural gas, often in association with crude petroleum. It is used as a petroleum refinery and petrochemical plant input and is also used directly for blending with motor spirit without further processing.

Petroleum products: Comprise the liquid fuels, lubricant oils and solid and semi-solid products obtained by distillation and cracking of crude petroleum, shale oil, or semi-refined and unfinished petroleum products. As far as possible the series include fuels consumed in refining, but exclude oil products obtained from natural gas, coal, lignite and their derivatives.

Aviation gasolene: Motor spirit prepared especially for aviation piston engines, with an octane number varying from 80 to 145 RON and a freezing point of -60°C.

Motor gasolene: Light hydrocarbon oil for use in internal combustion engines such as motor vehicles, excluding aircraft. It distils between 35°C and 200°C, and is treated to reach a sufficiently high octane number of generally between 80 and 100 RON. Treatment may be by reforming, blending with an aromatic fraction, or the addition of benzole or other additives (such as tetraethyl lead).

Jet fuel: Consists of gasolene-type jet fuel and kerosene-type jet fuel.

***Gasolene-type jet fuel**:* All light hydrocarbon oils for use in aviation gas-turbine engines. It distils between 100°C and 250°C with at least 20 per cent of volume distilling at 143°C. It is obtained by blending kerosene and gasolene or naphtha in such a way that the aromatic content does not exceed 25% in volume. Additives are included to reduce the freezing point to -58°C or lower, and to keep the Reid vapour pressure between 0.14 and 0.21 kg/cm^2.

***Kerosene-type jet fuel**:* Medium oil for use in aviation gas-turbine engines with the same distillation characteristics and flash point as kerosene, with a maximum aromatic content of 20% in volume. It is treated to give a kinematic viscosity of less than 15 cSt at -34°C and a freezing point below -50°C.

Kerosene: Medium oil distilling between 150°C and 300°C; at least 65 per cent of volume distills at 250°C. Its specific gravity is roughly 0.80 and its flash point is above 38°C. It is used as an illuminant and as a fuel in certain types of spark-ignition engines, such as those used for agricultural tractors and stationary engines. Other names for this product are burning oil, vapourising oil, power kerosene and illuminating oil.

Gas-diesel oil (distillate fuel oil): Heavy oils distilling between 200°C and 380°C, but distilling less than 65 per cent in volume at 250°C, including losses, and 85 per cent or more at 350°C. Its flash point is always above 50°C and its specific gravity is higher than 0.82. Heavy oils obtained by blending are grouped together with gas oils on the condition that their kinematic viscosity does not exceed 27.5 cSt at 38°C. Also included are middle distillates intended for the petrochemical industry. Gas-diesel oils are used as a fuel for internal combustion in diesel engines, as a burner fuel in heating installations, such as furnaces, and for enriching water gas to increase its luminosity. Other names for this product are diesel fuel, diesel oil and gas oil.

Residual fuel oil: A heavy oil that makes up the distillation residue. It comprises all fuels (including those obtained by blending) with a kinematic viscosity above 27.5 cSt at 38°C. Its flash point is always above 50°C and its specific gravity is higher than 0.90. It is commonly used by ships and industrial large-scale heating installations as a fuel in furnaces or boilers.

Liquefied petroleum gas (LPG): Hydrocarbons which are gaseous under conditions of normal temperature and pressure but are liquefied by compression or cooling to facilitate storage, handling and transportation. They are (i) extracted by stripping of natural gas at crude petroleum and natural gas sources; (ii) extracted by stripping of imported natural gas in installations of the importing country; and (iii) produced both in refineries and outside of refineries in the course of processing crude petroleum or its derivatives. It comprises propane (C_3H_8), butane (C_4H_{10}), or a combination of the two. Also included is ethane (C_2H_6) from petroleum refineries or natural gas producers' separation and stabilisation plants.

Refinery gas: Non-condensable gas obtained during distillation of crude oil or treatment of oil products (e.g. cracking) in refineries. It consists mainly of hydrogen, methane, ethane and olefins, and is used principally as a refinery fuel. Refinery gas is also known as still gas.

Feedstocks: Products or a combination of products derived from crude oil destined for further processing in the refining industry other than blending. They are transformed into one or more components and/or finished products. This definition covers naphtha imported for refinery intake and naphtha returned from the chemical industry to the refining industry.

Naphtha: Light or medium oil distilling between 30°C and 210°C, for which there is no official definition, but which does not meet the standards laid down for motor spirit. The properties depend upon consumer specification. The C:H ratio is usually 84:14 or 84:16, with a very low sulphur content. Naphtha may be further blended or mixed with other materials to make high-grade motor gasolene or jet fuel, or may be used as a raw material for manufactured gas. Naphtha is sometimes used as input to feedstocks to make various kinds of chemical products, or may be used as a solvent.

White spirit/industrial spirit: A highly refined distillate with a boiling point ranging from 135°C to 200°C, which is used as a paint solvent and for dry-cleaning purposes.

Lubricants - Viscous, liquid hydrocarbons rich in paraffin waxes, distilling between 380°C and 500°C, obtained by vacuum distillation of oil residues from atmospheric distillation. Additives may be included to alter their characteristics. Their main characteristics are: a flash point greater than 125°C; a pour point between -25°C and +5°C depending on the grade; a strong acid number (normally 0.5 mg/g); an ash content less than or equal to 0.3%; and a water content less than or equal to 0.2%. Included are cutting oils, white oils, insulating oils, spindle oils and lubricating greases.

Bitumen - Solid or viscous hydrocarbon with a colloidal structure, brown or black in colour, which is obtained as a residue by vacuum distillation of oil residues from atmospheric distillation. It is sometimes soluble in carbon bisulphite; non-volatile, thermoplastic (generally between 150°C and 200°C), often with insulating and adhesive properties. It is used mainly in road construction. Natural asphalt is excluded.

Petroleum waxes: Saturated aliphatic hydrocarbons obtained as residues extracted when dewaxing lubricant oils, with a crystalline structure with C greater than 12. Their main characteristics are as follows: they are colourless, in most cases odourless and translucent; they have a melting point above 45°C, a specific gravity of 0.76 to 0.78 at 80°C, and a kinematic viscosity between 3.7 and 5.5 cSt at 99°C. These waxes are used for candle manufacture, polishes and waterproofing of containers, wrappings, etc.

Petroleum coke: A shiny, black solid residue obtained by cracking and carbonisation in furnaces. It consists mainly of carbon (90 to 95 per cent) and generally burns without leaving any ash. It is used mainly in metallurgical processes. It excludes those solid residues obtained from carbonisation of coal.

Other petroleum products: Products of petroleum origin (including partially refined products) not otherwise specified.

Alcohol: Ethanol (ethyl alcohol) and methanol (methyl alcohol) for use as a fuel. Ethanol can be produced from sugar, starch and cellulose and is used mainly in transport (on its own or blended with gasolene). Methanol can be produced from wood, crop residues, grass, and the like and can be used in internal combustion engines.

Biodiesel: It refers to oil derived from biological sources and modified chemically so that it can be used as fuel in compression ignition (diesel) internal combustion engines, or for heating. Biological sources of biodiesel include, but are not limited to, vegetable oils made from canola (rapeseed), soybeans, corn, oil palm, peanut, or sunflower. Chemically, biodiesel is a linear alkyl ester made by transesterification of vegetable oils or animal fats with methanol. The transesterification distinguishes biodiesel from straight vegetable and waste oils. Straight oils can be used as fuel only in if the engine is modified; for this reason, it is not recommended to report them as biodiesel. Biodiesel has a flash point of around 150°C and a density of 0.86 kg/litre. When burned, some of the emissions (sulphur, carbon monoxide, and aromatic hydrocarbons) are lower than that of petroleum-derived gas-diesel oil, while some are higher (nitrogen oxides, particulate matter (sooth)). Biodiesel is biodegradable and non-toxic. It has higher cetane rating than petroleum diesel, with which it is often blended. For example, B20 is a fuel containing 20 per cent of biodiesel and 80 per cent or regular diesel; B100 refers to pure biodiesel.

Gaseous Fuels

Natural gas: Gases consisting mainly of methane occurring naturally in underground deposits. It includes both non-associated gas (originating from fields producing only hydrocarbons in gaseous form) and associated gas (originating from fields producing both liquid and gaseous hydrocarbons), as well as methane recovered from coal mines and sewage gas. Production of natural gas refers to dry marketable production, measured after purification and extraction of natural gas liquids and sulphur. Extraction losses and the amounts that have been reinjected, flared, and vented are excluded from the data on production.

Gasworks gas: Gas produced by public utilities or private plants whose main activity is the production, transport and distribution of such gas. It includes gas produced by carbonisation, by total gasification with or without enrichment with oil products, by cracking of natural gas, and by reforming or mixing gases.

Coke-oven gas: By-product of the carbonization process in the production of coke in coke ovens.

Blast furnace gas: By-product in blast furnaces recovered on leaving the furnace.

Biogas: By-product of the fermentation of biomass, principally animal wastes, by bacteria. It consists mainly of methane gas and carbon dioxide.

Electricity and Other Forms of Energy

Electricity production: Refers to gross production, which includes the consumption by station auxiliaries and any losses in the transformers that are considered integral parts of the station. Included also is total electric energy produced by pumping installations without deduction of electric energy absorbed by pumping.

Production data includes Solar, Tide, Wave, Wind, Wastes, Wood and Fuel cell production when reported.

Primary electricity refers to electrical energy of geothermal, hydro, nuclear, tide, wind, wave/ocean and solar origin. Its production is assessed at the heat value of electricity (3.6 TJ/million RWh).

Secondary electricity is defined as thermal electricity, which comprises conventional thermal plants of all types, whether or not equipped for the combined generation of heat and electric energy. Accordingly, they include steam-operated generating plants, with condensation (with or without extraction) or with back-pressure turbines and plants using internal combustion engines or gas turbines whether or not these are equipped for heat recovery.

Public utilities comprise the undertakings whose essential purpose is the production, transmission and distribution of electric energy, primarily for use by the public. These may be private companies, co-operative organisations, local or regional authorities, nationalised undertakings or governmental organisations.

Self-producers include undertakings which, in addition to their main activities, they produce (individually or in combination) electric energy intended, in whole or in part, to meet their own needs. They may be privately or publicly owned.

Net installed capacity is measured at the terminals of the stations, *i.e.*, after deduction of the power absorbed by the auxiliary installations and the losses in the station transformers, if any.

Imports and exports: Refer to the amounts of electric energy transferred to and from the country concerned, respectively, which are measured at the metering points on the lines crossing the frontiers. Included are imports and exports of electric energy made by means of high-voltage lines crossing frontiers as well as imports and exports made by means of low-voltage lines for use in the immediate vicinity of the frontier, if the quantities so transferred are known.

Heat: Heat obtained from (a) combined heat and power (CHP) plants generating electricity and useful heat in a single installation; (b) district heating (DH) plants and (c) nuclear power plants and geothermal sources. The heat may be in the form of steam, hot water or hot air.

Uranium (U) production: Comprises the U content of uranium ores and concentrates intended for treatment for uranium recovery.

Traditional Fuels

Fuelwood: All wood in the rough used for fuel purposes. Production data include the portion used for charcoal production, using a factor of 6 to convert from a weight basis to the volumetric equivalent (metric tons to cubic metres) of charcoal.

Bagasse: The cellulosic residue left after sugar is extracted from sugar cane. It is often used as a fuel within the sugar milling industry.

Charcoal: Solid residue, consisting mainly of carbon, obtained by the destructive distillation of wood in the absence of air.

Animal wastes: Excreta of cattle, horses, pigs, poultry, etc., and (in principle) excreta of humans, used as a fuel.

Vegetal wastes: Mainly crop residues (cereal straw from maize, wheat, paddy rice, etc.) and food processing wastes (rice hulls, coconut husks, ground-nut shells, etc.) used for fuel. Bagasse is excluded.

Municipal wastes: Consist of products that are combusted directly to produce heat and/or power and comprise wastes produced by the residential, commercial and public services sectors that are collected by local authorities for disposal in a central location. Hospital waste is included in this category.

Industrial wastes: Consist of solid and liquid products other than solid biomass and animal products mentioned above (e.g. tyres) combusted directly, usually in specialised plants, to produce heat and/or power.

Other wastes: Wastes not specifically defined above, such as pulp and paper wastes.

Transactions

The data on **production** refer to the first stage of production: accordingly, for hard coal the data refer to mine production; for briquettes to the output of briquetting plants; for crude petroleum and natural gas to production at oil and gas wells; for natural gas liquids to production at wells and processing plants; for refined petroleum products to gross refinery output; for cokes and coke-oven gas to the output of ovens; for other manufactured gas to production at gas works, blast furnaces or refineries; and for electricity to the gross production of generating plants.

The **international trade** of energy commodities is based on the "general trade" system, that is, all goods entering and leaving the national boundary of a country are recorded as imports and exports.

Bunkers refer to fuels supplied to ships and aircraft engaged in international transportation, irrespective of the carrier's flag.

In general, data on **stocks** refer to changes in stocks at producers, importers and/or industrial consumers at the beginning and end of each year. In some cases, however, stock series have been derived on the basis of the difference between gross availabilities for transformation or consumption and official or published data on actual consumption. A positive stock change (+) reflects additions to stocks which in effect decreases "apparent consumption"; while a negative stock change (-) creates exactly the opposite result.

Data on **consumption** refer to "apparent consumption" and are derived from the formula "production + imports – exports – bunkers +/– stock changes." Accordingly, the series on apparent consumption may occasionally represent only an indication of the magnitude of actual (*i.e.*, "measured") gross inland availability. This statement is particularly suitable either when stock data are unavailable or unreliable, or when apparent consumption is a small residual element derived from calculations between large aggregate series and thus is sensitive to small variations in these series. This latter point is also appropriate with respect to the *per capita* consumption calculations presented in some tables. Where the quantities involved are small, the series tend to exaggerate the effects of such elements as stock additions or withdrawals.

Energy Resources and Reserves

Hard Coal, Lignite and Peat

Proved amount in place is the tonnage that has been both carefully measured and assessed as being exploitable under present and expected local economic conditions with existing available technology.

Proved recoverable reserves are the tonnage of the proved amount in place that can be recovered (extracted from the earth in raw form) under present and expected local economic conditions with existing available technology.

Estimated additional amount in place is the indicated and inferred tonnage *additional* to the proved amount in place. It includes estimates of amounts which could exist in unexplored extensions of known deposits (and also in the case of coal, in undiscovered deposits in known coal-bearing areas), as well as amounts inferred through knowledge of favourable geological conditions. Deposits whose existence is entirely speculative are not included.

Crude Oil and Natural Gas Liquids

Proved recoverable reserves is the tonnage of the proved amount in place that can be recovered (extracted from the earth in raw form) in the future under present and expected economic conditions and existing technological limits.

The ratio of crude oil reserves to production (R/P ratio) is used to show the length of time those reserves would last in years if production continued at the then current level and there were no further increases in the proved recoverable reserves. The ratio is calculated by dividing the proved recoverable crude oil reserves (which for the most part refer to reserves at the end of 1995) by the production. *These R/P ratios should be viewed with extreme caution.* The definition used for proved recoverable reserves is very restrictive and confined to those known reserves which can be recovered with reasonable certainty under existing economic conditions. The R/P ratios, therefore, can frequently give a very pessimistic impression of the expected life of a country's reserves. In addition, for some of those countries whose R/P ratios appear very large, it can reasonably be assumed that the figures for proved recoverable reserves include some unproved reserves.

Oil Shale and Bituminous Sands

Proved recoverable reserves are the amount, expressed as tonnage of recoverable synthetic oil, that has been both carefully measured and has also been assessed as exploitable under present and expected local economic conditions with existing available technology.

Natural Gas

Proved recoverable reserves is the volume of the proved amount in place that can be recovered (in raw form) in the future under local economic conditions with existing available technology.

Uranium

Reasonably assured resources refer to recoverable uranium that occurs in known mineral deposits of such size, grade and configuration that it could be recovered with currently proven mining and processing technology, at a cost of between US $80 and $130 per kilogramme.

Estimated additional resources refer to recoverable uranium, in addition to reasonably assured resources, that is expected to occur, mostly on the basis of direct geological evidence in:

- extensions of well-explored deposits,
- little-explored deposits, and
- undiscovered deposits believed to exist along a well-defined geological trend with known deposits, recoverable at costs of up to US $130.

Hydropower

Gross theoretical capability is the annual energy potentially available in the country if all natural flows were turbined down to sea level or to the water level of the border of the country (if the water course extends into another country) with 100% efficiency from the machinery and driving water-works. Unless otherwise stated, the figures have been estimated on the basis of atmospheric precipitation and water run off.

Units of Measurement and Conversions

Metric units of measurement are used throughout the *Yearbook*. **Conversion Factor Tables** I through V provide the necessary factors for converting energy data from one measurement system (mass or weight, volume or heat) to another. Unless otherwise stated in the Table Notes, in the case of solid fuels, liquid fuels and gases, the conversions are based on the net calorific value.

The comparison between different fuels is presented in metric tons of coal equivalent (Tables 1 and 5), oil equivalent (Table 2), and terajoules (Tables 3 and 4) on the basis of the heat energy which may be obtained from each of them. In the case of solids fuels, liquid fuels and gases, this is represented by the heat energy obtained by burning an average grade of the fuel in a bomb calorimeter under ideal conditions.

A unit of primary electricity may be equated theoretically with the amount of coal or oil required to produce an equivalent unit of thermal electricity. In the case of hydro-electricity, the ideal condition (assuming 100% efficiency), is taken to be 3.6 TJ per million RWh which corresponds to 0.123 tons of coal equivalent or 0.086 tons of oil equivalent per 1,000 kWh. In the case of nuclear and geothermal electricity, the average condition is assumed (33 and 10% efficiency respectively) and is taken to be 10.909 and 36 TJ per million kWh which corresponds to 0.372 and 1.228 tons of coal equivalent or 0.261 and 0.860 tons of oil equivalent per 1,000 kWh.

The procedure to convert from original units to common units and from one common unit to another is as follows:

Data in original units (Metric tons, T.J. kWh, m^3)	Multiplied by factors in Table 1 →	=	TCE
TCE[1] →	multiplied by 0.0293076[2]	=	TJ
TCE[1] →	multiplied by 0.7[3]	=	TOE

1. The base used for coal equivalency comprises 7000 calories per gram
2. One TCE is defined as 7×10^6 kcal or 0.041868 TJ.
3. One TOE is defined as 10.0×10^6 kcal or 0.041868 TJ (1 calorie = 4.1868 joules).

III

Table Notes

Consumption

Consumption throughout the *Yearbook* is defined as: production + imports – exports – bunkers +/– stock changes.

Negative Consumption

Consumption for some of the petroleum products is negative due to the exclusion of inter-product transfers from the calculations.

Negative consumption of electricity is due to negligible or no primary electricity production and/or net exports.

Time Period

The period to which the data refer is the calendar year, with the exception of the data of the following countries which refer to the fiscal year:

Afghanistan and Iran (Islamic Rep. of) – beginning 21 March of the year stated;

Australia, Bangladesh, Egypt (electricity only), Nepal, Pakistan – ending June of the year stated;

India, Myanmar and New Zealand – beginning April of the year stated.

• • •

IV

Glossary of Oil Companies

Baikal Finance Group: An obscure company that was originally awarded Yuganskneftgaz in a controversial auction.

BPD: Barrels per day.

British Petroleum (BP): One of Britain's biggest companies and one of the world's largest oil and petrochemical groups.

China National Petroleum Corporation (CNPC): China's largest producer and supplier of crude oil and natural gas. A state-owned company.

China National Offshore Oil Corporation (CNOOC): A Chinese, state-run oil firm.

Gazprom: State-owned Russian giant, Gazprom, is the world's largest producer of gas.

ILSA: Iran-Libya Sanctions Act. An executive order signed in 1995 by President Clinton and renewed by President Bush in 2004, prohibits U.S. companies from doing business in Iran.

Lukoil: Russia's largest privately owned oil company, since the downfall of Yukos.

MBD: Million barrels per day.

MEG Energy Corp: A private energy company based in Calgary, Canada.

Menatep Group: An international holding company and investor in international financial and capital markets. Menatep Group is the core shareholder of Yukos' assets, this company has headquarters in London and Moscow.

OAO Sibneft: One of Russia's largest privately owned oil companies. Sibneft focuses on Russia and the CIS.

Oil and Natural Gas Corporation (ONGC) Limited: An Indian state-owned oil company.

Organisation of the Petroleum Exporting Countries (OPEC): A permanent, intergovernmental organisation created at the Baghdad Conference on September 10-14, 1960, by Iran, Iraq, Kuwait, Saudi Arabia and Venezuela. These countries were later joined by Qatar

(1961), Indonesia (1962), Libya (1962), United Arab Emirates (1967), Algeria (1969), Nigeria (1971), Ecuador (1973-1992) and Gabon (1975-1994). Angola has joined the OPEc in 2006.

Petroleos de Venezuela (PDVSA): A state-owned Venezuelan oil company.

Rosneft: The only Russian oil company that is completely state-owned.

Russian Railways: A state-owned railway mainline. Russia's only mainline running in the eastern direction.

Sibneft: See OAO Sibneft.

Sinopec: (Also known as China Petroleum & Chemical Corporation), one of China's largest integrated energy and chemical companies.

Surgutneftegas: A Russian-based oil company and the eleventh largest oil company in the world.

TNK - BP: A major oil company with the majority of its assets in Russia. It was formed in August 2003 from the assets of TNK (Tymen Oil Co.), Onako, Sidanco and the majority of BP's assets in Russia.

Transneft: Russia's oil pipeline monopoly.

Yuganskneftegas: Formerly Yukos' largest production asset, which some claim was illegally auctioned off, causing Yukos to collapse.

Yukos: A petroleum company in Russia. The company was, until recently, controlled by Russian billionaire Mikhail Khodorkovsky and a number of prominent Russian businessmen, or "oligarchs". Khodorkovsky was arrested on 25 October 2003 and has since been imprisoned, while others have fled Russia. The company was forced into bankruptcy.

• • •

V

Millennium Development Goals

Millennium Development Goals (MDGs): Goals and Targets Adopted by the United Nations, 2001

Goal 1: Eradicate extreme poverty and hunger

- Halve, between 1990 and 2015, the proportion of people whose income is less than $ 1 a day
- Halve, between 1990 and 2015, the proportion of people who suffer from hunger

Goal 2: Achieve universal primary education

- Ensure that, by 2015, children everywhere, boys and girls alike, will be able to complete a full course of primary schooling

Goal 3: Promote gender equality and empower women

- Eliminate gender disparity in primary and secondary education preferably by 2005 and in all levels of education no later than 2015.

Goal 4: Reduce child mortality

- Reduce by two-thirds, between 1990 and 2015, the under-five mortality rate

Goal 5: Improve maternal health

- Reduce by three-quarters, between 1990 and 2015, the maternal mortality ratio

Goal 6: Combat HIV/AIDS, malaria, and other diseases.

- Have halted by 2015 and begun to reverse the spread of HIV/AIDS
- Have halted by 2015 and begun to reverse the incidence of malaria and other major diseases

Goal 7: Ensure environmental sustainability

- Integrate the principles of sustainable development into country policies and programmes and reverse the loss of environmental resources

- Halve by 2015 the proportion of people without sustainable access to safe drinking water
- Have achieved by 2020 a significant improvement in the lives of at least 100 million slum dwellers

Goal 8: Develop a global partnership for development

- Develop further an open rule-based, predictable, nondiscriminatory trading and financial system (includes a commitment to good governance, development, and internationally)
- Address the special needs of the least developed countries (includes tariff- and quota-free access for exports, enhanced programme of debt relief for and cancellation of official bilateral debt, and more generous ODA for countries committed to poverty reduction)
- Address the special needs of landlocked countries and small island developing states (through the Programme of Action for the Sustainable Development of Small island Developing States and 22nd General Assembly provisions)
- Deal comprehensively with the debt problems of developing countries through national and international measures in order to make debt sustainable in the long term
- In cooperation with developing countries, develop and implement strategies for decent and productive work for youth
- In cooperation with pharmaceutical companies, provide access to affordable essential drugs in developing countries
- In cooperation with the private sector, make available the benefits of new technologies, especially information and communications technologies

Source: Mini Atlas of Global Development, the World Bank, Washington, D.C. 2004.

Bibliography

Aissaoui, Ali, 2001. *Algeria: The Political Economy of Oil and Gas,* Oxford University Press, Oxford.

Amouroux, Martin, and Marie, Jean, 2005. Le Charbon-Roi: Jusqu'a Quand?. *Revue de l'Energie,* 563 January-February, pp. 14-18.

Asia Pacific Energy Research Center, 2002. *Energy Security Initiative: Emergency Oil Stocks as an Option to Respond to Oil Supply Disruptions.* Asia Pacific Energy Research Center, Tokyo.

Bacon, Robert, 2005. The Impact of Higher Oil Prices on Low Income Countries and the Poor: Impacts and Policies. *Energy Secior Management Assistance Program Knowledge Exchange Series 1*, World Bank, Washington, DC.

Barton, Barry, Redgwell, C., Ronne, Anita and Zillman, Donald, N., 2004. *Energy Security: Managing Risk in a Dynamic Legal and Regulatory Enrolment*, Oxford University Press, New York.

Bowley, Graham, 1999. *Talisman May Not Find Good Fortune from Sudan Oil,* Financial Times, November 19.

BP Global. 2005. *Statistical Review of World Energy,* London: BP Global.

BP Global. 2006. *Statistical Review of World Energy*, London: BP Global.

Brzezinski, Zbigniew and Mearsheimer, John J., 2005. Clash of the Titans. *Foreign Policy,* January/February, pp. 46-9.

Buckley, Chris, 2004. China Gains Access to Venezuelan Oil. *The International Herald Tribune,* 28 December.

Center for Liquefied Natural Gas, 2005. *Updates on LNG Security and Safety.* Center for Liquefied Natural Gas, Washington, DC.

Chingendael International Energy Programme, 2004. *Study on Energy, Supply Security and Geopolitics.* The Hague, Netherlands.

Cody, Edward 2005. China Builds a Smaller, Stronger Military. *Washington Post,* 12 April.

Danforth, John C., 2002. Special Envoy for Peace. *Report to the President of the United States on the Outlook for Peace in Sudan,* at 8th April 26.

Dean, Jason, 2006. China's Planners Slow Timetable for Oil Reserves. *Wall Street Journal*, March 7.

Douglas A. Yates, 1996. *The Rentier Stale in Africa: Oil Rent Dependency and Neocolonialism in the Republic of Gabon,* Africa World Press, Trenton NJ.

DRC (Development Research Center), 2000. *Basic Conception of the National Energy Strategies.* Beijing: DRC.

Economist Intelligence Unit, 2005. *EIU Country Report Nigeria—November,* London.

Economist Intelligence Unit, 2006. *EIU Country Report Libya*–January, London.

Ellsworth, Brian and Patricia Vasquez, I. 2003. *CVP to Displace PDV in Handling Private Contracts in Venezuela,* oil daily, Aug. 26.

Esther Pan, 2006. China, Africa and Oil. *Council on Foreign Relations Home Page.*

Flynn, Martin, William, Imai, Ryukichi, Steeg, Helga, 1996. Maintaining Energy Security in a Global Context. *Trilateral Commission*, New York.

Foster, Peter, Editorial, 1999. *Talisman in Ethical No Man's Land,* Financial Post, Nov. 12.

French, Howard W., 2007. China and Africa. *African Affairs*, 106, pp. 127-132.

Frynas, Jedrzej George, 2005. The false developmental promise of corporate social responsibility: evidence from multinational oil companies. *International Affairs,* 81, pp. 581-98.

Frynas, Jedrzej George, 2000. *Oil in Nigeria: Conflict and Litigation between Oil Companies and Village Communities,* LIT Verlag/Transaction Publishers, Hamburg/New Brunswick, NJ/1-London.

Frynas, Jedrzej George, Beck, Matthias and Mellahi, Kamel, 2000. Maintaining corporate dominance after decolonization: the first mover advantage of Shell-BP in Nigeria. *Review of African Political Economy* 27, pp. 213-30.

Frynas, Jedrzej George, Wood, Geoffrey and R.M.S. Scares de Oliveira, 2003. Business and politics in Sào Tomé e Principe. *African Affairs:* 102, pp. 51-80.

Sanderson, G.N., 1974. The European Partition of Africa. *The Journal of Imperial and Commonwealth History,* 3, 1, pp. 1-54.

Gelb, Alan, 1988. Oil Windfalls: Blessing or Curse. Oxford University Press, New York.

Gillis, Charles, 1999. U.S. Pension Fund Dumps Its Stake in Talisman, post, Dec. 9.

Greenwald, Judy, 1985. Political Risk Insurers Owe Firm $162 Million, N.Y. Times, Dec. 23

Gurney, Judith, 1996. *Libya: The Political Economy of Oil.* Oxford University Press, Oxford.

Gylfason, Thorvaldur, 2001. Natural Resources, Education and Economic Development. *European Economic Review,* 45, pp. 847-859.

Haufler, Virginia, 1993. *Crossing the Boundary between Public and Private: International Regimes and Non-State Actors, in Regime Theory and International Relations,* 94, Volker Rittberger, ed.

Hilt, David, 2005. Impacts and Actions Resulting from the 14 August 2003 Blackout. *Paper presented at the North American Electric Reliability Council Research Teleseminar*, January 20.

Hojman, D.E., 2002. The Political Economy of Chile's Fast Growth: an Olsonian Interpretation. *Public Choice,* 111, pp. 155-78.

Hyne, Norman J., 1995. *Nontechnical Guide to Petroleum Geology, Exploration, Drilling and Production,* PennWell, Tulsa, p. 14.

IEA (International Energy Agency). 1993. Shared Goals. *Adopted in a Meeting of the IEA ministers*, Paris, June 4.

IEA (International Energy Agency). 2002. *World Energy Outlook*, Paris.

IEA (International Energy Agency). 2005. *Monthly Oil Market Report.* May.

International Energy Agency, 2004. *World Energy Outlook*, Paris.

International Energy Agency, Energy Technology Policy. *IEA*, Paris, 1985.

Jackson, Eric, 2005. China-Venezuela Oil and Telecom Deals will Affect Panama. *The Panama News*, 9 January.

Jacoby, Neil, H., 1974. *Multinational Oil: A Study in Industrial Dynamics.*

Jones, Jeffrey, 1998. *Talisman Chief Gets Quick Lesson in Risks of Sudan Oil*, J. Com Aug. 26.

Keenan, Jeremy, 2004. Terror in the Sahara: the implications of US imperialism for North and West Africa. *Review of African Political Economy*, 31, pp. 475-96.

Klare, Michael and Volman, Daniel, 2006. The African "Oil Rush" and American National Security. *Third World Quarterly*, 27, 4, pp. 609-628.

Klare, Michael, T., 2005. Oil, Geopolitics and War with Iran. *Asia Times*, 13 April.

Klare, Michael, 2004. *Blood and Oil: The Dangers and Consequences of America's growing Dependency on Imported Petroleum (The American Empire Project).* Metropolitan Books Publishers, New York, p. 144.

Kobrin, Stephen J., 1985. *Diffusion as an Explanation of Oil Nationalisation: Or the Domino Effect Rides Again*, 29 J. Conflict Resol. 3, 13.

Kobrin, Stephen J., 1997. *The Architecture of Globalization: State Sovereignty in a Networked Global Economy*, in Governments, Globalization and International Business 146, 148 *passim*, John H. Dunning, ed.

Kobrin, Stephen J., 1998. *Back to the Future: Neomedievalism and the Modern Digital World Economy*, 51.

Kuppuswamy, C.S., 2004. Straits of Malacca: Security Implications. *Paper*, 1033. South Asia Analysis Group, India.

Lacasse, Chantale and Ploude, Andre, 1995. On the Renewal of Concern for the security of Supply. *Energy Journal*, 16(2).

Lake, Anthony, Christine Todd Whitman, Princeton N. Lyman, Ralph Bunche and Stephen Morrison, 2006. More than Humanitarianism: A Strategic US approach Toward Africa. *Council on Foreign Relations*, 19 April.

Lamech, Ranjit and Saeed, Kazim, 2003. What International Investors Look for When Investing in Developing Countries. Results from a Survey of International Investors in the Power Sector. *Discussion Paper* 6, World Bank, Washington, DC.

Layne, Christopher, 1993. 'The Unipolar Illusion: Why New Great Powers will Arise', *International Security* 17, 4, pp. 5-51.

Leite, Carlos and Jens Weidmann, 1999. *Does Mother Nature Corrupt? Natural Resources, Corruption and Economic Growth*, International Monetary Fund, Washington, DC.

Li, Zhidong, 2003. An Econometric Study of China's Economy, Energy, and the Environment to the Year 2030. *Energy Policy*, 31, pp. 1137-50.

Littlejohns, Michael and Buchan, David, 1999. *Annan Backs 'Rights Beyond Borders*, Financial Times, Sept. 21.

Medciros, Evan S. and Fravel, M. Taylor, 2003. China's New Diplomacy. *Foreign Affairs*, 82, 6, pp. 22-35.

Neuffer, Elizabeth, 2001. Critics Decry Oil Investors' Link to Sudan War, Boston Globe, Mar. 26.

Neumeister, Larry, 2003 . Talisman Can Be Held Liable for Genocide: Judge, Gazette (Montreal), Mar. 20.

Pegg, Scott, 2006. Can policy intervention beat the resource curse? Evidence from the Chad-Cameroon pipeline project. *African Affairs,* 105, p. 22.

Peter Schraeder, 2000. Cold War to Cold Peace: explaining U.S.-French competition in Francophone; Africa. *Political Science Quarterly,* 115, 3, pp. 395-419.

Pugg, Scott, 2006. World leaders and bottom feeders: divergent strategies toward social responsibility and resource extraction. in Christopher May (ed.), *Global Corporate Power,* Lynne Rienner, Boulder.

Ross, M.L., 1999. The Political Economy of the Resource Curse. *World Politics,* 51, pp. 297-322.

Royan, R.P., 1999. From primary production to resource-based industrialization in Malaysia. In A. Farooq (ed.). *Development Policies in Natural Resource Economies,* Edward Elgar, Cheltenham.

Rubin, Richard, 2002. U.S. Firms Cleared to Negotiate With Libya, Platt's Oilgram News, Feb. 13.

Sachs, Jeffrey D. and Warner, Andrew M., 2001. Natural Resources and Economic Development: The Curse of Natural Resources. *European Economic Review,* 45, pp. 827-38.

Saghir, Jamal, 2005. Energy and Poverty: Myths, Links, and Policy Issues. *Energy Working,* Note 4, World Bank, Washington, DC.

Sarraf, M. and Jiwanji, M., 2001. *Beating the Resource Curse: The Case of Botswana,* The World Bank, Washington, DC.

Schwartz, Peter, 1996. *The Art of the Long View*, New York: Currency Double-day.

Shell Group, 2005. Visions of the Future: Shell Launches New Global Scenarios Looking Forward to 2025. Press release, June 6.

Sohn Se-joo, 2006. An Assistant Minister at the South Korean Foreign Ministry. *Yonhap News Home Page,* 5 April.

Spiro, Peter J., 2000. *Globalization, International Law, and the Academy,* 32 N.Y.U. *Journal of International Law and Politics,* 567, pp. 569-72.

Stem, Jonathan. 2006. The Russian Ukrainian Gas Crisis of January 2006. *Oil, Gas, and Energy Law Intelligence*, January: 1-17.

Strange, Susan, 1998. *Mad Money*, Manchester University Press, Manchester.

Taylor, Jerry, and Doren, Peter Van, 2005. The Case against the Strategic Petroleum Reserve. *Policy Analysis,* 555, Cato Institute, Washington, DC.

Tohmatsu, Deloitte Touche, 2004. Sustainable Power Sector Reform in Emerging Markets—Financial Issues and Options. *Joint World Bank/U.S. Agency for International Development Policy Paper*, Washington, DC.

Toyo Engineering Corporation and others. 2005. Technical and Economic Assessment: Off Grid, Mini-Grid and Grid Electrification Technologies. *Discussion Paper, Energy Unit, Energy and Water Department*, World Bank, Washington, DC.

UNCTAD, 2005. *World Investment Report: Transnational Corporation and Internationalisation of R&D.* Geneva, 10 April 2006, pp. 42-43.

United Nations Development Programme and World Bank Energy Sector Management Assistance Programme. 2005. The Impact of Higher Oil Prices on Low Income Countries and on the Poor. *Energy Sector Management Assistance Programme and World Bank*, Washington, DC.

Wolhforth, William C., 1990. The Stability of a Unipolar World. *International Security*, 24, 1, pp. 5-41.

World Bank and IESM (Institute for Economic System and Management). 2000. A Comparative Analysis of the Upstream Fiscal Terms for China. In *Modernizing China's Oil and Gas Sector: Structure, Reform, and Regulation.*

World Bank. 2000. *Fuel for Thought: An Environmental Strategy for the Energy Sector*. Washington, DC.

World Bank. 2004. *Toward a Sustainable Coal Sector in China*. Washington, DC: World Bank.

Yadav, Surya Narain, 2005. Shanghai Cooperation Organisation: Strategic, economic and political implications for India, Approach paper submitted to the institute of Chinese studies, Delhi, August 2005.

Yadav, Surya Narain, 2006. "Shanghai Five: Issues, Achievements and Prospects", Occasional Paper, Institute of Chines Studies, Delhi, May 2006.

Yadav, Surya Narain, 2007. Energy Security and Foreign Policy : A Comparative Study of China and India in African Perspective. *Approach Paper, Presented at the Institute of Chinese Studies*, Delhi, April 10.

Zweig, David and Bi Jianhai, 2005. China's global hunt for energy. *Foreign Affairs* 84, 5, September/ October, pp. 25-38.

• • •

Index

D

E

F

G

H

I

J

K

L

M

N

O

P

R

S

T